3000 800013 63???
St. Louis Community College

D1238714

F V

WITHDRAWN

St. Louis Community
College

Library

5801 Wilson Avenue
St. Louis, Missouri 63110

THIS GUY HAS ALSO WRITTEN:

The Number One Best Seller

You Can't Judge a Book by Its Cover

The Red Chinese Air Force Exercise, Diet and Sex Book
*(with Victor Navasky and Richard Lingeman, using
the pseudonym William Randolph Hirsch)*

George Washington's Expense Account
(with Gen. George Washington)

The Marvin Kitman TV Show

The Coward's Almanac

I AM A VCR

THE KITMAN TAPES

I AM A VCR

A BOOK BY TV'S NUMBER 1 CRITIC*
ABOUT SEX & VIOLENCE,
DYNASTY & DALLAS,
T&A, N.Y. & L.A., DRUGS,
ROONE ARLEDGE, & HERO CARS

MARVIN KITMAN

WELL, ALL RIGHT, MAYBE NUMBER 6

RANDOM HOUSE 🏠 *NEW YORK*

Copyright © 1988 by Marvin Kitman
All rights reserved under International and Pan-American Copyright Conventions.
Published in the United States by Random House, Inc., New York, and
simultaneously in Canada by Random House of Canada Limited, Toronto.

Library of Congress Catloging-in-Publication Data

Kitman, Marvin, 1929–
I am a VCR.

1. Television broadcasting—United States.
I. Title.
PN1992.3.U5K54   1988   791.45′0973   87-43237
ISBN 0-394-56001-9

Manufactured in the United States of America
24689753
First Edition

For Carol Kitman, without whom none of this would have been possible. For living through the whole twenty years of the experience; for providing me with love and understanding and patience and some of my best jokes; for her insights, editing help, and for sharing with me her technical abilities, such as reading the manuals and knowing how to set the VCR; and who, when the writing was finished, took the show biz tradition of saying "Good luck" to its extreme by breaking her leg. Thank you for everything.

CONTENTS

I AM A VCR

PROMO

This is a book about sex, soaps, violence, drugs, money, and rock and roll. Okay, not rock and roll. My kids said to put that in: It would help sales.

The book *is* about sex, violence, and drugs. It is, thus, autobiographical, as anyone who knows me can attest. You thought it was going to be about television? No, you don't understand. Page 1 and we're having problems.

Sex, violence, and drugs—three words that can sum up all of TV and life. The getting of those things, and even worse, the not getting of them, is what life is all about.

This is the most important thought I've had about the nature of things since the insight that the decline of Western civilization dates back to the day Arky Vaughn died. Why? Because the great shortstop of the Pittsburgh Pirates and my boyhood idol will never get into baseball's Hall of Fame and Phil Rizzuto will someday. Because the world's greatest shortstop didn't play in New York, and had the chutzpah to drown while on a fishing trip in the Ozarks at the end of the 1943 major league baseball season while in his prime. Since then, it's all been downhill.

This is a book about television, in one sense. It is about what having to watch all that sex and violence has done to the American people, meaning me. What it is doing to your average—no, above average; there is no such thing as a merely average TV critic—meaning me.

The book is also about my life, the story of what made me *meshugge*.* Also what made other people *meshugge*: the stars, and executives, and institutions in the most profound medium for education and information ever invented. And the poor people at home who watch it. It's also about my TV sets, and how I drove them *meshugge*.

---

* Pronounced m'SHU-geh. Rhymes, approximately, with *Paducah*. Well-known Yiddish word, meaning crazy. Funny-crazy, not insane. Defined here for my *meshugge* WASP editor, one of three people in the United States today who didn't know that.

It is my autobiography because somebody, I felt, had to write it, and it might as well be me.

It's an insider's view of what it's really like to be Marvin Kitman, the one subject on which I am a leading authority, next to Carol Kitman, my wife (where I often find myself), and without whom none of this would have been written. Whenever I use the phrase *my wife* in the following narrative, I refer to Carol Kitman.

Whenever I mention *mistress*, I am referring to Lynda Carter (Wonder Woman) with whom I have had a relationship, as you'll see, and Mary Tyler Moore, the thin woman, and Susan Dey, the L.A. Lawwoman. When I say I "woke up" with Diane Sawyer I'm referring to Anchorwoman, the only woman who ever did the *CBS Morning News* in basic black dress and pearls. Also Lindsay Wagner (Bionic Woman), who taught me everything I know about jogging, mostly how to run at 60 mph; Erma Bombeck (generously made, funny woman), the person I made into a star on *Good Morning America*; and Elizabeth Taylor (Woman).

Space limitations prevent me from mentioning the Dallas Cowgirls, all forty-four of them. I'm a sucker for pompoms.

By my *psychiatrist* I mean Dr. Marlene Brady (Deidre Hall) on *Days of Our Lives*.

In this cast, my three children will be played by my three children, who are now . . . I can never remember their ages. Someone once suggested that as you and the kids get on in years, it is easier to remember them as car models. Therefore, I have a 1957, a '59, and a '64. Jamie, Suzy, and Andrea—was there another? Edsel?—have survived television a lot better than I have, as you'll see.

This is necessarily a long story, like TV itself. And if the writing that follows can be termed mediocre, I am writing about the world's most mediocre medium. This proves what a good reporter and sensitive stylist I am.

Of course, I don't have to tell anyone who can still read that it's not really about TV. I'm writing about the "Great American Metaphor," as Marshall McLuhan said. TV is the dominant center of everybody's universe today, the sun in our solar system. We all revolve around the set.

Every day I see how powerful television is. In this book I am trying to capture the TV changes in people, again meaning me but also you, many of which have happened subtly. There are few complaints about commercials anymore, for example. It's the program in between they complain about now. The commercials are often more interesting. As a TV critic, I find that more and more I write about the unthinkable. What

I can think about, with you, is the new American made by TV, the brilliance and the blindness, the numbness and the new values and no-values we have absorbed since the advent of commercial television—that rising sun in our living rooms. I will think about the universe, and Copernicus, watching events and programs revolve around me.

PROMO II

(THE BOOK WILL BE RIGHT BACK . . .)

I would like to apologize in advance for the discursive nature of this account of television in our national life, meaning mine. My attention span grows shorter. Every eight minutes, my mind wanders. I get the urge to go into the kitchen or to the bathroom or to go outside and buy something. The same thing, educators observe, happens to young children in classrooms. It's too quiet sitting here writing. The voices inside my head are only my own. Where is the sound track? I need music to tell me when something is important. How can I tell when a bad person enters my room, or a crisis is occurring, without the bongos and synthesizers up? How can I tell when something I have just written is funny? There is no laugh track. But, as promised, I digress.

If I seem distracted at times in doing this book it has taken me away from my lifetime vocation, which is looking at TV. Earlier, for example, I was doing truly important work, watching *General Hospital*. I love to watch hospitals in soap operas. They have eight doctors and nurses for every patient. If I ever get sick, I want Blue Cross to cover thirty-two days at General Hospital. I would rather have my nerves X-rayed at "Hospital," (as it's known by the cognoscenti in Port Charles) than at St. Elsewhere in Boston, where everybody dies, including the doctors.

Today, I am especially excited, because as soon as my basic task, seeing the day's soaps, is over, I have something even more significant to do. Cassettes of *Hollywood Wives* have arrived from ABC and are waiting on the floor by my VCR. *Hollywood Wives* is, of course, an epochal event. It is by a member of TV's literary establishment, Jackie Collins, a best-selling miniseries, a powerful drama that drove some TV viewers into puberty.

What was I saying? You see? I have difficulty finishing a thought. My mind keeps starting and stopping. If a problem isn't solved in sixty min-

utes, thirty minutes, or thirty seconds, I lose patience with it. I'm powerless. It's almost as if a third force is starting and stopping me, as if
somebody were tuning me. What is really strange about this is that we're
not talking about some dope. We're talking about one of the finest minds
in the aforementioned Western civilization. It's as if all the TV watching
I am required to do in this line of work could be changing me.

I don't want to alarm anybody, but have you ever considered that we
might be *mutating* as a resulting of all this TV? Biologically, I know my
kidneys are not the same. I can no longer sit and watch an entire movie
through without commercials. As our kidneys shrink, our stomachs grow.
How else can you explain the need to nosh so often? The next development
is bigger eyeballs.* I'm no authority on science. Heck, I thought a chromosome was Zenith's new TV tube. But who is to say one day little antenna
will *not* grow on the head? When was the last time you checked for
bumps?

Forget physicality. My mind has definitely been altered. I used to read
a lot, but now I only read during commercials. I've been reading *War
and Peace* since 1969. I'm doing it all wrong: I should be reading during
the programs. That way I won't miss the good stuff.

TV affects spelling. And I don't mean just Aaron. How do you spell,
they are always asking on TV, R-E-L-I-E-F? "R-O-L-A-I-D-S," they say.
I say T-U-M-S. I'm an independent thinker. Did you know that Tums
spelled backward is Smut? These are the uses of TV dyslexia.

My neighbor, Professor Marshall Hurwitz of the Department of Classical Languages and Hebrew at City College of New York, thinks it is all
of us, not just me. He got a paper last term from a student in mythology,
discussing the significance of "Jason and the Goldon Fleas [sic]", as if
they were a rock group. But there are those who will set us straight. I
once received an angry letter from a reader of my column: "Linda Evans's
role in 'Dynasty' is *Krystle*, not whatever spellings [and not Aaron] you
use in your essays [Crystal, et al.]."

Of course, I occasionally misspell a word on purpose, just to see if
anybody is reading. But I can't help wondering—how do those smart-
aleck English professors who complain know how, in a visual medium, a
character spells her name? And it is not only academics who make one

---

* The size of cantaloupes, Fred Allen used to predict, to go with brains the size of peas.
And then smaller ears, like corn kernels. But what did Allen know? He also said those
people on the screen in the musical-variety format who replaced his comedy program (*The
Fred Allen Show*) in the late 1940's were a special tribe of pygmies, like small gypsy bands.
To this day some people think that little people enter the TV set from the rear, while we're
not watching.

wonder about television's impact on our ability to read and reason. I get mail from readers of my column, which is titled "The Marvin Kitman Show," who address me as "Dear Mr. Show."

Not just ordinary amateurs are affected by the new television illiteracy. I called the research library at *Newsday* the other day, checking the spelling of Scheherazade—somehow I had forgotten—and the young research assistant asked, "Do you have a first name on that?"

Language usage has been altered. I used to say, when stepping on a foot in an elevator, subway, or movie, "Pardon me." Now I say, "Well, excuuussse-e-e me." (When I used the correct expression "Well, excuuussse-e-e me" in a recent scholarly essay in the *New Leader*, the copy editor changed it to "pardon me." Intellectuals!) Our heroes, even our celebrities, have been altered in value. "More people know Fonzie," Martin Garbus once told me, "than Brezhnev, Andropov, Nicaragua, and George Washington combined." Garbus is a first-rate civil-liberties lawyer who is famous for having grown up with Gary Marshall, creator of *Happy Days*. TV makes us all a family, the world's largest extended family. Or extruded.

We gain and we lose. Watching TV is causing us to gradually lose a few minor faculties, such as word recognition. A writing teacher at East Stroudsburg (Pa.) State College conducted an analysis of 8 *Charlie's Angels* scripts, and discovered that there were a total of 5,312 words in the average hour-long program. But there were only 1,000 discrete words; the others were discrete sounds such as grunts. The 8 shows together used a vocabulary of 3,350 words, about that of a child entering school in the first grade. So much for those who say TV isn't an educational tool. Those kids know more words than your average chimpanzee.

The missing words reappear elsewhere in our lives, thanks to TV. Should I be lucky enough to ever receive an award, mere thank-yous would not suffice. I would want to thank: "my executive producer, Gordon Slotkin; my assistant producer, Sy (Rip) Schwartz; my director, Harold Levenworth; my wife for giving me zero support. I did it anyway, Sheila. My mother, Esther, who really believed in me. Ma, you've got your condominium. . . . And last but not least, my kindergarten teacher whose advice I'll never forget: 'Sidney, a success you'll never be.' Go to hell, Sadie Glockenspiel. I'm glad I received this honor tonight. I deserved it."

We can thank the TV award shows for expanding the meaning of "a few words." (I'd better not.) But watching TV talk shows I learn all kinds of new words, such as "awesome." This is a California word meaning some awe, as in "this salad is awesome."

These days, my writing is filled with obscure classical references. "I'm not as neat as Felix," I write, immediately losing a certain number of the uneducated, unfamiliar with *The Odd Couple*.

In coping with major emotional problems in my life, I find myself saying, "Oh, yeah, they had that on *Growing Pains*." Kirk Cameron and I have a lot in common in our lives. More and more people use the emotional problems raised in soap operas as a guide to life. Infidelity, incest, alcoholism, miscegenation, incontinence, premature ejaculation— they say, "Oh, yeah, they had that on *All My Children*." When I ponder the larger questions, viz., "What is art?" I find myself saying, "As one of the major thinkers in our industry, Cher, explained in *People* magazine . . ." (What did Cher say about the meaning of art, you ask? "If Michelangelo painted in Caesar's Palace, would that make it any less 'art'?")

Today, as you will come to see, I am virtually illiterate. What an incredible achievement this has been, and in such a short time. (I became a TV critic in 1969.) The de-learning curve has been remarkable. I have become, in my way, without meaning to be boastful, beyond literacy. I am truly an audiovisual person.

The comforting aspect of these achievements is that one is not alone. The last words of the great choreographer Balanchine, when asked if there was anything that might make him happy, were: "Yes, I'd like to meet Lynda." That my Wonder Woman, Lynda Carter, was George Balanchine's, too, comforts me.

You never know where the marks of TV will impact, as they say. "Eric," my friend Max, a former public TV executive, wrote one day, "is hooked on *I, Claudius*." Eric was five months old at the time and a hefty eleven pounds, ten ounces, the worried father explained: "He will eat only while watching the excesses of our pizza parlor's forebears. This proves conclusively that watching television is an inherited trait, carried in chromosome 13 (or 2, 4, 7, 5, 9, 11, or up to 84 if you're a type UHF)."

Life is just full of such mysteries. A National Geographic Special will clear each of them up one day.

Once I had a steel-trap mind. Today it's a steel sieve. Some people have total memory, or as Oscar Levant said, "total recoil." I have total forgetfulness. This, however, is not a loss. It's a defense mechanism, I'm convinced, which has allowed me to remain a TV critic for nineteen years already.

If I remembered every plot of *Growing Pains*, I'd wake up screaming. It's essential to sanity not to remember or dwell on these things. It's also embarrassing. Do you know what it's like to have some thirteen-year-old punk write you a letter that informs you that the episode you thought was swell in *Charlie's Angels* was actually the same story used in *Mod Squad* and before that *The Fugitive*? It becomes difficult to take yourself seriously as an authority figure. Yet I am in possession of arcane facts. Georg Stanford Brown spells his Christian name without a final *e*. To my mind, however, he was in *Mod Squad*, not *The Rookies*. One out of two ain't bad.

Our onetime president Gerald Ford—or was it President Chevy Chase?—taught us it was not easy to walk and chew gum. "I find that I used to be able to think and write at the same time," explained Tony Prizendorf, a newsman then at Channel 5 in New York. We need consolation for memory loss, especially when one suddenly asks himself, "What time does the seven o'clock news come on?"

As I lie on the beach at East Hampton, the hot sun will boil the vegetable oil in my brain, and I gain fresh insights into how TV changes us. It's not only that I care who shot J.R. and that it was only a dream that Bobby died, or whether a great actress like Joan Collins should have posed in the nude for *Playboy*. The way I see things is different. Before I became a critic, I was an old-fashioned kind of guy. I thought in a linear mode. I moved from idea A to idea B in a straight line. Now, I have gone from linear reasoning to the other type, circular reasoning, or TV reasoning, TV-think. I used to be a normal writer. Dostoyevsky and Conrad come to mind. I wrote stories that moved in a logical progression. Today, I'm beyond that. My style is more MTV. I find myself thinking in terms of sequential bits, scenes (rather than stories or chapters), segments, none of which is more than ninety seconds.

Every story has a beginning, middle, and end, said Aristotle in *Poetics*. "And a tag," according to my friend Alan Alda. But lately I've developed this manner: A story starts in the middle and jumps back to the beginning, a form I call "Rewind." Or it jumps ahead, a literary device called "Fast Forward." I pause. Stop. Erase. Dubover, instead of rewriting. I tend to think in Slow Motion, even Super-Slo Mo, something most of the world may have first become aware of during the 1984 Olympics.*

Stop. Start. Fast forward. Replay. Pause. Rewind. Click. Click. Everything I do now at the typewriter is so fragmented.

Even the most serious of writers, Renata Adler, is stylistically in synch. Nobody writes a story with a beginning, a middle, and an end anymore. There is a fragmentation in society as in the arts, which affects writers

---

* It is a technique invented by an obscure camera-store janitor musician in the Fairfax Avenue section of Los Angeles named Super Schlomo. Yes, the man who used to play with the Izzie Gillespie Band.

like Adler. Novels like her *Pitch Dark* provoked debate about "whether it was a brilliantly constructed mosaic or a random collection of deft snippets." But none of those naysayers were TV viewers. It's "modernist in form," said Adler of the style.

The changes were complete, I decided, after buying my first VCR. It was as if a cassette had been inserted in my brain, a continuous tape, a compilation of everything experienced on television. Characters in commercials, like Fred the Furrier, or the two stoical, splendid spokesmen for Bartles & Jaymes, are as memorable as characters in the dramas and sitcoms. At first, I doubted myself; it was as if, in the words of the noted merchant and motivational researcher Crazy Eddie, I had gone totally insane. Then, by God, I got it! Isherwood had written *I Am a Camera*; suddenly I knew that I was a VCR.

As a video recorder, I immediately had my first identity crisis: was I a JVC or a Panasonic?

This realization has become pervasive. That I have become a machine, much like Gregor What's-His-Face in Kafka's *Metamorphosis*, who woke one morning to find that he was a cockroach, was a fact I just had to face. The sum of my life was being stored, as bits and snatches of television, cassettelike in my mind. I had become the living personification of MTV.

And what has happened to me is happening to you. This book is a warning. I am what I see on TV, as Descartes might have said. We are all half-sleeping giants who are going to explode, or implode, one day. When Peter Finch in *Network* cried "Wake up!" he was ahead of his time, by five minutes.

What you are about to read are my tapes, and so are my pearls preserved for *Posterity* (follows *Jeopardy!* in prime time). Here you will find my analyses of the great issues of our time—whatever happened to Moldavia in *Dynasty*, should Rona Barrett be declared legally inane, and did Lassie take cocaine?

There are others who would tell my story. The first time my son Jamie used the cash machine at the bank, he came to Step 3, which directed him to a button he was told to "Depress." So he told the story of how much money he owed MasterCard and how he had gotten a parking ticket that morning as well as a flat tire.

But I must tell my own story, for it may be yours, too.

And getting it all off my tape is terrific. There is nothing so refreshing as degaussing if you have become a tape. Erasing gives you, as we say, the wonderful feeling of being clean for the first time.

START TAPE 1

(ON)

I have no patience with those who would attack TV for having no educational value. My own life is testimony to its uplifting, upgrading powers. Consider what happened to me on a weekend in the country. (STOP) (REWIND)

THE DUKE OF JERSEY
(MY ADVENTURE AT *DITCHLEY*)

(PLAY)

In 1977, I was invited to attend a conference, "The Impact of Television on Human Behaviour," at Ditchley Park, an olde English country house (built between 1720 and 1730) in Oxfordshire, 72 miles from London and 3,258 miles from New Jersey. Queen Anne slept there. So did Sir Winston Churchill, whose own country place, Checquers, was down the road. Blenheim Palace was a neighbor to Ditchley. Some neighborhood.

So you see how educational this is already?

The weekend meeting was sponsored by the prestigious Ditchley Foundation, and was attended by distinguished leaders of the television community in Great Britain and the United States. These included Sir Michael Swann, then chairman of the BBC, and Lady Swann; Lord Windlesham, P.C., managing director of the ATV; Lady Plowden, D.B.E., chairman, Independent Broadcast Authority; Lord Aldington, K.C.M.G., C.B.E., D.S.O., P.C., T.D., D.L., chairman of the BBC General Advisory Council, and Lady Aldington; and me, Marvin, with my lady, Carol.

Oh, yes, there were several scholars from English institutions. Professor

James D. Halloran, director, Centre for Mass Communication Research, University of Leicester, was on hand. One guy, Rt. Hon. Lord Harris of Greenwich, minister of state, the Home Office, actually had to leave the conference one day to sit in the House of Lords. The equally distinguished American delegation included Arthur R. Taylor, then president of CBS and onetime heir apparent to the throne of Paley I; Chairman Richard W. Wiley of the Federal Communications Commission; Donald H. McGannon, president of Westinghouse Broadcasting; John Jay Iselin, president of WNET/13; Professor Percy Tannenbaum of the University of California at Berkeley; Eli Evans, of the Carnegie Commission, and other members of our intellectual TV royalty.

I suppose I was there as a case study in altered behavior. Besides, they needed someone who actually watched television. I was, at the time, kind of a walking case, living testimony that TV has considerable impact on human behavior. Every eight minutes or so at the conference, my attention wandered. I became listless, needed a sweet or a nosh, had to go to the bathroom.

They might also have needed someone to answer technical questions, such as: Who is in Grant's tomb? (a) Lee Grant (b) Lou Grant (c) Bob Grant (d) Grant Tinker (e) all of the above.

As you may not have suspected, I had never been invited to a stately English country house for a weekend before. Or during the week, for that matter. I don't think a Kitman has been invited for a weekend in England (or anywhere else) in the last hundred years.

The terrors of country life are well known, and the English weekend terrifies even the English. They did not give courses in English country weekends at the City College of New York. I was a nervous wreck even before the weekend started. (See my monograph *How to Wear a Jacket While at University.*)

The Ditchley Foundation driver picked us up at Heathrow in the Daimler. I was genuinely miserable, looking over the gray countryside that January morning motoring out to the house, even when passing Checquers. When the moon was up during World War II and the Germans could see clearly, we were told, Churchill would sleep at Ditchley on weekends. (Clever. So, that's why he didn't sleep at home. But it probably didn't do a lot for Lady Churchill.)

We drove onto the pebbled serpentine driveway of the magnificent former residence of Sir Henry Lee, Knight of the Garter, and the second Earl of Litchfield, whose father, Francis Henry Lee, the first Earl, had married Lady Charlotte Fitzroy, natural daughter of Charles II by Barbara Villiers, Duchess of Cleveland. (*Cleveland?*) It looked like a nice place, said to have 38 bedrooms in the manor house, surrounded by 150 acres. It may have been 150 bedrooms and 38 acres. The place is so big and so stately and of so much historic interest, they have guidebooks to it. I am not in them, even now.

I do believe I was the first member of my class (1953) at City College who had graduated without honors, with a B.A. in only six years, who later attended the U.S. Army and rose to Pfc through the ranks in only two years; member, Brooklyn Tech Alumni Association; member, AFTRA; member, FDIC; to visit Ditchley. Through the front door.

Sir Philip Adams, K.C.M.G., ambassador to Cairo, now the director of the Ditchley Foundation, was on hand outside to greet us. So was Lady Adams. And butlers, footmen, and maids, all lined up like in a movie. The footman threw open the great oak door. We went into the central hallway. It was roughly the size of my house in New Jersey. There was a fire crackling in the fireplace large enough to roast Brandon Tartikoff *and* Johnny Carson, with Don Rickles, Joey Bishop, and Sammy Davis, Jr., on the dais. As a footman or batman or tight end took our luggage up to our room, miraculous things had already begun to happen. I suddenly knew how to act.

When this guy in dinner clothes first came down the steps to the manor house to greet us, I didn't try to shake his hand. (The low point of my life had been once when I thought the fellow in the black tie was the host of a dinner party I was invited to. He was, of course, a butler. No resemblance at all to the host I was to meet for the first time, Herb Schmertz, the Duke, as in put up your dukes, of Mobil Oil.)

At dinner the first night, with all the lords and ladies, sirs and siresses, I was sensational. The first course was announced as a fish mousse. I had never seen a fish mousse before—did it have antlers instead of gills? Is it hung on the wall?—much less dream that I would ever be eating one. But I knew the proper utensils, somehow, of the eighteen surrounding my plate like a model of the Dunkirk evacuation.

And I didn't lick the fork afterward, even though it was a first-rate fish mousse. I didn't use my fingers on the lamb chops. I didn't slurp my soup, which came as the last course, which I didn't laugh at. When they passed the port, I knew it went to the right, sliding it along to Lord Wilderpointshaver. My elbows weren't on the table once.

During conversational lulls I knew how to say things like "Up with the Raj, down with the peasants." I'm joking, of course. You didn't talk politics in genteel company with the ladies present. You made chit-chat, polite talk.

I tell you not since Woodrow Wilson had a New Jersey fellow handled himself so correctly at dinner, making his debut in polite society. I just knew to do all the right things. Not once did I err. It was almost as if knowing how to handle myself on a weekend in a stately English country house had been in my genes. That's absurd, of course. No, something bigger had intervened.

Despite my humble origins, I seemed to know exactly how to comport myself in a stately house, and at its stately dinner table, *thanks to educational TV*, in the form of *Masterpiece Theatre*. All the time I had been sitting there wasting my time, watching what I considered a soap opera— a British soap (Yardley's) opera—*Upstairs, Downstairs* was teaching me. Miraculously, I had become to the manor reborn.

Not that I was without culture or couth. My parents had taken me during my childhood years from Pittsburgh to Brooklyn—where I could have the advantages of the public-school system (P.S. 186)—for polishing. Other parents took their children to the Continent. Then there was the culture acquired in the shopping-mall culture of Paramus and Mahwah, New Jersey. It had all come togther importantly in *Upstairs, Downstairs*, making my manners in the manor shine like the patina of old silver.

To be sure, in the first season of *Upstairs, Downstairs* (1974), I used to joke about how my wife and I would handle the servants, if we ever got one. Whenever there was a family crisis, I would start wiping the wineglasses like 'Udson. I guess I carried it a little too far sometimes. "Will you *stop* calling me Rose," my wife once said sharply when I asked that the bed be made and fluffed for a change. After Lady Margery died, I wore a black armband for a week.

"Rest assured, Sir Geoffrey Dillon will be in touch concerning your libelous statements," I wrote often when anyone criticized my criticism.

My favorite new activity was decanting the port, an elaborate ritual with candles. In a hundred years, dating back to Vilna in Lithuania, ancestral home of the Kitmans, there has never been a Kitman who decanted port in his leisure time. Or one with leisure time. On occasion, I've been a little absurd in pushing port. The thing is, none of my friends drink port.

Still, life was easier when I was 'Udson, running 165 Eaton Place. Yet I had no idea how all of this miserable, pretentious playacting would work, if ever there was a time to put it in practice. I didn't laugh when people at Ditchley said *izzue* or *shedule*. I went right along with it, saying *shool* as in "What shool did you attend—Eton or Harrod's?" Never once saying I had gone up to Yeshiva of Bensonhurst.

The major item on everybody's agenda at the conference was talk. They do so much with talk as to make everybody who isn't English feel inadequate. But somehow I could speak English, finally. Said *bawth* for bath (which was something you didn't put into practice that weekend because it was so cold). And like 'Udson, you didn't speak unless spoken to, or had something crashingly important to say, such as "There is a bit of a snake on your foot, Lady Grassmere."

Still, the tensions were constant. The conference consisted of a series of luncheon and dinner parties, each designed to expose me as an imposter. Every day we would be awakened at 6:30 A.M.—in one of the colder of the thirty-eight bedrooms—by our chambermaid, Rose (as I persisted in calling our chambermaid, Millicent), with tea. "India or China?" she would call cheerfully from the hallway as we hopped around, putting on enough bathrobes. "Make mine iced," I would mumble agreeably. It would never melt. They had turned on the heat for Queen Anne, sometime before 1714, and it still hadn't come up to our room on the second floor, a bracing 45 degrees in January-February.*

The aforementioned *bawth* would then be drawn or sketched. Either way, it was too cold to believe. Then we would dress quickly in our tweeds and run down the stairs for breakfast, served from the sideboard as had been our custom at Eaton Place, too, and buried our heads in *The Times*'s English football (soccer) standings and in soft-boiled eggs and bangers. This was before they had morning television in England, incidentally, before *A.M. London* or *Good Morning U.K.* or *Dukes of Hazzard* reruns or old movies. I don't know how they survived all those years. You were not supposed to talk to anyone at breakfast; just keep your mouth shut, except for inserting food. Why? Because at lunch and dinner you were expected to talk your head off.

An agenda was posted in the grand hall for the day's scholarly events. My own hidden agenda read:

1. keep warm.
2. check seating arrangements

I didn't want to be seated next to one of the other Americans, like the lord of CBS, Arthur Taylor, who was still acting as if he hadn't been fired a week before the conference began; or Peggy Charren, the Queen Mother of Good Children's TV, who would chew my ear off about how kids want to see more *Hansel and Gretel* when the truth is they love programs like *Three's Company* and *I Dream of Jeannie*, and all other

---

* Later, I learned that Queen Anne had slept, actually, or *eckchewaly*, in an older home on the Ditchley grounds, one built in the fourteenth century. We were staying at the "new" house. She died in 1714, undoubtedly from a chill.

shows made for adults. (Somebody was wrong about the age groups at which network prime-time shows were aimed.) I preferred sitting next to the Marquis of Television Reruns, the Viscount of London Weekend TV. Within hours after arrival, I had become an insufferable snob.

I did love the mealtimes, breaking bread with my newfound peers. "The wines of Cleveland are famous," I would comment as they poured the wine. "Oh?" Lord Pound Sterling would say.

(Bill Beutel of ABC had told me the week before the conference that the official wine of Cleveland was slivovitz.)

And they, in turn, would lay information on me, complaining about how the Kuwaiti were buying up all our institutions, like the Ritz. At the white sale at Harrod's, Marghanita Laski explained, "There wasn't a thing left to buy. Not even for ready money. Not a washcloth." The Kuwaiti cartel had cornered the market in towels! See what I mean? Learning, learning . . . all the time.

The conference broke into a number of study groups, which met between meals, where you could catch up on your sleep to be fresh for the next meal. You quickly learned that the Tapestry Room, where a plenary session was being held, was the only room in the house that didn't have a tapestry on the wall. Here they discussed such matters as "whether TV was having as much impact on public behaviour as the petrol engine."

Many of the social scientists seemed to know each other from previous conferences, where they had also studied the impact of TV. One old chap said, if I'm not mistaken, that he had done a paper for a Visigoth conference on TV's impact in 476, right after the Roman Empire fell. Rome, he explained, fell because of violence at the Coliseum with the Christians and lions. Everybody went to see the lions eating the Christians in the so-called family hour. Anyhow, the point that I think he was making was that he'd been around for a long time.

We had predecessors, of course. There had been an earlier conference on TV at Ditchley in the 1970's when some sociologist did a paper about American imperialism. This involved a plot to destroy the minds of the Third World with *Charlie's Angels*. The show had obviously been designed by the CIA to warp the minds of African and English kids. He really believed that. Nobody wanted to disabuse him of the notion, either. Ridiculous. To think there were people in TV intelligent enough to have dreamed up such a plot.

A vow of confidentiality was taken. We were not supposed to say what went on at Ditchley meetings. Otherwise, an exchange of views would be inhibited. We were allowed to say such things as the crowd attending the conference was mainly British and titled, and an enormous proportion of the nontitled were Jews and had a lot of hair. I shall protect the *privvacy* of the institution to this day. (Many of the participants are still living, despite the temperature.)

But a number of important discussions about television took place outside the official sessions. I remember asking Lady Plowden, famous in the United States for her landmark study on childhood education, why she had bought *Charlie's Angels* for ITV (the British independent telly, or commercial network). She liked it personally, she said.

Shivering and eating aside, the major business of the conference seemed to be drinking. I knew why they plied the guests with so much alcohol. As Lord Leyland Land-Rover told me, "Brandy is Nature's own antifreeze." Delicacy, tact, and good breeding prevent mentioning a fallacy in his scientific reasoning: Alcohol makes you colder. Still, with my exquisite new manners, I never complained. I kept a stiff upper and lower lip; frozen, in fact. In another week I'd have been praising the lack of heat, to the extent that I could still speak at all.

So, gossiping, shivering, talking, and drinking. That's what the feared English country weekend boiled down to. I kept expecting that the pressure would get to me. I'd blow my cool at some minor contretemps, like the time I didn't seem to have a spoon for the cake, and Colonel Gye (a Ditchley administration official assigned to guard me, or so it seemed) said, somewhat miffed, "That's because you ate your potted shrimp with it." At no time did I say, "Well, excuuussse-e-e me."

Despite a wretched upbringing, despite being beneath the salt, I could hack it. The House of Kitman, in North America, was not shamed. But Monday morning, as we were taking our leave and Lady and Sir Philip were saying "Do come again," Carol and I talked about their coming over for a weekend. If only my poor mother were alive, I mused as the Daimler tooled back to Heathrow. As she said once, counseling me gently in the finer points, "Use your napkin, Marvin, that's what they're made for."

(STOP) (PAUSE)

(PLAY)

Not all of us are lucky enough to be able to attend Big Think conferences. There is a principle guiding attendance; as the prominent New York analyst and shrink-about-conferences Dr. Donald Kaplan said: "It's the leisure of the theory class."

Conferences began in early times as a defense. After the Middle Ages, instead of throwing down boiling oil on the enemy, they began to throw research papers. Delivering papers is the seeming purpose of conferences. But any conference worth its salt, including SALT talks, has hidden agendas.

At Ditchley, for example, the powerful media and communications moguls were setting the course for the British Empire for the next five years. Everybody was out for things not listed in the conference title or agenda—better jobs, more power, more money. Eli Evans of the Carnegie Commission, for example, was there to determine the need for a new Carnegie Commission on Public Television—which would spend five years studying the need—and then appoint himself to the commission. Professor Percy H. Tannenbaum of the Graduate School of Public Policy at the University of California, Berkeley, was there to trace his roots back to the House of Windsor. Everybody had some ulterior motive. They all wanted something and knew how to get it. It was a little frightening to me, seeing a game being played without a ball.

My only problem was that I never knew what I was doing there. My fellow conferees knew their agendas. I didn't want any of their jobs, all of which seemed boring compared to mine. They all wanted something. My agenda was getting a free trip abroad. That was not much of an agenda, and it had been accomplished once we were under way. I reminded myself of Milt Kamen, who used to say, "I want to sell out to Hollywood. But they never ask."

(STOP) (REWIND)

MY LIÈGE, BELGIUM
(PUBLIC TV CONFERENCES/THRILLS)

(PLAY)

Every seven years or so, I manage to put it all together, though, and get asked to a conference. In the spring of 1983, I was invited to attend a second—a public TV conference in Liège, Belgium, called Input/83, which was designed to deal with such pressing issues as *Video, avez-vous dit video?*

A public TV conference in Belgium? What a good place for it. Speaking of pressing issues, at least I could get a waffle or two out of it. And see some TV. I love TV in Europe. You get to see *Dallas* in other languages, and a lot of the classics, like *Lassie*. She barks in Italian. It's dubbed.

Liège turns out to be a wonderful place to visit, a small city on the

River Meuse. On Sunday the major form of entertainment is window shopping for arms. It's a terrorist arms center. But when you really get to know it, in a few hours or so, it is clearly the Pittsburgh of Belgium. Downstream, the Meuse is lined with steel mills, relieved only by what looks like atomic reactors. But Liège itself is *Nowheresville de Cité*, the original nothing town in Belgium.

The conferences, an annual event, are sponsored by the public-television systems of Belgium, Italy, West Germany, the Netherlands, Canada, Hungary, France, Denmark, the U.K., and the United States. They are attended by public-TV network station executives, scholars, independent film-makers and disinterested observers such as myself. It has the distinction of being different. The founding fathers of Input sat down in 1978 (Input/78) in Milan and figured out a conference that included all the elements not found in other conferences. By putting together all the missing disparate elements, they created a whole new concept for a conference. That's what I call real input. It shows what the human mind can do when it wants to travel on an expense account.

Input/83 was hosted/sponsored this year by Radio-Télévision Belge de la Communauté Culturelle Française-Liège (RTBF, the Belgian public-TV system in the southern part of the country) and was being held at the most fashionable hotel in town, the Holiday Inn. This spa represents New World charm to the Belgians. We were all free to stay at the other exotic foreign place in town, the Ramada Inn, further down the Meuse, near the McDonald's.

It didn't matter what the hotels were like. We were there for business— to watch TV shows for a full week. They had three screening rooms going in the basement of the Palais de Congrès, adjoining the Holiday. And they weren't showing *Dynasty*, the most popular show in Europe in March 1983, but public-TV programs. You got to see documentaries and public-affairs shows from SNTF (Société Nationale Télévision Française), ZDF (Zweites Deutsches Fernsehen), Magyar Televiso, RAI (Radiotelevisione Italiana), not to mention WNET/13, WETA/Washington, and KQED/Pittsburgh.

The way the conference worked was through the viewing and discussion method, preceded by confusion. First you were in conflict about which of the three screening rooms to go to in the morning and afternoon sessions. It wore me down deciding. This needn't have been a problem; they had "demand" screenings so you could watch cassettes in little private cabinets after dinner and throughout the night. Then the viewers could ask profound questions of the film-makers, producers, network executives. Why did they do it that way?, and so forth. American public-TV people tended to ask only how much everything cost, and where did they get the money? This bored the hell out of the European public-TV people, who are artists, not fund-raisers.

Sometimes the discussions were quite lively. Once, they showed *Working*, the musical based on Studs Terkel's book, the most prestigious production in the *American Playhouse* (season of 1983). This jewel cost millions, raised from five or six foundations. The gist of the discussion was that the music was lousy but that was okay, the production was lousy, too. The British, in particular, could be very candid at these conferences.

The programs, as noted, were translated into many languages. Belgian TV shows alone were broadcast in Walloon, Flemish, and French. They really rub it in in Belgium, making you feel inferior—illiterate in three languages.

Yet anything seems possible in a Holiday Inn in Liège, in the heart of the coal-rich Ardennes area, and anything tends to happen. You sense this, lifting an occasional glass of the favorite local drink, what they call an "anthracite," a martinilike drink, very volatile clear liquid with a prune, representing a lump of coal.

The conference was run by a consortium of powerful brass from the world's biggest public-broadcasting systems, RAI and RFE, ZDF, SNTF, BBC, RTBF, and RSVP. But it was really run by the Rockefeller Foundation man, Howard Klein. He supplied the money for the American public-TV film-makers' and others' travel grants to attend. The Rockefeller man was the guiding light of the convention. His job is to travel around the world to see what's going on at the events he funds. He was more popular and more heavily attended than any of the TV shows.

With multitranslations blaring away, it was a media experience. Also, it seemed a little silly sitting in the basement of a Holiday Inn on the River Meuse watching public-TV shows I had already missed or planned to miss at home. It was one thing to be in my TV den in New Jersey watching TV and pondering the meaning of life and art and whether *My Little Margie* was the first sitcom about a girl on speed. But here in the heart (and gallbladder) of Flemish culture, with food only a short distance away, TV finally palled for me.

We started taking café-au-lait breaks in the morning, leaving the screening rooms and driving to the other end of Belgium, some eighty-two kilometers away. It's a civilized country in which you can drive from end to end in less time than it takes you to get to East Hampton on a Friday afternoon.

To forget TV, we relaxed by going to cathedrals. Of special interest there was religious art. I am something of a specialist. You can always tell a religious painting by the gold halos. There is more gold in some of those pictures than in a Fortunoff's window. Mark Twain once said that if you've seen one martyr you've seen them all. He was wrong. We looked at a lot of pictures with a lot of blood spurting. Flemish art seemed like a metaphor for public TV's problems.

To lighten the Christian misery of our illicit mornings, we went to chocolate shoppes. They have them in Belgium the way we have bars in Jersey, on every corner. And we researched the cuisine. The first day we had some *frites.* That's the national dish of Belgium—fried potatoes— with mayo. They serve them in wax-paper cones—with a dollop the size of half a bottle of mayonaise. "Fries and mayo," my wife said. "That's why the Belgians look that way."

Belgian fries are such a craze these days, they are specifically forbidden at the Waterloo battlefield. At the entrance to the steps (222 of them) up to the butte where a huge stone lion honors the duke of Wellington, a sign reads: *FRITES INTERDITES.*

In addition, we went to dinner a lot with Mr. and Mrs. Rockefeller, as we thought of them. They were vegetarians, and they discovered this wonderful Vietnamese restaurant in downtown Liège. Every dish had bean sprouts in it, or sprouts of something. The names of the dishes were exotic, the food even more mysterious, and altogether it reminded me of a Chinese restaurant in Roscoe, New York.

They used to say a six-course meal in Belgium was steak, fries, and four bottles of beer. But apart from the mysteries and miseries of Southeast Asian cooking transplanted, the best restaurants of Belgium were sinfully good, and we spent more and more conference time conferring in them. After all that public TV, you needed some private time.

(STOP)

END TAPE 1 (EJECT)

START TAPE 2

COVERED WITH HONORS:
(THE FIRST ANNUAL KITMAN LECTURE AT
BROOKE SHIELDS MEMORIAL HIGH SCHOOL)

(PLAY)

All is not foreign travel and heavy-breathing intellectual conferences. One of the greatest honors I've had so far in my career is being invited to address the student body at a private school in northern New Jersey, the Dwight-Englewood School, known locally as Brooke Shields Memorial High School. (Yes, it is the school Brooke herself attended.) The big money in lecturing is at the women's clubs or synagogues or the colleges. For a TV critic at my level, though, visiting high schools is the most aesthetically rewarding experience.

It has been said that in my columns, I tend to be writing over people's heads. If the average age of TV viewers (my readers) is twelve, I write for the fourteen-year-old mind. Thus, the accusation has some merit. I am too highbrow. But if there is one thing these young people know, whatever their teachers say about them, it's TV. Nothing is too obscure for these high-school kids. Any reference to *Air Wolf* or *Knight Rider* or other shows you may have never heard of hits the mark. These kids are the true scholars in our field. Going to your average high school for a TV critic is going to the Groves of Academe.

Should I want to discuss KITT, the wonderful car in *Knight Rider* (the car talks: more intelligently than any of the actors in the show), and compare it to, say, the helicopter in *Blue Thunder?*—they know what I'm talking about.

It's not like trying to have an intelligent conversation with those adults you run into at lectures elsewhere, who say the only thing they watch on TV is *The MacNeil/Lehrer NewsHour*. And maybe, for laughs, a presidential press conference or State of the Union address. I have no problems communicating with my audiences at your average high school. We talk fluent TV together. We are bilingual.

"Today, we are going to discuss one of the great unanswered questions of our times," my lecture begins. "What is the name of the family in *The Brady Bunch?* Is it: (a) Kelly (b) Bunche, as in Ralph Bunche (c) Schwartz (d) Partridge (e) none of the above."

The resulting discussion is stimulating. You'd be amazed at the philosophical ramifications of the question. These kids know where it's at (culturally). And it's not at Elaine's or at the Aspen Institute.

The students at Shields Memorial are special. The crème de la crème of northern New Jersey and New York City youth are sent here for finishing. There are more BMWs in the parking lot per student capita (1.4—some leave their second cars at school) than in any high school east of Beverly Hills.

Indeed, it was a career-opportunities-day convocation at Beverly Hills East, in which the school administrators had invited distinguished representatives of the tristate area in the arts and business to tell the young scholars about challenging positions that might inspire them. Other addresses that day were delivered by a fellow who I believe was related to the De Beers family (they're in diamonds), and another chap, who owns Wall Street. His great-grandfather invented the stock exchange, and every time a share was bought or sold he got a small royalty, I think. Anything is possible for these kids.

As I looked out over the student body, my mind could not help but go to Brooke. Only a year earlier she had been sitting in these very seats, thinking, probably, about what sat between her and her Calvins.

I used to find myself hanging on every word of those Brooke Shields commercials for Calvin Klein. They were pearls for posteriority. My favorite was the one where she reads a book. It looked like a classic. Maybe it was the dictionary. She liked the plot. Or maybe it was something really heavy, a Sidney Sheldon. Then she stops and looks up. She is thinking. This may have been a very hard thing for her to do.

Finally she says, "Reading is to the mind . . ."

There is a long pause. You can almost hear the director (Richard Avedon) say, "Now take a long, philosophical look at your pants, kid." You think she is going to say something important. And she does:

"As Calvin is to the body."

This had to be the most memorable line in TV advertising since Orson Welles spoke for Paul Masson. Only I forget it. Oh, yes: "I will eat no crow* before its time."

Reading is to the mind as Calvin is to the body? Didn't I hear that before in a Bob Dylan song? The only trouble is, what did it mean? Was she trying to encourage reading? If I ever read a book, the youth of America may be thinking, I'll look like Brooke Shields.

Then there was the famous New Math commercial, the one in which she explains that whenever she gets some money, she buys Calvins. If there is any left over, she pays the rent.

* Or was it cow?

She was fourteen when she made that commercial. What fourteen-year-old pays the rent? Besides, the whole thing sounds like baloney. Mommy pays. Or her manager. At least she didn't imply that anybody else was paying the rent.

And do you know how inadequate this commercial makes the average kid feel? Brooke is counting her money to buy Calvins, playing with the nice little budget of $2 million a year. And they are baby-sitting at two dollars an hour. My sixteen-year-old daughter Andrea, who gave me these facts, was especially pissed.

Then there was the one where she is talking about how there are two kinds of people who wear his stuff: those who want to remember and those who want to forget. I mean, Brooke is really deep, a regular Camus in Calvins. Another couple of commercials in this vein, and she would be offered a chair in philosophy at Harvard. And if the chair fits, wear it . . . outside you and your Calvins.

With each new major philosophical statement she was making for Calvin Klein back in 1980–81, Brooke seemed to be changing. Originally she was made up to look like an innocent, one who was filmed nude as a nine-year-old, at her mother's suggestion. She matured before our eyes (my lenses) in commercials. By the third one, she was wearing her hair in an older fashion. Her hair was frizzier in the budget/rent spot. "La Creepella," as Andrea and her friends said of her new creepier look. Kids are jealous and cruel, not like me, Marvin.

And then there was her frankly autobiographical "Wanna know what comes between me and my Calvins? Nothing." I get it, I said to myself, a few days later. *They are implying Brooke Shields doesn't wear underwear.* Bad taste! This one should win her the Mendel* Award for cheap genes.

And then Brookie began singing. No harm done; she sounded like a dolphin. It was the same song she sang in the movie *Pretty Baby*. A song that is historically sung in New Orleans brothels, an authority once told me. No matter. There always seemed to be a last line missing in whatever she had to say for Calvins. Yes, baby, go on . . . Finish your thought . . .

I saw one empty chair in the school auditorium. Could that be where Brookie sat figuring out her budget? Some day they would put up a plaque: THE BROOKE SHIELDS CHAIR OF MATHEMATICS. Future scholars will visit. It could be a shrine.

---

* The Henri Mendel prize in biological retailing.

All of this was before Brooke went off to Princeton. But who knows, I thought: Today there could be another major figure in that student body whom I might now influence.

I was warned by a school administrator that the body was interested in two subjects: cars and money. They were also very laid back.

First of all, I apologized for being so distracted. At this very moment a show, the daytime version of *Wheel of Fortune*, was going on without me. There was a sitting ovation.

I was especially dazed, I explained, because I had just returned from the dentist. It was nothing. Root-canal work. No worse than a brain transplant. And I was still under the influence of drugs.

That got the biggest hand of the day.

"The subject of this mini-course," I explained, "is How to Be a TV Critic. It is the world's most exciting profession. When your fathers rush to work in the morning, I rush to the TV set. All day and night. Nobody can say, 'Are you watching TV, again? You'll ruin your mind. Your brain will turn to mush. Why don't you read a book?' If I read books instead of watching TV, I'd lose my job. I'd have to go on welfare, and sit at home and watch TV."

Then the real talk began.

"Do you know me?"

You have to talk as people do in the commercials. It's the lingua franca, which allows one to be understood in the East, West, North, and selected cities in the South at the same time. Yet why lecture at all? I should have just played my video. How important can you be without having your own video today?

I continued the guessing game about my identity in the American Express commercial manner. I was someone half-famous, someone whose name was known but whose face wasn't. But because I do some TV, this becomes doubly confusing. People often look at me and say, "You're somebody," but they haven't got the foggiest notion *which* body. As one fan said to me after the night I knocked them dead on the *Tomorrow Show* with Tom Snyder, "Are you somebody?" Yes, I assured them, and signed their autograph books, *Somebody*.

"My name is Marvin Kitman," I lectured on. "I write a newspaper column called 'The Marvin Kitman Show.' I don't call myself a columnist or a writer. I am identified as 'executive producer' under the picture in the space."

My show started in 1969. It has already outlasted a number of other important shows of the period. *The Merv Griffin Show, The David Frost Show, The Mike Douglas Show, Captain and Tennille, Thicke of the Night.*

I write five columns, or episodes, a week, in my house in northern New Jersey. They are sent to a newspaper called *Newsday* in Long Island over a telephone wire, where it is then published and forwarded to the Los Angeles Times Syndicate, which sends it to other enlightened papers across the nation. My column is seen—I don't know about read—by millions. My whole life, I explained, is a miracle of technology.

For many years I was also the TV critic on a New York news show—*The Ten O'Clock News*—on WNYW-TV (Channel 5), where I was known to a whole other new set of people who don't read *Newsday* or maybe, judging the response, anything. I was on every Saturday night, right before Lotto at 10:15. Every parking-lot attendant, night watchman, Con Ed repairman, elevator operator, and sanitation man knew me instantly. To them, I was as big as Walter Cronkite. That's because they only tuned in the news a few minutes early so they wouldn't miss Lotto. Quite accidentally, they heard my commentaries on the medium of TV. The resultant fame, I found, could be scary.

One day I was walking along Columbus Avenue in Manhattan after dinner, before resuming my duties at home in front of the set, when a long lavender-and-flamingo Lincoln Continental with white sheepskin fenders came to a screeching halt in front of me. A dude in flashy clothes rushed out of this pimpmobile, and right at me. I could see the headlines: TV CRITIC ASSAULTED, SOLD INTO WHITE SLAVERY IN BEIRUT. The man would flash a gun and I'd die. Instead, he flashed a grin that sparkled. He had diamonds in his teeth instead of gold. "Hey, Mr. TV Man," he shouted, "I know you." He pumped my hand so hard it bled. He had five diamond rings on his hand.

The school official had asked me to tell the children a little about my work, what I like about it and why.

"So you want to be a famous newspaper critic like me? First of all," I patiently explained, "there are no openings at my paper, and won't be for twenty-five or thirty years. You may as well be brain surgeons or used-car salesmen." I knew these kids. They ask a lot of questions, as if they were really interested in the medium as an art form, but all they want is your job. They're always these young punks who are hot writers, with new insights, wanting to steal your bread. These are rotten kids.

As I went on to tell the students, a lot of people think that because they have a TV set that makes them a critic. This is a common misconception. You can't expect to be a critic just like that. What do you think this is—the presidency? You have to have qualifications.

First, you must develop a working understanding of technology. Van Gordon Sauter, when president of CBS News, told a man he was hiring as the producer of the *CBS Evening News* with Dan Rather, "All you have to know about TV is that when you turn the knob to the right, the volume goes up." He is a well-known kidder. You also have to know how to turn the set on. And off.

Second, you have to be able to be over people's heads sometimes. You don't want them to understand everything. Be obscure. Otherwise how can you be taken seriously?

This is the Andrew Sarris school of movie criticism. We don't have any really obscure writers in TV since Marshall McLuhan died. He was always saying those wild things like the invention of lasagna made the Pullman car obsolete. Mac was our field's leading thinker.

Not just anybody, as I've been trying to say without hurting your feelings, can be a critic. You have to have a gift for words. An important part of your job every year is finding new ways to say *garbage*, as in "This is the worst garbage." Some of the words I've coined over the years include *junk, trash, rubbish, drek, pure garbage*, and *impure garbage*.

You also have to have an historical sense. You must be able to say, as I have on occasion, "This is the worst season since 1982." Or "the worst since 1981." Or 1980, 1979, or 1978, from a random list of the worst seasons taken from my files. You need a rich background in the art of television to draw on.

You can't fool people about TV. It's not like the theater or dance, where nobody really knows anything. Theater, especially, is a tiny art form. You can fit the whole Broadway audience for a year into a closet. TV is a mass art, where everybody is an expert because everybody is involved.

The people at home are genuine authorities, experts in their fields. The average person who makes *Mr. Belvedere* his life's work knows more about it than Albert Einstein in his prime knew about the universe.

(STOP) (PAUSE)

I then paused to tell the inspiring story of my daughter Suzy, who, like thousands of young people, took time off from television one spring as she prepared to take the S.A.T.'s, the ticket of admission to college. Half the time she told me how dumb and irrelevant the tests were, the other half she worried that she wouldn't do well enough to get into the college of her choice. Only two things stood in her way of becoming the first Harvard woman in the Kitman family: the verbal and math parts of the tests.

The S.A.T. (Scholastic Aptitude Test) has various virtues. It is a terrific money-maker for the E.T.S. (Educational Testing Service) people in

Princeton. But are the S.A.T.'s a good thing in themselves, and do they adequately judge skills relevant to the culture of the electronic age students like my daughter have grown up in?

Every year there are reports in the papers about how S.A.T.'s are coming in below pinball scores. At UCLA in one year, for example, verbal scores for incoming freshman had dropped an average of sixty-one points in ten years, while those for math were down twenty-seven points. Eugen Weber, dean of the College of Letters and Sciences, blamed secondary schools for deemphasizing basic skills because "they just aren't fun to learn." Pedagogues gave us another reason. Today's students are easily distracted. At UCLA, for instance, *Los Angeles* magazine reported in 1979 that pinball had in fact reached such "manic popularity that students regularly cut class to compete in tournaments in which the winner gets to take home his favorite machine." But in later years the blame was laid to video games and then to cutting classes to watch *General Hospital*.

I offered my major theory that explains why S.A.T. scores are dropping. The tests are not relevant. They ask students questions in subjects for which high-school students are not prepared. It is like sitting for an examination in economics after taking philosophy all year. I went on to explain that as a concerned parent, I feel the Benevento-Schmid Test is more relevant than the S.A.T.'s.

The Benevento-Schmid is named after John R. Benevento, a teacher at Adelphi College, and Glen Schmid, then a student at Port Washington (N.Y.) high school, who worked independently to discover a method of testing that would provide colleges with students who meet the high standards they desire.

This battery of tests, known collectively as the S.A.T.V.'s, tests students on the subjects they have been studying diligently for years. Here, for example, is the European History section:

1. What are the names of the Spanish Inquisitor's two assistants?
    (a) Pither and Gulliver (b) Frank and Dinsdale (c) Biggles and Fang (d) Balfour and Gilliam (e) Eric and Ian
2. Which has never appeared on Monty Python's Flying Circus?
    (a) Royal Hospital for Over-Acting (b) Ideal Loon Exhibition (c) Ministry of Silly Walks (d) London Toad Jumping (e) All-England Summarized Proust Competition
3. What did Dennis Moore originally steal?
    (a) ducats (b) lupins (c) costume jewelry (d) bishops (e) doormats
4. Where was "Scott of the Antarctic" relocated?
    (a) London (b) Australia (c) South Pacific (d) Arctic (e) Sahara
5. Who sang the Spam song?

    (a) hairdressers (b) Vikings (c) lumberjacks (d) Gumbys (e) policemen

6. Which of the following was not the subject of a Monty Python sketch?
   (a) mollusks (b) storage jars (c) enraged leprechauns (d) Beethoven (e) crackpot religions
7. What finally destroyed the Killer Rabbit?
   (a) holy crossbow (b) holy hand grenade (c) Holy Grail (d) Holy Bible (e) holy H-bomb
8. Which Monty Python album has three sides?
   (a) *Monty Python's Previous Album* (b) *Matching Tie and Handkerchief* (c) *Another Monty Python Album* (d) *The Worst of Monty Python* (e) *Monty Python and the Holy Grail*
9. Which of the following was not named Eric?
   (a) the bee (b) the fish (c) the sheep (d) the dog (e) the cat
10. Which of these occurred in a sketch as a radio program?
    (a) "Njoles Saga" (b) "Death of Mary Queen of Scots" (c) "Tale of Two Cities for Parrots" (d) "Life of Sir Philip Sidney" (e) "Wuthering Heights"
11. Nobody expects
    (a) the cheap laughs (b) the bishop (c) the Spanish Inquisition (d) the pantomime horses (e) the Gumbys
12. A man returns to the pet shop to complain about his parrot because it's
    (a) stunned (b) pining (c) dead (d) sleeping (e) stuffed
13. What was the fat man eating during the "Disgusting Family of the Year" sketch?
    (a) Spam (b) marshmallows (c) beans (d) cabbage (e) fish
14. What did the knights who say "Ni!" want from King Arthur's band?
    (a) shrubbery (b) lupins (c) a gas cooker (d) the Holy Grail (e) a parrot
15. In the "Attila the Hun Show," what did Attila bring home for his family?
    (a) a dead Christian (b) a severed head (c) a lemon-custard pie (d) a new sword (e) tickets for a soccer match

Another part of the Benevento-Schmid Test is even more taxing to the human brain. The Science Section (twelve of one hundred questions):

1. A tribble predator is called a
   (a) Gloma (b) Kzin (c) Quadro-pod
2. Code Factor One is
   (a) invasion status (b) code broken by the Romulans (c) code name for destruct sequence
3. The Horta is a life-form based on
   (a) carbon (b) silicon (c) fluorine

4. How many years did Spock say it would take Cyrano Jones to clear Space Station K-7 of tribbles?
   (a) 19.3 (b) 16.5 (c) 17.9
5. Tal Saya is
   (a) an ancient form of Vulcan execution (b) the name of Spock's pet sehlat (c) a Vulcan city
6. Who called Kirk "a swaggering, overbearing tin-plated dictator with delusions of godhood"?
   (a) Koloth (b) Kor (c) Korax
7. Blue-skinned aliens with antennae are known as
   (a) Tellarites (b) Andorians (c) Brions (d) Television critics
8. Dr. McCoy used ____ to bandage the Horta?
   (a) plaster (b) thermal concrete (c) bandages and tape
9. Who, at the age of twenty-four, made the discovery that won him the Nobel and Z-Magnee prizes?
   (a) Dr. Richard Daystrom (b) Zephram Cochrane (c) Jackson Roykirk
10. What is the antidote to Rigelin Fever?
    (a) Rytalin (b) Adrenalin (c) a Theragin derivative
11. What is the serial number of the *Enterprise*?
    (a) NCC-1170 (b) NCC-1017 (c) NCC-1701
12. Which of the following is not a Klingon?
    (a) Kodos (b) Korax (c) Kor (d) Kitman

The answers to the two parts of the Benevento-Schmid Tests are printed below. John Benevento, who has devoted his life to Pythonianism (i.e., the study of Monty Python), explains that any student who is in the ninety-ninth percentile of the European History section is entitled to receive a genuine stuffed penguin guaranteed to explode when placed on any TV set.

Certain generalizations about a person's qualifications for college on the basis of their Benevento-Schmid scores can be made:

• If you didn't actually take the test (above) it means that you're afraid of intellectual challenges and you shouldn't be allowed into any college.

• If you took the test and got a score in the ninetieth percentile or better, you are good college material, a credit to any seat of higher learning. The reasoning behind this assumption:

A high score on Part I (European History) indicates that the testee:

1. watches public television and must be an intellectual (either embryonic or already hatched). Ordinary people, everybody knows, don't watch public television.
2. understands the English language, as spoken at Oxford and Cambridge (where the Python boys learned how to speak like that);

probably also has an open mind about sex, religion, and British politics (which are sometimes the same).
3. has a good sense of humor, and probably will find a lot to laugh about at college.
4. can stay up late at night, so can study hard for exams.

Those who have passed the second part of the Benevento-Schmid Test (Science) with flying colors reveal the following favorable qualities:

1. the ability to count to, say, eleven (on the TV dial);*
2. loyalty;
3. dedication to the truth, as it is written in science fiction;
4. memories like computers;
5. the ability to grasp symbolic concepts and to find hidden meanings on a TV show, the rarest skill of all.

A college filled with *Monty Python* and *Star Trek* freaks may not win many football games, but I would be proud to have my daughter attend what might be the electronic age's first institution of truly higher learning.

(PAUSE)

BENEVENTO-SCHMID TEST ANSWERS

European History:
1. (c) 2. (a) 3. (b) 4. (e) 5. (b) 6. (c) 7. (b) 8. (b) 9. (c) 10. (b) 11. (c) 12. (c) 13. (c) 14. (a) 15. (b)

Science:
1. (c) 2. (a) 3. (b) 4. (c) 5. (a) 6. (c) 7. (b) 8. (b) 9. (a) 10 (a) 11. (c) 12 (a)

(STOP)

(PLAY)

What drew me to the profession, I also said in my lecture, was the danger. Being a TV critic is one of the most hazardous jobs in the world, following only work as a test pilot, president of the United States, and a rock star at concerts in South Philadelphia.

It is, first off, dangerous being subjected to all that sex and violence.

---

* *Star Trek* played on WPIX/11 in the New York market for 111 years in the late twentieth century.

Second, you can gain weight. Is there a connection between violence and obesity? Grants are being given to study this. Meanwhile, look at me. Before I became a TV critic, I used to look somewhat like Robert Redford. That is, male, two eyes, etc.

And then there is the damage to the mind. A writer's mind is very important to him. Next to his fingers, which he needs for typing, there is nothing more important to a writer than his mind. (I never do any fixing around the house, for fear of hurting my fingers. Horowitz, Rubinstein, Van Cliburn, J. D. Salinger, Liz Smith—we're all the same way.) I'm always worried about losing my mind. Carol tells me, "You have already lost your mind, and you should start looking for it."

Some day soon I'm going to take my case to the State Workmen's Compensation Board. Pressmen and delivery guys at the paper are always claiming a loss of a finger or an arm or an eye. But no one has ever put in for a whole mind before. And I have my work record to prove it. All I have to do is show as evidence what I wrote before becoming a TV critic.

"You can't lose," my lawyer tells me.

It's a race whether I will lose my mind or hair first. This is not just paranoia. Of course, the movies have destroyed more writers than TV. Look at Pauline Kael. Where did she get her enthusiasm for garbage? From TV. But first you have to have a garbage gene, a trash chromosome, which TV brings out.

And then there is the danger of going friendless, certainly in the industry. This, however, is a blessing in disguise.

We haven't discussed the problem of radiation coming off the set. The consequences are too frightening to contemplate. Anyway, I wear a lead smoking jacket while I watch. It may work.

This is really nothing to be laughed at, I explained to the young people. The suspicion is growing that TV critics have a shorter life-span than music critics or architectural critics. There has not been enough time to compute actuarial tables; TV as a popular medium is only about forty years old.

Still, I've studied what happened to other critics. Jack Gould of *The New York Times*, founding father of TV criticism in the early 1950's, became an insomniac. Why? From watching TV. I knew his mind was shot back in the 1960's when he started urging more opera in prime time. When last heard from, Gould was in Connecticut repairing TV sets.

But at Shield Memorial you could see the question in their handsome, pimpled young faces. If it's such a terrible job, why would anybody want it?

Power, I explained. Five of the shows I have praised this season have already gone off the air. This is what we call *negative power*. All I have to do is say something is good and the show gets canceled. Conversely, I pan something I hate and it stays on. I tell you, sometimes I don't know how I can sleep at night, living with all that power.

A second reason is that the job is beautifully theoretical. One theory I worked on (see above) is that the shows I like get canceled. (That's how you know they're good.) On the other hand, a lot of terrible shows get canceled, too. So much for this theory.

Third, there is the thrill of digging out big stories. For example, I was the first to solve the mystery—this was back in the early 1970's—of Lieutenant Columbo's first name. We were all intrigued by the fact that his given name was never mentioned on *Columbo* in all the years it was on NBC.

I discovered that it had been. It was, in fact, "Lieutenant." Is "Lieutenant" an Italian name? No, it is of Bosnian-Herzegovnian (two former countries on the border of Trieste) origin. Indeed, Lieutenant Columbo is distantly related to Sargent Shriver and Major Major.

And then there are the firsts. I've had a lot of thrills in my nineteen years as a TV critic. I was in attendance on the day they first ran six commercials in a row during a single "pause for a message" from a station (a pause more like an interregnum than one that refreshes). The old record had been five. It has been broken many times since.

I also had the thrill to have been the first to notice Marcus Welby's hair changing—from silver to brown. Usually, in life, it's the opposite, as you will observe. I thought he had contracted some rare disease. Perhaps *optionitis*, fear that your option won't be picked up if you look too old. I also saw him paid for a case. Admittedly, it was only once. And they gave him an apple pie. But it represented a serious conflict-of-interest charge. All TV doctors, it's well known, work for nothing.

In TV journalism I was the first to discover why they laughed so much on our local *Eyewitness News* show: Roger Grimsby (anchorman at the time) wasn't wearing his pants under the desk. I don't know why. I was also the first to suggest they hire better joke writers for that show, which is my favorite sitcom. They don't call it *Eyewitless News* for nothing.

On the other hand, I was the last to notice that Howard Cosell was wearing a rug. I thought he was born looking like that, just as he always tells it the way it is.

The best part of all those aspects, I explained, was coming up with new theories. TV is a new medium, still in its infancy, compared to print. I mean, it took print 132 years to think of numbering the pages in a book, for example. Here was TV still in swaddling clothes, relatively, a bouncing baby forty-two years old. There is a lot of room for being first. That appeals to me.

I am most proud of a basic law about the medium now known as Kitman's Law. It took years to discover this distillation of wisdom. Kitman's Law reads:

If it moves, the public will watch it.

Actually that should be known as Mrs. Kitman's Law, because Carol first noticed it. And she told me about it. But I was the first to recognize her insight. Kitman's Second Law:

Behind every great TV critic there is a great woman (usually asleep).

One of my most important later discoveries (1983) is: *The only way to enjoy TV is with the eyes shut.* This controversial theory posits that it's at least 40 percent better without actually seeing the picture. This technique makes you use the imagination, like radio. It's also better, I've discovered, with the sound off. Which is better—picture off or sound off? It depends on which show you're talking about. The important thing here is that the networks have demonstrated that you can't improve the programs. The way we *perceive* them is the hope for the future of TV. But there I go, over people's heads again.

Through the years I have been dedicating my life to coming up with basic truths and new theories of criticism to explain the inexplicable, or TV programming. A bright example: *Each new season is worse than the one preceding it* (Kitman's Third Law). And why is it that *there is never anything on* (Kitman's Fourth Law).

I was the first critic to postulate that programming is probably so bad because they're all on cocaine in Hollynose (southern California). Did you ever notice, I asked rhetorically of the student body, that the comedies aren't very funny. And yet they must have seemed funny when the networks bought them from the producers, who also must have thought they were funny. Theory-in-the-making: The average length of a sitcom is twenty-three minutes—or just as long as your average cocaine high. Could it be the writers, actors, producers, network executives who bought the shows, and the people on the laugh tracks were all on cocaine? And at the same time? The only one left out of the process is the poor viewer at home, who watched the shows in stunned incomprehension. It was following this insight that I advocated a free coke plan, with drug stamps, like food stamps for the needy.

Remember, I explained, *TV causes TV.*

I'll be mentioning other theories and laws from time to time in this book. But here I want to add the law that gave me the most satisfaction. As I told the students that day, it's something I frankly stumbled on in my very first season as a professional watcher:

Pure drivel drives out absolute drivel. And vice versa.

(PAUSE)

It is a difficult life. People are always demanding to know:

• If I've stayed awake through any *Masterpiece Theatre* episodes lately.
• If I felt "Mr. Belvedere" was worth watching.
• Why I hadn't panned the daytime soaps.
• Why I didn't write about Mason Reese anymore.

This sort of thing, accompanied by incessant Channel 13 invitations to see a Frederick Wiseman Festival, goes on all the time. Ours is indeed such a difficult, perilous profession, there should be a drama series based on the TV critic's life. I wrote one the other day. It's called *One of Our Pilots Is Missing.* I commissioned Gene Shalit to write the review of it, or the script. I forget which. Then I was doing a sitcom called *The Nielsen Family,* about Vic and Sade Nielsen, or *Share and Share Alike.*

One of the problems as a critic is that you start to get delusions of grandeur. You think you can do anything, especially make better TV programs than the network executives. That isn't saying much, but it points to mind damage and a severe limitation of vision and ambition.

The most difficult part of the job, I concluded, is being able to relax at the end of the day. You can't watch TV. Video games are not stimulating enough. Staring at the wall is more stimulating after a long, hot day at the set. My favorite hobbies are playing the flügelhorn and the flaut (I'm a flautist), and writing complaining letters to Nabisco (why don't they make Mallomars like they used to?).

The more one thinks of it, the more one recognizes the difficulty of becoming a TV critic. There should be a Famous TV Critics School of Westport, Connecticut, where budding young critics could go. I may start one next summer during a commercial break.

The speech was successful. "They are not interested in anything," the school administrator had said on the stage, "besides cars and money." And we now know, TV.

Afterward, one of the students walked with me to his BMW in the school car park. The sun was setting on the cloistered campus. I knew that this was a youngster who had been dwelling on the deeper theoretical and philosophical questions raised by my lecture. "Tell me again," he said, and I felt like his old professor/mentor, "what you said about how everybody in L.A. is on drugs?"

Then he drove off, westward, presumably to L.A. For all I know, he is now right nostril to some big-shot TV executive in California. So you see, that's one of the things I like most about the job—it gives you the chance to shape young minds.

(STOP) (PAUSE)

But enough about me. (As the ancient response has it, "What do *you* think about me?") Eventually, I want to tell you how some of those on television react to me on the subject. That's for later. No more about me.

For now. My autobiography will be woven throughout the book as the seamless story it is. The more important tapes will tell how I came apart at the seams, after which I became a VCR, an instrument of the instrument I was watching.

Let us, instead, reel on to one of our most significant subjects, as promised in the trailer tease at the outset. It is the three-letter word that follows TV's two letters.

(STOP)

END TAPE 2 (EJECT)

4

THE SEX TAPES I

TEASE

(PLAY)

One of the significant parts of my work, as noted, is postulating theories and laws and discovering trends. I can spot a trend at fifty feet. Across a crowded, darkened room. Yes, sir, I can trip over a trend with the best of them.

Two basic trends obtain in TV. Sometimes the trend in programming is sex. Sometimes it's violence. Some years it might be sex *and* violence. Or, in alternate seasons, violence and sex.

I can predict it as the weather prognosticator does in the *Farmer's Almanac*, only I am more accurate. Check it out: You saw it here first:

1991   Major new trend in TV, newspapers will say: more sex.
1992   Major new trend in TV: more violence.
1993   More sex and more violence.
1994   More violence and more sex.

Programming is like a sausage. You push at one end, and it expands on the other. One corollary: There is never too little sex or too little violence. It's always too much.

You have to be careful when attacking these trends in American culture. As a network executive (Paul Klein) once told me, "That's how Hitler came to power, attacking the media. He was always complaining they had too much sex in the theater." I think it was Isherwood's play (*I Am a Camera*) to which he was referring.

That is no cause for concern. Being subjected to all that sex and violence is one of the most dangerous things about TV criticism.

(STOP) (REWIND)

SPELLING LESSON (AARON'S ANGELS)

(PLAY)

We're good at trash. That's our contribution to culture. Even the British appreciate such skill. They love *Dynasty* and *Dallas*. *Hollywood Wives* was watched as reverentially as *The Jewel in the Crown*. The whole world is counting on us.

And the American public needs trash. Put on a *Mountbatten: The Final Years in India*, and a *Harem*, and we naturally go to the trash. We all have a yearning for it. This comes from a mineral deficiency as children. We didn't get enough dirt in the clean sandboxes. Our need is as basic, and as American, as mud, Mudder, or apple pie.

I've always been a student of Aaron Spelling. Aaron is one of the most prolific producers in America, with a knack for picking hits. There were times when he did *all* the programs on Saturday night for ABC. One third of the ABC movies-of-the-week some seasons were made by Spelling. *Hotel, The Love Boat, Fantasy Island, Charlie's Angels*, and *Dynasty* are among his shows, in case you haven't kept up with the arts. His name is, in short, synonymous with *trash*.

Spelling's work has made it hard for critics. What can we say about his shows? "Oh, that's trash!" Higher praise you can't give it! *Trash* today is not a pejorative. It's the ultimate superlative, like the word *escapist* was ten years ago. (*Escapist trash* is a meaningless double superlative today.)

Not that I would want to criticize anything as trash. Trashy is one of the basic programming forms, thanks to Spelling and others of his ilk. (The Benevolent Protective Order of the Ilk meets Tuesdays at the Polo Lounge of the Beverly Hills Hotel.)

He has that touch. Everything he touches turns to trash. Spelling is trashmaster of American culture.

Other producers make trash, and I can't even remember their names. But Spelling! He has the gift. What is his secret?

I first began thinking about this while working on my book *A Boy's Life of Aaron Spelling*.

This was back in the days when he first caught the imagination and was the envy of every red-blooded American. I mean, here is the man who actually *picked* the Charlie's Angels. Not three times, but four and five. Here is the man who thought Shelly Hack was an actress.

Now fifty-nine, and only slightly richer than God, Aaron Spelling started

the same way, as the son of a poor immigrant Jewish family. Only in
Texas. He was a starving respectable writer at SMU, the first playwright
since Eugene O'Neill to twice receive the Harvard Award for the best
original one-act play. In 1953, he arrived in Hollywood with his big Texas
accent, his suitcase, and, as the press releases say, "his talent in hand."
The rest is part of our cultural heritage.

Aaron Spelling is one of the most admired figures in California. . . . A
friend who is a writer-creator told me, "I have a development deal at
Aaron Spelling Productions, which is like seeing Mecca." I haven't seen
Mecca yet, have not had the pleasure of making Aaron Spelling's ac-
quaintance. In dreams I see myself going into his office someday and
telling of my aspirations to be a producer like him. His office is of legendary proportions. "It's enormous," one of my sources says. "Any moment you expect Mussolini will return."

The guy is big, too. At home, he has an indoor bowling alley, a private
zoo, and his own skating rink in his bedroom. He's so rich he once gave
his kids snow for Christmas. Trucks filled up the Spelling lawn in Beverly
Hills with white stuff. He bought Bing Crosby's old house for $10 million,
and tore it down to build a new $25 million house.

His wife, Candy, the former hand model, and most famous of Hollywood wives, wears diamonds—to breakfast. Everytime she wears one of
her $4 million worth of jewels, she explains, "This one is *Starsky & Hutch*.
. . . This one is *Love Boat*. . . . This one is *Dynasty*." Candy is also the
one who after spending $5,000 for Christmas cards (1987) had customized
cards made for her poodles to send to the pooches of her friends. Each
card, it is said, arrived with a bone.

Candy Spelling is the big fashion trend-setter in L.A. today. Now that's
depressing.

The Spellings travel with 160 trunks. He hires a train, I'm told, and
converts it. He has a pathological fear of flying. Good. That's the first
thing we have in common.

Aaron Spelling is potentate in the Rich People's Republic of L.A. He
has more money than Kuwait. He's the sultan of trash. Nobody upsets
the big guy.

A story in *The Wall Street Journal* says that he conducts business in
his bedroom in his mansion. (Sound familiar, Hef?) He sits in his Louis
XV bed, and has the ABC officials come in to talk to him. "Only when
he's sick," one ABC official said. But he seems to be sick often, the *Journal*
notes. Maybe Spelling's heroine is Colette.

I decided to study his work, to look for the clues to what makes Spelling's stuff, but not Spelling, run. What makes his trash better than the other trash? Over the years, as they say in the garment center, I have begun to see a pattern.

The essence of the Spelling mystique, the magic, the Spelling style, what makes his shows such a success, is the establishing shot. Every eleven seconds, there is a picture of where you are. "Here is the building," the cameras say, "where all of these fabulous romantic people are going to be uttering fabulous romantic banal dialogue in a second." . . . Cut to the banal dialogue . . . Cut to the next establishing shot . . . follow by banal dialogue. It's always a glamorous modern building in Denver or San Francisco or L.A., or a glamorous boat or island. It gives you a vicarious feeling, as if you are there, as if Edward R. Murrow were, too.

(The reason *Hotel* is less of a hit than, say, *Dynasty*, and certainly than *Love Boat*, is that *The Love Boat* moves you around and brings you back home. *Hotel* is stationary. It doesn't go anywhere.)

Spelling is better at establishing shots than anybody. *Super Train*, for example, was supposed to be *The Love Boat* on land. Freddie Silverman at NBC was trying to do *Love Train*. But the train he used had too much steel. And that's why it failed. If it had been an old train, the Orient Express or something, it would have worked.

The establishing shot? That's *it*?

What do you mean, "that's *it*?" TV is a very small medium. All the ideas are smaller. Any idea becomes magnified. The establishing shot is a very big thing in a tiny medium for tiny brains.

It's not the stories. A debate in a Los Angeles paper took place recently about a writer who said he was unable to recall one of Aaron Spelling's shows. A reader wrote in angrily, saying that he could remember three memorable *Love Boats*: "The warm episode where the captain falls in love, but can't give up the sea. Then there was the touching one where Doc falls in love, but can't leave the sea. And what about the poignant episode where Gopher falls in love, but can't give up the sea," wrote Charles Gould of Los Angeles.

Oh, yes—the lighting makes a difference, too. Spelling's shows always use a lot of lights. The scenes are always light and cheerful. None of the dark, broody, arty stuff like you see in the work of Levinson and Link (*Columbo, Ellery Queen*, et al.), those two boys from Philadelphia whom I'd really rather use as role models. But their shows were always being canceled. Why? Because they're *dark*, and have a sense of mystery and intrigue. They're too heavy for the people.

By being associated with quality of sorts, Levinson and Link were only millionaires. In this age, you model yourself after a mere millionaire, and you might as well model yourself after some Sanskrit translator. That's really sick and self-destructive.

"Trash," I say to you as the old man said to Dustin Hoffman about plastics in *The Graduate*, "go into trash. It's the medium of the future." And hasn't done so poorly in the past.

(STOP) (REWIND)

(PLAY)

Someday I will lecture on the mythic significance of *Charlie's Angels*, the definitive Aaron Spelling contribution to civilization as we know it. *Charlie's Angels,* on or off the air, remains an institution, like Roger's Rangers or Nader's Raiders.

Since no reader has ever watched this program, let us first review how it achieved its stature:

A seven-minute segment at the start of each hour-long episode on Wednesdays on ABC from 10:02 to 10:09 P.M. from September 22, 1976, to August 19, 1981, had at least one private investigator trying on a wet T-shirt, or jumping up and down to test Newton's Law of Gravity, or answering the doorbell in a towel after showering, or running down the esplanade in Encino in high-heeled shoes yelling "Don't move!" at criminals. The situation didn't matter: the only important thing was that the girl wore different T-shirts every week—and was braless.

Demographic studies of the period found 92 percent of all American males between the ages of eighteen and thirty-seven at home on Wednesdays at 10:00 P.M. watching the program. The other 8 percent were in the hospital recovering from auto crashes incurred while trying to get home to watch the opening. In the thirty-eight to sixty-five age bracket, almost 100 percent were tuned to watch *Charlie's Angels*. The rest had been told by their physicians that one more peek at an angel could mean . . . the Big One.

The number of angels became a cause for National Concern in 1977 when Spelling-Goldberg Productions sent shock waves by hiring a fourth angel, Cheryl Ladd. She was to play Kris Munroe, sister of archangel (others feel she was the devil incarnate) Jill Munroe, otherwise known as Farrah Fawcett-Majors (at the time). By hiring a fourth, Spelling-Goldberg had elected a daring course, artistically, and were at the same time covering their rears, for there was a chance that Farrah would not be returning to the show when taping began for the second season. The talk was she had acting aspirations that were going unfulfilled in the show, a reasonable complaint, as well as in her Wella commercials.

With so much that was major, or Majors, at stake, ABC had to be careful. Would four instead of three angels ruin that show, disturb its balance? Clearly, then, the number of angels who can dance on the head of a pin, or on the head of an ABC programming executive (to get the right answer you have to ask the right question) was not only of philosophical but of theological import as well.

Questions of equal import flew through the air: Was there any truth to the rumour (in some British paper) that Farrah Majors wears a wig? The same people asking this question were also asking if Alex Haley was really an orphan and if Lassie was Jewish.

Another crucial risk for Spelling-Goldberg was that the magic number on television had been three. In the beginning there was *Rock Follies*, the mid-1970's Thames TV (of the U.K.) series featuring three girls trying to make it small in the rock-music industry. That begat ABC's *Sugar Time* (originally titled *Girls Girls Girls*), a series about three maidens trying to make it small in the American music business, and NBC's *3 Girls 3*, about guess what trying to make it in TV. And there was, of course, also a show called *Three's Company* (ABC).

Previously, two was the highest number TV audiences could cope with. There were two cops, as in *Dragnet* or *Adam-12*, and two sex partners, just as there were on Noah's ark. Then *Mod Squad* brought it up to three: two minorities (woman and black) and one WASP.

Yet if the hiring of Cheryl Ladd that spring was risky, it also held out the promise of another monumental breakthrough. It would give *Charlie's Angels* four of a kind, a pretty good hand in any game. But all that depended on Farrah Fawcett-Majors coming back to the show.

Production for *Angels* was scheduled to begin June 1, and I fully expected Farrah to be on the set. I expected this because she had a contract with Spelling and Goldberg that specified she was to report for work on June 1. Come September, I assured everyone, we would once more see her on our home sets, her lovely hair flying naturally in the wind being whipped up by supertornado fans off camera.

Farrah is a citizen of good character, not a lawless person. Anyone so beautiful, I kept telling myself, wouldn't do anything so ugly as ignoring a contract. Besides, she would never disappoint her fans, who are legion. Still, I must admit that it was with trepidation, not to mention trembling, that I picked up the June 1 newspapers. And my worst secret fears were confirmed: There would be no Farrah for Charlie anymore.

Had the incredible and unexpected occurred? Did Farrah wake up at

5:00 A.M. that day and decide to enroll in the Actor's Studio with Lee Strasberg? Had she run off to join the Peace Corps and teach Third World children how to do their hair? The correct answer, as everyone now knows, is that the hirsute lovely simply couldn't get along on her weekly TV salary of seventy-five hundred to ten thousand dollars. The price of a bottle of shampoo in Beverly Hills these days was outrageous.

So there would be only three angels on the show, after all. Artistic breakthroughs would have to wait. On September 14, the two-hour premiere night, my heart went out to Cheryl Ladd as she tried to fill Farrah's clogs.

The qualifications for the role are as follows:

1. Actress must have genuine imitation blond hair that she is willing to grow longer if necessary, especially late in the season, as the public forgets what's-her-name.
2. Teeth. Many. All same size and white.
3. Ability to bounce bountifully in a T-shirt.
4. The acting talent of a snail.

Cheryl fit the bill (as could thousands of actresses in the greater Los Angeles area), but, in all honesty, was not Marvin's angel. My first choice would have been that then-southern-fried and affordable angel Dolly Parton. Despite this bias, I could see that Cheryl had her strong points. Of course, I am not implying that she matched the standard set by Farrah, which is to acting as scaling Washington Heights is to mountain climbing.

Yet Cheryl could read her lines, and no one will forget her immortal first words (as Kris Munroe): "Hi! I'm here."

To such lines Cheryl added a certain depth. She was probably preoccupied with getting her hair the right shade and the right tousle, and she seemed genuinely concerned about the danger her boss, Charlie Townsend, was in (he had been kidnapped from his yacht in Hawaii). Maybe she was just pulling my leg, or acting.

While Cheryl did not resemble Farrah Majors (she looks more like Peter Frampton), she has better individual features—eyes, ears, nose, and teeth. It's no contest in the hair department, though. Farrah had easily copped the Emmy for the best head of hair on a cop show that season, beating out James (hot comb) Garner of *The Rockford Files*. Nevertheless, Cheryl's hair was nice, and far better for detective work. She could run faster with shorter hair. Less drag. More important, the ratings indicated that Cheryl had not hurt the show's popularity. The public obviously felt that it had seen enough of Farrah on her commercials and wanted to leave Wella enough alone.

Sure, it was easy to make fun of *Charlie's Angels*. Don Imus, the early-morning New York disc jockey, used to recite the synopsis of an imaginary program entitled *Frankie's Angels*, starring Linda Lovelace, Marilyn Chambers, and Glorious Bliven. "In tonight's episode," Imus would announce, "we'll see Frankie's angels corner the bad guys and yell, 'Don't move—or we'll blow your head off.' "

But at least *Charlie's Angels* was nonviolent. True, the girls carried guns, but hardly used them, content to stop criminals by throwing sugar in their eyes or hitting a man on the back of the head with a purse. In one of my favorite episodes one season, a guy with a .44 magnum was going to shoot the angels. They prevented disaster by casting a net over his head. Do you know—the fellow couldn't figure out how to shoot through the net?

Usually, the girls did not have to go to such elaborate lengths to foil the heavies. It was enough for Kate Jackson, the angel who comes closest to looking like a person, to shout, "Don't move!" (The angels never chased anybody in cars, although they did use skateboards.) Their most effective strategy for bringing desperadoes to their knees, however, was making eyes at them.

And the program was always educational, and concerned with the public welfare. I still remember the episode when the bad guys fed Jackie Smith some heroin in her tea. She acted as if she were high for an hour, her impression resembling a high-school sophomore having her first gin and tonic. The performance gave a new definition to the word *acting* and new meaning to the word *heroin*, and probably was responsible for its disappearance as a drug in the 1980's.

(STOP) (FAST FORWARD)

(PLAY)

It developed later that all along *Angels*, the trash classic, was more than a glorified peep show. It was an acting school. Unbeknown to great minds of the times, like mine, *Charlie's Angels* was an incubator of talent, like the Old Vic in London or the WPA Theatre in the 1930's.

Everywhere these days we see the graduates of Aaron Spelling's Repertory Theater getting big roles in our most distinguished productions. Cheryl Ladd, for example, played Princess Grace Kelly on ABC in February 1983. Clearly an honor. They could have given the role to Christie Brinkley.

Ladd made Grace Kelly seem like two of the ten dullest people in the world. She played this, her role of the century, mostly with her eyes. They had been through so much, all those scrapes with the criminal element on TV, and the anxiety of never seeing Charlie Townsend.

The real Grace Kelly was, in fact, a terrible actress in *High Noon*. But after she went to Broadway to do Strindberg, something happened to her. She blossomed as an actress.

Cheryl Ladd played it steadily all the way. She didn't improve as an actress. The high emotional peaks of *Charlie's Angels* were not seen in this performance. She was cool, a piece of steel, as they called Grace, or dead.

The legendary Cheryl was fresh from her triumph as a coal miner in *Kentucky Woman* a few weeks earlier on CBS. Cheryl Ladd as a coal miner was a very moving television experience. It made me want to convert to nuclear power.

Ladd played a waitress whose ambition was to be a miner like her daddy. But he wouldn't let her use his lunch bucket. This was fraught with psychological meaning. It was deep as a strip mine.

It was okay for New York TV critics to exult in her verisimilitude as a coal miner. But back home in Allegheny County, around the Pittsburgh Consolidated Coal Company mines in Library, Pennsylvania, her interpretation doubled them over.

In fact, my pet canary, who once worked in the mines, laughed for the first time that night.

On the up side, Cheryl did show the nation's female coal miners, or minerettes, that it is possible to look FRESH after a long day in a filthy environment. She also demonstrated the proper use of eyeliner below ground.

All you teenage girls out there who may have been inspired by Cheryl's story—don't go into the mines. It's overrated. It does nothing for the complexion or the lungs. The work is the pits.

Angel Jackie Smith played Jackie Kennedy, our first lady, in "Jacqueline Bouvier Kennedy." Her serious acting debut was as a whore in *The Users*. And then she played a beautiful lawyer in the miniseries on NBC based on Sidney Sheldon's seminal work *Rage of Angels*, and *Rage of Angels: The Show Goes On and On*, showing again why she is known as Plastic Woman.

Going from the ridiculous to the ridiculous, Shelly Hack appears in a movie about Queen Victoria. I think she plays a piano.

And remember the mane—Farrah, the first of the angels, the archangel, and first of the angels to have serious acting aspirations.

Eli Evans, formerly of the Carnegie Commission on Public TV and now the head of the Revson Foundation, thought the reason the show was so successful was because of Farrah Fawcett-Majors's smile. This scholarly foundation official had a woman friend who was writing the script for the first Farrah Fawcett-Majors–Lee Majors movie. She met the actress for the first time in a Hollywood restaurant. "Farrah flashed that smile," he recalled, "and my girl said it lit up the restaurant like an electric sign. My girl is attractive, but seeing Farrah smile made her feel like a hunchback in an Eastern Europe *shtetl*."

I didn't think much of her acting, her personality, or body. Her taste in husbands was terrible. But I had always been a great admirer of the way she fixed her hair.

In the 1980's she resurfaced with new hair and new ability. This is not the same Farrah; a simple chromosome test, like they give Olympic athletes, will prove it. This new so-called Farrah who acted so brilliantly in *The Burning Bed* or *Extremities* is an imposter. Arrest that woman.

Noting all the acting plums that have fallen into the laps of the angels may sound like sexist claptrap. But John Forsythe got his biggest job in TV because of *Charlie's Angels*, too. And he wasn't even seen.

If it's any consolation, Forsythe is not very good on *Dynasty*, either. But with him, at least, it's a form of self-protection. He has achieved a certain level. He doesn't want to be too good on a network series; that's why he is still working. You can achieve yourself out of a job on TV.

So the angels glow on and on in our miniseries and movies and minds. They are like radioactive waste. We can't get rid of them. Is this radioactive, retroactive punishment inflicted on society for the crimes of watching them so intently in the mid seventies?

They are, in a TV sense, our royalty. There is a danger of in-breeding. The same ones get the choice roles. There is nothing nefarious or corrupt about this. The network executives who make the choices grew up watching *Charlie's Angels*. They're fixated on these girls. That's the reason all the roles go to angels and to Ali MacGraw. She died in *Love Story*. On an unconscious level, where they operate best, they still feel sorry for her.

(STOP) (PAUSE)

(PLAY)

In 1986, *People* magazine had a cover proclaiming that season as "The Summer of Trash." But the only thing they could come up with to justify that claim was a picture of Abby Ewing (Donna Mills) of *Knots Landing*, Miss Trash herself. Was theirs a trashy, even sleazy, reporting job? They missed so much that was truly trashy all around them, starting with the magazine itself. Things may be changing. I don't want to alarm anyone. But there is a serious shortage of trashy TV today. Not since *The Cartier Affair*, starring Joan Collins, has there been a really great trashy show.

I watched that show, accidentally, for two hours, in 1984. I thought it was the news.

The increase in disease-of-the-week and pressing social-issues-of-the-minute TV movies is made at the expense of trash. The situation at ABC has become especially critical. You could always count on ABC for the best in trash. Where is *Malibu II*?" Or *Lace III*? ABC used to be the national archives of trash, a central repository. It wasn't called ABSleaze for nothing. You could always count on them for the lowest. Do you know what it was like to have your favorite trashy series preempted by an even trashier ABC TV movie-of-the-week? In recent times, ABC fights internally over whether *Amerika*, about the Russians taking over Kansas, should run thirty-two nights or the whole season from September to June.

The failure of Joan Collins as a producer of trashy films—*Sins*, in 1985— is a particular downer.

The trouble with Joan in her early years was that she was too good an actress for the trash she usually did (the B-movies, or before *Dynasty*), and not good enough to be Vanessa Redgrave. She wants to be taken seriously. That's one of the penalties of being British. They are all so educated, and class conscious. She would like to be Dame Joan someday, instead of Joan, the dame.

There ought to be a special Trash Day on American TV, when all the networks would put out their best shows. Or *Saturday Night Trash*. We must *encourage* young trash makers.

(STOP) (REWIND)

THE TV SEX & MISCEGENATION TIME LINE

(PLAY)

Some important dates to remember in TV broadcasting history:

    1947   Milton Berle wears dress for first time on TV.

    1948   Dagmar wears dress for first time on TV. Fills it.

1949   First wrestling match with strapless gown. Denise Darcell. She loses, 2–0.

1949   First nude shown on television (CBS). A man, and naked from the waist up.

1950   Plunging neckline introduced by Faye Emerson. Said to be the first to fill ten-inch screen.

1951   Jonathan Winters wears dress on TV for first time.

1951   Network Standards and Practices Department (censor) approved first black woman to go topless on TV. National Geographic Special, naturally.

1955   Sex discussed for the first time on a David Susskind show.

1956   Premiere. First deodorant-soap commercial featuring model with naked back. Killed by censor.

1959   Networks begin to allow scenes of people taking showers—behind opaque glass doors. Networks rationalize it is acceptable on serious-drama shows because nudity has to do with cleanliness.

1960   Barbara Eden not allowed to show her navel on *I Dream of Jeannie*. NBC. Program, network feels, is watched by children. Network feels not TV's job to tell kids that grown-ups have navels.

1961   Jack Parr uses initials *W.C.*

1964   Jackie Mason gives Ed Sullivan the finger.

1967   Nureyev dances on Sullivan show first time. Sponsor's account executive tells him his pants are too tight.

1968   First show on BBC (England) featuring topless witches in documentary: When the spirit moves them, the BBC public-affairs unit reports, witches run around that way. American observer says sexless, like people in nudist camps running around playing volleyball.

1968   Harry Belafonte puts his arm around Petula Clark while saying good-bye at end of special. Account executive fired.

1969   Several networks show documentaries about Michelangelo's life. Photographing his work on Sistine Chapel, nudes are finally shown on American TV.

1969   ABC features movie titled *Naked Prey*. Stars Cornel Wilde in the nude. He is seen once running through the jungle naked, but long shot from the rear, and rear obscured by foliage (camera obscura).

1970   Shirley Jones appears nude in a serious drama (*Silent Night, Lonely Night*). Censor forces producer to put in scene a fence that covers parts of actress below shoulders.

1970   Engelbert Humperdinck kisses Dionne Warwick on camera. Account executive not fired.

1971   First feminine personal spray advertised.

1971 Censorship of movies dropped for the first time by independent station. *Damn* is heard on TV for first time (WOR-TV, N.Y.). Trade sources suggest that damnable words let go by at Channel 9 because it's cheaper not to censor than to censor.

1972 First homosexual relationship implied on detective show (*Madigan*, NBC).

1972 First doctor show about lesbians (*Bold Ones*, NBC).

1972 First movie about homosexuality (*That Certain Summer*, ABC).

(STOP) (PAUSE)

June 1973

Dear Mr. [V.P. of P.R. at major network]:

For a scholarly work I am preparing on the history of broadcasting—the first 25 years—would you be good enough to read this sexual timetable over with a special eye for errors of commission and omission.

Your colleague,

Marvin Kitman

Dear Sir,

Appears quite accurate. You are to be commended for undertaking such a long needed history. Is yours an oral history? Have you any idea when we can expect oral sex?

Sincerely,

Signed
[V.P., P.R., major network]

(STOP) (REWIND)

THE SLEAZE FACTOR (THE GOLD OF THE AM-AZON WOMEN & JUDITH KRANTZ'S GOLD)

(PLAY)

I was in my office, as I call our bed, one night in the spring of 1979. My wife came into the office and asked, "Why are you watching that crap?"

That was her mini-review of all the miniseries and drama shows then current—*79 Park Avenue, Aspen, Loose Change, Scruples, Sharon: Portrait of a Mistress, Portrait of a Stripper*. Sight unseen, this woman has the gall to use the colloquial *crap*. Often, she is right. It occurs: She must be a very smart person.

"Pardon me," I explained this night. "This is Arthur Hailey. It may or may not be sleaze, depending on what they do to the novel, but it's not crap. While I personally may find this particularly 'World Premiere Presentation' at NBC positively revolting, and would prefer to be writing about Eugene Ormandy and the Philadelphia Orchestra in *Great Performances*, my readers will be watching *Wheels* tonight. And I should be reporting on it exactly as I see it. I see my duty plain as a newspaper man and citizen."

"My God," she said. "You're becoming just like Freddie Silverman."

Those are three fighting words in our hourse: Fred, Dee, and Silverman.

"Hold on there," I said, "watch your mouth."

"You're reviewing not on the basis of quality but on the basis of what people may be watching. And that's as bad as making programs on the basis of what the public will watch. You're turning into your average viewer."

I turned her off.

Actually, it was a rerun of the miniseries *Wheels* that I was researching. It was one of those dramas that we critics usually describe as "taut and gripping," the story of a man (top auto executive Rock Hudson) and his love for a car (the all-new Hawk) and a new-model woman. The love that Adam Trent (Hudson) was demonstrating for his mistress (Blair Brown) was not as much as he displayed for his car. And anyone who takes umbrage at that hates cars. And deserves to drive a 1956 Umbrage.

Wheels was also the story of the making of the Mustang, sort of. It loosely paralleled the real-life struggle of the Ford Motor Company. Rock was playing Lee Iacocca in his attempt to introduce a new car for the young market, a kind of sports car on the outside, though basically the Ford Fairlane underneath. A smash success in the marketplace, he wound up getting purged in real life. *Wheels* was loosely based on reality. Very loosely. But this was the educational underpinning of the eight-hour, four-night drama.

Naturally, as I insisted to Carol, the banished, I would rather have been watching Itzhak Perlman on *Live from Lincoln Center, The MacNeil/ Lehrer NewsHour,* reruns of *Wall Street Week, Mourning Becomes Electra,* Shakespeare, the ballet, and for laughs, an occasional presidential press conference—my usual diet. But I found that I often turned to shows like *Harem, Seventh Avenue, Dawn: Portrait of a Teen-Age Runaway, North Atlantic Affair, Condo, The Pirate, Moneychangers*—anything Harold Robbins. I do sometimes, somehow, find myself watching sleazy programs.

Hasn't that happened to you? After a long day in the operating room, you want to step into something really sleazy? Junk television is like junk food. You just want a Big Mac, even though you know it isn't good for you. I won't even mention the times you want to double-dip sleaze, like watching all five hours of *Valley of the Dolls* on CBS, so boring it could have been called *Valley of the Dulls.*

Sometimes I start to suspect that I must be a sleazy person. Except I also like TV that is trashy, tacky, smarmy, kinky, which along with dopey and sleepy are the seven dwarfs of programming. Heck, without those characteristics, there wouldn't be much on TV.

It used to bother me in the beginning when I found that I no longer was watching as much religious programming as I should, or *Camera Three* or *Meet the Press.* My idea of heavy, at least in the 1970's, was *Family.* But it was my job. I was just keeping up with popular culture. I had to watch all the so-called "sleaze" just to be *au courant.* It's like being a journalism professor and discussing magazines and not mentioning *People*—just because it's unmentionable.

Sleaze relates to life—to life in general, not just television. Sleaze is really in. It's big in literature, in politics, in business, in the movies, and even in the prestigious public arts. Is there anything more sadly sleazy than a public-TV station making Itzhak Perlman beg for money during pledge breaks, or begathons?

The periodic oil crises are sleazy. Balancing the budget and buying bombs while cutting down on food stamps is sleazy. Early American history is filled with sleaze. Rita Jenrette is sleazy. Margaret Trudeau is sleazy. Bianca Jagger is sleazy. Richard Nixon is sleazy, but Pat Nixon is poor. Jaclyn Smith is sleazy playing poor Jackie Kennedy Onassis. Irving

Mansfield is sleazy trying to squeeze more money out of *Valley of the Dolls*. Sleaze is Robert Evans getting out of a jail sentence just for doing a TV special about not getting high on drugs. Ted Nugent on the special telling us not to use drugs is sleazy.

The American TV public is one of the leading authorities on sleaze, especially in our TV dramas, still the leading purveyors of sleaze. Call it *kitsch*, or call it *trasch*, as I sometimes do when putting on airs. Like pornography, it may be difficult to define, but we all know the kind of *trasch* I'm talking about.

It's almost as if we have a built-in crap detector that tells us what's sleazy. *Three's Company* is stupid, not sleazy. There's a difference.

You can be reading Liz Smith's syndicated column, for example. So-and-so network is buying the TV rights to Irving Wallace's next big novel—what was it again?—*Creels*, the steamy inside story about the fishing-pole business. Or *Garden City*, an exposé of the sordid publishing world. Or could it be the new Irwin Allen disaster movie, *Burps*, the story of the nuclear-power plant that had a bubble in the reactor? Fifteen thousand die. But thirty-seven times excess acid is reduced.

You just hear the name and you can damn well tell what the TV mini-series will be like.

If you're really slow, the promos for the latest sleaze series confirm what really sleazy people already know. Remember: All sleaze series have kissing scenes in the Coming Attractions. Every time two big-name stars are kissing in the promos—provided they are of the opposite or same sex—you know it's sleaze. It means your sleaze hormones are functioning normally.

The sleaze hormone is that certain something that causes intelligent people to be drawn to programs they consider below their intellectual level. The brain surgeon who wants something mindless when he gets home from the operating room, and so forth. Having the sleaze hormone means not having to say you're sorry.

Some people are SH (sleaze hormone) frigid. In order to avoid becoming as vapid as TV itself, at some point in their post-adolescent years they practiced restraint, and holding back and after years of this self-abuse became SH frigid. When Merv Griffin used to butter up some celebrity who was on his way to Vegas, Sleaze Central, they started to shudder. They don't get chills up their spine when reading about whether Philip Michael Thomas or Don Johnson of *Miami Vice* has a bigger ego or wardrobe in the *National Enquirer*, the sleaze bible. In other words, they don't care about sleaze and might just as well be brain dead. (Though it is not the brain that dies: It is the taste bud.) Someday there will be a telethon for SH frigidity, and it will be recognized as the sleazy disease it is.

Some of us have the sleaze hormone and some of us don't. Why worry about the poor wretches who are missing everything without this secret love? If you fell asleep during *Mistral's Daughter*, it probably means that you still have something in you that is counteracting the hormones, i.e., sleaze antibodies. You're in trouble. Call your doctor, or see your sleaze specialist.

(STOP) (PAUSE)

But, to fine distinctions: There is good sleaze and bad sleaze. *Aspen* and *Seventh Avenue* were what I call bad sleaze. Looked sleazy, sounded sleazy, but were too predictable. This is unrealized sleaze. Sometimes I get the feeling that commercial-network television major dramas are just a game of Madlibs, where the writers get five thousand dollars a page to fill in the correct answers:

Adam Trent works in: (a) Detroit (b) Aspen (c) Las Vegas (d) Park Avenue (e) 30 Rockefeller Plaza (f) a hot tub.

His wife is: (a) a nymphomaniac (b) lesbian (c) frigid (d) dead (e) Republican (f) all of the above.

She is on: (a) pills (b) booze (c) pills and booze.

The hidden motivation of the major character is: (a) he is running away because he is gay (b) he is not gay (c) he wants to be gay, or not gay.

In the first episode: (a) the old man falls in love with the young woman (b) the young woman falls in love with the old man (c) the old woman falls in love with the young man (d) . . . you get the idea. Mainly, the plot is to get to a big kiss-off one night, which can be used for the promos.

There is also a difference between class, or quality, sleaze, and real sleaze.

Attempts at class sleaze are the kind of shows where people who have sex take off their Ralph Laurens or Giorgio Armanis. They don't drink beer in class sleaze, they drink Moët. But whatever the artifacts, they might as well drink the champagne from a bottle with a straw. Class sleaze is going to the Four Seasons and ordering a cheeseburger with a side of fries.

Lillie with Francesca Annis was an example of British class sleaze. (La Grande Horizontale, as Lillie Langtry was called behind her back, about being on her back.) *Edward and Mrs. Simpson* was class sleaze. So is *Upstairs, Downstairs* and other British soaps. Anything with an accent is class, not soap opera, to public TV viewers. *General Hospital* with British accents could play on *Masterpiece Theatre.*

American sleaze is earnest, serious. You sleep with somebody—something terrible will be sure to happen to you. You get killed or die. In British sleaze, you don't get invited to the queen's party. Which is, I suppose, as bad as being dead.

Yet the question is subtle. In *Dallas* they speak with a foreign accent (Texan). In *Dallas* they never take off their clothes. Just their hats. And maybe their shoes—when they get into bed. And after they've scraped off the mud. Granted, the shoes are Guccis. But that doesn't make it class sleaze. Can you see how complicated this subject is?

But is *Dallas* good sleaze? Does Howdy Doody have a nose?

Carol doesn't understand any of this. I explained that's because she is not a sleazy person.

(STOP) (REWIND)

(PLAY)

Two other types of sleaze mark television today. The first is found sleaze. It's like found art, except it's found on TV, as the happy accident, or unintentional sleaze. Then there is deliberate sleaze, or what we call "real sleaze." Both can be defined as sleazy, and the act of creating them as sleazifying. Still, I doubt if there is any show that is as sleazy as what passes for an idea in the average TV producer's mind.

Charlie's Angels was too slick to be called sleazy. Close, but not sleaze. Real sleaze has no pretensions. It's right up front. You can see it. And I usually love it.

An all-time classic example of *echt* sleaze was *The Gold of the Amazon Women*, a two-hour made-for-TV movie on NBC, a "Big Event" first presented the night of March 6, 1979. This was the winner of the Kitman Prize, The Sleazy, awarded annually to the TV show that makes going to a low-rent disco at night look good.

The award was presented, coincidentally, the week of the Festival of Brazilian Arts at Avery Fisher Hall in Lincoln Center. The night before, I had attended the Rede Globo retrospective of Brazilian TV shows. *The Gold of the Amazon Women* wasn't one of them. We are lucky Brazil did not declare war on us as a result of it.

Gold, etc., was one of what is called tits-and-jaguars pictures. Takes place, in principle, in the Amazon. The jungle used in the TV movie was more of a wood, which looked rather like a park I once saw in Altoona,

Pennsylvania. This is an example of geographical sleaze, when the producers are so sleazy they can't even approximate the real scenery as
advertised.

At the beginning two Amazon women are seen in Gramercy Park in
Manhattan, stalking an old explorer at his club in their little outfits, which
look like seconds from Fred the Furrier's kinky bathing-suit shop. They
are climbing rooftops overlooking Gramercy Park and the Players Club,
and nobody notices them until they hit the old explorer with two arrows
in the back. Then Bo Svenson chases the two female aborigine thugs, or
thugettes, and corners them on Nineteenth Street, where they shoot each
other point blank with bow and arrows. A poisoning and taxi-hitting,
then a fleeing killer quickly follow. Five dead in fourteen minutes, according to my body count, like a typical night on the eleven o'clock
news.

Then there is some nonsense about the lost city of Eldorado where
the gold is hidden, which came from somebody in Hollywood reading
too many Tarzan novels. An Eldorado is a car and an apartment house
on Central Park West. And we are swiftly carried to "Brazil." (I later
found out it was Trinidad.) Finally, we get to the sleazy part of the
picture.

The Gold of the Amazon Women starred Anita Ekberg in her return
to TV movies. The year before, she had played middle linebacker for the
Steelers. For this movie, she weighed 250 pounds, 100 pounds of which
was in eye makeup alone.

Actually, Ekberg is thin now, comparatively. She has been on the
Paramus Diet, which requires that you only can eat whatever is served
at every fast-food franchise along the quarter-mile stretch of Route 4
between Hackensack and Paramus, New Jersey. If Bo Derek is a ten,
then Anita Ekberg—who was the Bo Derek of my dreams in the 1960's—
is a twenty. In her next picture, I'm told, she is playing the airship
Hindenburg.

In *Gold, etc.*, Ekberg is queen of a primitive tribe of statuesque women
hidden deep in the South American jungle, a place where women are
women. She is the one who is always seen running barefoot through the
vines, wearing what looks like somebody's living-room rug. The film also
stars the other Bo—Bo Svenson. He is a safari guide and prominent
explorer-around-the-jungle. He is looking for gold in the Amazon hills,
and finds abject humiliation as an actor.

But who are those people who run with Queen Anita? Anthropologists
will tell you they are Amazons. There is a blond one, a redhead, a silver

blonde, an ash blonde, a strawberry one, a candy one, a raven-haired one, and so forth. Those native berries and roots really worked wonders in primitive times. They had also invented lip gloss in the early days.

All the natives in the jungle speak English. Why don't the anthropologists just accept that?

Queen Anita the Fat and her people live together in straw huts in some remote area, which now, on reflection, looks more like the ramble in Central Park than Altoona. They resembled a consciousness-raising group to me, but others might have thought of them as members of an urban rehabilitation project for old hookers. The primary occupation in this model society was waylaying the guys who just happen to be passing by their neck of the park . . . sorry, jungle.

What the Swedish bomber has gained in weight, she has lost in the ability to speak lines. "In old world men used women," the queen says, as if translating from Portuguese on the TelePrompTer. "Here women use men." This may have been NBC's major statement on women's rights for the 1970's.

What makes this a sleaze classic is that the story, or plot, means nothing. It's an excuse for action. We see two Amazon women fighting for the right to spend the night with Bo Svenson, the larger lug. An alligator waits expectantly on the bank of the Amazon as the two juicy beauties fight on a rafter with poles. Clearly, a rough-enough life being an Amazon. It's a jungle out there. But a river with alligators—it's too much. Rank discrimination.

One woman finally falls into the water, to the almost total indifference of the local alligator. He might have been a gay alligator. Or he ate already. Or perhaps he was put off by the chemical additives in her hair.

"How far is it to Eldorado?" asks Bo, after rescuing the vanquished Amazonian from the unsnapping jaws of the listless alligator. Queen Anita, the Blast from the Past, utters, "Is half-day's run." It has to be one of the great sleazy lines of all time.

And off the plot runs. They run instead of walk in TV's Amazon country. This movie demonstrates one of the major principles of how TV programming has been running, too, the principles of bralessness discovered by Freddie Silverman at ABC in the mid-1970's. Running is the real point to the whole movie.

According to the credits, *The Gold of the Amazon Women* was written by one "Sue Donem." Examine the name closely: Could this have been the great Vietnamese writer Pseu Do Nym? There we have a perfect example of sleaze writing. Not only has some fellow—and I couldn't believe any woman, even in California, would give her name to a piece of sl---- like this—collected money for the script, but he has run away from accepting credit for the script. Run, "Sue," run. However, he turned out to be okay. Or almost.

(STOP) (PAUSE)

Later, a writer-producer named Stanley Ralph Ross of Beverly Hills, California, confessed he was "Sue." He had left his real name on as executive producer, he explained in a letter, because he had written the original script, which was intended as a send-up of all tits-and-jaguar movies. But it was only later, when the words had to come out of Anita Ekberg and Bo Svenson, and he detected the directorial style of Mark Lester (Ross reminded me that Lester produced the unforgettable—unfortunately—*Roller Boogie*) that the international comedy went off.

But, as he asked me rhetorically, whoever saw a funny film out of Sweden? Ingmar, his letter reminded me, was not exactly a bundle of laughs and Ingrid no Goldie Hawn.

His letter was amusing and I'd reproduce it here except that he refused to allow this, probably because he wants to work again. Or maybe he is just kind. But he ended by asking whether I wasn't the guy who had been mixed up in a show called *Ball Four* and who was I to go around criticizing anybody? Or anyone else's comedy?

Well, now, that was real sleaze. First, calling his show a "comedy." It was so bad it really *was* funny. And then smearing the other fellow's efforts, which also may not have worked out as planned. I don't mention a CBS sitcom I co-created with a baseball player, and why should he?

And then there is the other sleaze, unreal sleaze, pretentious sleaze that puts on airs, or smog, since it's often made in L.A. In TV, this takes the form of literature, or novels, which sometimes seem as if they are written for TV, so perfect are they for the medium.

(STOP) (REWIND)

(PLAY)

I have always been a great admirer of Judith Krantz. What I admire most about her is her sales. The same thing could be said, I guess, about Admiral Farragut, John Paul Jones, or Filene's basement. She is the only writer since the invention of the pencil to have every one of her novels turned into miniseries. A classic example of the Krantz novel for television was *Mistral's Daughter*, the major event of the 1984 video literary season.

Back in 1984, I used to get *Mistral's Daughter* confused with that other literary classic, *Lace*. *Lace*, a four-hour movie on ABC, was the only miniseries I know ever based on one line: "Incidentally, which one of you bitches is my mother?" It led to a sequel, *Lace II*, which in 1985 ensured a place in TV history permanently carved in stone by asking, "Which one of you bastards is my father?"

The author of both these burning questions is Shirley Conran, the British novelist who wrote the original best-selling novel, which won the Queen's Award for Industry and Exports. *Lace II* is not based on the novel called *Lace II*. It's only "suggested by." "Written by" is becoming vestigial in TV arts and sciences. Soon we will be seeing on the credits: "Based on an idle remark over breakfast at the Connaught by . . ."

The two *Lace* works succeeded in giving ABC the heavy literature prize for 1985. Imagine getting Jackie Collins (*Hollywood Wives*) and Shirley Conran in the same year. Not since Jane Austen and Charlotte Brontë were scribbling away at their Chippendale desks can there have been such a confluence.

What will *Lace II* be like? Somebody on the set said he overheard a colleague ask, in a restaurant where the crew was having lunch, "Which bitch is my waiter?" The people at Lorimar jotted it down for the *Lace III* story line.

Sure, I suppose it's sleaze compared to, say, *Hollywood Wives*. That's high level socio-anthropological stuff. *Lace* is very, very TV. It smells like perfume, actually a cheap toilet water, eau de sleaze. It brings them out in droves. But all pale beside Krantz and her classic *Mistral's Daughter*, which ran eight hours on CBS.

Marcel Proust's *Swann's Way* only ran three hours or so in the movie-movie. Does Krantz have almost three times as much to say as Proust? This one is the story of Stacy Keach, and his impact on three generations of women . . . for eight hours, starting with Stefanie Powers. He is a painter named Mistral in the Paris of 1925, and she is a young orphan girl from the provinces who comes to the big city to make it as an artist's model. She won't drop her knickers. No nudes was good nudes in the 1920's.

As if Stefanie didn't have enough troubles, she is also Jewish. You can tell by the way she lights candles and puts the candelabra in the window every Friday night, which must have been a custom in France.

Stefanie Powers as a nine-year-old (or whatever) is enough to give child abuse a bad name. Keach as Mistral the painter is dedicated. For eight hours, painting is his whole life.*

And what paintings! His major work, a nude protrait of Stefanie Powers, didn't look like her. His paintings looked like Chagall's, dipped in water. But he talks a lot about painting as the hours go by. Keach must have been the first artist to say "light passes over your body like light." Must have lost something in the translation.

Bad dialogue passes from his lips like bad dialogue.

I like to think that Keach, my idea of a good TV actor, was driven to drink by his role in *Mistral's Daughter*. It may have been that he allowed himself to be cast in this role because his mind was once befuddled by chemical substances. In any case, these were not his finest eight hours.

After I had watched for a while, a phenomenon occurred: I began to hallucinate. I thought for sure I was watching *Saturday Night Live*, and that Bill Murray was doing a great impression of a lousy but vain French painter. Was Stacy Keach the guest host this week, maybe?

Mistral's Daughter is the book Judith Krantz wrote, as she has explained, in her sweat pants. She writes them all that way. It's also the first book to come out of her experience of living in Paris. It's her "Paris novel." Every writer has one. A story dating back to the 1920's makes trips to France tax deductible, back to the 1920's (according to my accountant, Shifty Lazar). A former member of the group of writers from New York who moved to California (the Bloomsbury set in Beverly), she says she went to Paris to do research for *Mistral's Daughter*. Now, people who go to France sometimes discover things. For example, you can go to the Rhône River Valley and find the great truth about *foie gras*. Which is: "It ain't chopped liver," as Reuven Frank of NBC News told me after a research trip.

But what eternal truths did Krantz discover and report?

I almost read the book. It's an almost-read book. More people almost read it. I read forty pages of it from time to time standing at airports and in drugstores, which raises questions about what constitutes reading a book today. If you pass it in the drugstores, and see the title twice or three times, is that beginning to read it? If you see it on TV, is that reading it? What are the criteria for today?

And what if you *finish* a book in twenty minutes standing in the drugstore? Does stand-up, fast-food reading qualify?

---

* Mistral named his daughter Fauve, after the painting of that period. "Just think," as Harvey Jacobs, the novelist, has explained, "if she had been born later, he would have named her Minimalist."

I do know that Krantz's literary works have not been improved by TV. Her books when read have a pretentious quality. On TV, they become shallow and dull.

She really does research, I read. *Princess Daisy*, for example, has detail about the making of commercials. Princess Daisy, the ad woman, arranging a shoot for a dog-food commercial, makes sure a dog is hungry so it will jump up in front of the camera. Also that the crew have sandwiches so they *won't* jump in front of the cameras. She has piled two and three details on top of each other like that in each of her novels.

In TV terms, *Mistral's Daughter* could even be called sleazy trash. That does not rule it out; it rules it in. It rules, in fact, since, as I explained, trash is what TV is about. We can tell, i.e., smell, sleazy trash immediately.

I'm not talking about garbage. All networks make garbage. There is a special art form to making great trash programs.

Harem, an ABC miniseries of 1985, was trash. You could tell from the name.

The story of an American damsel in distress, in the midst of all those Turkish water pipes and veils and dancing girls of the sheik. Hey, you don't even have to see it to know how great it will be. What do you think a four-hour movie called *Harem* is going to be—a study of working conditions in multiple-wife dwellings? A portrait of early Utah? Gloria Steinem's doctoral dissertation?

The title tells you when something is *supposed* to be trash: *Paper Dolls*, *Glitter*, *Malibu*, *Sins*. *Moon for the Misbegotten* is not supposed to be trash. *Mourning Becomes Electra* is not supposed to be trash.

Every so often we like to look at a nothing TV movie with no socially redeeming or any other values. We like to watch them. Often they stress clothes. There is nothing more taxing to character development than the query Which dress will be worn? Trash covers the glittery, glitzy side of life or fantasy that means absolutely nothing. But it's fun and relaxing, an escape from the reality of the world we all see too much at times.

Trash movies are honest. They merely appeal to our lowest common instincts, the basement of the base emotions.

It's supposed to be bad. That's what trash is all about.

But it is also true that you can never be sure.

Sins—a story about clothes, starring Joan Collins—sounded as if it was going to be the ultimate in trash, perhaps pure trash. And the seven-hour miniseries on CBS (1986) turned out to be one of the great trash failures of the century.

At its best, *Sins* was a TV experience like wandering in some rich woman's clothes closet, a chance to look at the thirty Valentino costumes she had; to feel the material, so to speak. Whenever it was being nice and trashy, showing the life-style of the mannequins, like Capucine and Lauren Hutton, who were trying to act like real people, it was fun. But it kept getting serious, in huge half-hour chunks.

What was wrong with Joan? This was her first TV movie as the executive producer. So suddenly she had entered her *auteur* stage?

She had bought a book called *Sins*, written by two guys hiding behind the name of "Judith Gould." And suddenly she was turning it into Dreiser. Now, Dreiser had a problem, being Dreiser. And Joan's problem is that she's British, as I've observed, which makes it worse. In England, you have to understand, they laugh at her. Clearly she had decided they would never make her Dame Joan if she just had a normal trashy TV show about the fashion-magazine business, with the usual power struggles and jetting around from Milan and Venice to Paris to New York. She had to have a serious side in her trash.

Apart from committing the deadliest sin of all, being boring, *Sins* made the mistake of interjecting harsh realities. All that stuff about the Nazis, especially the incredible brutality demonstrated in some of the scenes— punching a pregnant woman in the stomach—was jarring and counter-productive. The war-criminal trial, which cut the glitter and glitz, also trivialized history.

Sins made me want to escape from the escape of *Sins*. As trash, it was too serious. Serious trash is not just moronic, it is oxymoronic, a contra-diction in terms.

At any rate, there was no denying that *Mistral's Daughter* was trash. But not just trash alone. Other writers also write trash, and I can't even remember their names. There's only one Judith Krantz. What is the "secret" secret of her success?

I first discovered how trashy Krantz could be with *Scruples*, the major literary event of the 1980 season.

Scruples was a hot-hot book. People were said to have gone into puberty just looking at the title page. They said it was absolutely the worst trash ever written. That meant only one thing to TV viewers of a literary bent like myself: smut, filth, dirt, bliss, nirvana.

The six-hour CBS blockbuster *Scruples* series starred Lindsay Wagner, the only actress in the history of TV to be named after two New York City mayors. The bionic actress played Billy Ikehorn, sex-starved, crazed proprietress of a boutique on Rodeo Drive called Scruples.

The book was basically a story about buying silk blouses, the second leading indoor sport in the Los Angeles area. Shopping, the hidden meaning of *Scruples* suggests, leads to sex and other kinkiness, something I've always argued in my house. The same thing can be said about dancing. But that's an oversimplification of the book's theme. The message of Krantz's work is: *If you're rich and beautiful and have a husband who adores you and encourages you to have lovers on the side, and these lovers give you multiple orgasms, then you can be happy. Buy a blouse and celebrate.*

The book was read, however, for the sex scenes, not its philosophy. Such scenes were not marred by the heavy transcendentalism and obsessive character development that marred Jackie Susann's coverage of the same ground in such seminal works as *Valley of the Dolls.* Krantz's sex scenes were sordid, explicit. Yet romantic. Every time her characters did "it," it was the greatest. The earth stood still forty-nine times in *Scruples*, the novel.

There I go putting on smog again as any lofty discussion in Los Angeles is characterized. It makes it sound as if I've read the book. Ever since I became a critic, I've gradually been forgetting how to read. Not just books. I mean reading itself. It's a little like long division. Does anybody still know how to do that, with the divisor, etc.? Usually, not reading is no problem, with TV making miniseries on the latest major books and all.

I made an exception, though, with *Scruples*. It was, after all, duty. But I maintained my integrity by only reading the dirty parts.

CBS advertised the series for weeks in advance, as *Scruples—The Searing Novel.* My glasses fogged in anticipation.

They only had sex eighteen times in the first two-hour episode. Things picked up in the two later installments, however.

At least I *think* they were having sex. The beautiful Californians in those jeans . . . which gave them the look you wanted to know better . . . tended to kiss once. Or give a smoldering look. And then a door closes. A wave crashes. A fire crackles in the hearth. Or there is a commercial or two or three—multiples, you see?

You know, as a result of seeing the sex act consummated in commercial breaks, millions of kids today probably think Wisk, Parkay, or Lite beer* causes babies, and sex, it's well known, never takes more than thirty seconds. (An orgy would take a minute and a half.)

The cloud passing over the moon I found especially erotic. It sends shivers down my skin. I'm a sensitive writer.

But something strange happened when they turned a trashy novel into an even trashier miniseries. All the dirty stuff, the sex sex, got left out.

---

* In fact, scientific studies prove that Lite beer does.

Left in was serious stuff. You would think that Judith Krantz was the new Renata Adler, for godsake. Such a lack of sin and sensationalism was sickening.

It was still the same basic story about the way the real people in Los Angeles live: shop, sex, shop, sex, shop, sex . . . But it had a new literary tone, as it explored the glamorous world of glamour, high finance and low fashion, photography, modeling, merchandising, media, celebrities. It was like having one of the great pastry chefs of France explain how to make a Twinkie in two hours.

But where was page 8 (paperback edition)? And the unforgettable pages 13, 14, 18, 19, 23, 25, 26, 29, and 30—the so-called "dirty parts," to use the correct critical term. And that was only the first chapter.

What happened to those missing pages of *Scruples* at the hands of Warner Brothers? Had they become the Dead Sea Scrolls of TV? Were they lost in the Hollywood Hills, hidden in some condo cave?

I couldn't believe what they did to a classic work like *Scruples.*

Scruples was so tame, I'd have wakened the kids to see it. A night at your neighborhood laundromat was sexier.

Searing? The promos on TV and radio had pounded away. *Scruples,* the miniseries, wouldn't arouse the prurient interest of a prune. They turned Billy Ikehorn, the book's sex machine, into the El Encino Mother of the Year. How low could CBS sink?

Sordidness, white heat, steam—why else would anyone want to see *Scruples,* except to see in pictures what they'd read or heard about? Filthy pictures. That's what a visual medium should be about. That's what all of us macho types who live life to the fullest in front of the TV set want from the medium. Gusto. CBS didn't *go* for it. They ran away from it.

What else was the point of all that hype? To show us what an actress Lindsay Wagner was? Come on. She's a real berry. She was more sedative than seductive.

Night after night I ducked out of events like *The DuPont-Columbia Journalism Awards* to see if the show was going to take a proper turn to filth. How cruel CBS was, playing with viewers' emotions. They knew what emotional zombies we can be, mostly from watching TV; they know sex is just about the only thing we still care about. Forget the other stuff, the eternals, like truth, beauty, integrity in government, and a good whopper from McDonald's.

Scruples is an example of what Evelyn Sarason, one of the founding mothers of ACT (Action for Children's Television) calls "chastity-belt TV." For years it tried to protect the audience from real-life sex. Cleaning up

Scruples so that you could eat off of it was sleazy, not just artistically, but morally—the worst sort of sleaze.

It was also bad for the nation's health. Promising smut and not giving it makes TV viewers feel vaguely disappointed and horny all the time. They don't have the slightest idea why they're so frustrated and blame it on their mates, and eventually kill.

(STOP) (REWIND)

NOVEL TV

(PLAY)

It was in 1975 that Frederick Pierce, then a lowly president at ABC Television, explained, "The novel is a natural source of material for television, which could make for superior programming." No anthology of *The World's Great TV Executives' Sayings* would be complete without that observation. It had taken only thirty years for television to make the discovery.

What they call "the print world" had suspected the possibilities of the novel since it was invented in 1740, by Samuel Richardson. (Some say the first novel was by Cervantes, but that's quixotic.) His four-volume *Pamela, or Virtue Rewarded* was a well-known miniseries at the time.

One wondered, while reading of Pierce's excitement, if the discovery was made by one person, who had taken a wrong turn into the stacks of the Beverly Hills Public Library, or by a committee sitting around a swimming pool. Perhaps a committee sitting around a computer printout?

Pierce delivered his novel statement at a press conference announcing the revolutionary concept in programming, "ABC Novels for Television." Since *QB VII* was a hit the previous season, ABC had been buying novels like a grad student with an open account at Dalton's: James Michener's *Hawaii*, Irwin Shaw's *Rich Man, Poor Man*, John Dos Passos's *U.S.A.*, Gore Vidal's *Burr*, and Alex Haley's history-with-imagination, *Roots*.

Other networks also were discovering novels in a big way back in 1975. NBC and CBS, for example, were sparing no expense, i.e., paying on royalties, acquiring novels in the public domain: *The Prisoner of Zenda, Les Misérables, The Adventures of the Scarlet Pimpernel, The Corsican Brothers*. Any day, then, I expected to hear that a network had acquired the rights to *Beowulf* with a sequel by Cliffs Notes.

By 1976, "the Year of the Novel in Television," the fall schedule looked like the rack in an airport drugstore: Taylor Caldwell's *Captain and the Kings*, Cameron Hawley's *Executive Suite*, Robert Ludlum's *The Rhinemann Exchange*.

Courses in the schools surely followed. "TV Lit I, the Test":

> 1. What were the Nielsen ratings of *Captain and the Kings*? (a) 55 (b) 40.2 (c) 9 (d) 14.7 (e) 99
> 2. In *Rich Man, Poor Man*, Book I, which brother dies at the end? (a) Rudy (b) Tom (c) Joyce

Literature itself was affected. Two kinds of novels were written in the late 1970's: short form (three hours) or long form (three-to-thirteen hours). Characters in the new novels thought to themselves in dialogue, "He said . . ." "Then I said . . ." Monologues, which had served a purpose for several hundred years, were on the way out. Prime-time novels, critics said, were more deeply conceived than fringe-time novels. Also, the "now"novel tended toward climaxes. Instead of one at the end, they now had a climax at the end of each episode ("chapter," as they were once called). Avant-garde novelists worked directly on the storyboard, as a means of preserving the organic wholeness of their work.

The most significant of the novels on television in my opinion was *Rich Man, Poor Man*, which began running in February 1976. This series represented a breakthrough in television's traditional thinking about audience mentality. Once, the industry had thought us to have the span of interest of a child (thirty minutes). The new novel would run for twelve hours (with intermissions or commercial breaks for school, sleep, life, etc.). That television, a new medium, had such fixed ideas about the length of time we could be involved in a story always seemed to me amazing. It was as if when Don Ameche invented the telephone, he believed people would only talk for three minutes.

The new long-story form introduced by ABC with *Rich Man, Poor Man* took an even longer time for commercial television to arrive at, which shouldn't be surprising. Look at how many years it took for the medium to go to the sixty-minute and then the ninety-minute forms.

In the early 1950's, nobody thought we would watch any one thing for an hour, unless it was variety. They just didn't do hour-long dramatic shows. The thirty-minute playlet was the thing.

When TV started doing sixty-minute drama, prestigious cultural figures like Loretta Young or Ronald Reagan or Dick Powell were summoned to serve as hosts. The next breakthrough in drama occurred when somebody said, Why do we need a host? You could go right into the show. (So, Loretta and Ron and Dick went on to host elsewhere.)

These ideas took ages to discover because of the nature of television. They are not into creating new ideas that might contribute only to the quality of life. But by 1978, literature on television was no longer considered an impossibility. Literature and television could go hand in hand.

(STOP) (PAUSE)

So, it never ceases to amaze me how television people can take a bad book or a good book, and by spending only $10 million or $15 million, manage to turn it into a bad miniseries. No matter who the authors are— Harold Robbins, Leo Tolstoy, or Sidney Sheldon—their work all comes out looking like your average movie-of-the-week.

Not that it is easy to do. Writing for the movie-of-the-week is an art form, like haiku. It all comes back to the aforementioned playlet. A movie-of-the-week consists of a series of short plays, each lasting about twelve minutes, each with a beginning, middle, and end. The playlet has to build to a climax before every commercial break. So there were about eighteen or twenty crashing climaxes per night, for example, for *Winds of War*. Not even Hercules can do that—or, more to the point, Mrs. Hercules. In effect, *Winds of War*, based on Herman Wouk's novel of the same name, which ran for seven consecutive nights in February 1983, was like writing seventy-five plays in one week. No wonder it was close-captioned for the deaf. "Several hearing-impaired people I know stuffed cotton in their eyes," explained Harvey Jacobs, the novelist. In 1983, jokes about *The Winds of Bore* were a leading growth industry. Still, there are those who would jest and those of us who are serious. Even as the novel moves in and out of favor, as TV executives move in and out of jobs, the major question raised by the use of classics on television persists:

Will TV ruin the novel as an art form the way it ruined the movie?

I first began worrying about the future of the novel in November 1978, with the playing of *The Word*, an eight-hour miniseries on CBS based on Irving Wallace's novel.

To me, Wallace is one of the admirable novelists. What I admire most about him is his sales. *The Word* was, however, not one of his better books to start with. The television version was produced by an organization named, appropriately, Stonehenge. The script played as if written or carved out of stone by Druids. And David Janssen, who searched for the word for eight hours, used this occasion to officially give up acting. The feared word all were searching for must have been *borrrrrrinnnnnnggggggg*.

If Wallace's *Word* suffered in the process of translation to the small screen, Harold Robbins's *The Pirate* met another fate. That was a laugh-a-minute. One problem, however: It was supposed to be a serious novel.

The secret of failure in the process of turning a best-selling novel into a TV dud is in the writing. Here is how the magical formula works:

First, spend millions buying the hot property. Then discard it. Consider yourself lucky if you use one word, like the title. This is what happened in the case of *Hotel*, Arthur Hailey's novel that was so-honored by Aaron Spelling—for ABC's *Hotel*. I'm exaggerating of course: they also use a lot of *the*'s and *and*'s.

Second, assign the novel to a competent hack to write the teleplay. Then throw away his work, also.

The real creative work begins in committee. These are usually informal groups of TV executives, each ready to put out his own "input" on a script. A novel, traditionally the product of a single mind, a single point of view, a vision, an obsession, is for TV a matter of the more minds involved the better.

Lighting on a show is left to the lighting men. They never tell the lighting director you need another seventy-five-watt bulb in this scene. The cinematography on a show is considered complex. Nobody says, "This scene will work better with a 2.8 aperture opening." But everybody gets involved in the writing. That's because almost everybody in the meeting knows the alphabet. That's how they qualified to attend in the first place, unless they have the same name as the chairman, producer, director, or star.

Nearly all the miniseries and shows you see on the air have story editors, one of whose jobs is to make final revisions. "In theory these changes should be made only for budgetary or production reasons, when it is impractical to recall the original writer," explains Shimon Wincelberg, novelist and playwright and three-time winner of the Writer's Guild of America Award for Year's Best-Written TV Script. "What happens, though, is that the story editor or producer has his own creative itch. Sometimes he may also want to share in credit and residuals. But I think they mainly just regard writing as unskilled labor, and anything one of their overpaid hired hands can do they can do better. Anybody who has written a letter or shopping list can fix a script today."

Often a script is given a "little polish." The process of polishing can mean rewriting every line of the dialogue. "And this kind of thing happens when they say they like what you have done," Wincelberg says.

You must not misinterpret this as signifying that to television minds, writing is inconsequential. No. It means that in TV, the writing is too important to be left to the writers.

The executives from advertising and sales who rose to power at the networks were bad enough. Now the executives who sit in the committees and rewrite the writers are young M.B.A.'s from NYU.

"Television sucks," as one novelist-in-residence on the planet of Los Angeles explained. "I went in to pitch a miniseries idea to executives at a network that shall remain initialless. I told the woman in charge that I wanted to do a film based on the original novel used to make the movie *The Man in the White Suit*. They looked at each other for a fleeting moment, then back at me, and asked, 'What's *The Man in the White Suit*?' This is from a woman in her late thirties. Her assistant was twenty-two, so she may be forgiven."

The novelist continued, "I described the movie stars and the plot and told them I believe it could be gotten from J. Arthur Rank. They had no idea who *he* was, either. It was only when I described the title sequence (gong) that they recalled the Rank Organization. They vaguely seemed to have heard of Alec Guinness. These executives were born and raised in TV, and know nothing else. They have never seen Shakespeare, unless it has been made into a rock musical, and they have never read a book by anyone other than Harold Robbins."

The only thing that upsets me about the Creative Process is that it's misleading and frustrating and uncreative. Or do I mean de-creative? If I watch a novel-on-TV, even *Princess Daisy* or *Scruples*, it's for Krantz, or her way of looking at the world. I don't want Krantz as seen through the eyes of some TV mini-mogul, leading the life of a grapefruit in southern California. I want my hacks pure. *The worst novel*, Kitman's Fifth Law runs, *is better than anything written especially for TV*.

(STOP)

THE CHIDING OF THE CHILDREN OF TV
(PARENTAL GUIDANCE ADVISED)

(PLAY)

With all the gradual loosening of attitudes toward sex, a question I as an authority am often asked is how I control the viewing of "mature" programming by immature children.

The only known way modern man has ever invented to effectively control viewing by the young during the prime-time evening hours is to make kids go to sleep at the dot of 7:30 P.M. This can be done two or three times if the child is under three.

Unfortunately, I no longer have any kids under three. Older ones are a little more difficult to regulate.

The basic rule at our house is that nobody is allowed to watch a so-called adult program without a parent in attendance. We know what is best for our kids.

Specifically forbidden is the viewing by the children of any program—regardless of the hour—dealing with the subject of girls behind bars. Anything having to do with heterosexuality is also banned. Nothing on a Friday night on ABC aimed at baby-sitters can be watched.

My reasons for being so firm in these matters are perhaps a little different from those of the average parent. I don't want my kids to learn anything about "mature" subjects from television. The networks are too immature in their approach to deal with such subject matter. I'd rather my kids learn about "it" in the streets.

Anyway, children in my house must have a talk with parentals on any program with a disclaimer suggesting as much. A *parental*, incidentally, is a humanoid, the TV version of a father or mother. We are trained in something called *discretion*.

One problem here is that like some other parentals, we tend to fall asleep before ten o'clock, when the programs that everybody is so worried about (the good stuff) usually go on. This is a loophole in the rules established at my house. I am convinced that children, like the Strategic Air Command, never sleep.

The networks' advance warning system about "mature" programs (begun in 1975) has caused major changes in viewing patterns and household behavior. Whenever such a useful announcement is made before a major filthy program, we rarely have a child to advise. They are up in their rooms already—studying.

According to my admittedly somewhat localized research, most big tests in school are given the day after the raunchiest, most "mature" TV shows run. These are the nights, too, when American children finally get to reading *War and Peace*. But I may be deluding myself here.

Children no longer ask whether a show is suitable for them. They just automatically assume that it is unsuitable and perfect for them.

Parental discretion advised, indeed, seems to have become a useful teenage slang expression: It means, don't miss, or you'll be culturally disadvantaged at school tomorrow morning.

Children don't mind at all the inconvenience of watching programs on the second set, usually the older, smaller, often black-and-white set discarded by the downstairs people. Black-and-white makes a show seem even more risqué, smuttier, like a stag movie. In fact, they seem to prefer it. It's the electronic equivalent of reading dirty books (*Studs Lonigan*, de Maupassant, *Maggie and Jiggs*, or whatever was selling in plain covers in your day) under the covers by flashlight. The invention of the battery-operated portable TV set has been a boon to undercover viewing.

I discovered this fact of life at my house quite by accident. This was at a time when that noted sociologist the Happy Hooker was making the rounds of the more highbrow talk shows, like *Merv Griffin*.

There was a discussion one late afternoon at a cocktail party at our house about the sociological implications of Xaviera Hollander's research with our neighbor, a Guggenheim Fellow, a professor of history, and the dean of inhumanities at SUNY (Purchase), and my wife quoted a passage she thought she had heard from Merv Griffin's show the previous night. Our daughter, Suzy, ten at the time, explained, no, we had gotten it all wrong. What the Happy Hooker had actually said was . . .

Suzy, of course, didn't understand a word that she was saying. Like most children of the TV age, she was a tape recorder and could rattle off many of Merv's greatest lines. Much to our surprise, she had watched the same show, but we had fallen asleep. We have been watching this child very carefully. One wrong move, and we will sue Metromedia for every penny they've got.

The parental-discretion advisory warning is one of the most dangerous inventions since television itself. Suppose your child is sitting there looking at the screen, instead of reading Aristotle and Schopenhauer. You're in the other room, fighting with your spouse. Does the TV network expect the kid to cry out, "Mommy, Daddy, they're having a show about Linda

Blair getting raped in the women's prison. Get me out of the room quick!"?

Have the network psychologists considered the possible damage to the child if a parental comes rushing into the room like a bat out of hell and grabs the kid out of the room where the child has spent more time than in public school or church? I would imagine that such an action, at the least, would be traumatic, doing more harm than good.

And what happens when your child misses the warning, which is on the first thirty seconds of a "mature" show, wanders innocently by, bouncing a ball or reciting his Keats, and suddenly, in the midst of "Ode to a Nightingale," he is zapped by immoral stuff? (A similar thing must have happened to me in the days of radio. It's the only way I can explain my interest in sex and nudity in all media.)

The program should pause for a moment or two after the warning to give a parent a chance to deal with the problem of what to do with the kids. Right now everything happens so fast we are often forced to accept a *fait accompli*.

Needed: a brief musical interlude between the warning and the show, with "Music to Get Rid of the Kids By." The pause could run as long as five minutes. The moment could even be brought to us by various advertisers of sexually oriented products, such as Summer's Eve and Femsweet.

Why not have an announcer come on the air before the "mature" movie begins? "You are about to see a documentary about brushing teeth," the voice would say. All children in their right minds would leave the room. For the few who are transfixed: "Parental discretion is advised on whether you should be allowed to see such dull programs."

Long pause.

"No, that's not so, adult viewers," the announcer whispers then. "Stay tuned for some really hot stuff."

On CBS they might have the eye winking at adults. On NBC the peacock could be shown laughing up his feathers.

The parental-discretion warning in use today—words on the screen for a few moments or the announcer voice-over—is sadly inadequate. A dot in the corner of the screen for "mature" programming was discussed in the mid 1970's. Technically, it was not feasible. On older sets it would look like snow.

There could be a light blinking in the corner of the screen continuously on all prime-time TV programs. A red light is for "danger, immoral programming ahead." Yellow: "exercise caution." Green: "mindless pap." These advisory lights could be regulated as the program progressed in and out of the shoals of potentially harmful material, the network censor at throttle or tiller.

The whole warning system is a can of worms.

I've adjusted to it, nevertheless. When in doubt about "mature" programming, I ask my children for guidance about whether I should watch.

At my house, when I really don't want my kids to watch a program, I simply confront the need to assert myself, to recognize my rights and my obligations as Father, and I go down to the basement and pull the circuit breaker.

(STOP) (EJECT)

(At this point my VCR taping instructions will be dropped for a time. I had to send my mind—or my set—out for repair.)

5

CRITICISM AND ITS CRITICS

PART I: ANCHORS AWRY
(BROKAW TURNS HIS BACK ON ME)

The selection and seating of a new network evening news anchorman is a ritual in TV and American society parallel to that of picking a new pope.

I was at the "21" Club in Manhattan for what they said would be a major TV news announcement during the last week of March 1982. As of April 5, Tom Brokaw would be joining Roger Mudd as the new anchor of *The NBC Nightly News.* Everybody knew that already. But a major TV announcement about TV news has to be made, preferably at a ridiculously expensive former speakeasy, or it isn't official.

John Chancellor had previously announced he was jumping, or perhaps throwing himself, from the seat of power as Anchorman. He was becoming, instead, the Commentator. It's what he always wanted to do, or so he was told when NBC announced six months earlier that Tom Brokaw would be replacing him.

John was soon telling us at "21" how thrilled he was about becoming the new Eric Sevareid sans white hair. He had once said he wanted to leave the anchor job after the 1982 elections. So it was a little early. One has to be flexible in the news biz.

I like Chancellor. He was like my old college professor. I knew I'd miss him.

Everybody had shown up to meet, or re-meet, Tom Brokaw. I think even Tom's father and his uncles had come to meet him.

I went up to Brokaw, the former weekend weather reporter from KTIV in Sioux Falls, Iowa, who made good, to wish him well in what we all knew also was the coming battle with CBS and ABC for supremacy in the nightly network news wars, and he turned his back on me before I could say a word.

This had happened to me before. Every time I'm at some party with Brokaw, in fact, he turns his back on me.

I'm used to reactions from the people I write about. Roger Mudpie, as I sometimes call him in print, makes believe he doesn't recognize me. That's funny. The most powerful TV critic in America, or at least in parts of Long Island, Manhattan, and New Jersey, and he looks right through me. Dumb. Morley Safer raises his nose a little at my presence. He doesn't like my shirts, it's been said. Lesley Stahl asks me where I have my hair done. Sue Simmons, a New York anchor, bats her eyelashes at me. If looks could kill, I'd be as dead as the *CBS Evening News with Dan Blather* had seemed on some nights. The way Dan was forcing his smile, even when reporting a mine cave-in, he looks like he's on some kind of drugs [laughing gas]. I had been calling him the Manchurian candidate of news. I'm always afraid somebody will do a John Simon on me, a form of criticism pioneered by Sylvia Miles when she dumped a dinner tray on the head of the vitriolic theater critic as he waited on a buffet line. I don't know what Simon Says when digging out from under the *plat du jour*, but my reactions are personal. I'm always expecting interface, the word for a relationship in the electronic era, followed by interpersonal trauma, or at least a punch in the face, (plastic surgeons' technical phrase). But turning your back on me? How small can you get.

Back then, with Reagan's budget problems, Nicaragua, the Falklands, the Mideast, and the threat of nuclear extinction, I was bemused that one of the up-and-coming anchormen/journalists/opinion-makers/agenda-setters for the nation and world would turn his back on me. There were greater matters in the air.

But what do you expect from a hick from South Dakota? He doesn't know you're not supposed to turn your back on somebody just because they criticize you. So I hadn't fawned over Tom Brokaw as the greatest white man since white bread. So I didn't butter him up like Tom Shales of the *Washington Post*. Big deal.

Sure, I'd poked a little fun at him in the past with, for example, a few choice words in the days of Tom-Tom Communications, Inc. (1979). That was the name of Brokaw's mini-broadcasting conglomerate, which had bought a radio station, KTOQ, in Rapid City, South Dakota. A mini-furor occurred when it turned out that Tom-Tom had received $345,000 in a Small Business Administration loan guarantee to buy the station. It was part of the SBA's program to encourage minorities getting into broadcasting. That Tom-Tom (of which Tom Brokaw owned 94 percent) qualified for the program, puzzled some. The silly SBA probably thought it was encouraging a native American company (because of the old Indian name

Tom-Tom) to buy a radio station. It looked to a lot of critics that Tom was taking loan money away from real Indians. He could have been accidentally on welfare, too, for all we know.

The SBA wound up denying it had such a program for minorities, since that discriminated against majorities like Tom Brokaw. And when last heard from, Tom-Tom's KTOQ in Rapid City was playing country music twenty-four hours a day.

Sure, I needled him a little for not wanting to do the *Today* show anymore. It wasn't worth the money (half a million dollars per year), he explained, having to get up at 4:30 A.M. every morning. I know several people who would do it for a quarter of a million.

They're up already.

Sure, I had written that Tom was as warm as a fish on television, with an aloof, cold, mechanical, snooty air about him. What was he—some kind of Brahmin from the Dakotas? Life was grim enough without having to wake up to Tom gritting his teeth at me in the morning.

Sure, I made fun of a few of the words he used. He was talking to a guy one morning about condominiums. And he used *symbiomatic*. "What the hell is symbiomatic?" producer Paul Friedman called out in the control room. "It's an Egyptian word," a messenger passing by explained. "Meaning: to get hit over the head with a symbol."

"He's from South Dakota," I explained.

"Condominium," somebody else said. "What's that?" (This was some time ago.)

Gene Shalit said, "A small condom?"

Sure, I used to rib Brokaw about his compensation demands during the panic sale created when it looked like Roone Arledge might steal him away from NBC as anchorman for *ABC World News Tonight*. Some steal. His agents said he wanted a small royalty every time NBC used the "B" for Brokaw on the air.

But I never mentioned his speech impediment. Brokaw was the first male TV personality with a subliminal diction defect. He sounds as if he's about to choke on his *l*'s, which he pronounces *gl*, as in glitch. My friend Robert J. McLaughton told me, "I knew a kid who did the same thing. His name was Leo. We used to call him Gleo." I get absolutely fixated waiting for the next L-word to roll around TB's mouth.

But that wouldn't break Brokaw at NBC anyway. Since Barbara Walters's eminence, everybody seems to have speech impediments. Walters has a lateral lisp, made famous by Gilda Wadner.

Still, I was too easy on him. The thing about Tom is that he still speaks as if his jaws are wired. He drinks the news between two straws. The British influence again. Never use the upper lip while talking (stiff upper lip and all that). Also, he never shows any feeling about the news. He reads the prompter, each story, picnic or catastrophe, all the same way.

What *was* the secret of Brokaw's success? Well, he is one of those people who really auditions well. He looks good the first time, and doesn't grow a millimeter in the job all year. What you see the first day is what you get. He's the Vicki Lawrence of the news business. You can't tell what their talent is.

How a man rises through the ranks with nothing on the ball is a genuine, untold news story. Telling TV news is tough business. You have to go through the minors, the local stations, and then low network jobs. And there he sat on top. A man who had managed to bring the previously top-ranked *Today* show into a distant second, behind *Good Morning America* . . . and he becomes anchor of nightly news.

True, I had been no help at all to Tom Brokaw as he fought his way down the ladder. But those were my opinions. They're what I got paid to have. I didn't expect everyone to agree with me. I didn't expect Tom Brokaw, for one, to share my opinions.

True, I can sound cruel sometimes, perhaps. But at least I'm out front about how I feel. Nobody can accuse me of saying bad things in print and then going behind their back and saying nice things about them in private.

I tend to divide the world into two groups—us and them; sort of the haves and have-nots. Those who have salaries of $1 million-plus a year, and those of us who don't.

Now I believe in capitalism. Anybody should be free to make $1 million or more. But once they do, that's it. They're on their own. Expect nothing from me. Criticism goes with the territory. Traditionally critics are either jealous or trying to make their own million at the rich fellow's expense. We are quick to find fault, nitpick, to be unfair, unfeeling, too. That's the nature of the justice system.

My compassion for the poor is boundless.

I never pick on anybody who makes less than a quarter of a million a year for doing nothing. Don't waste time on pikers—one of my basic principles of criticism. I also believe that anyone earning over a million a year should smile, whatever I say about him. What does he have to be sad about, anyway? The FCC should make a rule: News readers should be fined for not smiling. Then they'd have a real reason for looking as if their chairwarmers had blown their thermostats.

Look, it's no great loss not being able to talk to Tom Brokaw at a party in the Hunt Room. He is a cold fish on TV, as I've explained, and he is sincere, in that he's exactly the same off camera.

Ed Murrow never would have turned his back on a critic. He wouldn't have bothered. (He might have exhaled smoke and squinted, though.) Qualified people have their priorities in order. Barbara Walters wouldn't have turned her back on me. She is a real gentleman.

Starting to leave the NBC News party at "21" that afternoon—I had a deadline to meet—I accidentally bumped into somebody, with my glass of Seven-Up. "Excuse me," I said.

Without turning his head as he went by, the voice, which I recognized from my TV life, said, "You've dumped everything else on me, Kitman, why not your drink?"

Good grief, it was Tom Brokaw. If he said that spontaneously, without a TelePrompTer, that was pretty funny. Underneath that cold façade, he may have a lukewarm sense of humor.

I decided to keep up my Blue Cross payments anyway.

PART II: THE BIG CHILL (JENSEN KNOCKS MY BLOCK OFF)

One of the genuine chills I've had was the day Jim Jensen, one of the nation's most famous local anchormen—at Channel 2 News (WCBS-TV) in New York—called me from the newsroom to report, "The next time I see you, I'm going to knock your block off."

Jensen, my local TV market's most distinguished anchorman: a handsome, square-jawed, authoritative figure who earned hundreds of thousands of dollars a minute more than I did, for reading the news at six o'clock. He became, in his way, a victim of the happy-talk revolution. In the early 1970's, anchormen were chattering away inanely, making banal remarks and jokes, off the cuff and on the cuff. News writers at the stations would type up small talk for the anchors. Ad-libbing was "in." Ad libs were, of course, too important to be left to chance.

Jensen was, at the time, your classical serious anchorman. Stone-faced. His phiz was carved out of granite cliffs, taken from Washington Heights and brought all the way downtown to the CBS Broadcast Center on West Fifty-seventh Street. Jensen didn't just read the news—he intoned it, sonorously, as if reading from the bottom of the well or the top of a mount.

The news by Jensen sounded like somebody reading from tablets, handing down sins, not commandments.

Apparently, Jensen hadn't liked my column of three days earlier. It wasn't even a column about him, just a history of the first forty years of TV news. He was only a footnote in the history. Thank God. Otherwise he might have put out a contract on me.

I didn't know what he was getting so upset about. What I had written was nothing. A few references to Jensen's difficulties with ad-libbing. They once wrote in a stage direction for Jim on the TelePrompTer, and he had read aloud, "Ad-lib to sports here." Then he realized the line wasn't part of the news. I had also mentioned, in passing, another of Jim's contributions to journalism. In his early interview shows he had a writer put down questions for him, such as "How old are you?" But I *never* wrote that Jim Jensen was the model for Ted Baxter. That comic figure, the inept anchorman in *The Mary Tyler Moore Show*? I didn't believe that. He had much more depth than Ted. Also, different-color hair.

So what if ad-libbing small talk was not Jensen's forte? That's no crime. Not everyone can do it. It's an art. Not everyone can crack an egg. And now he was threatening to crack my block?

I was surprised. Was this to be the "in" thing in TV journalism, all the anchorpeople threatening to knock all the blocks off critics? Was Channel 7's Rose Ann Scamardella—it was said that she was the prototype for Rosanne Rosanna-Dana on *Saturday Night Live*, at least her name— calling to de-block John O'Connor, my colleague at *The New York Times*? Was Chuck Scarborough, of WNBC-TV, threatening to knock the *Daily News*'s Kay Gardella's block back on?

Was this some kind of custom in New York TV journalism I hadn't heard about (it was only my second or third year), just something you said and didn't do? Or was knocking blocks off the tradition, now that dueling was outlawed except in subways?

I had heard of Greek editors and journalists getting the soles of their feet thwacked by the military when somebody didn't like what they wrote about the regime. As I began thinking about it, which interfered with the normal progress of my work, I grew righteously indignant.

What kind of block was he talking about? Momentarily I had a bad case of writer's block, and if Jensen was going to knock *that* off, okay. But if he intended to knock the block off the writer, instead of the writer's block, if you get my drift . . . I was drifting, as fear materialized to match my indignation . . . then perhaps we had a problem. Maybe it was a bad phone connection. Could he have said he had read my column and loved it and it "knocked my socks off"? Or had his hairdresser read it and dropped his locks off? Was the reference to Zabar's and "drop my lox off"? Get my "rocks off"? Visit my discount Chinese kitchenware outlet, the Woks Loft?

Or was he actually threatening to knock my head off?

My block is not easily replaced. I don't know about you, but to a writer, his head is very important. Next to his typing fingers. And here is this madman, a large and respected journalist, going to knock my block off. He might just as well have said he was going to hit me in the eyes so I couldn't watch TV.

In Los Angeles, the TV people don't get upset about what you say about them in the papers. They are thrilled to see anything in print. At the Evelyn Woods School in L.A., they teach speed reading of columns so you only see the name.

But New York is a much tenser and more demanding environment. People rub up against each other in the subways, with knives. Everybody is bristling. And Jensen, who I always wrote was just in from Peoria (actually, he was a Kenosha, Wisconsin, boy) must have been one of those hotheads, quicker to take umbrage than your average neighbor on the A train.

Well, during the call, the first thing I did in this major confrontation with temperamental talent was take notes. "You say you're going to block my knock off, Jim?" I asked on the phone. I was nervous. "I mean, knock my stock up?" I wanted, at all costs, to keep him talking. "Can you repeat that, Jim?" A critic didn't get threats like this every day. If you were going to get threats, get them right.

He repeated everything in his refreshingly frank, direct language. Exactly what I thought I heard the first time. Only scarier the second time.

Well, now, there were journalistic principles involved. "What a true journalist does in a case like this," explained Reuven Frank, then president of NBC News, "is research. Find out the man's background. Was he active in college sports? Was he, for example, an intercollegiate heavyweight boxing champion?" This helps you frame an appropriate response.

The CBS press releases in my files didn't give Jensen's height, weight, or reach. They were filled with journalistic achievements, this award and that, Sigma Delta Chi, and all that nonsense.

But there was one ad from *TV Guide*, featuring Jensen, which explained that: (1) as a youngster, Jensen had developed an arm so strong from throwing newspapers up the steps in Kenosha that the Chicago Cubs had offered him a job throwing baseballs instead, and (2) he turned it down, taking a dollar-an-hour job with a small CBS-Radio network affiliate when he was nineteen. Imagine, passing up a chance to play ball for the Cubs in order to push a broom for CBS. "While other kids ran home to listen to the thrilling adventures of Jack Armstrong," the official biography read, "Jim Jensen ran home to the thrilling adventures of Edward R. Murrow as he covered the London blitz. He could have had shorter hours playing baseball, but to him, the news was a lot more fun." Good God, I was going to have to fight Jack Armstrong and the ghost of Ed Murrow? After reading that, if he wasn't out to get me, I'd have run for president of the Jim Jensen Fan Club. What a guy. Fabulous.

As things stood, I didn't want to stand—I wanted to run.

I found myself watching the next day's news wondering how tall Jensen really was. You can't tell from TV. One of the eye-opening experiences on the TV beat is seeing how tall, say, Howard Cosell is off camera. You imagine he is one of those pushy little shyster-lawyer guys with a big mouth? He is six-foot-three but stooped, so he can fit on the screen.

In my mounting anxiety, I remembered Abbie Hoffman, who told a crowd of young people in 1968—I was young then, too . . . would I ever live to get old?—that Eric Sevareid was a paraplegic; you never saw his legs. A crude joke, but that was 1968, a crude year. Still, an element of truth. Your local anchorwoman could be a mermaid, for all you know. Part of the power of TV is its ability to give you part of the picture, fragments of the truth. Pictures are always, intended or not, deceiving. And deception is the new reality.

The new reality, I discovered upon further research, was unnerving.

Jensen, it turned out, was six-foot-three, too, and not stooped—and all muscle.

Sure, he was graying at the temples. But, again, you can't tell about these older guys. He had fists the size of suitcases. I happened to notice them the next night as he shuffled papers into mincemeat. My sources said he had a tendency to scream at stagehands through clenched teeth before the show. The stagehands had a tendency to drop dead.

Reuven Frank offered to send over an NBC News crew to cover my next meeting with Jensen. "It's a slow news time," he explained.

Should I get a disguise? "Sit tight," Frank advised. "And it won't hurt to take a few boxing lessons."

Well, I would get to that bridgework when I crossed it.

The whole thing upset me. Jensen's proposed action violated all the rules of the game. We live in a society of paper exchange. He should have sent a letter or, if truly aggrieved, one from his lawyers.

Nevertheless, I found my mind writing newspaper headlines as it struggled to escape from inside my block. The heads were all for the sports pages:

JENSEN K.O.'S CRITIC
BLOCK KNOCKED OFF
IN 1:32 OF FIRST ROUND

I would like to report that my worst fears came true. The Incredible Hulk of TV journalism finally caught up to me on famous West Fifty-seventh.

But all my fears came to naught, which is what I had believed would come to occupy the space formerly taken up by my head.

My editor is very upset that nothing happened. It ruins the story, Jensen's not killing me. It doesn't have a punch line, he says.

Jensen must have mellowed. Or bellowed and killed another electrician, instead.

He never phoned again. In fact, we're sort of friends now. It was just a cloud that had passed over the horizon. Knocking my block off was not the issue; it was merely something he had to do to get it over with. He made the offer—and he didn't do it.

I'm glad he came to his senses. Jim knows the pen is mightier than the fist.

PART III: THE DENTIST AS CRITIC (SUE SIMMONS FAN CLUB)

Root-canal work is much less painful than it's supposed to be, all the endodontics experts say. It hurts less than, for instance, brain removal (formerly known as blockestomy).

I'm something of an expert on all forms of dentistry. My mouth has had so much work done on it over the years that it is an urban-renewal project. Reconstruction began when they were building the TVA, during the New Deal, continued through the hot and cold wars, and should be finished roughly the same time as the West Side Highway or Richard Nixon's rehabilitation.

I've known some great dentists. The most unforgettable was the one referred to as "the Communist dentist" in Bensonhurst. Alright, if not Communist, very "left." He was the one who didn't believe in Novocain. It was a capitalist tool, he said, which weakened the nerve of the middle class in the fight against . . . whom? I wasn't sure. I was only eleven or twelve, and I didn't want to fight anyone then, either.

Except him. While drilling, he used to tell me about the latest outrage

against decency he had read in the *Reader's Digest* article by Max East-
man, a fallen-away Communist who moved "right." He was always telling
me that Molotov was a swine: He would be coming to the United States
in a sub, and would be teaching at Fordham.

Mulling over some doctrinal dispute you didn't understand took your
mind off things, even at eleven years. "That sonofabitch," I still remember
him muttering as he began my first wisdom-tooth extraction. Or was that
about the latest apostate convert to capitalism, Eugene Lyons? Was he
Leonard Lyons's brother? I used to wonder about such abstruse issues
as Dr. Komrade Dentist hovered over me with the drill.

I was once going to write an article for *Monocle Magazine* about another
great dentist in history, Dr. Major Peress. He was the army officer in
the 1950's who got a million dollars' worth of free publicity from Senator
McCarthy. "Who promoted Major Peress?" Joe McCarthy kept asking in
the 1950's when I was stationed at Fort Dix. Later, in the sixties, somebody with a toothache went to him, and came out convinced he was a
good dentist. He had offices on West Fifty-seventh Street. If that didn't
prove it, wouldn't it be a great idea, my editor Victor Navasky suggested,
if I went to Peress, complaining of a toothache? On the left side of my
mouth, get it? See if I could prove retroactively that the army was right
to have promoted him, or not. Navasky was pioneering a new form of
reporting, investigative dentistry. But thoughts of my Dr. Capitalist Pigs
in Bensonhurst kept coming back to me, like a throbbing ache. Although
a credentialed investigative reporter, I'm also a famous coward. So I never
opened my mouth to Peress or my mind to Navasky's idea.

But I like going to dentists today. It's the only time I get to read *Esquire*
and *US* and *U.S. News & World Report*. I read faster at the dentist's.

So when my regular guy, who is working on my bridges in much the
same efficient, inexpensive manner as the Triborough Bridge and Tunnel
Authority, says I have to go for root canal, I'm cool. Hey, hey, root canal;
I had it once already. It's overrated. The book was better. No big deal;
piece of cake.

But a funny thing happened to me on the way to the specialist in
Manhattan. No, not on the way—as I was being strapped into the chair.
I lie there, a reclining, quaking shell of jellyfish mousse, and he asks,
"Well, what's new with our friend Sue Simmons?"

I feel a twinge in my diseased canal. I look up at the dentist for the
first time. Until now, my eyes have been shut. What's to see in a dentist's
office, anyway? You've seen one chamber of horrors, you've seen them
all.

It turns out that this new dentist I'm visiting is one of my readers who lives on Long Island. He says he loves my stories in the papers about Sue Simmons, the earlier-mentioned anchorwoman of *News 4 New York*. Now you don't have to live in New York—thank God, you say?—to know that Sue Simmons represents a certain breed of anchorperson found in most major markets, and all minor ones, throughout the U.S.A. She is pleasantly pretty but not alarmingly beautiful. The upper half of her body rests neatly on the desk. She looks at the camera. There is some suspicion that she reads the words left to right, as written, though this is less certain. Ever since I started writing about the way she bumps into the English language while trying to decipher the TelePrompTer on the eleven o'clock news, my dentist says he can't look at her without laughing. It's funnier than some of the entertainment shows, he says, chuckling good-naturedly, letting me have it with the Novocain.

Ahhh, Novocain. Ah, Sue Simmons. One of the great unanswered questions of North America, I had written, was Ms. Simmons. Hardly a night goes by without a noteworthy contribution, all of which I jot down for a book, *The Wit and Wisdom of Sue Simmons*.

He stepped back to put down the needle. "Remember the time," I said, trying to relax for the first time with a kind of colleague, "when she said, 'The roads are slippery and icy, hopefully'?"

Hopefully? What does she own—a tow truck?

Even her co-anchor, Chuck Scarborough, said, "Hopefully?"

"What a peabrain," the dentist said, reapproaching.

"And remember the time she was doing a story about a famous person she called Carol Kennedy? Either Caroline was a close personal friend, or it's a new nickname."

"Or she didn't know who Caroline Kennedy was," the dentist offered, grinning. "Yah, and remember the time she called the eighteen-month-old baby—the son of Prince Charles and Lady Di—*Princess* William? That was premature."

Now if there's one thing I can't stand, it's a talkative dentist. It's bad enough when the dentist tells you jokes, when you're a prisoner, a captive audience. Most dentists also write songs on the side, for some reason. They must minor in it at dental school.

But I don't mind a talkative patient. It's whistling against the dark, delaying something.

"My favorite encounter of Sue's with the English language," I said hurriedly, "was the sad night when six people were killed in a fiery car crash. An oil truck had plowed into the cars as they waited to pay the toll at the Connecticut Turnpike. Sue was giving the story as if chatting.

Then she read off the TelePrompTer that the six victims had been in-
carcerated in the crash."

I thought the police were adding insult to injury. Wasn't it bad enough
that they had died?

"What she meant, of course," said the driller, with great understanding,
"was *incinerated.*"

"And I don't mean to imply that reading is her only problem. She has
trouble with names. Remember on *Live at Five*, they were discussing
Gone With the Wind. The best-known line of the movie came up, the
one where Clark Gable said, 'Frankly . . .' And Sue, after someone said,
'Frankly, ____ , I don't give a damn,' filled in the missing name—with
'Charlotte.' "

"Yah," the dentist said, giggling away as he bent to the attack. "She
also had a lot of trouble last baseball season with 'Billy Martin,' " I went
on babbling. "Talk about your tough names. She kept confusing Billy
Martin with Billie Holiday. That's what she said. She actually admitted
confusing the two names in her mind." He leaned back for a moment,
reflecting. "They are alike, I suppose."

"Yeah," I said. "And the time she called Gary Bussey 'Harry,' which
is a lot better than Barry Gussey. Then there was her mispronunciation
of the station's star city reporter, Gabe Pressman, calling him 'Gabe
Pregnant.' The other night she called Scarborough 'Jack.' Sue may not
be that close to Chuck Scarborough—she only works with him five days
a week. Still, she's supposed to know his name sooner or later."

I kind of like Sue Simmons, and have no reason to feel superior to
anyone, but I pressed on.

"My favorite moment of all was the time she began a report, 'Traffic
on the brudges and tinnels' . . ."

"She meant *bridges* and *tunnels*," he told me.

Her problem, I explained to my new friend, was trying to think of
something to say while reading—some put-down, *shtick*, *nudge*, *shtup*
to needle her fellow news-team members. But she could also have an
impediment. Not everybody can talk and read, or chew gum, or think at
the same time.

The dentist smiled. "Or drill," he said. "Or be drilled."

He bent over, but I put my hand on his chest. "In baseball they have
designated hitters," I explained. "Channel Four could call a pinch reader,
a designated reader, for her whenever she has to deal with the
TelePrompTer."

"What really cracked me up was the time . . ." the dentist said, and suddenly he drills for the first time. He went straight forward to the floor, and I went straight up to the ceiling.

Hours or seconds later, when the same progression of Sue Simmons's great bobbles alternated with drilling, I managed to say, "Is this a big job or something?"

"*Triple* canal."

At least that's what I think he said. I had never heard of a triple canal. Was it like a bypass? But what did I know? "Dig you must," I said cheerfully. Con Ed slogans were dredged up from my murky past, along with more of Sue's miscues, but he went on. And on.

Say, this was the Panama Canal of root jobs, I began to think.

As the pain increased to isthmus proportions, I wondered, Wouldn't it be funny if Mr. Dr. Dentist here was really not simpatico with my editorial criticism of newspeople? Had he genuinely agreed with me? Or was he baiting me? A lot of people must like Sue. Identify with her errors. Look, nobody is perfect. Leave the poor thing alone. She's just trying to make an honest $475,000 a year without being able to read English so good.

Above me, in the hot light, like a TV apparition, his face moved. Who is this masked stranger, anyway? Is he trustworthy? Is he a TV dentist or a real one? Did he study under Woody Allen? He says "triple canal." What does that *mean*? All I know is that my mouth is hurting more than three times as much as usual.

What if he is really Sue Simmons's press agent's cousin? A lot of letters complaining about what I said about Sue and her Channel 4 news show the last time were written by Sue's relatives and by Channel 4 press agents. (Who do you think writes all those letters to the editor, anyway?) What if this guy was president of her fan club—"the Long Island Dentists Luv Sue and Her Big Bad Mouth"?

Maybe they were having—a cold chill ran down my spine to parallel the hot pain near my tonsils—an affair. Other unlikely couples came to mind. Sex makes strange bedfellows. Beds make strange sex fellows. Fellows make strange beds . . . Ow!

What nerve this dentist had! What nerves I had—and he had found all of their endings. By now I was convinced he and Sue were engaged. He should have declared a conflict of interest, and given the case to a dentist who could be objective.

I realized I was getting a whole paranoid fantasy going as he turned my mouth into Venice.

But not all is paranoia. There is a long list of others trying to "get" me because of statements about various artists. I had scarcely sat down to lunch before delivering a speech to the SCOPE conference of teachers and librarians at the Smithtown (L.I.), New York, Sheraton, when a waitress, serving the rubber roast beef, hit me in the head, dropping the meat in my lap. If anyone had asked, "Where's the beef?" it would have been easy to display. Clearly, she was a Sue Simmons fan. Everybody's a critic these days. You can't be too vigilant.

Several years later, when the dentist finished his triple play, I got up out of the chair. He was ready to resume the assault on Sue, I could see by his devilish smirk. "Remember when she . . ." he began—but I flung myself out of the room, shouting unintelligible imprecations. Also insults.

"What's wrong with him?" the driller asked his receptionist, "what's he saying?"

With her experience, she could tell what I meant with what was left of my mouth. "He's saying that Sue Simmons is a jewel, a national resource, a much-put-upon woman. And at least she limits her tortures to five and eleven o'clock."

6

THE MAD (FLIPPER) FLICKER
(HOW TO WORK THE DIAL)

Enough of the dangers of being a critic. Now I want to get down to basic theory, such as how to work the dial.

The most stimulating thing that has happened in all my years as a TV critic—not counting the time Valerie Bertinelli invited me to do her algebra homework—was getting cable. It gave me (sound gong) Multi-channel Capability. It now takes thirty-six changes of the dial before I can say there is nothing on.

Soon it will take eighty-four. And then, someday, 207. When we have seven hundred channels, will we still be saying, "God, there's nothing on—except a tit or two"? It may be that there never will be anything on TV.

I'm talking about the new remote control my cable company lent me. It's hardware that you have to master to get maximum enjoyment out of TV. You know, it's that—to use the technical word—gizmo, with the long wires you pull over to the bed when you want to watch TV. Or, it could be a wireless remote-control device like mine. Can you imagine getting up every time you wanted to change channels? Without these break-throughs, somebody would have had to invent reading books in bed, or sex, or something.

In the old days, before remote control, you went over to the set and changed the dial manually. Then you had to return and sit down on the edge of the bed to see if it was tuned properly. Then you'd lie down and get under the covers until your wife would tell you there was nothing on. Or until the picture slipped. Then you'd get up, walk over and change the dial to another channel, or return to adjust the focus or the vertical hold, and so on into the night, eliminating any horizontal hold you might

have gotten on your wife. No wonder the birthrate fell. The first days—
and nights—of TV were exhausting.

Remote control is the biggest boon to society since sliced bread.

What I usually do, if I may share some of my trade secrets as a critic,
is punch the dial until there something interesting on the screen, or
Casablanca. Usually I watch a program for as long as I am entranced,
maybe ten or fifteen seconds. Then, when it finally palls, I move on. Life
is too short to just lie there.

Besides, I have to keep up. So it's ten seconds of a taut and gripping
drama about the cops or robbers. Then ten seconds of a documentary
about saving endangered alligators (why?). Two seconds of a crusading
editorial. Ten seconds of a commercial.

Sometimes I go directly to the MTV channel. That's the incredible spot
on the dial where they play only commercials for record albums. The
hottest new concept in cable broadcasting in the 1980's is based on the
principle of taking the worst of radio and putting it on television.

I always stop by the Playboy channel. You never know when they will
be having an important public-affairs show or documentary, like the "Miss
Playboy Interview." That's heavy. You have to be sick or dead not to find
that—or them—significant.

The biggest event of the night on TV for me is nine o'clock. That's
when a new set of programs start, replacing the ones that began at eight-
thirty. This thrill lasts sometimes until 9:03. Then you say nothing is on
again.

Ten o'clock is also important. Not to mention the ever-popular eight
o'clock and eleven o'clock.

There are several accepted ways of "going around the dial," as it is
called, successor activity to rocking around the clock. Most people start
by going across the top row (from Channel 2 to Channel 13). Then there
are those who go directly to the second row, also starting at the left. And
then on the third row, starting at the left.

Certain scholars I know who have studied Hebrew do each row from
right to left.

Still another method of working the dial is the up-and-down method,
going through all the channels in the first rank, or column, second rank,
and so forth. You can choose one from Column A, two from Column B.
There is a correlation between this method of watching TV and dining in
Chinese restaurants, and about as much enduring satisfaction.

Some people like to be flexible, or just hop around frivolously, as the
spirit moves them. It's like in dance: Some like modern, free-form, others
classical ballet, with its set patterns and rules. I favor a more rigid system,

moving along rows the same way each time. I'm always afraid of losing my place. Or missing something on one of the thirty-six channels.

New push-button controls have made me, as you may have guessed by now, one of the dreaded channel flickers, or (in honor of a past television hero) Flipper, dreaded by those who like to watch one program at a time, good or bad, as God or the network programmers intended.

God would be an improvement. Flickers or clickers find there is not enough on most TV programs to occupy the human mind.

The first person to discover flicking as a way of life was Susan Grossman's husband, back in 1974. He perfected switching in six nights, raising it to a fine art, according to Mrs. Grossman, who now lives with her husband, his remote-control box, and their dog, Vanna, in Plantation, Florida, some forty minutes from the heartland of America's Southeastern Tourist and Riot Center, Miami.

"My husband can watch three programs simultaneously without missing more than a moment of any," she says proudly.

He could not perform this feat, needless to say, without the aid of predictable commercials and station breaks.

"As much as this habit of his annoyed me," Ms. Grossman told me, "I now credit my husband for obliterating any desire I ever had to watch TV. Because after a half hour I became totally confused. And I missed the commercials."

More recently, a crisis in American TV took place. My remote control broke. What had happened, again to use the unavoidable technical term, is that the gizmo fratzed out.

This meant I had to change channels by *hand*. Actually, by foot, first. I had to get out of bed, walk nine or ten steps to the TV set, and manually make the moves.

What a mixed-media experience! Did people really do that all the time before remote control? No. TV never would have survived.

Without the remote, it was as if my fingers were broken. The nature of my viewing changed. I found myself watching one program. It was awful.

For the first time, I had to ask myself: Is this trip necessary? Do I really want to change the dial? And whom was I kidding, besides myself? Was it really worth getting up to see some classic movie edited with a chain saw or an *MTM* rerun I had seen twelve times anyway?

Several nights without a remote control, I'm ashamed to say, led to desperate measures. I did push-ups. Wrote my father. Kissed my wife. Read four chapters.

Going around the dial, or doing laps, as we say, is what makes TV remotely, so to speak, engrossing.

And the great quality of channel flicking is that it's wildly idiosyncratic. Everybody travels around the dial at his own speed. And timing reveals a personality: A two-minute lap, you are sensitive, warm, and compassionate; three minutes, thoughtful; four minutes, curious about the world around you; and so forth.

As the fastest dial switcher in New Jersey, I'll match my threshold of pain against any man's. I can do seven laps around the dial in five minutes—and when I'm restless, forget it. Old Trigger Fingers, they call me. I've got the hands of a surgeon, when needed.

All of this is a little disconcerting to my mate. She has a linear mind, not a circular one like mine. Carol likes to watch one program, good or bad. Thus, if I'm a sadist, she's a masochist. She can't follow the shows in such short takes and bits. Anyway, she feels sorry for the actors. I have to remind her they can't see us; it's not like in a theater.

"Will you change the dial to Two?" one wife asked her husband, a top TV executive in New York City.

"What are you doing?" she cried.

"I am. I'm getting there."

What happened was that he had stopped off at 26, 35, 24, 33, 14, on the way to 2.

The remote control is the other cause of friction in the American home today, one of the dark secrets of the bedroom nobody discusses—except your correspondent.

Some bed mates become despondent and dizzy when the set's pictures change so fast as somebody else runs the dial. They get headaches, real headaches, but they want to have sex. Where are their priorities? David Letterman or fornication? It's sickening.

Who will control the dial?—the basic marital question of our time many young, impetuous kids rushing into marriage never ask. Forget how the kids will be raised, in which church, etc. Are they remote-control compatible?

Many couples are seriously mismatched. I have two friends, call them Susana and Jeffrey, largely because those are their names. She is an artist from Argentina—impetuous, sensitive, foreign. He is a brilliant architect who designed Freddie Silverman's home in Westchester— skittish, hot-tempered, well paid, when paid. He watches news at five, six, seven, ten, eleven. "It's always the same thing, anyway," she says. "I like sitcoms," she says. "He doesn't like sitcoms. I like to laugh."

So every night they battle over who watches what with the dial. She laughs at the news. He thinks sitcoms are tragic.

"I get up and paint," Susana confesses. "I put up a screen so I can't see it. Then I plug up my ears so I can't hear it."

Fighting over who controls the dial has a remedy. The solution is to have two sets of controls, as in jet planes. Who is the pilot and who the co-pilot? Who actually flies the plane and has his hands on the throttle and gives it the gas, so to speak?

"She who controls the dial controls destiny," I think Mrs. Stalin said. Can you imagine negotiating channel changes with Stalin? He eliminated people faster than ABC does pilot programs.

In fact, the fairest solution is probably the two-control house. Not that this eliminates competition. Instead, it becomes built in. The process is called dueling remote controls, and can be a lot of fun to play. But what happens when you hit a 2 and a 7 at the same time? Do you get 9?

Nonetheless, I love my wife *and* my remote control. Especially digital numbers lit up in the corner of my set. Have you ever wondered what that green light is? Where it comes from? I know you have enough to worry about besides strange green lights emanating from your TV set, but how do you know it's not a signal for space ships? What color *is* a UFO? How do you know that isn't an alien staring at you in the night, sending back a televised transmission on you to spaceship computers named Spielberg while you sleep?

Still, conflicts or not, the creativity in TV today is the way you go around the dial. The control box is the key to enhancing one's appreciation of TV and of TV itself. You are creating your own program by juxtaposing images. It makes you creative, alive, involved. Are you best from the prone position? Or do you like to sit? Standing is nice. You are the artist, painting with the palette of push buttons, you are the Olympic athlete, skiing the dials as fast or as slowly as you like, and in the direction that befits your personality.

Channel hopping takes many forms. Try to switch channels so the dialogue goes from one show into another, like a sitcom rerun with *MacNeil/Lehrer*. You have to be *really* bored to play this game. But I live in the suburbs and my kids are grown. A man has needs.

You are your own director. Fellini said, "Because they can use the TV as an editing machine . . . they change to another film, they cut whenever they like . . . The atmosphere of what we have meant as cinema has been corrupted, destroyed, frustrated."

Bitter old man. Fellini was against the invention of popcorn, too.

Sure, you are the creative person. You are, in effect, writing a televised book, using the same devices John Dos Passos did in *U.S.A.* Picasso himself did it, only he called it "montage."

The medium, as I believe I said first, is the medium. *You* are the video revolution they are always talking about. You channel clickers are putting together the really big show. You're making the mosaic called TV. This is how you can love TV. As your own executive producer, your own Grant Tinker, you tinker with your toys. You are making TV remotely interesting.

SANITARY TV, OR, SAFER THAN SEX (R RAYS AND Z RAYS)

1.

One other thing I forgot to mention. Wash your hands before you watch TV.

Why? I don't know. There may be germs on the dial. My mother always was telling me to wash my hands. Like standing up straight. It figures. You could grow up to be Johnny Carson, who is starched up straight. But wash your hands before watching TV, anyway. Look, it can't hurt. I, for one, am willing to try anything.

2.

Everybody knows that you're safe if you sit six feet away from the TV set. You can put your TV set at one end of the apartment and sit with your back against the wall at the other end, putting you beyond the maximum safe distance from the set. But then what happens when your neighbor on the other side of the wall turns on his set? Zap: The rays go right through the wall.

Over the years the government has tried to get manufacturers to reduce the X rays emanating from our TV sets to the point where they are no longer considered dangerous. But by reducing the X rays, are our sets now producing more gamma rays? As a matter of fact, when was the last time anybody checked your set for gamma rays (which scientists describe as "very high energy X rays")? Gamma rays are emitted by decaying radioactive substances, and there's a very high percentage of decayed and dead material on television.

It is the gamma rays, perhaps, which make TV so faintly nauseating.

Documentaries make us listless. Commercials leave us irritable and jumpy. Late-night talk shows have been known to give *men* a headache before bed. Perhaps such physical by-products of television watching have nothing to do with the programs, as has been assumed. But who knows? Show me one laboratory, one university, that is investigating what the programs, rather than the sets, do to us?

At this very moment, we are definitely mutating. Our stomachs, as noted, have grown larger since the electronic age began. (See my episode, I mean chapter, on eating and TV.) Is our mental capacity smaller? (See my chapter on TV and mentality. It's short, two words.) Many of us, of course, have already forgotten how to read. Except for books about TV like this, and maybe the classics, like Vanna White's autobiography. And how do you *know* little antennae aren't growing on top of your head? What did you think those bumps on your skull were—information pods or floppy disks? If I were the Surgeon General, I would order the nation's 113,200,000 TV sets recalled until they have been properly tested.

Less is known about R rays than about gamma or X rays. But anyone who has ever had a TV repairman in the house knows how R rays work: (a) Sets repaired at home always work perfectly, while the repairman is on the premises, even though he may have removed your set's best components to sell to another customer. That is because the repairman exudes Rays, another less publicized ray of the electromagnetic spectrum; (b) conversely, the TV sets stop working perfectly as soon as the TV repairman leaves. This may be caused by the absence of R rays.

I may have alarmed you enough. It is, however, the Z rays I'm concerned with lately, in any case. These are the rays coming off the electromagnetic spectrum, which go from the On-Off button on the set directly to the hypothalamus of the brain, the so-called Z-*spot*. This is located in the unconscious, or the television sector of the brain, where the mindless trivia masses, such as names of all of the Brady kids, the facts about Oscar and Felix, and Monty Python, *Saturday Night Live*, Steve Allen, Garroway, Paar, and other buried icons.

The Z-spot has its uses. It produces a very deep, drugged form of pleasurable sleep. These Z rays are emitted in a set pattern, as: Z-Z-Z-Z-Z-Z-z-z-z-z—z——z————z————————z. . . . like zo. Or the pattern of distribution is sometimes like zis: z-z-z-z-z-z—Z—ZZZ-ZZZZZ! (If the person is znoring).

Sleep is more intense when you fall asleep watching TV, many say. You also dream better. Often, one dreams in living color. I know the scientists say you don't dream in color but in black and white, but that's easy for them to say. Such doctors didn't watch sufficient TV when growing up; otherwise they wouldn't have become doctors. It depends on whether you had a color or a black-and-white set in the formative childhood years. Not only are dreams, among active modern viewers, in full color, but my dreams tend to be rectangular and frequently interrupted by commercial messages (REM sleep). My dreams have ghosts and double focus and flecks of snow, or tape "noise," whenever something irritating crosses my mind. And I can't see certain dreams because the World Trade Center gets in the way.

Once a week, a network should run the last ten minutes of the week's previous movies in prime time. Why? Old movies were made for viewing in theaters. They usually start off fast, then bog down in frills, like character development. Once they have you in a theater, there's nothing to do but sit patiently, waiting for the story to move to its dramatic finish. But watching these slower developing pre-TV movies in bed, many viewers fall asleep. Many people are walking around wondering how *The Vampire and the Ballerina* ended. They can't sleep.

A festival of the last ten minutes of all the week's previous movies would also appeal to that crowd who enjoy reading the last three pages of mysteries.

Another constructive suggestion about dealing with TV-induced mental health problems is the Geraghty Plan, named after James Geraghty, a confessed insomniac. "I refuse to use drugs," he explained. "What sleep I get is induced . . . The series 'Winds of War' gave me an idea that perhaps you could abet. Could not a public service station be set up to show—on a twenty-four-hour basis—shows like 'Winds of War,' Board of Estimate hearings, you know the types of presentations I mean. It would be a boon to swing-shift people, like policemen, firemen, nurses, newspapermen, and people like me who have difficulty falling asleep. Those hyperactive kids who cause trouble in school and in zoos would become calm. There is no end to benefits. Think about it, Mr. Kitman."

The only trouble is that thinking about it is making me sleepy.

Final health note: TV causes snoring. Now why is this universal, especially among men over forty? I can finally declassify the data. The reason men snore on the couch when they have fallen asleep watching TV is to alert the Strategic Air Command in Omaha so that B-52's can home in on the sounds en route between Indianapolis and Murmansk. If you must know. Nosy.

TV EATING:
THE OFFICIAL GOURMET SNACK GUIDE

Watching TV is America's second favorite indoor sport. Eating while watching TV is first.

I have the evidence. Once, I was well-built. A bite-size Arnold Schwarzenegger, whom I resemble to this day around the nostrils. But I am also mistaken for Henry Kissinger.

One of the consequences and dangers of practicing TV criticism. ("You'll practice till you get it right!")

An analysis:

There are two major causes of TV eating: (1) When there is something bad on (to drown our sorrows), and (2) When there is something good on (to celebrate our good fortune). Number 1 is the primary cause. Number 2 is so rare as to be statistically negligible.

"The beat generation" of the 1950's has been succeeded by the eat generation of today.

So much eating goes on, I have concluded that there is a kind of physiological relationship involved, some link in the food chain, a chromosomal tie between the TV electronic impulse, or wave, as the rheostat and the appestat, i.e., the salivary glands and taste buds. Why else should TV remind us, or cause us, to eat so often? Why do we settle down after dinner with supper? Follow Saturday brunch with lunch? These could be conditioned reflexes. TV is the bell.

Reading a book doesn't make you hungry. Sitting in a churchyard thinking, writing a sonnet, listening to the radio, even exercise—nothing makes us as hungry as watching that tube.

Quite possibly, the human body NEEDS food while watching TV. It may be NECESSARY to eat. You could be endangering your health by not eating while watching. I don't know. I never actually tried it that way.

TV was invented, of course, for thin people, during the Depression (in the days of radio) when one third of the nation, as President Roosevelt said, was "ill fed," as well as ill clothed, ill housed, etc. This was before the invention of the malted, McDonald's, or the condo. The improvements got out of hand, like kudzu.

At any rate, there is now such a direct link between eating and TV, I have put in for a patent on a set that will microwave hot dogs while you watch. Or with a corn-popping attachment. That's thought for food.

Everybody has their favorite foods while watching TV. Anthony, my friend Tony Gentile's son, has a favorite thing to eat while watching TV, his father told me, spaghetti.

"But I'm not talking about eating meals while watching TV," I told Tony. "That's a whole other subject. I'm talking about the stuff you eat before and after regular meals, you know, the good stuff, snacks."

"That's what Anthony eats as a snack," Tony said.

I mean, naturally, the basic survival foods—anchovy paste on crackers, a Ring Ding remnants, the bottom of the barrel of Kentucky-fried Gino's chicken, a Mounds bar, a Milky Way, five or six Mallomars with milk, staff-of-life stuff, staples, the kind of food that made the poet write "A bag of pretzels, a Fig Newton, some Old Milwaukee, and thou."

Research shows that certain foods go with certain shows. In the old days, when you saw *Rhoda*, you automatically wanted a piece of fruit.

I pride myself on knowing wines. My speciality is the colors (red and white). I can always tell a red from the white, for example. In the same way, TV critics know that certain principles apply to eating snacks with TV. Have you ever noticed how *Moonlighting* was more enjoyable when you were eating sweet things? Sweet things also taste better when you're not watching TV. But that's another issue.

It is natural to eat hot dogs while watching a baseball game on TV. Popcorn goes with *The ABC Friday Night Movie*. Certain foods are unnatural. Nothing goes with celery and carrot sticks.

"What goes with Szechuan, or peanuts?" you might ask, listening to the discussion so far. You begin to feel in the mood. That's a reverse problem and skews the statistics. Sometimes we unconsciously *pick a program to watch*, based on the subliminal *unconscious desire to eat certain foods*.

What I'm leading to now is presenting the first Official Guide to TV-Watching Nutrition, or what goes with what show.

"You are what you eat," as Brillat-Savarin said. Or was that the lovable but less-brillat Julia Child? Maybe he said, instead, "You are what you watch." At any rate, what you eat with what shows is revealing. You don't want to seem like an unlettered oaf and munch away without a sense of where you are, your culture, your heritage.

Remember, you can trust me. I'm a man of taste. I will eat no food before its time.

Kitman's* Official TV Gourmet Snack & Nutrition Guide, 1988 Edition
(Pat. Pending)
[WARNING: For Prime Time & Rerun Eating Only]

L.A. Law . . . Leftover quiche.

Moonlighting . . . Mounds bars, chocolate kisses, and Seagram's Wine Coolers.

Murder, She Wrote . . . Mysterious green salads with curious ingredients you can't identify, like the red-edge lettuce that you think may be rotten around the edges. Also, chicken soup (homemade).

Cosby . . . Jell-O pudding.

A Different World . . . Oreos.

Golden Girls . . . Borscht with jalapeño peppers, caramels, nougats, M&M's.

Family Ties . . . Cold cereal.

Growing Pains . . . Cold cereal, choice of fruits. Also, Yodels and Ring Dings.

Who's the Boss? . . . Snickers.

My Two Dads . . . Sunny Doodles, Suzy Q's.

60 Minutes . . . Tums, because you're stuffed from eating during the football games and have *agita* from the exposés.

I Love Lucy reruns . . . Arroz con pollo, with bread and butter.

The Odd Couple . . . Beer, potato chips with relish, cold pizza, or *anything* with ketchup on it that doesn't really taste good with ketchup. Also, a stale salami sandwich from under the bed is nice, is in fact of the essence.

The Mary Tyler Moore Show . . . Little watercress sandwiches on white bread.

Dukes of Hazzard . . . Moon pie and RC.

Kojak . . . Souvlaki.

Dynasty . . . Champagne and Beluga caviar. TV Munch.

The Colbys . . . Ritz crackers. Diet Coke.

Dallas . . . Pit-style barbecued ribs flown in from Nieman-Marcus, Godiva chocolates.

SCTV . . . Six-pack of Moosehead beer.

Highway to Heaven . . . Apple pie and American cheese (individual slices).

Wheel of Fortune . . . Fish sticks, canned tuna, sardines on soda crackers, any kind of cheap fish, brain food to help you solve the word puzzles. Campbell's Chunky alphabet soup.

---

* Many of the recipes here were tested by the noted eater Martin Solow.

Kate & Allie . . . Chicken broth made from a bouillon cube. Chocolate cake from the box, just add one egg.

Designing Women . . . Who has time to prepare a snack? Anything that can be microwaved.

Johnny Carson . . . Milk and cookies, Fig Newtons, Vienna Fingers, Sugar Wafers, and Lorna Doones.

Late movies . . . Smoked Fiddler's Creek turkey, chopped liver, cole slaw, Russian dressing, with sour kosher pickles. Any big sandwich, which can be eaten at one sitting, so you then suffer. With an Alka-Seltzer chaser.

MacNeil/Lehrer . . . Thunder tea, or any special blend of herb teas with extra caffeine. Coke *with* caffeine. Coffee with *extra* caffeine *plus* on the side. All the caffeine they take out of the caffeine-free sodas and coffees goes with *NewsHour*.

Cagney & Lacey . . . Corned beef (slightly fatty) and cabbage. Irish stew. Jameson's chasers.

Twilight Zone (original black and whites) . . . Moxie, Nehi Orange, Horlick's Malted Milk Tablets and Mello-Rolls.

Twilight (new) . . . Carvel's Flying Saucers.

Hooperman . . . Reese's Peanut Butter Cups, Milk Duds.

Nova . . . Bagels, cream cheese.

Wall Street Week (with Louis Rukeyser) . . . Apples.

Hogan's Heroes . . . Knockwurst and sauerkraut. Subs, torpedos and hoagies.

St. Elsewhere . . . No food. You'll vomit. You can be watching even a party at the old St. E., and somebody will be in the next bedroom doing something sickening, like bleeding to death.

Laverne & Shirley . . . Any kind of nuts.

Sgt. Bilko . . . Chipped beef (all brands).

Upstairs, Downstairs . . . Warm beer, cold roast beef.

Firing Line with William F. Buckley . . . Sour balls, peanut butter.

Three's Company . . . Doritos and nachos. Anything with a loud crackling sound is good. It should drown out the dialogue.

Slap Maxwell . . . Buffalo Bill Chicken Wings. Milky Ways.

Popeye cartoons . . . Spinach.

Lou Grant . . . Scotch, from the bottom drawer of the desk, near the old manual typewriter.

Werewolf . . . Col. Sanders's Kentucky Fried Chicken, breasts and thighs.

*M*A*S*H* . . . Martinis, Dim Sum, and fresh fruit salad from the Korean market.

Star Trek . . . Tang, with spacefood sticks.

Newhart . . . Waffles (frozen) with Vermont maple syrup, honey nougats.

Perry Mason . . . Diet food. Weight Watcher's Lean Cuisine specials. Lite beer only.

Dark Shadows . . . Tomato juice, cranberry juice, Hi-C, any red-colored drink.

The Equalizer . . . Cadbury's Fruit & Nut Bars. Cadbury's Brazil Almond Bars. Yorkie bars.

MacGyver . . . Granola.

Fantasy Island . . . Beef jerky.

Barney Miller . . . Fish. And chips, Lay's or Wise.

Cheers . . . Pretzels (Bachman's Pennsylvania Dutch) and beer, Lowenbrau, if you're with good friends, but Molson Golden, St. Pauli Girl, Grolsch, and Dos Equis if you're your own best friend.

Happy Days . . . Burger, fries, and a malted.

Gilligan's Island . . . Coconuts, berries, soybean and sunflower seeds.

Presidential press conferences and State of the Union addresses, starring Ronald Reagan . . . Jelly beans. Grains of salt.

Addams Family . . . Chocolate-covered grasshoppers, ants, frogs' legs. Anything from K mart's discount "delicacy" shelf, or too long in the supermarket freezer.

Facts of Life . . . A Twinkie and a Tab.

Married . . . with Children . . . Take-out Chinese food (anything, as long as it's not too exotic). Baby Ruths.

Thirtysomething . . . Orville Redenbacher's popcorn. Perrier and water.

Morton Downey, Jr. . . . Cuchifritos, or a fried gall bladder attack.

Spenser: For Hire . . . Boston baked beans.

Knots Landing . . . A nice salad, with alfalfa, bean sprouts, and kale. Three Musketeers and Mason Dots.

Falcon Crest . . . Cheez Whiz and wine.

Mr. Ed . . . Grass, or hay, juice.

Magnum, P.I. . . . Your heart out, if you're into Tom Selleck.

Rumpole of the Bailey . . . A glass of wine, either a Château Thames Embankment 1988 or a Cabernet Fleet Street from last month.

Hill Street Blues . . . Pizza from the Pizzaman & New York City-style hot dogs, with mustard and sauerkraut.

Frank's Place . . . Pralines, gumbo, jambalaya, and burnt blackened fish cakes.

Oprah Winfrey . . . Fried chicken steak, smothered with mashed potatoes and creamy gravy, cornbread, black-eyed peas, okra greens, as a starter. Anything you can get your teeth into afterward.

Donahue . . . Coffee cake and coffee.

Mr. Belvedere . . . Recommended for diabetics only, an alternative to ingesting sweets.

Lassie . . . Chili dogs with the works. Noodles and cheese.

Miami Vice . . . Nose candy.

WKRP in Cincinnati . . . Mallomars.

Taxi . . . Mallomars.

The Honeymooners . . . Mallomars.

Car 54, Where Are You? . . . Mallomars.

Fawlty Towers . . . Bass Ale and Mallomars.

The Love Boat . . . Dramamine. So you don't get seasick just watching.

Swiss milk chocolate, especially Chocolat au Lait Suisse by Lindt & Sprüngli, goes well with everything on this century's schedule. Also cashew nuts, David's Cookies [when fully baked], and Häagen Dazs.

Häagen Dazs vanilla ice cream tastes good without TV. It's amazing how most of the things on my list taste better alfresco or al TV ("without TV" in Italian).

I must leave off this subject with one final, important, scientific question. Are they making smaller Mallomars these days, or am I getting bigger?

7

THE SEX TAPES II

DEEP RIVERS (EXPURGATING JOANIE)

I was watching Joanie sit in for Johnny one night. You know the Joanie I mean, the one who sounds like a horse with a cough. Joan Rivers, the first half-woman, half-snake, half-Republican, who so often seems like some kind of mythological figure, a Sagittarius who smokes three packs a day and has been inflicted on us from another planet as a curse for inventing atomic energy or panty hose.

The one thing that I like about the mouth-running Rivers is that she is courageous, fearless, and honest. "Don't go to college," she said to young women on the *Tonight* show one night. "Men like morons."

Joanie was being her usual hilarious self, explaining how much she admired Bo Derek: She's gorgeous. But stupid. She thinks *Lord of the Rings* is a book about Sammy Davis, Jr. There was a woman in Hollywood who went to a hospital and told the surgeon to make her look like Bo Derek. So they gave her a lobotomy. Etc.

"Can we talk?" Joan then said, leaning to the camera.

And suddenly her lips were moving . . . but no words were coming out of her mouth.

I sat up. I couldn't believe it. They were actually censoring her. Was she advising TV viewers to eat plenty of fresh vegetables? Get lots of rest, grow up to be healthy and normal?

No, presumably what she wanted to talk about was sex. She had already been mentioning funny things like having attended a small school in a Westchester town, Our Lady of Perpetual Herpes. It was such a small school they had to take turns having herpes. She stooped so low as to joke about Helen Keller, Eleanor Roosevelt, Mamie Eisenhower, the tragic death of Karen Carpenter, the Holocaust, and calling all young

Jewish girls whores. But that's our Joanie—a little on the foul side, almost always in bad taste. Why else would anybody watch her?

What could she possibly be saying, I wondered, in this day of blue movies on cable, of permissiveness in the arts as well as society at large? What could Joan Rivers have been saying at *midnight*, following the sorts of things she had already said, that NBC found offensive enough to censor?

Ah. First of all, it's not midnight in California. When they tape, it's still late afternoon. It's before they all have whatever it is that makes them so laid-back out there in Hollynose.

Was it something new in sex, some kinky development we hadn't heard about on *Donahue* in the morning, or during the soaps, or during the news on *Live at Five*?

Was it some new dirty word that our Miss Joanie had invented on the spot?

This pointed up a serious crisis in obscenity. There hasn't been anything new, actually, since the days of the Vandals and Goths who went around vandalizing and writing Gothic novels. Not to mention the Fucks, a lesser-known tribe than the Angles and Saxons, for whom the sex act was named. Which came first, the tribe or the act? How the Fuck do I know?

It was catching. . . . In the silence, I was going over to the other side . . .

Whom are they trying to protect at this hour? I thought. All the older people in the audience had fallen asleep watching *MacNeil/Lehrer* or Ted Koppel. Young people were watching the *Tonight* show, waiting impatiently for Letterman. Was NBC trying to protect the kids who had been sleeping with girl friends since they were fifteen?

I assumed ultimately that NBC was trying to protect innocent bystanders, like me. Thanks a lot.

First of all, anything Joan Rivers might have said I have heard before, on the streets, in the army, or the nursery.

Second, the censoring itself aroused my prurient interest. What word did she actually use? My imagination is more lurid than Joan Rivers's best.

I don't condone the use of four-letter words or four-letter ideas in comedy. In the early TV days, the only time they were used was on Dean Martin's show. Traditionally, when a comedian was in trouble and wanted to kick an audience into gear, he would say something dirty. It may not have been funny, but it sure woke up the audience.

Younger audiences at the clubs today don't understand something is funny until they say (insert favorite dirty word here). Drugs and *schmutz*.

That's all they know. There is a different style of comedy since the days of Sid Caesar. His old sketches would work today, if they just threw in *schmutz*. They don't care what they watch, it has been said of young audiences, as long as they use *bleep* or *bleeping*.

Obscenity is so unimaginative. It's the mark of a truly barren mind, or poor writing. I try not to use it myself, and don't especially want to hear it. However, I like to decide that for myself. I don't want some network official who has the intellectual capacity of a grapefruit telling me which bad-taste remark of Joan Rivers's I can hear and which I can't.

Artistically, the way they censored Joan Rivers was offensive. Although the process is called bleeping, which harks back to the days when there actually was a sound like *bleep* superimposed, what they did to Rivers was actually silencing, or cutting out the sound track. It's the most obvious, crude, uncreative, and unfair method of censorship.

For one thing, this left the unhandicapped viewers in the dark, and the lip readers in the audience vulnerable. Hard-of-hearing or hearing-impaired viewers didn't know Rivers was censored at this point. They just kept reading along, not knowing that what followed was deemed not good for good ears.

Instead of silencing only the audio, why not insert a slide on the screen reading:

$$\#*\$\#\&!!\&\%\$\#!!!$$

When I see those substitutes for cursing in the comic books—I still light up. Those expressions on the typewriter key say it all.

It also would be better if they were more creative about cutting—and did some substituting.

Why not the New York Philharmonic, playing the first three chords of Beethoven's Fifth Symphony, for example, superimposed over the offending words? Then you would get some culture in lieu of the bleeped filth. Sort of like reading D. H. Lawrence or Henry Miller while listening to Mozart.

Or:

- a visual fast-cut to a train entering into a tunnel;
- a mortar round coming in and exploding;
- a foghorn;
- a cuckoo bird sounding the hour on a clock;
- a daffodil blowing in a field of grass;
- the Mormon Tabernacle Choir singing "Nearer My God to Thee."

Any of these would protect the viewer from the offensive words or pictures but not from imagination.

My own favorite method is self-censorship. The comedian, if he must use *outré* words, should come up with new ways of expressing old ideas. I'd never be sure what they mean. For example, Mel Brooks is always talking about *shtupping*. He even used the expression on the *Today* show, and everybody either had a good laugh or didn't know what the *bleep* he was talking about.

TV has come a long way since the days when they couldn't use the word *bleep*, as in "*bleep* the torpedos, full speed ahead." Now you can say "*shtup* the torpedos" with impunity.

The big danger in all censorship is that the device or method itself arouses prurient interest. As soon as I hear a *bleep* or see Joan Rivers's lips flapping away without sound, it runs the risk of becoming a turn-on. It could even make Joan Rivers desirable.

T&A, J&J: (I DREAMED I WAS WATCHING TV WITHOUT HER MAIDENFORM ON)

A curious phenomenon was occurring in the ratings, during the spring of 1977. The new ABC fourth season ten o'clock shows, such as *The Feather and Father Gang* and *Dog and Cat* seemed to score well with the public, while the CBS ten o'clock shows, like *Hunter*, starring James Franciscus, or NBC's ten o'clock shows, like *Kingston: Confidential* did less well. Why?

It was doubtful if the viewing differential was related to the quality of the shows involved. None of those ABC ten o'clock shows will be remembered long after eleven o'clock in the historical sense. The NBC and CBS shows were just as unimportant and unimaginative.

Yet people preferred ABC to NBC and CBS. Most curious.

The answer to this mystery was right before our eyes, ignored precisely because of its simple nature.

What the new ABC new shows had in common: There was always a young, sexy actress-thing, jumping up and down to call our attention to something. Stefanie Powers, brilliant young attorney in *The Feather and Father Gang*, and Kim Basinger, the brilliant policewoman in *Dog and Cat*, jumping and jiggling.

"This is not a sheer accident," explained an NBC official who first noticed the trend. "ABC is beating our brains out with bralessness."

Research by this writer confirmed that ABC had somehow magically developed a reputation for unharnessed girls on its shows. Toni Tenille, a majority of viewers interviewed believed, went braless. Even Eleanor, in *Eleanor and Franklin*, was thought to have been braless on ABC. One had to go back to *Beat the Clock*, a syndicated game show on local TV, for a similar breakthrough in programming. The highlight of that show, younger scholars tell me, were the girls in tight sweaters running down the aisle to participate in the game. You'd be amazed how many men showed an interest in fashion and game shows in the early years of *Beat the Clock* Now, ABC was being watched as closely as *Women's Wear Daily*.

On the other hand, the public seemed to think that NBC had a reputation for girls with bras. Not true, of course. "We still do it in the daytime—have girls wear tight sweaters and bras on our game shows," one NBC official said. "But in the nighttime, we don't wear bras, either." Very democratic of him, that "we," or queenly.

CBS was in the worst shape of all, thanks to Maude, Rhoda, and Miss Junior Sophisticate herself, Mary Tyler Moore. "Even if the censor made Maude, Rhoda, and Cloris Leachman go braless, it wouldn't matter," one authority said. CBS has a frankly asexual image that will take a decade to change.

ABC began taking the lead in freedom as a programming tool early in the season when they introduced bralessness between 10:00 and 11:00 P.M. on *Charlie's Angels*. Every episode of *Charlie's Angels*, scholars say, had at least one braless girl on display from 10:03 to 10:11 P.M. It was a major plot element—that one girl be braless. Or if not plot, it was part of the set design.

One could be skipping rope or answering the door in a wet T-shirt or a towel. It need not be crucial to the story. It could be the same plot every week. It didn't matter if *Charlie's Angels* went on *The Love Boat*— and who will ever forget that meeting of minds?—the only important thing was that the girls have different T-shirts every week. They could also run down a street, in their high heels, pulling out their guns from little pocketbooks that wouldn't hold a lipstick.

The shows started off with the girls asking, "What do I do today?" "You got to go undercover as a go-go girl." One script told Farrah Fawcett-Majors to go undercover as a call girl. Farrah said (at the time) she thought *Charlie's Angels* success was based on the fact that she didn't wear a bra. Talk about your falsies modesty.

The trend may have started on ABC in 1975 with the debut of *The Bionic Woman*. Technically speaking, she does not appear exactly braless, but rather seemed to be wearing a special running bra with steel-span suspension. Engineers tell me it was based on the cantilever principle first introduced in the Brooklyn Bridge project of 1899. If you have ever seen the Brooklyn Bridge sway, you'll understand what the engineers are talking about.

The bionic-breasted Jaime Sommers (Lindsay Wagner) on *The Bionic Woman* was widely studied in the 1970's. They don't bounce when she runs because, some insiders say, they are made of surgical steel, with radial no-sway treads.

ABC's impressive collection of unfettered wonders also included Wonder Woman herself (Lynda Carter); an example of the curious phenomenon that psychiatrists call *wunderfräuleinmitdiegrossebosoms.*

The way it worked (in the series titled *The New Original Wonder Woman*, 1976–78) was as follows:

Diana Prince (a.k.a. Wonder Woman and Lynda Carter) is in her U.S. Navy uniform. Her hair pulled back, she's wearing horn-rimmed glasses and an innocent look. She is alert, hanging on to every word, like the superstenographer that she is. An emergency occurs. The Nazis are trying to seize some emissary from outer space so they can get the advance scientific secrets he may possess. Yeoperson First Class Prince lets her hair down. She twirls like a top. And suddenly becomes Wonder Woman, with that lasso around her waist.

For those of you who watched this classic series—just to keep up with the kids—you may well have asked, what was the lasso for? It didn't hold in her stomach, as some envious women liked to believe. Wonder Woman was all muscle; the only flab in that show was in the writing.

Now, she is standing there in her bracelets. What a wonderful pair. And wearing the famed breastplate. As one who studied this phenomenon, I am reminded of a night spent at the Playboy Convention in Chicago in 1972. Between John Kenneth Galbraith and Hugh Hefner at our dinner table, sat a wonder woman who was, I think, Hefner's date. She wore a dress very much like Wonder Woman's costume. It had no other visible means of support. Dan Greenberg, the humorist, leaned over the table and said to the women present, "How would you feel if those were twin brains?"

Back to the set: The plain Diana Prince has miraculously been transformed into the gaudy Wonder Woman. Naturally, at first nobody can recognize the connection between the two people. To find her face takes enormous powers of concentration. How can she run with that shelf? one muses. It's a miracle she doesn't pitch over on her head.

Here's what I also never understood: How was it possible that nobody could recognize Wonder Woman behind Diana's glasses? Couldn't anybody see that she had the same nose, the same lips, the same eyes, the same cheekbones, jaw, neck, etc.? Especially etc.?

In particular, Lyle Waggoner, better known as Major Steve Trevor. Such a jerk.

So much is written about offensive female stereotypes. I wish somebody had protested what that show did to male stereotypes. Has there ever been such a vicious anti-male macho put-down as Major Trevor, World War II hero? That a beautiful person with superhuman qualities is shown actually pining away for that military drip is the penultimate reverse putdown, almost as bad as Jeannie calling that dummy colonel "Master" in *I Dream of Jeannie.*

But this inability to recognize the two sides of Diana Prince may not be as farfetched as I make it. It could be based on a phenomenon of the physical sciences, the Superhuman Syndrome. "All Clark Kent did was take off his glasses," Helayne Gordon observed at a seminar on the "Wonder Women in American Culture" at Mepham High School in Long Island. "He didn't even let his hair down. And after all those years Lois Lane never came close to suspecting the connection."

Then there was the original version of *Sugar Time*—starring those three comic bombshells, Barbi Benton (as Maxx), Marianne Black (Maggie), and Didi Carr (Diane)—which introduced (in August 1977) three new forms to situation comedy: trampoline, volleyball, and horseback riding. The plots of the show always had something to do with its three stars going up and down.

It was said at the time that Jimmy Komack, *Sugar Time* producer, had to do about twenty hours of videotaping to make a half-hour episode. They were striving for perfection. Those hours of tape should go to the Smithsonian. Future generations could see an artist like Barbi Benton in progress. I would kill to see those tapes, to see Barbi Benton forget her immortal lines, such as, "A girl like I." Or: "I saw *Jaws* twice and screamed both times." According to my notes, the highlight of each comedy segment was the closeup shots of Barbi Benton's nipples. It was a landmark, a new high in TV comedy—and jumping.

Bralessness, scholars now say, was all a kind of *Reader's Digest* pornography, i.e., covered, but you know it's them. Pornography is often in the eyes of the beholder. And there were a lot of beholders for ABC's ten o'clock shows—rilly bigg shews—in 1977.

FREDDIE, PURE SILVER
(HI HO SILVERMAN, AWAY)

The genius who thought of all this was Freddie (Heigh-ho) Silverman, at the time vice-president in charge of programming at ABC.

Silverman, father of modern bralessness, who grew up to be president of NBC, was the first superstar TV executive, a true celebrity. When RCA got a new chairman in 1981 (Thornton Bradshaw), the papers used it as an excuse to write more (again) about Freddie. You walked on the street with Freddie, and people recognized him. In fact, he may have been the only corporate executive the public knew, besides Lee Iacocca and Frank Borman. And Freddie did it without commercials—that is, commercials for or by him. He became a household name, like Drāno.

At NBC, Silverman took a third-place network, and in only three years managed to keep it there, third spot in a three-team race.

What explains the success of Freddie Silverman, the only man ever to head programming at all three major commercial networks? One might just as well try to explain the success of Wonder Bread.

There were for one thing, the techniques Silverman had mastered at ABC:

1. What works once (*Six Million Dollar Man*) will work twice (*Six Million Dollar Man* and *Bionic Woman*).

2. What works in a half hour (*Happy Days*) will work in an hour (*Happy Days* and its spin-off, *Laverne & Shirley*).

3. What works at one length can work at another. Some shows he stretched out (*Rich Man, Poor Man*), others he squeezed together (*Roots*).

He was into ratings in such a big way that I expected him to change NBC's address to 30.4 Rockefeller Plaza.

Yes, the secret to Freddie's success or failure was his programming ability. He was the man who invented *schlock* therapy and trading down. Take what worked as quality programming, cheapen and degrade it somewhat so that it meets the mass taste, all the while promoting it till you scream. (*Laverne & Shirley*, one of Freddie's successes at ABC, was a failed *Mary Tyler Moore*.) He also had the insight that the American public loves double entendre (*Three's Company*) and enjoys nothing more than looking at double entendres (*Charlie's Angels*).

Uncle Freddie discovered that baby-sitters at home like salaciousness passed off as social documentaries, like *Little Ladies of the Night*, the story of teens who became hookers in Times Square. Silverman was the man who made it possible for ABC to be called "the Pimple Network," specializing in programming for kids and dummies, and was the acknowledged king not of popcorn, but of kiddie porn, turning sitcoms into soft-core pop porn. In *Three's Company* every second line was about (a) the guy's impotence; (b) the guy is queer; and (c) the girls are trying to make the guy.

Not all was pure dirt. He was a master of making things *seem* dirty. When the wonderfully satirical *Soap* came out, Freddie promoted it instead as dirty. Even when *Roots* was starting on ABC, they were taking the sex tack.

One morning before the greatest drama in TV history began, I remember reading on the front page of the *Times* that a woman was suing the producer, David Wolper, for depicting her daughter in the nude. ("We knew we were finished as soon as we saw that story," an NBC P.R. executive said.) The story suggested that girls were lined up, showing almost all. "They didn't tell me I'd have to expose my breasts," said the poor girl, reportedly.

There was, it turned out, no such suit. There was no such person in the show.

That Freddie was something. His accession to the throne at NBC—the pinnacle of his power when he, more than any person, had his fingers on the throat—sorry, pulse—of American culture—could be called the triumph of the common man. Every so often, somebody in history has the good fortune to embody the people he is leading. There was Hugh Hefner, in his day. Harry Truman. Ronald Reagan. Silverman was the Everyman of the 1970's–80's, successful because he *was* his audience.

Silverman actually liked TV. While other top TV executives have had exotic tastes, Silverman's greatest perversion was watching television shows.

He watched TV at the office and at home. He watched his wife and kids watching TV.

Sooner or later, one of us was going to seize control of the apparatus. It's the TV version of the Horatio Alger story. Here was this son of a TV repairman in Queens, who did his master thesis on ABC's programming in the 1950's, who started out in the mail room at ABC, who within a few years became network president. It shows the power of a good education.

Herb Schlosser, the man Freddie replaced at NBC, was an old-fashioned person. He thought the genius of programming lay in spending big money. His coups included laying out $100 million (that was a fortune in the 1970's) to get the Olympics. He also bought Betty Ford, the ballet, and Dr. Charisma, Henry (Hank) Kissinger. Schlosser was a highbrow, to whom those names meant something. It was impossible to imagine Schlosser sitting in his office watching a Saturday-morning cartoon, as Silverman did. And laughing out loud.

Freddie Silverman's only problem was a slight one of taste. His taste was in his mouth.

Silverman's favorite show at ABC was not *Roots*. It was *The Captain and Tennille*. He poured energy and ABC money (five hundred thousand dollars an episode) into that dog, and yet it still never became *Lassie*. Freddie's idea of a great entertainer was Marie Osmond, who he believed was to be the superstar of the next twenty years, the Tennille of the 1980's. He liked cute. I still remember his tendency to like Sandy Duncan at CBS. These are genuine problems; he was a truly disadvantaged man.

In drama, Silverman excelled especially in lowering taste by expanding the time allotted. Let any greasy-kid-stuff program, like *Having Babies*, get good ratings once, and it was a series.

While at CBS, Freddie got all the credit for *M*A*S*H*, *All in the Family*, *Mary Tyler Moore*—a claim that some at CBS disputed—he was also the one who discovered *Me and the Chimp*, *Big Eddie*, *Khan*, *Dirty Sally*, and *Planet of the Apes*.

Rationalizations about television are everywhere in the industry, but the Silverman Response to Carping Critics, in defense of the cultural classics mentioned (*Laverne & Shirley*, *Charlie's Angels*, *Three's Company*, and such) was: "If the American people live with these kinds of programs, presumably they want them, and should have them." The statement was a model of impeccable logic, undeniability, and the same sort of argument that could be made for giving them heart disease and acne.

Silverman so lowered the tone at ABC, where he was discovered by NBC, that the shortsighted said he could go no lower. They were wrong. *Roller Girls* (1978)—the story of the Pittsburgh Pitts, an all-girl roller-derby team led by towering Mongo Sue (Rhonda Bates) and Pipeline (Marilyn Tokuda), the only Eskimo-American in the history of sitcom—was a new low, until *Hello, Larry* (1979), McLean Stevenson's tragic attempt to get a fresh start as a radio talk-show host in Portland, Oregon, after his previous death as Colonel Blake in *M*A*S*H*.

Freddie reached the zenith, no, the RCA, at NBC, where he single-handedly managed to ruin comedy *and* variety in an immortal show, *Pink Lady & Jeff*, starring the Japanese lock and lollers Pink Lady. "They can't even speak English," Brandon Tartikoff, then Freddie's assistant, warned. "Don't worry," Freddie explained. "They can go to Berlitz before the season starts."

I dwell too much, possibly, on his achievements, like *Facts of Life*, a spin-off from the already creatively dreary *Diff'rent Strokes*; or his loyalty and devotion to *Hello, Larry*, which said good-bye to McLean Stevenson as a comic artist. At NBC he was the one who introduced female truckers (truckettes) to shows like *B.J. and the Bear*. Chimps were not enough. *Three's Company*, which made him famous when he started at ABC in 1976, was Molière by the time he finished at NBC in 1983.

But enough of the shows. Freddie Silverman's real skill, anyway, was in programming wizardry, they said: picking time slots (putting the right program against the rival program where the competition is vulnerable, etc.). But that turned out to be something computers could do.

For a further discussion, see Dr. Don MacLeod's definitive work on what went wrong with Silverman in "The Theory of Manifest Destiny as Evidenced by Archetypal Symbolism in Modern NBC Programming: An Autopsy of *Supertrain*" (the feature piece in next month's *Better Homes and Sitcoms*).

Still, nothing was more original than Silverman's *Supertrain*. He spent $12 million on the train, and then had nothing to put in the cars. It never even occurred to him to put McLean Stevenson in the train with his insipid "bachelor" crowd of kids. They could have traveled across the country, stopping for visits with Gary Coleman's family, Archie Bunker's, and Robert Young's (the kids are all sixty-six or so now). The Harlem Globetrotters could have come on board, playing exhibition games in the train's gym. No, sadly, Freddie seemed to go blank in his three years as resident programming genius at NBC.

For three years people kept trying to read hidden meanings into Freddie's actions. It was like the content of the cars on the train: There wasn't any. The new Freddie Silverman was the old Freddie Silverman.

I remember the time he suddenly began reading. It was the new James Clavell novel. This was after the smash success of *Shogun*, which he hated—before the ratings came in. There was talk that NBC was going to do more "quality miniseries" like the new Clavell. But he read the twelve hundred pages in one day. "That's how deeply he gets into things," explained vice-president Irwin Segelstein, his friend and co-worker at NBC.

I was lucky to be at NBC the day they bought the TV rights to *Shogun* in August 1977, B.S. (Before Silverman). Robert E. Mulholland, then president of the NBC Television Network, had heard the news a few minutes before I did. He was rushing breathlessly into the office of Paul Klein, then vice-president in charge of programming at NBC. Mulholland had that shocked look of the captain who occasionally comes down to the boiler room of the ship. So this is where the real work goes on, this is where it all happens when I say "full speed ahead." Klein, with three phones by his ears, had the harassed, sweaty look of the engine-room chief who is pouring more coal on, always afraid that the coal (the books purchased for miniseries) was going into the wrong furnace door, or out the porthole.

"What's this about *Shogun?*" Mulholland yelled. "What's a shogun?"

"It's about a family," Klein said.

"Oh, that's good," Mulholland said. At the time *family* was the hot word in television. Mulholland seemed relieved at the word *family*.

Klein may have said that it was "a Japanese family living in Connecticut." I couldn't swear to it. There was a lot of mumble-mumble cross talk going on, which I couldn't overhear innocently. But he gave the boss the distinct impression that *Shogun* wasn't something for him to worry about.

Freddie was very worried three years later when he realized he would be starting his first fall season at NBC with a TV show about feudal Japanese society in the sixteenth century, a twelve-hour movie, half of which was in Japanese, without subtitles. He had been on the phone all weekend from the beach in Hawaii, interrupting a vacation to denounce executives who had betrayed him in what he considered his personal Pearl Harbor.

Well, if the truth must come out, let me be the first to reveal it. Fred was not a cultured person. In 1978, when he started at NBC, one suspects he had never heard of Molière. Or thought he was Norman Lear's brother, Moe Lear. But it was Silverman who brought back live theater and live concerts. It was Silverman, too, who seemed genuinely surprised at the low ratings.

He was a fast-thinking executive with lots of ideas and didn't know the good ones from the bad. His success at ABC, some said, was because of the other Freddie. Not his alter ego—his boss. Fred Pierce, president of ABC-Television when Freddie S. was head of programming for the network, used to say to Silverman yes, no, no, no, yes, no. At NBC, where Freddie became boss, there was nobody to say no, until they said good-bye.

The reason Silverman failed had nothing to do with the quality of his mind or programs. He failed because he had absolutely no background in running a multibillion-dollar corporation like NBC. He had zero training for such a job.

I'm a superb critic and a perceptive writer. (Also, a swell fellow.) But if they made me president and chief operating officer of the *New York Times* Corporation, I'd probably blow it.

Look, here was a guy with absolutely no bureaucratic executive experience responsible for the bottom line, hiring executives who did all of the nonprogramming functions. And the firing. Soon there was more job security in the Shiite militia than at NBC.

Most of all, I resented Silverman because he gave TV back to the kids. After all those years of fighting to prove to TV networks that adults were not thirteen-year-olds, victory came in the early 1970's. Sitcoms and dramas began growing up with the arrival of *All in the Family, The Execution of Private Slovik,* and *The Autobiography of Miss Jane Pittman.* We had won the battle—and suddenly Silverman sold us out. He was nothing but a Trojan pony, a kid disguised in adult's clothing. And in his career, he traveled around like a contagious disease, spreading his form of infantile paralysis.

In the end, Silverman was alone at NBC. Nobody could talk to him, nor would he talk to anybody. He was like the boy in the bubble sealed off from germs. The closest thing to a real person he ever spoke to was his chauffeur, who drove his limo from the apartment on Central Park West to 30 Rock. He was out of touch with the great mass audience, with himself.

Still, sad in its way. The last time we lunched in his vast office on the sixth floor of the RCA Building, he wouldn't let me go, pressing question after question about what was wrong with TV. He had it all worked out: NBC shows were failing because of the promotion.

NBC's P.R. was superb, compared to its product.

They were calling his office Grant's Tomb, because Grant Tinker, who was his summer, winter, and long-run replacement, was to spend much of his time in California, it was said. (They were right. He does. He's gone, too.) Yet I felt a pang. How could I write on television without having Freddie to kick around? It is part of the American tradition with presidents, national or network, to kick a man on his way down—gives him a little momentum.

There were, again, those contributions, those wünderful bosoms, jugs, T & A. He was the one who stuck his neck out to give us Barbi Benton, for what she stuck out, and who saw talent in Susan Anton where others did not. Anton, the idealized woman of all Silverman's shows, was long,

long legs and an overbite. At NBC, under Fred, Secretariat could have been a star.

KILLING THE JIGGLE?

One night in 1981, I realized, there are no more private detectives on *Charlie's Angels* running after the crooks in their high-heel shoes. No more cute little wet T-shirts . . . no more *B.J. and the Bear*, with those seven female truckers, or truckettes, including Randi and Candy . . . no more sitcoms where the whole plot was "the girls play a volleyball game or practice the trampoline" . . . no more Suzanne Somers and her shorty pajamas . . .

What's going on here? I asked myself.

They were *killing* jiggly. Disgusting!

The age of the new wholesomeness had begun.

Three's Company, in that awful winter of my discontent, began stressing wit, not fit (of the clothes). Oh, brother. Had anyone actually ever *listened* to *Three's Company*?

Were they crazy, eliminating jiggly so suddenly, cold turkey? They didn't just ease off. A little topless, maybe, buried in *Sermonette* early in the morning . . . ? No.

The end of jiggly could affect the people much more than the new tax law or corruption in high places. Another setback to the nation's youth, for instance. Now the kids were going to have to learn about sex in the streets.

I had been on the wrong side of the controversy, for jiggling was the major social issue of the decade (1970–80). In 1978, I was writing these learned essays about how the networks were into jiggling, and wasn't it depraved. All the critics sang the same song. I remember one night all three networks had jigglers on at the same time, including the National Collegiate Cheerleaders Contest. I was livid, with rage. They were turning the TV audience into a booboisie.

But it occurred to me one day, I have nothing against boobs on TV. Didn't our forefathers call it the boob tube? Klutz, I said to myself, what is really wrong with jiggling?

Nothing is wrong with jiggling, given the attention in previous ages to, say, juggling; what is wrong is the complete lack of historical perspective. In late 1978, I began a study of the subject that is not, to this day, complete, and that has, of course, labeled me as one of your highbrow critics. Me, who haven't looked at a brow in years.

My interest goes back in time. Puberty was a factor, of course, but I was watching something called *American Girls* on CBS in 1978, the one viewer in the New York market to do so, according to the Nielsens. I also followed a little number called *Flying High*, well named, on CBS, and for comparative analysis studied the godmother of the movement, *Charlie's Angels*, as well as the important primal company, or scream, *Three's Company*. True scholarship, like the subject itself, knows no bounds.

What I saw, frankly, was appalling. The jiggling perpetrated by Pam Dawber, for example, Mindy of *Mork & Mindy* [now *My Sister Sam*] startled me, because I had thought of Dawber as the Carrie Nye of commercial broadcasting, a really thin, serious Artist. Pat Klous of *Flying High* was a sweetie, but, no offense intended, she didn't have much to work with. Yet even I make the classic mistake when shouting *J'accuse!* at *Charlie's Angels* . . . because with the exception of Cheryl Ladd, they were an insult to the activity. Skinny women can't really jiggle. It's an anatomical impossibility, a simple fact.

But, anatomy apart, my study and others' criticisms came too late. Students of the deep divide over such matters must be reminded of the riches of the 1950's: Faye Emerson, in her low-cut gowns; Denise Darcel, Diana Dors, Jane (the Body) MacDonald, Jane Russell, and the last of the red-hot jigglers and still the classiest of them all, Marilyn. Monroe kept 20th Century-Fox *together* until they got to *Star Wars*.

Yet none of the big-time jigglers could ever measure up, in a manner of speaking, to Adrienne Barbeau of *Maude*, unsung heroine of the modern movement. A. B. is unsung because she was not of her time; she was ahead of it, well out in front. In those days, the calculated jiggle was in limbo or unthought of; or, if thought of, unheard of. Yet Barbeau was major league. "Adrienne Barbells," they called her backstage. To be sure, there was always (or so it seemed) Suzanne Somers with her Two on *Three's Company* but to my shocked disbelief, as I really researched the matter, she stopped jiggling in 1978.

Again, let us remember the pioneers, even pre-1978. There was a brief golden age of J in 1977 with a show called *Sugar Time*. One entire episode was a volleyball game. That was *serious* jiggling because of the constant jumping; it is difficult to plot a show that calls for all the female characters to leap into the air for thirty minutes or so. And we have made scant progress. Mary Hartman's pigtails jiggled more seductively than the modest movers on some of today's shows.

The top three jiggling incidents in one sample year were:

- *60 Minutes*, when Mike Wallace, in his disapproving, disbelieving tone, was the voice-over as the cameras showed the stars of *Flying High* and *American Girls*, parading onstage at CBS affiliates' meetings, no bras, high heels, the look. Another example of the fearless exposés of renowned TV journalism.
- For the best jiggling incident not in a regular network series, *The Merv Griffin Show*, November 1978, an interview with Big Loni Anderson, then star of *WKRP in Cincinnati*. Loni was supreme, a trip to the bountiful who jiggled as she just sat there quietly, being interviewed. Then the cameras came in on—how to say it? Well, Loni's nipples. No parental-guidance warning, to get the adults out of the room. No nothing, except . . .

    "The studio must have been very cold," said one industry observer, who suggested the producer had turned the studio thermostat down to fifty-two degrees. But this observer, me, Marvin, knew the hard truth—intellectual shows are a turn-on for girls like Loni.
- Johnny Carson has to make the list. The master of sly innuendo (is there any other kind?), and pale blue material, can get almost prudish, and did, when Lesley Ann Warren came on the *Tonight* show promoting NBC's movie-of-the-week, *Night of Betrayal*. That lovely little girl sat there and claimed that her psychiatrist, played appropriately enough by an actor named Rip Torn, seduced her into having sex. Warren's concern was reflected in the demureness of her costume, a black dress rip-torned down to the belly button. Carson's concern came when he warned her to be cautious. You can't bleep a ---. Anyhow, the cameras zoomed in on her face and stayed there. (All except the spare camera the director monitored back there in the dark.)

Of course, for true students of the subject, nothing can compare—thank God—with the *Battle of the Network Stars*, the Valhalla, the Super Bowl of big-time jiggling. Not a single competitor wore a bra in the 1977 battle, not even Jane Seymour. Oh, maybe Kristy McNichol, but who cares?

You have to sit through the tedious parts in any *Battle of the Network Stars*, when somebody like McLean Stevenson, the perennial coach, tries to be funny with somebody like Robert Conrad, the perennial. And you have to sit through the second-rate jigglers, like McNichol or Valerie Bertinelli. But you know that—yes—sooner or later, the main event, Adrienne the B., will pop up and run a relay race, or climb a fence, or dive through an inner tube, and get drenched and interviewed, breathlessly.

In my sample year, however, the wet-shirt number was performed not by Barbeau but by the aforementioned Pat Klous, who got soaked in the Baseball Dunk event. "She has," said Howard Cosell, in a classic of misstatement, "a lot of grit."

Other scholars claim that Bette Midler is the most moving of the big-time jigglers. And she is not widely thought of as a jiggler, nor does she compete with Elizabeth Taylor, of the set-in-cement school. But Midler brought jiggling to the danger point in the *Bette Midler Special* on NBC, or what was called the "Oh-my-God-did-you-see-that-show?" It was a coming-out party, and anybody watching felt the earth move.

But enough of sex, of this coarse talk, for now. Let us turn to a safer and more substantial subject, the opera.

8

NIGHTS AT THE OPERA

THE DYNASTY OF *DALLAS* AND SUCH (MY NIGHT OUT WITH KRYSTLE, QUEEN ESTHER, KING BRANDON & THE MERRY MOLDAVIANS)

One of the problems of the TV critic is that we have to go out with the stars. Susan Lucci wants advice on whether she should play in *Medea*. Morgan Fairchild wants me to come to a candlelit breakfast. Generally speaking, I don't go. "It's not necessary," my wife explains, after her judo lesson, "to get that involved with your work."

Yes, but . . .

One day I received an invitation more intriguing than most:

BLAKE AND KRYSTLE CARRINGTON
(JOHN FORSYTHE AND LINDA EVANS)
CORDIALLY INVITE YOU TO JOIN THEM FOR

A

GALA EVENING
AT REGINE'S
59TH STREET AND PARK AVENUE
ON
SATURDAY NIGHT, OCTOBER 19, 1985
COCKTAILS AT 8:00 P.M.
FOLLOWED BY DINNER AND DANCING
THE PARTY, CO-HOSTED BY CHARLES OF THE RITZ AND REGINE,
WILL CELEBRATE THE INTRODUCTION OF THE NEW COLOGNE
CARRINGTON

THE ESSENCE OF A MAN
BLACK TIE REQUIRED

Carrington. The essence of a man? As cologne?

Just as we were recovering from the opportunity to buy Krystle's perfume—and who would not remember Forever Krystle's immortal line, "A woman's scent is her identity"?—they would treat us to a new Blake Carrington fragrance. What was this, a new TV series, *Smells of the Rich and Famous*?

Bad enough that you had to watch and talk about *Dynasty*, but now you'd be smelling it everywhere?

What would be next—Forever Esther Shapiro? (the *Dynasty* producer-genius behind the merchandising plan, which drove rival TV executives mad—with greed, if not passion.)

One Sunday a woman I know was going to work on the subway on the East Side of Manhattan. At the Bloomingdale's stop, a crowd swept her out of the train, along the station, and *into* the store. She fought against the tide of shoppers. But she couldn't get away. She found herself at a counter. It was crazy, a nightmare. She had accidentally become engulfed in the uncontrollable mob that was pushing to attend a major cultural event—the opening of "the *Dynasty* line" at Bloomingdale's. On a Sunday, yet.

In the Great Dynasty Sales Riot of 1984, as historians call it, people pushed and shoved and fought their way into the store. A hundred private security guards were inadequate. The New York Police Department was called in to control the crowds. It was, in fact, a very scary example of the power of TV. Ten guards were trampled by hundreds of crazed TV viewers-shoppers going berserk trying to buy, among other things, the first vials of Forever Krystle as if it were the secret of Linda Evans's perpetual, golden middle age.

My friend, that poor woman, was frightened. So deranged by the experience, she bought two *Dynasty* items.

Now, "the *Dynasty* line" is not just the famous Nolan Miller dresses—you know, the fashions that 1940 movie stars used to wear when they were being buried. The marketing of "the *Dynasty* line"—some one hundred products besides the Miller dresses; luxurious bedding, glassware, and china, bath towels, wallpaper, and men's evening suits in a color that the advertising declared "is richer than royal and darker than midnight—it's Dynasty Blue."

At one end of the line they were selling *Dynasty* ermine at $200,000 a pop. That's not twenty thou, love, but two hundred big ones. Not for the ranch. But each coat.

They were selling fake oil-company certificates at my end of the line, Denver Carrington (preferred) at ten dollars a share. Some regular stocks cost even less, and can be worth something.

Other bonbons included a gold-lamé dress with a matching jacket with fur cuffs that costs . . . for you . . . a paltry twelve hundred dollars. For cheapskates there were hundred-dollar silk blouses, or the *Dynasty* perfume—at $150 a *whole* ounce.

Clearly, it was a demonstration of the major link between art and mercantilism, the ultimate in TV as mannequin.

What I always liked about *Dallas* in the first couple of seasons was that everybody was so rich. Whenever they wanted a new fur coat, a car, a speedboat, they had it sent over. Nobody had to talk about how they were going to pay for the stuff. I especially loved their discussions of money. It was always in nice round numbers like "fifteen million" or "twenty million." "That's Ewing money," a paragon like J.R. used to say. "Your mamma's money." This was well before Cosby's commercials, in which he immortalized the line "Because it's *my* money."

The Ewing house at Southfork was a suburban branch of Neiman-Marcus. They seemed to have everything. Still, now and then one of the Ewing women, the lush, Sue Ellen, or the little tub, Lucy, would actually go to the store. "I'll take one of those," they'd say in the fur department, "and two of these." This was only prudent. You never knew when a frost was going to hit Dallas.

The Ewings were like kin to me week after week, as the story developed. Like others, I lived and consumed with them vicariously. I, of course, was the poor relation.

What I was discovering, naturally, was the TV prime-time soap as merchandising vehicle. The soap unconsciously set an agenda of things I might want to get some day. It told people what they could dream of. It was, in effect, a video of the Neiman-Marcus mail-order catalog. I am convinced it was the central reason why *Dallas* was so popular.

It's well known that there is a relationship between TV and the desire to buy things. TV causes shopping. I also had to realize that the art of programming is not just in writing or telling good stories. The plot of *Dynasty* is as predictable, with as many surprises, as reading the *Farmer's Almanac*. TV success is not about good acting or directing or breakthroughs in camera lenses and aperture openings.

The merchandising of products is what TV is all about.

Every show, except maybe for *60 Minutes*, is selling. (*60 Minutes* is indicting.)

The link between shopping and programming first discovered in *Dallas* was seen in *Dynasty* and the other soaps. They are as different from each other as L. L. Bean, Norm Thompson, and Eddie Bauer catalogs, with *Dynasty* the richest of the shows, halfway between Horchow, Victoria's Secret, and Frederick's of Hollywood.

The major dramatic achievement of *Dynasty* was the sheer number of products being marketed at the same time. The selling of *Dynasty* was a gang bang of merchandising, a World Series of product pushing. What happened that Sunday was, artistically, a smash success, the ultimate art and act of TV—driving people from the sets to the stores.

Dynasty, in the beginning, was smarter than *Dallas*. Instead of just displaying products on screen for viewers to covet, they went a step further and put out their own line of products. The latent relationship between selling and soaps had become overt. But *Dallas* quickly caught up. A few months earlier they had unveiled the South Fork Collection, the *Dallas* merchandise.

So many things were endorsed and merchandised by the *Dallas* and *Dynasty* stars in the stories that at Christmas I expected to be able to buy a J. R. Ewing or a Blake Carrington carved out of chopped liver.

My favorite explanation for this phenomenon, though heavily intellectual, was delivered by Esther Shapiro, who, as noted, created the series, working also with her husband, Richard, and Aaron Spelling. She explained the selling of the clothes and such as a public service. So many requests came in from viewers asking "Where can I get Krystle's earrings" or "Alexis's jewelry?" Somebody else was putting out unauthorized products, she explained. We deserve a piece of the action, I mean profit, from our artists' endeavors . . . "It was an outrage they should do it, and not us," she said. "There was no way to manage quality control."

Well, not a bad idea perhaps, marketing-wise, that is. They'd had Mr. T dolls and a *Knight Rider* sleeping bag, which was really cool—it had a dashboard in it—and God knows what for kids. Now adults were getting a chance.

TV raises everybody to the same level.

The great, you might say, Equalizer.

They were trying to use me, I knew, with this invitation to Regine's. I, too, was a merchandising tool. They were trying to use my famous nose for news (and sniffing out the corrupt and meretricious) for their nefarious commercial schemes. No way!

But a night out with Krystle . . . even if there might be a few others along . . . ? How often does one get such a chance? It was Regine's. And my tux was clean. I decided to put aside my principles and go.

I told my wife to grab her cameras, and how would she like to see John Forsythe, live and in person? Foolishly, I had given our limo driver the night off. We were just about the only ones who arrived on foot from a parking lot.

There was a madding crowd in front of Regine's on Park Avenue. The paparazzi were there *trenta, quaranta* deep. And fans! How did they know Krystle and Blake were coming? Apparently they just know. Nobody tells them. There is a jungle telegraph that spreads the word about where the celebrities are, the P.R. people said, in awe themselves.

Krystle was late for our date. I stood at the back of the crowd waiting for her limo, watching the TV cameramen and still photographers neatly standing their ground. In such combat situations, they make an agreement in advance about who shoots first, still photographers, TV cameras, and so forth. And then, as soon as the limo carrying Krystle and Blake arrived, they broke the agreements.

These two groups sometimes come to blows. A Channel 4 cameraman, Chuck Scarborough's brother Jeff, once had his jaw broken at a party like this. It's scary.

When the Krystle-and-Blake limo door opened, the crowd parted, as if the Red Sea and Charlton Heston had arrived. Suddenly they were engulfed by a wave of photographers. I was pushed up against the wall of Regine's entrance, in danger of becoming a pressed duck. Only to be saved in the vacuum created by the crowd, and swept in as part of the Carrington inner circle.

That's why I'm in the background of most of the pictures with Krystle and Blake. I'm the one whose eyes are shut all the time. I'd never been hit by nine hundred flashbulbs going off at the same time. If your favorite stars looked drugged in those supermarket tabloids, they're just trying to keep their eyes open.

I was then swept by the phalanx into the private room set aside for interviews before the Carringtons were scheduled to meet the common people, Marvin Traub, president of Bloomingdale's, and other corporate types, whom, I soon saw, Linda had also invited on our date.

I found myself locked into an all-mirrored room with crystal chandeliers with Krystle and Blake. Also with *Entertainment Tonight*, CNN, and the Regis Philbin show camera crews. That's about as private as you can get these days. There was the legendary Kathie Lee Johnson, formerly of

Good Morning America, now co-hosting with Regis Philbin, in a fabulous Nolan Miller girl reporter's dress.

Philbin himself would have died to have been there. But, as he explained on his local morning show the following Monday, his wife had insisted on looking at the leaves upstate instead. He was bitter about it, as well he might be. "Leaves are pretty," as the noted garment manufacturer Bob Goldstein once said, "but I prefer to look at the color-swatch book instead."

Also caught in the crush with the cameras was Robert Merrill, the opera singer. Every time I see Merrill I feel like standing up and saluting. He has made "The Star-Spangled Banner" *his* aria. He was at the party this night to sing "The Star-Spangled Banner" before dinner. Merrill was from my wife's home territory, Borough Park in Brooklyn. So she had a lot to sing about and talk about while I was otherwise occupied as a journalist.

It's not every day that I get to meet my wildest fantasy, even if this was to be only for a moment. For the time being, there were so many other important guests she had to curry favor with.

She moved among them in her silver-lamé gown, with the side slashed up to her eyes. She was also in her Charles of the Ritz perfume. I was in my Sam of Teaneck (N. J.) rental tux, with the dashing ripped seam under the arm.

And then the fuses started blowing. The multicamera crews were drawing too much electricity. Krystle and I were locked in that room, with only about ten or eleven people, for seventy-five minutes. This is the way the end of the world will come, I'm sure. This is how it *should* end. Me, with Krystle and Blake and Merrill to sing "Nearer My God to Thee," as the world goes under.

But the lights came on again. After a time Blake said, "It smells like a French whorehouse in here," as the heat of the lights and interviews progressed. Not that I'd know. Charles of the Ritz, apparently a fellow named Miller, had been running around spritzing the room with Carrington, the fragrance.

I myself chose to smell Krystle's perfume; she was calmly standing by. "Two scents off for your thoughts," I whispered into her beautiful ear. My dream girl, live and in color, was everything I had imagined. And more. This was the woman, I kept saying to myself, that John Derek threw *out?* The dope! And for what—too old? For that BimBo Derek?

While Forsythe was doing his thing before the *ET* cameras—"Don't describe me as a horse lover," he said, gently chiding the reporter, "I am not seeing any horse at this time; I never even went out with one"— I managed to monopolize Linda for what seemed like an hour.

What I always loved about Krystle Carrington was that she was always so easy to get along with. Blake does something she disagrees with violently, and she says, "Oh, Blake." And Blake says, "Krystle, I must." And she goes along. Blake tells her to do something, she whimpers, "No." He says, "*Do* it, Krystle," and she does it. That is more than you can say for the woman in my house.

"What do you expect," said the woman in my house, my wife, the photographer. "She is Blake's former secretary, and she still takes orders."

As a person, Linda/Krystle was everything I dreamed of, except for one dimension. She is skinnier than I had imagined. I would have thought Linda more *zaftig*. The cameras exaggerate, add from ten to twenty pounds.

After seventeen years, I should have known that TV appearances can be misleading. As I said, TV makes you think Howard Cosell is a little weasly rat. Then, when you see him off-camera, he is a giant, stoop-shouldered from looking down at us lesser worms. He's a tower, like Dave DeBusschere or Bill Bradley.

Does that mean we are all overweight? No, we're just in good shape. They're too thin.

The media are, in fact, anorectic. All the macho-man types, like Tom Selleck, have skinny little pipestem legs like *GQ* models. So my Linda is not perfect. She is only a $9^{15}/_{16}$ out of 10. She has flaws like any other person, and if you give me twelve or thirteen years, I can think of two.

I'm a hard man to please, when it comes to actresses, as anybody who has read my criticism knows. I'm especially hard on gorgeous blondes. I make fun of everybody except Elizabeth Taylor, who reminds me of my mother.

There is nothing funny about Linda Evans in person.

Of course, I was as stunned by her beauty in person as on TV. I always try to talk slowly—very slowly—to blondes. But she made me feel very foolish. Meeting her for the first time I was even more stunned to find that she is also warm, wise, sensitive, intelligent, humane, courteous, brave, and a real person. Otherwise, I was unimpressed.

The thing about actresses is that they are a little self-involved, with a limited repertoire of interests. Valerie Bertinelli is known in the trade as a two-minute interview: She discusses her latest health food, the exercise she is into, and that's it. But Linda! You could talk to Linda about the Punic Wars, and she would discuss strategy and tactics and be engaging and charming, as well.

At first I was amazed to see how a person with so many professional problems could be so relaxed. She had just been kidnapped by George

Hamilton on *Dynasty*, and she was being replaced by her double, Rita, in a plot hatched by her niece, Sammy Jo, the slut, to get even with Auntie Krystle.

So there was a pair of Krystles that season, the good Krystle who had returned to Denver after being locked up in a Moldavian dungeon without her eyeliner, and another actress who looked like her, named Rita. This was the famous two-Krystle period in *Dynasty* history . . .

Both Krystles were being played by Linda Evans. One had red hair, the other was the original, striking blonde. There were those who said you couldn't tell the difference: They were each bad. I liked them both, although the red-haired one sometimes made the blonde seem a little . . . dumb. Krystle is an idiot, some women were saying. "She could have gotten out of the ranch just by starting a fire." The dumb side of her character was underlined by those positively withering lines from Joan Collins's Alexis, as in "Take the mud out of your ears, Krystle."

But if she was dumb, what about that Blake? He's living with this complete stranger (Rita) for weeks, and he couldn't even tell it was not his wife?

Just that week I had read that Krystle, in captivity, had her lights punched out by Hamilton. While he was trying to kiss her, he accidentally knocked her over. The papers said they sent Linda home from the set. So, she took the cure. She went shopping. The best remedy for headaches. The best therapy, they say. Some doctor on Rodeo Drive, that is, with a half interest in Gucci, said it.

But here she was, this one evening, chatting away with the nation's most powerful television critic as if nothing had happened. She was utterly calm, as we had a lengthy discussion about criticism. She never reads reviews, she explained. While I was completely against what she was saying, in principle, her arguments were persuasive. Also, her nostrils.

Linda, it became clear, was above all the madness of being a superstar. It did not turn her beautiful head. She has an inner beauty, a tranquillity that drew me. Forget the gorgeous long legs, the low-cut gowns, all that superficial stuff. Forget her millions, her incredible good looks. Underneath all that, she is a nice person—engaging, charming, witty.

That must have been *some* perfume she was wearing.

Blake smiled at us knowingly as we talked for a half hour. Nothing fazes him. Not even on the show. Not only was he living with Krystle's double, the double now had a headache ten nights in a row. No problem. He tells her to see a doctor. He's so unflappable. If Rita and Krystle showed up in the same bed, he would not have been surprised.

I know there are those who say Linda Evans is not much of an actress to start with. There are even those who say that Linda Evans is not the most beautiful. "She is so, what do you say . . ." explained Michel Sobrane, a French writer ". . . so *plastique*. Collins, she may have a waist that starts under the armpits, but she is more beautiful."

That's one Frenchman's taste.

All that beauty and brains, too. A woman can feel inferior around her.

Whatever else Linda said to me on our date is private. It's in my diary. I am a gentleman.

I can tell you what we had for dinner.

Congealed—something, for a first course, And veal, although many thought it was lamb or beef or fish or chicken. Regine's cuisine is not up to her dance floor.

Wordlessly, Linda and I decided to sit at separate tables. To avoid gossip, suspicion. She was at the next table, with a few of the corporate types, Charles of the Ritz, and the other Marvin (Traub) of Bloomingdale's.

The only average person at the dinner besides me was Boy George. He crashed. He came with the fabulous, vacuous Cornelia Guest, daughter of C. Z. Guest and professional party attender. She also brought the fabulous, vacuous Ann Turkel, the ex-Mrs. Richard Harris.

Boy's lipstick was on straight. If not his, as my wife explained, who else's? He made most of the women look frumpy.

One of the other average persons at my table was Miss Universe, the former Miss Puerto Rico. And then there was Kathie Lee Johnson, the TV journalist and friend-in-waiting of Frank Gifford. And the editor of *Woman's Wear Daily*, Michael Coady, who was complaining about everything, even the place cards! He kept saying that if Regine herself was running this, it would be done right.

Then there was the excitement of seeing a fellow in shades with a thin tie carrying an Instamatic camera, followed by three others who looked exactly like him. It was like four Andy Warhols. Turned out to be the cultural reporter of the *Los Angeles Times*—and three clones.

After Robert Merrill sang "The Star-Spangled Banner," and there were speeches in praise of Charles of the Ritz, the dancing started. I decided against dancing the night away with Linda. My principles had already been compromised. I would be a hopeless wreck. At midnight I rushed out of Regine's and was handed bags containing the essence, my brush with greatness, my date with pure beauty and fantasy, over.

Life for me would never be the same. Every time I watched *Dynasty* now, I would not smell the bad scripts or the overacting. Forever Krystle, the scent, doesn't remind me of a cheap perfume, but rather of Krystle.

And Blake. And the night I went out with the Carringtons. My date not with *Dynasty* but with Destiny.

Parties are such sweet sorrow, but they are part of the business. A critic with a true vocation goes—often against his will, often when he'd rather be curling up with a good book or an iced drink, but he goes.

The first time I went to Hollywood, back in 1980, I stayed at the Beverly Hills Hotel with all the other big stars and powerful men in broadcasting. I assumed that I would be invited to swinging cocaine parties, with starlets wearing sheets, popping ludes, and in and out of hot tubs. I had read *Hollywood Wives*. I wore my shirt open (with no tie) and had Italian loafers . . . casual shoes, I mean. I was ready for action. And I am a party kind of guy.

It turned out that the only party I was invited to on that first trip to the planet Los Angeles, Los Paradiso, the Big Grapefruit, the land of silk and money—was to a bagel-and-lox bash on a Sunday morning.

Of course, bagels and lox in L.A. are *vieux chapeau*, as they say where French is spoken. Also served was chili-cheese kugel.

The event was at the home of TV writer Shimon Wincelberg, a graying, distinguished author of scripts for such shows as *Star Trek*, *Trapper John, M.D.*, *Mannix*, *Have Gun, Will Travel*, and a host of other popular programs in the first golden age of TV, before television programs made you lose brain cells. He lives with his wife, Anita, about three miles south of the Beverly Hills Hotel, in his costly mansion on the Lower East Side of the Hills, within comfortable striking distance of synagogue and tennis courts, to which he haughtily withdrew upon reaching the compulsory retirement age of thirty-five. He had gotten out of TV entirely the year I visited with him, word having gone about that his characterization for *Fantasy Island* (or whatever Aaron Spelling hit it was that year) "lacked profundity"—which in the TV business earns you an automatic twelve-month suspension. "A status characterized," Wincelberg explained, "by each executive's secretary, who goes back to making you spell your name when you call."

"The day I flunked acne inspection," as he put it, "the internetwork computer erased my name from the dreaded 'Network Acceptability List,' and I was left alone to choose between finding honest work or going back to being a writer." Possessed of no other marketable skills, he settled down to polishing his tennis game, finishing a second novel, and awaiting the fate of three plays under options, a living reminder of a time when not everything for TV was written on Kleenex.

A typical Hollywood Saturday night? As the late Bernard Herman once noted about greater Los Angeles, "No matter how hot it gets in the daytime, there's nothing to do at night."

This was, however, a Sunday brunch.

Usually in these hours the Wincelbergs are obtaining instruction in Talmud, aerobics, and hatha-yoga. But on this Sunday morning they had gathered a group of "like-minded types," a cross section of L.A. dissidents in the TV business, cranks, complainers—sort of an emergency meeting of the dissident underground to immunize me with a necessary grain of salt. To give me, as he put it, "a chance to decompress, debrief, or merely regurgitate your first impressions of Tinsel Town."

Anita Wincelberg is a sociologist who has done important studies on the local fauna, i.e., writers and producers, many of whom suffer from the pain and angst of bruising experiences, the small price being paid by some of these guys for taking home their hundred-plus grand a year. "A select company I have managed thus far carefully to avoid," Shimon Wincelberg said. Six out of seven of these complainers in Anita's landmark study of kvetchers are now cheerfully writing, producing, and in one case, directing. One is even a VP at ABC.

The cosmopolite group that had gathered at the Wincelbergs' writers' circle included Michael Medved, the co-author of *Whatever Really Happened to the Class of 1965?*, which had been a big miniseries on NBC that year. There was a *Charlie's Angels* line producer who regaled the group with stories about Jaclyn Smith and Shelly Hack, in their high heels trying to run after the bad guys up in Holmby Hills. And there was a mystery woman, my host explained, currently working on a series proposal for Aaron Spelling.

The talk of the day was the big social event that season, the bar mitzvah of Jason, son of Barbra Streisand by Elliott Gould. Yentel the Yeshiva Girl Herself! Medved had actually *attended* the event, which took place at his synagogue in Venice, California. It was an Orthodox service. That means, in Venice, that the congregation was not on roller skates. And the reception, too, was quite simple: The likeness of the boy was not done in chopped liver, as in certain Beverly Hills bar mitzvahs, but in halvah.

Jason is a good kid. When he went to Serendipity, an à la mode restaurant-store in New York, a week later with his father, the actor, management asked him to pick out a present from their exotic merchandise. According to Liz Smith's column, the bar mitzvah boy answered, "All I want is money."

Everybody talked that morning, too, about how difficult it was in Los Angeles for serious writers, for people who didn't play the game, for people who wanted to fight the system, not go along. It was like being on the Left Bank in Paris in 1920 with the exiles, the good and true people. It also felt in a small way like being in a crowded room in Moscow with the drapes drawn tight, the secret police hovering to barge in at any moment and send us all to the gulag in Encino.

The only one who didn't say much was the mystery woman, who was, as we say, working on a pilot for a miniseries that could become a series. Her name, which meant nothing to me at the time, was Esther Shapiro. She had chipped nail polish. Her hair was tousled. She was wearing what seemed to be a housedress that didn't come from any of the houses on Rodeo Drive.

The series she was creating was then called *Oil*. "What's it about?" I remember asking her. "A big family in Texas?"

"No, Denver," she said.

"*Oil*? It won't work," I explained. "Shows beginning with a vowel never succeed. Unless they are preceded by a *the*."

She obviously listened to me. *Oil* was later changed to *Dynasty*. The *D* in the title reminded people of *Dallas*. The rest is history.

But at that moment, Esther Shapiro sat quietly in the corner, a very unglitzy woman who obviously was too busy to go to the nail salon.

Appearances are deceiving. You don't have to look like Joan Collins to write about Alexis. Writers often have rich fantasy lives. In the same way, you don't have to be a great ballplayer to win pennants as a manager. What an imagination this Esther Shapiro woman had.

She seemed to be the epitome of the middle-aged, middle-class, liberal Jewish woman/television producer. Yet she wrote stories of the rich, glitzy, power-mad, avaricious, amoral, goyish families that are the Carringtons and the Colbys.

After a while, she announced that she had to go back to her desk at Aaron Spelling Productions to finish the script for the pilot show. I realize now she was, that very morning, doing research for *Dynasty*. I wonder for which character I was the prototype—Blake Carrington? Dex Dexter?

In a small way, I had played a part in the success of a major dramatic breakthrough in its formative year. A small part, I say, in all modesty.

I was the one who said it would never work. I had also been the one who told my neighbor in New Jersey, when we were both starting out— he as an actor-turned-novelist, I as an illiterate-turned-critic—that he would never make it as a writer. Robert Ludlum, for reasons of his own, ignored me and was never heard from again.

In technical terms, what I was giving Shapiro was negative input. This, too, has real power. You can make nuclear explosions from negative, reverse polarity, and all that. Black holes were caused by a caustic TV critic disappearing into space. It fills the creative people with resolve. And they go out and prove me wrong. Little did I know this straight, down-to-earth woman with chipped nails would turn out to be Queen Esther, Hurricane Esther, Aaron Spelling's right-hand woman, who with her taciturn husband, Richard, the silent partner who was at home playing the guitar that morning, would revolutionize prime time, soap operas, and give us a dynasty of programs, *Dynasty I* and *Dynasty II*. (*The Colbys*).

I reminded Esther Shapiro of this one night in 1985, as we sat in her Jaguar Saloon XJ-6, customized, specially painted to match the color of her green eyes, or money. Remembering the chili-cheese kugel, she got a distant look in her eyes.

"I showed you," she said.

Oh, yes: the problem about not getting invited to the sex-and-drug parties, I found out later—my shirt wasn't opened three buttons. Also, I wasn't wearing chains.

In 1985, there was a shocking announcement out of L.A. Ordinarily, no shocking news issues from L.A. Of course, nothing they do in Hollyweird surprises us. But this was something: Moldavia was going under. ABC was writing out the segments in *Dynasty* dealing with the country they had put on the map.

King Galen, the Sponger, was being thrown out of his expensive digs at Denver's La Mirage Hotel (the Carrington Arms). When last seen, he was on his way into exile with Papa Doc and the Marcoses. Prince Michael was on the verge of suicide. Even his hair looked depressed. And just when the underground had been established in Denver with his old sweetheart. Amanda was so broken up by this turn of events she started sleeping with Dex, her stepfather, who had been thrown out by Alexis.

Esther Sharpiro and her Dancing Moldavians, finished on network TV?

Moldavia! Gone? A sad day in the geopolitics of television. I still can't believe that they blew Moldavia off the map.

What is a Moldavia? you ask. Most people think that it is a fictional country located somewhere between the principalities of Beverly Hills and Bel Air in the Rich People's Republic of Los Angeles. Wrong. Look it up in *The World Book Encyclopedia*:

Your *World Book* will show you that Moldavia is located to the south of **MOLD** and just north of **MOLE**.

Moldavia is also a region in southcentral Europe. Part of it consists of the Moldavian Soviet Socialist Republic in the southwest corner of Russia. It includes Bessarabia, formerly in Romania, whose leading export was some of my wife's relatives.

What Moldavia doesn't have is the Riverialike coastline seen in *Dynasty*. In fact, if you look closely at a map of Moldavia, you'll observe that it doesn't have a coastline at all. But then, as one L.A. newspaper writer observed, "What does that matter to a show that uses major downtown (L.A.) skyscrapers as stand-ins for Denver architecture?"

As you recall, the residents of Denver had been attending a wedding in Moldavia during the 1985 cliff-hanger. A Carrington daughter, Amanda, was being married to the prince of Moldavia, and the wedding was rudely interrupted by uninvited guests, paratroopers of the Moldavian Provisional Government, crashing through the windows of the chapel in their cute Nolan Miller jump suits, spraying the wedding party with lead. All the bodies were piled upon each other. It looked like Jonestown.

When the show came back in September with the first pictures from strife-ridden Moldavia, it gave the answer to the question that kept TV viewers going all summer: Who lived and who died in *Dynasty*?

The casualties included three Nolan Miller dresses smudged. One sleeve (belonging to Alexis) was badly ripped. Missing in action was Krystle's silly little hat.

The only people killed in the storming of the palace by the armed insurrectionists were a couple of actors whose contracts were up for renewal. Steven Carrington's friend, Luke, and the noted international photographer and bad actress Ali Guffaw (MacGraw).

In May it had looked like everybody was dead. But in late September (1985), when the show returned, the residents of Denver were amazingly hearty and healthy. There is an old Moldavian folk expression, *"Brnyzwzmyg drewytzqkly brnwp,"* which means: "How the hell did that happen?"

Those Moldavian marksmen should have taken more target practice.

The beginning of the end for Moldavia began with the accession to the throne of King Brandon II in January 1986. His rise was due to a shift in television-industry credentialing.

The trend in 1986 was the code name "Brandon." Two out of three network-programming departments were headed by men named Brandon—Brandon Tartikoff at NBC and Brandon Stoddard at ABC. It was the hottest thing in TV management since its executives discovered Perrier. No wonder CBS was in such bad shape creatively. It was stuck with a Harvey (!) as head of its programming department.

CBS, the only network without its own Brandon in charge, reportedly looked for a Brandon to replace Harvey Shepherd. They rejected Brandon de Wilde out of hand. Marlon Brando was a near-miss. Still, there is a "Brandon X," out there, its headhunters said.

There were, seriously, a Brandon Wojecocichowic, a Brandon Cohen, a Brandon O'Toole, and a Brandon Gall (no relation to *The New Yorker*'s Brendan Gill) working in the William Morris Agency and MCA mail rooms. "Brandon" 's time had come.

I can still remember when Brandon was revolutionary, a name to conjure with when it first burst on the scene. Brandon Tartikoff was the talk of TV. ("Brandon Tartikoff?" they were saying. "Isn't he a football star?" "No, that's Fran Tarkenton, turkey.")

When Tartikoff first surfaced, he was associated with Freddie Silverman in the NBC programming department. He was the one carrying the water pitcher.

Silverman had hired him when he was at ABC in the 1970's, after an undistinguished career as a *Newsday* copyboy. Tartikoff was promotion director. His first job was at an ABC affiliate in Chicago doing on-the-air promotion spots. One of his best-known promotions was "Ape Week." (ABC owned the rights to *Planet of the* . . . movies.) Instead of just running them for the sixty-fourth time, Brandon's promos included songs like "Gorilla of My Dreams." Silverman went ape over them, and him.

The original Brandon had some rough years at NBC. No one could fire him, it was said, because they couldn't pronounce his name. But he hung in there. The newest Brandon at ABC has more substantial credentials, as the former vice-president in charge of all miniseries and drama. Further, he was a classmate of C.D.B. Bryan III, Dick Cavett, and Bobby Zarem at Yale. This Brandon replaced Tony Thomopolous as boss.

What happened to Tony T., as he is called in Hollywood? Rona B. (Barrett) explained: Tony T. was fired by Fred P. (Pierce). Nevertheless, they were the best of friends. But Fred P. had to do something to show Cap Cities (Capital Cities Broadcasting) that he (Fred P.) was an action-oriented executive. He fired Tony T. to get rid of some extra layers of F. (Fat).

Also, it was reported, Brandon S. said, when Freddy P. offered him the job, "I want to take the job. But you'll have to get rid of Tony T. I'll only take the job if I can report to Freddy P. (you) personally."

So Freddy P. had to get rid of Tony T.

Meanwhile, Christina DeL. (Ferrare DeLorean) was left wondering why she married Tony T.

They are, as you gathered, big into initials in L.A., which shouldn't surprise anybody who has heard of the expression L.A.

The creative community in L.A. is also into first-name dropping in a big way. As soon as a stranger to L.A. walks through LAX (the airport), he or she suddenly starts dropping names like "I wonder if Lew [Wasserman] sent the limo?" Last names are something they check with their neckties at the airport.

It's always, "Grant said Mary was not good in bed." Or, "Harvey told me Bud (Donald Grant, then head of CBS Entertainment) was the king of beers." Or "Brandon told me shows about apes are 'in' . . ." All the big executives in TV seem to have given their last names away; there may be a tax write-off, a charitable deduction.

So you can imagine the crisis that took place after the appointment of Brandon Stoddard at ABC. When they say, "Brandon said . . ." or "Brandon told me he loved it," or "All we need is Tom Selleck to play the rabbi," people don't know which Brandon they are dropping.

One seer suggested we call them Brandon the Tall and Brandon the Short. Tall Brandon and Shorter Brandon, or B.T. and . . . B.S.? A pejorative?

It is true that Brandon S. is not the world's tallest TV executive. He has an office at ABC the size of Mussolini's office. In that office, he looks short. True, he tends to disappear behind the desk. When he gets down off the chair, his head doesn't go over the desk.

But in his way, this Brandon is a giant. His ideas are big. Start with *Roots*. If you said "Brandon the Tall," I think of Brandon Stoddard.

On the other foot, Brandon Tartikoff, who may be physically taller, has some very small ideas. He personally thought of *The Misfits of Science*, for example, not to mention *Mr. Smith*, which gave us talking chimps ("Gorilla of His Dreams," scholars will remind us, a leitmotif in Brandon T.'s career).

My own solution is to call them Mr. Stoddard and Mr. Tartikoff. After all, we barely know these people.

In his inaugural address to the nation's TV critics assembled in L.A. on an ABC junket, Brandon the Short declared the Moldavian segments as a major cause of the decline in *Dynasty* ratings, which at the time were falling faster than Brandon's stock.

There were other problems with *Dynasty* story lines, King Brandon the Second said. Not only was the whole Moldavian thing a mistake, there was the Krystle-Rita doubles thing.

As you may recall, at the time Linda Evans was playing two characters, neither of them well. She looked the same and acted the same way in both parts.

You could so get too much of Linda Evans. Sob.

Some authorities saw Queen Esther's fine Italian fingernails in these machinations on *Dynasty*. But it was all part of Brandon's game plan. Here was the hottest creative mind in the business, as yet untested in the world of realpolitik, and the new leader was turning on his network's number-one show. This was more the traditional Hollybabble or Hollywoodthink.

They fired Sigmund Romberg, or whoever was writing those operettas about what seemed like a little town in Europe, those *Prisoner of Zenda* outtakes.

To further rectify that problem, Queen Esther called herself back from active duty on *The Colbys* and started to write her way out of the mess:

- King Galen . . . out!
- Prince Michael. Forget building our underground. We'll take the IRT to Moldavia.
- The whole country of Moldavia? Erased. Degaussed. Neato.

But did they ever consider that the real problem might not have been Moldavia? This aspect of the show added class, a touch of internationalism. It was like the *Foreign Affairs* of prime-time TV, with Joan Collins, banker, deeply involved in high finance in Moldavia. A sadness. And just when they were going to put her picture on the Moldavian kopeck.

Kopeck? That is what they call Kojak on Moldavian TV (MTV)? *Tiev, baby, who loves ya?*

THE COLBYS MEET THE CARRINGTONS

Television history was made the night of November 18, 1985, when the Colbys met the Carringtons in a special two-hour spectacular block-buster *Dynasty*. Not since Godzilla met King Kong, or the Hatfields the McCoys, had we seen anything of such magnitude.

It was "the largest all-star cast in the history of series television," the ABC ads said. The purpose of the meeting was to introduce the characters who would be appearing in *Dynasty II: The Colbys*, the spin-off of *Dynasty I* that was to start a few weeks later.

It was an example of classic programming principles: Two *Dynasty*s are twice as good as one.

ABC could not, of course, just call it *Dynasty II*. That sounded too much like the Super Bowl the day after, or a Chinese antique vase, as in Ming Dynasty V, the series that ran so long—through several civilizations—in China. So Queen Esther, the Creator, along with husband Richard the Silent, came up with the idea of calling the spin-off *Dynasty II: The Colbys*. She is some smart fortune cookie.

It made for a month that went down in history as Dynastic. Double doses of *Dynasty* were commonplace now on Wednesdays and Thursdays. ABC even got President Reagan to postpone the Geneva Summit address one night because it conflicted with a *Dynasty* promotion, according to Walter Fishon, Dynastyologist at the State University of New York at Stony Brook (near Moldavia).

Dynasty mania hit a peak at Thanksgiving time that year. Every ten minutes an episode popped up. What Esther was doing was running two episodes of the two *Dynastys* together, *Dynasty I* (the Carringtons) and *Dynasty II* (the Colbys) back to back. One Wednesday it would be I & II, and next II & I. Then they moved it from Wednesday to Thursday and back to Wednesday. The Carringtons and Colbys were busy visiting back and forth. What Hurricane Esther was trying to do was confuse me. And she succeeded. Then, suddenly, the first week in December, on a Thursday, one hour only? The answer came from on high. We had gotten an hour off for good behavior.

To me, the programs were so similar I had trouble keeping them apart, or staying awake. Any scholar could tell the difference, though. The Colbys were richer. The Carringtons of Denver were, compared to the Colbys of California, welfare cases. Poor relations in the hills. Where *Dynasty* was a fantasy about the rich, *The Colbys* became a fantasy of the extremely rich. Denver Carrington was running a corner grocery store of a corporation compared to Jason Colby's operations. Their office is on the sixtieth floor of Century City, *which they own*. That's all you have to know.

Otherwise they're the same *mishpokhe*.

But I digress. The meeting of the Colbys and Carringtons, the summit, more important to the American people than the Geneva arms talks, had as its purpose the announcing of the new joint Colby-Carrington pipeline that Jason Colby was forcing Blake Carrington to build, one that would run from Denver to Shanghai, or some such. The Carringtons' hidden agenda of the summit meeting, though, was to meet the Colbys.

Of course, we had met many of the Colbys already. There was the night that art and *Dynasty* met, when Charlton Heston, who plays Jason Colby, first confronted his lifelong adversary, Blake Carrington, on the October 9 episode of *Dynasty I*.

Heston, in so-called real life—it had been revealed during the summer of 1985—had decided to give up a chance to run for the U.S. Senate and appear in the *Dynasty* spin-off. Well, the country couldn't have everything. Imagine, the man who parted the Red Sea . . . God, or Moses, himself . . . the man who could have been an instant fifth on Mt. Rushmore . . . coming back to the mainstream of American culture to be the John Forsythe of the second *Dynasty*. Heston would rather be a TV character in a soap than be right—or president, I guess.

Heston, as Jason Colby, did not do his usual Moses interpretation. He did his Ben Hur.

Immediately, the first night, we found out he was dying. Incurably ill. That was a heck of a way to start a spin-off. It certainly added to the suspense. You didn't know whether he could make it to the end of the hour, much less to the start of the spin-off in November.

Unfortunately, I missed his second appearance on *Dynasty* the next week. They were preempting *Dynasty* with baseball (the World Series) in October, and it happened so often that I thought I saw Charlton playing third for the Cardinals one Wednesday night. It was a bad camera angle. I couldn't be sure. Nevertheless, it was clear from all the pre-introductions before the premiere of *The Colbys* itself on November 25 that his Jason Colby would live in the annals of acting with his El Sid. (No, not El *Cid*—this was his El *Sid* of Mosholu Parkway.)

But when they told us Jason Colby was dying . . . How dare he? Sure, he had an incurable disease. But he could get a second opinion. In fact, he did, a few episodes later. And you guessed it—he was still dying. That's the thing about these incurable diseases: They don't clear up fast.

Then he got a third opinion. The rich can do that. Sure enough, they had the wrong X rays or tests, or the wrong Jason. Jason Colby should have sued that doctor for malpractice and for ruining six minutes of his life on TV, striking a blow for better medical care, while maintaining his credentials as a mean SOB. But the show had other pressing matters.

In the first month *The Colbys* was still introducing its forty-eight obnoxious new characters, none of whom had any redeeming social values, except that they were rich.

I used to love it when Sable Colby went out shopping with Fallon to the Rodeo Drive collections in Beverly Hills.

You had to love the names on *Dynasty*. They were so middle class. Blake . . . Krystle . . . Fallon. And now Sable. Where I grew up, *sable* was a coat, or a fish. Today, it's also a car.

This Sable Colby (played by Stephanie Beacham) gardens in a low-cut gown. I loved it. And while I'm confessing, I hated Miles Colby, the polo player, but I adored his red Ferrari. Great car, great polo player, but also an insufferable snot. When father Jason was dying and was trying to tell him something about the business, Miles took it as a personal rebuke. Really immature.

"I never thought I'd be saying this," I wrote in my diary of Nov. 12, 1985, "but I think I've finally OD'd on *Dynasty*."

I didn't like *Dynasty II* much, either. I could not get interested in them as people. They talk too much at the Colbys or something. The original *Dynasty* had flair, a sauciness. And it was lacking in *Dynasty II*.

The writing in *Dynasty Dos* was not as good, either. There were none of the great lines from Alexis, like her immortal remark to Dex, who had accused her of ulterior motives for housing King Galen the Sponger, of Moldavia: "Why do I need a kingdom when I already have an empire?"

"Please be careful," she said to the moving men who are bringing in the royal couch for King Galen the Deadbeat. "It's Ninth-century Ming."

Joan Collins's commercials for Sanyo, in fact, were more fascinating than *The Colbys*, the ones in which she tried to act like the perfect little homebody, meanwhile blundering that body through the kitchen, clearly a turf as unfamiliar to her as a Moldavian dungeon.

Then it all came clear.

The Colbys, I finally realized, was hurting *Dynasty*. The Double Dose was draining its vital juices, its creative energy.

Alexis could have figured it all out. But she was too busy trying to talk her husband, Dex Dexter, into taking the 8:42 back to Moldavia so she could rescue King Galen (who everybody thought was dead). Which eventually she did. That was the famous episode in which Joan Collins got to a nunnery—and was soon Nun of the Year in that habit, designed by Nolan Miller.

The plots in *Dynasty* were just plain bad, as thick as crankcase oil before a twelve thousand-mile change. Sludge.

But Moldavia took it in the neck for all the *Dynasty* blunders.

Moldavia, a country as scapegoat (the national mascot).

So Theodore Bikel was an idiot. King Galen was conniving. Still, Moldavia was a high price to pay.

I could understand what Brandon Stoddard was doing. He was playing a role, his Neville Chamberlain. And this move was his Munich. It was the first week of his reign, and all the critics were around. He had to do something big. So he sold Moldavia, the Czechoslovakia of TV soap operas, down the River Moldavia.

It was a safe call on Brandon's part. All he had to see was the ratings go down, and he knew it was the fault of the Moldavian story line. The fact that *Dynasty* itself had changed, become totally unbelievable, absurd, dragged out, painfully attenuated—that was nothing.

The real tragedy of the demise of Moldavia was executive producer and power behind the throne [Queen Esther] Aaron Spelling, who gets no respect in Hollywood. He was now out as possible ambassador to Moldavia, something to which his wife, Candy, was looking forward.

No matter that she could buy and sell Moldavia, make her children knights and dukes. Aaron is so rich, he could bring the country here, and put it in his house. "He has a lot of room," explained one father, whose child was in the same school as a Spelling child, in admiration. "For a man who brought winter to his kids in Beverly Hills by trucking in snow, anything is possible."

The Spellings are widely discussed at the school, the Center for Early Materialism in Beverly Hills, where they graduate kids at seven. The graduation exercise is going out to shop alone on Rodeo Drive.

Moldavia gone? Oh, well, you can't make an omelet, as Marshal Pétain said at Verdun (or was it Brillat-Savarin in the kitchen?) without breaking some *oeufs*.

I had the feeling we had not heard the last of Moldavia yet. You just don't start a country and forget it as if it were chopped liver. TV viewers are impressionable. There are people today who are planning to buy a split-level in Knots Landing, California. There are Moldavian partisans in the hills. There is a Moldavian underground movement, the FMN (Free Moldavia Now), that is going to make the Star Trek movement seem like small galactic potatoes.

What they don't understand is that a lot of people got involved emotionally in Moldavia while it was on TV. It was the perfect couch-potato way of following international affairs. More people know of Moldavia today, I say, than Bosnia and Herzegovina combined.

Moldavia lives.

SUMMER SHOW (TV IN EUROPE)

The big show in England the summer of 1985 was not *The Jewel in the Crown*, David Attenborough's *The Living Planet*, or even C. P. Snow's *Strangers and Brothers*. It was, as they mispronounce it, *Dinn-istee*.

At a round of dinners during a busman's holiday I took (as a TV critic, I always go back to England, as an art critic might go to the Uffizi, to see the best television in the world live and on the screen)—I was the life of the parties because I had seen the latest *Dynasty* episodes. Everybody wanted to talk to me because I was *au courant* about *Dynasty*.

It was so *brilliant*, they said, that I knew all about *Dynasty*.

I noticed this strange "behavior" at the first dinner party I attended at the home of Lady LeGallais in fashionable Chelsea. She had just recently returned to England after years in the colonies. Her husband, a legal man, was the chief magistrate who set up judicial systems in Kenya, Aden, the Gulf States, and theirs was a fabulous life spent abroad at the end of the empire. From the little I heard about her, she would have made a miniseries for Granada TV. A visually striking woman with a life-style that would have stunned Robin Leach, and all she wanted to talk about was *Dynasty*.

Lady LeGallais was showing us pictures of the time Rita Hayworth and the Aga Khan had been her guests at the Mogassa Club in Kenya while the Mau Mau were brandishing their knives. She was a woman who had known Isak Dinesen, if not Robert Redford, in the flesh. And she was pumping me for news on the expatriate British woman Alexis.

It was appalling.

Theater directors, wives of major generals, playwrights, educators, editors, research scientists, gynecologists . . . everybody wanted to know what was happening in *Dynasty*. Not a Leo, I was nonetheless lionized in England, because I *knew*. Talk about cultural exchange.

As I said, I love TV in Europe. When we travel, I get to see *Dallas* in a dozen languages. The big hit show in Italy one year was *Dynasty*, on the fourth channel, Wednesday nights at 20:30. It got blockbuster ratings in Rome, in Milan, in Firenze (Florence). Wherever you went in Tuscany, along the River Po, everybody was talking about *Dynasty*. They were concerned about that *beetch* Alexis, spitting at her, giving her the evil eye, a curse on future generations, muttering. It was like being at home.

It gives you a funny feeling to be in a city like Florence, center of fifteenth-century Renaissance culture, the streets lined with glorious buildings, the Cathedral of Santa Maria del Fiore, the Medici Riccardi Palace, the Uffizi Gallery, the Bargello, the Palazzo Vecchio, the Strozzi Palace, with the people in their houses sitting around watching *Dynasty*.

At first it bothered me that they even *had* TV sets in Firenze, much less watched them. But when in Firenze, do what the Florentines do.

And *Dynasty*, it turned out, was bigger in Belgium than waffles. I had gone to Liège to attend a public-TV conference. What concerned the public there was enlightenment—about John Forsythe.

I turned on the TV set in my Holiday Inn room. They had twelve channels from all the Benelux Nations plus Germany and England. And they all had *Dynasty*, *Quark*, *The Stepford Wives*, and *Vegas*.

We may have our shortcomings, politically, as a faltering democracy. In two hundred years to have gone from Washington, Jefferson, and Madison, to Nixon, Ford, Carter, and Reagan is not evolution but devaluation. We can't make other countries do what we want by sending a gunboat up the Rhine or reflagging tankers.

But we are still able to capture the battle for the minds of men. Or what there is of them.

MOBILVISION
(THE SUN NEVER SETS ON *DYNASTY*)

I had mixed feelings about this discovery that the upper classes of the U.K. and Europe were so into our soaps. Back home in New Jersey, I would have felt unpatriotic to admit this, a traitor to my class. Even worse, I was being disloyal to the company I keep, which is Mobil.

I feared punishment for what I was going to confess: I have had this secret thing for *Masterpiece Theatre* for fifteen years now. I even watch reruns. For me it's always been *Masterpiece Theatre*, right or wrong.

I didn't dare mention any of this, of course, as I looked at the dinner tables waiting to hear the latest from *Dinnistee*. I would seem like such a drag.

On the other hand, in all modesty, it made me seem an intellectual among the Brits. That, for a change, was nice. I usually feel inferior with all these Oxbridge and Eton graduates at dinner parties. Even the so-called Redbrick University people can make me feel bad. So I liked the way the Brits were eating up *Dynasty*.

It's not only that they watch the episodes religiously; they seem to know details of stars and characters. One doctor I sat next to at dinner seemed to know more about the American prime-time soaps than about her medical specialty. They are totally fascinated by the entire enterprise, even to the producer's family. They write stories about Candy Spelling in the London *Times*. She symbolizes the show to them. They all know she is really Krystle, with her diamonds for breakfast. "She is not nouveau riche," one Cambridge chap, a biophysicist, explained, "she is arriviste [beyond nouveau]."

The sordid truth is that we probably watch more English television in

New Jersey than they do in England. BBC-1 was broadcasting *The Towering Inferno* around Christmas time, and the announcer described it as
"a masterpiece." Was this an attempt at sarcasm? Or were such shows
their Masterpiece Theatre? Was it being introduced by Alistair Cooke?
Could they understand Cooke's accent? Or did they get the stories un-
Cooked?

I liked to think—at first—that they watch *Dynasty* as comedy.

No, they are very serious about it.

"What do you think of it?" my hostess said, turning to me one night.

"It?"

"*Dinn-is-tee*, of course."

"Well, it's a genre we call a comadrama," I explained. "You sit there
stupefied at how overbad it is. But you talk about it. Because so little
else is on."

"Really," she said coldly. "We think it frightfully interesting."

"Really," I said.

There was a chill at the table, cooler than the vichyssoise. What an
impossible snob I had turned into. I was ruining the party. Bad manners.
Criticizing someone else's taste in TV shows is like questioning the choice
of wine. "But I watch it anyway," I assured them. "It's a nice little
domestic, with just a hint of tannin."

"What happens in the trial?" she asked.

Which trial? I had to think.

The poor wretches, it turned out, were only up to Alexis's trial. It was
the trial (they have almost as many trials on *Dynasty* as on *Rumpole of
the Bailey*) for the murder of Mark Jennings, the late tennis pro.

"Oh, it would be unsporting to say. Ruining your chance to enjoy the
suspense." I drifted off into a reverie about the law and the soaps. (But
I would relent.)

There should be a TV version of Lexus (a computerized legal retrieval
system indexing every case in history and leading law reviews) that com-
piles all the law cases litigated in *Dynasty*. Even the characters forget
details of evidence, and give false testimony. I cite the famous trial of
Carrington v. *Carrington* (1986), where brother Ben came back to claim
his share of the inheritance ($40 million) from their father's will, which
appellant declared defendant (Blake) had glommed. The legal arguments
central to the trial dwelt on which of the two brothers had left the invalid
mother alone the night she perished in the big oil fire. One or the other
had abandoned their mother for a night of sex with some tramp.

"I was watching the late night reruns of *Dynasty* one night in April,"
explained the legal scholar Marcia Karsch, "and I nearly fell out of bed.

Blake Carrington was telling the original Fallon (Pamela Sue Martin) that he was *four years old* when his mother died. Don't they read the old scripts when they write the new ones? Which Blake is telling the truth? Or was he a very precocious four-year-old, who was sleeping with a woman? If not, didn't they have child-labor laws which prevented four-year-olds from working in the oil fields?"

My hostess had turned away. Too bad. I was about to compare notes with her about the *People of Denver* v. *Joan Collins* for the murder of Mark Jennings. The trial had been a long one, putting a tremendous strain on Joan's wardrobe. It also tested the range of her emotions as an actress. For weeks she had been sitting at the defendant's table, trying to look innocent until proven guilty. That was the Joan Collins open-mouth look. Words fail her; she listens incredulously to incriminating, damning evidence with—what range—wide eyes. Her eyes ask: How could you do that to me, your own mother?

Her open-mouthed, open-eyed look is one of her two major expressions. The other is, naturally, her "I'm-so-sexy-you-could-die" look, in which those eyes become slits, the mouth mocking. She is a genuine Sarah Heartburn, if not Bernhardt.

What bravura testimony in her own behalf. "Me, guilty?" she asked the ladies and gentlemen of the jury. (I ask you—*moi*?) "Trust me," she said. "I wouldn't do anything that bad."

Then she went into the *mea no culpa* defense, *theya culpa*. Unknown others were out to get her. Sure, she might have sinned. Who's perfect? Basically, she is a woman who has too much and who lives too well. The victimized are also victims.

I knew then that Alexis Carrington Colby is one of the great innocents of our time. Right up there with John DeLorean, Oliver North, and Richard N.

As she spoke to the jury on her own behalf, you could, despite the music in the background, hear the sounds of hearts breaking. Then the jury found her guilty.

Alexis guilty! It was too much. I still hadn't recovered from the shock of finding out that Diahann Carroll (Julia) and John Forsythe were sister and brother.

I spoke of this.

"You mean she did it?" my British peers of the table asked, prawn forks poised in the air.

"Yes. But she'll never rot in jail, don't worry. Joan Collins wouldn't let Alexis spend the rest of her youth in jail; they don't have a Nolan Miller boutique."

They seemed to admire Collins, not as a British comedienne second only to Penelope Keith, as I do. They take her seriously. Joan and her sister Jackie. They are the eighties Brontë sisters, two Jewish girls from the East End of London who made it in the United States, revered in their way as Jane Austin, who manufactured little cars, and what was the other famous one—Patty Duke Austin?—are.

When I told them about Jeff getting married (to some minor character), a glass of port spilled like blood. "And poor Fallon still warm in her grave." They had seen the funeral scene, which looked convincing to them.

"Oh, don't worry about Fallon," I explained to the table. "She is not dead."

"Not dead!" A lady from Heathcliffshire fainted dead away.

"Quite right," I said twirling my port glass to starboard. "Un-dead."

Me and my big mouth. Now, I realized I had gone too far with these poor provincials. They were not ready for Fallon, and certainly not the face-transplant operation from Pamela Sue Martin to Emma Samms.

I shuddered to think what they would make of the Moldavian attack when the insurrectionists crash the wedding party in the final episode, coming to them later that winter. There would be a House of Commons debate, the MP from Worcestershire demanding to know what Mrs. Thatcher will be doing about the Moldavian reprisals.

It is, they say, the queen's favorite show, next to *Starsky & Hutch*.

Well, I thought, with *Dynasty* we're finally getting even. They'll think twice before they burn our White House again.

DALLASTY (HAGMAN)

Inevitably, my studies of American sleaze and trash led to *Dallas*.

Here was a show that rose above routine sleaze, even trash: It was raunch, which is better still. It is a modern classic.

When I first found *Dallas* in my office in the spring of 1978, it was a throwaway program, a miniseries of six parts, one of those potboilers added to the summer schedule by CBS to vamp until the fall season started—the lull before the lull. Lorimar, the producer, had money left over from the budget of the made-for-TV miniseries based on the novel *Executive Suite*, which had been run at the same time, Friday nights at 10:00 P.M., a sacred spot in trashology. Fridays at ten is when people really need infusions of pure trash, apparently. It's like low blood sugar, the end of the work week, the start of weekend fun—and so, desperate measures are called for.

Few believed *Dallas* would succeed. Nobody in 1978 understood the trash-sleaze–hormone factor. The best executives money could buy didn't understand the tawdry, tacky, smarmy quality of the show. *Dallas* was a slutzier version of *Executive Suite*, the founding grandfather of modern sleaze. It had adulterated sex—the worst kind: expurgated sex. (I'm convinced that if you censored movies and put them on TV with the title *Expurgated Theatre* it would get huge ratings. Expurgated sounds dirty, like adulterated.) *Dallas* also had infidelity, in and out of bed like the Revolving Door Motel. The show was right down the American people's gutter. And I loved it on sight.

It was a modern family drama. That meant a guy slept with his wife and his sister-in-law at the same time.

The Ewings' place, Southfork, was my dream house. Did you ever *see* so much naugahyde? Why, to do the downstairs alone, they must have wiped out a whole herd of naugas. (They're on the endangered species list along with the poor polyesters.) What I loved most about the Ewings was that everybody had such nice manners and was so polite. When J. R. Ewing would leave the table at breakfast, he would say "Mamma? Daddy?" Getting permission to leave the table, as he's off to make a phone call that will break some guy or talk him into taking cyanide. J.R. was a good boy.

And so neat! Even late at night, while J.R. is stalking around making trouble, he is wearing a three-piece suit. He even sleeps in his clothes, I bet, like in the old westerns.

The Ewings eventually became like kin to me. I was from the poorer branch of the family, of course. There was Sue (hic!) Ellen, mother and lush of the year. And Lucy, the spoiled little rich fat brat, who modeled herself after Miss Piggy. There was Bobby, memorable in *The Man from Atlantis*. What a bummer. And Miss Ellie, who was always crying and looking concerned. And my special favorite, J.R., TV's man—also swine— of the year.

There had never been a character like J.R. on television. Mean, malevolent in a gleeful way, corrupt, selfish, a liar, and a cheat, the sort of person who reminds you of the traditional Chinese dish sweet-and-rotten pork. The man of whom his own dear Mamma, Miss Ellie, once said, "J.R., you don't have a redeeming bone in your body." The character is so perfectly realized, as they say at the Yale Drama School, that his own mother thinks he is a worm.

She is too kind. J.R. is a rat. A skunk. A varmint. And absolutely wonderful as a sleazoid.

An average day for J.R. would wilt most men. Down in Houston on business, he cheats on his wife, Sue Ellen the alcoholic, with the help of her kid sister, then working as his secretary (the family that lays together stays together). He also was fooling around with an oil millionaire's wife and his gorgeous assistant, cheating on the one he has been cheating with.

J.R. also slept with Lucy's sister-in-law, Afton, his P.R. consultant, Leslie Stewart, and a widow, Marilee Stone—though not all in the same day. There are limits. J.R. is a very busy boy. But he still found time in that episode, before lunch, to break up Ray and Donna, Bobby and Pam, squeeze in a few minutes to ruin two business associates, and make Kristin's other lover, the young lawyer, persona non grata in every known law office.

The man's meanness knows no bounds! And it's delicious. Remember the night he arranged for his wife's arrest on suspicion of drunk driving? He then worked at getting her back on the booze, planting a bottle of gin in her undies drawer and whispering sweet nothings in her ear: "Sue Ellen, you're a drunk and a tramp and no court in the world will let you have my son." A real sweetheart.

J.R. was always smiling, calling everybody "honey" or "little darling." Whether he was saying "I'm going to break you" to his rivals, or betraying his friends and loved ones, he always had this Twinkie-eating grin on his face.

What I liked about the show also was that it was so complicated. And so pervasive. To understand something in *Knots Landing*, the spin-off, you had to know all the episodes of *Dallas*, you couldn't be just a moron who watched TV. You had to *retain* things. You had to have watched *Dallas* itself for two years. That's too complex for some people.

For two seasons *Dallas* was a private thing, a vice. Sleaze-loving people watched in the closet, in the bedrooms. One didn't talk about being into *Dallas*; it was some kind of perversion. Suddenly it became okay.

I'm almost ashamed to say this, but I was at Elaine's on the Friday night in the spring of 1980 when *Dallas* became fashionable. Elaine's was the "in" literary watering hole on New York's East Side, where the average customer is Woody Allen. I was in a corner trying to look unimportant, my big trick in such scenes.

A famous person—I think it was Vladimir Nabokov, William F. Buckley, Jr., Updike, Steinem, or Isaac Bashevis Singer—looked at his watch. It was nearly nine-thirty. "Look, I can't rationalize this," he said. "But I have to go home to see *Dallas*. I'm not hooked per se. I just want to see what's going on."

It was the ninth-rated show in Buenos Aires that season; but in New York at Elaine's it had finally arrived. *Dallas* chic had started.

J.R. was the most despicable person in the history of TV drama. The man you love to hate. How sleazy could the country get? I suffered from that love-hate complex myself. Whenever he entered a scene, J.R. was pure nastiness and masterly malevolence ("a breath of fresh manure," as one western critic put it). But the hatred you felt needed some release, and I soon started to laugh. Lorimar, the producers, should have considered the shark music from *Jaws*. The famous *dah-dum* could have begun to beat whenever J.R. pulled up in his long Lincoln. Yet even that wouldn't have stopped me from loving him—as did millions of other Americans if the number of get-well cards flooding into Dallas General Hospital in the summer of 1980, when J.R. had his accident, were any indication.

Who would have wanted to shoot J.R.?

Maybe fifty thousand people had a motive. And that was in downtown Dallas alone. I suspect a lot of people in the TV audience also wanted to pull the trigger that night. What a catharsis it would have been for the nation. "Take that, J.R., and that . . . pow . . . biff . . . bang." It could have been a scene right out of *Julius Caesar*: *et tu*, Mystery Marksman?

Anyway, shooting was too good for J.R. He should have been boiled in oil. Or forced to spend the night with Mrs. Roper (in *The Ropers*). Punishment should fit the crime.

WHO MET J.R.?

The whole J.R. fuss that season—cover stories in *People, Farm Journal, TV Guide*, et al.—bordered on a national disgrace. It reflected a significant change in the nation's values. I knew just how sick the society had become when, on a first visit to Los Angeles in ten years as a TV critic, I ordered CBS and Lorimar to produce Larry Hagman for lunch. The power of the pen.

It had been an extra shock, seeing Larry Hagman in *Dallas* on Friday nights, for it was hard to believe this mean s.o.b., this Eric Von Stroheim of the 1980's, was the same nice, sweet guy who had been Colonel Nelson. The astronaut in *I Dream of Jeannie* had turned into the world's most contemptible lout, the metamorphosis of the century, right up there with Franz Kafka's character in *Metamorphosis*, who had changed from a Czechoslovakian into a cockroach. During those first couple of *Dallas* seasons I kept thinking that Dr. Bellows was going to pull up in the driveway of Southfork at any moment and say, "Colonel Nelson, what are you doing in this series? General Peterson wants to see you in his office immediately." You don't see thirty thousand episodes of a thing for nothing.

And now it was a shock seeing him off-camera. *He looked and sounded like J.R. on-screen.*

He was probably just as surprised at my appearance. I don't think J.R. had ever met any critic as mean and nasty and as sleazy. We understood each other. It was a true meeting of minds, sleaze at the summit.

I met the swine at an oily little Japanese restaurant near the Lorimar Studios on the old MGM lot in Culver City, a short walk from where he was filming an episode. *Dallas* is not done in Texas. I brought my taster, my wife. Hagman is a gourmet. Japanese and western cuisines. We shared recipes for currying favor: take two critics to lunch, spread it on thick.

Hagman brought along his food taster, too, a flack from Lorimar. Larry didn't eat anything, anyway. He was on a diet, which was a good thing. "I'd become a regular tub of lard," he explained. "Fasted for seventeen days, shitfire. Gone from two twenty-two to one ninety-eight. No drink. Just living on stored fat and alcohol. Whenever I feel myself going downhill, I take a supplement for the fast—made of a billion pounds of water and eggs." He ordered a sumptuous sushi-sashimi combination, negimaki, shrimp tempura, yamamoto yama, for my wife and myself. He took nothing for himself, only a little sake for nourishment.

Hagman is, even in La La Land, a famous weirdo. He wants people to smoke at his table so he can operate one of those little battery-run Japanese fans that blows the smoke back in the smokers' faces. It really disappoints him if you don't. "Dang," he said, giving us the fan to take home to our kids as a present.

Then he has this germ theory of food. People cough on Kentucky Fried Chicken and other fast foods before they are frozen. And that's how you catch a cold today.

He also has a crazy gleam in his eyes off-screen, as on the show. He was talking in a wild way about how "I scared the shit out of my local Mercedes dealer yesterday. Maj [his wife, whose name is pronounced My] owned a Rabbit diesel, gets sixty miles per gallon, dual turbochargers, that lasts forever, or at least a year. But we're switching to a diesel

Mercedes that gets twelve hundred miles on a tank of gas, or enough to get to Texas and back. Anthracite gray. The dealer said he needed time to wash the car and service it. 'I don't want to haggle,' I told him on the phone. 'Pick up your certified check at my office at five P.M. My wife wants the car *now*.' He came for it, too. That was right smart. There's an old saying, 'Always cash an actor's check right away.' "

Hagman and J.R. each have strong telephone personalities. They'd never have to take assertiveness-training courses. I told him that I loved the way he got on the phone in one episode and fixed the wagon of Alan (Kristin's boyfriend) while still in bed with her. J.R. had phoned to make sure old Alan wouldn't get a job in a law firm "from Dallas to Atlanta." "Fuckfire," Hagman said proudly. "Old Alan was trying to marry my little sister-in-law. I did everything but call him a *kike*, and he's a goy."

That was very real, I said.

"I've seen it happen in this town," Larry said. "I've even done it myself."

He walked, afterward, from the restaurant to the studio set. Sue Ellen is in her curlers. A sign over the living room of Southfork says HAPPY NINTH ANNIVERSARY, J.R. AND SUE ELLEN. He looks up at the sign, kisses Sue Ellen on the cheek, and says, "Mahzel Tohv, dahlin'." With scarcely a pause in his conversation with me, he does his lines as the mean and rotten J.R. It was incredible to see the lack of transition.

For a moment it seemed that Larry Hagman and J.R. were the same person. Hagman knew people like J.R., all the Ewings, and their business rivals when he was growing up in "Weatherford Shitfire Texas" (as he gives the full name of the town where he grew up). His father, Ben Hagman, was a lawyer in Weatherford, while his mother made another name for herself, as Mary Martin, on the Broadway stage.

Larry told me about a summer job he had while going to high school, with the Weatherford Oil Tool Company. "It was in a Quonset hut. A hundred and twenty degrees. I used to sit there with a two-foot-long piece of wire, stick it into a little hole, five times front, one time back, then hand it to this guy and he would bend it a different way. Every half hour we'd switch. Maybe we'd do ten a minute. In back of us was a machine this old guy had invented, did two thousand bends a minute. It was one of those useful jobs that drive a man crazy, that a machine can do five thousand times faster. Old man Mr. Hall invented this little tool for cleaning out the well, called the scratcher. It went around the pipestem of the tool drill. They're very expensive pipes. You have to case the well, force cement down. There would be little knobs on the side of the well wall. The scratcher would go down and get them out. If you didn't, the oil flow would pile up on it, the residue would build. You push a scratcher down, clean out the hole, saves twenty percent more oil."

Why did Hagman do it? "My daddy was this brilliant old guy's lawyer. I needed a summer job. They was just making work for me. But it was thirty-five cents an hour. And steady."

The Texas people put him down when he was a teenager, he recalls, treated him like dirt. Is that what gives Hagman this strange hypnotic power on the screen in the show? He doesn't have to put on that awful grin. He doesn't have to get into the role. He doesn't have to psych himself. He never has to ask, What is my motivation? He is not getting mad at the past: He is getting even.

Could it also be the man is absolutely insane, a perfect loony? Is that what the camera picks up in those wonderful scenes where he is destroying his loved ones and friends? It could be a performance, in the sense that he is having an analytic session with the camera. In an existential way, he could be J.R. without being him.

Behind those icy blues, I was to learn, nobody could be further from J.R.

The next time I met Mr. Rotten was in New York at Hisae's, in 1982. I had turned down a lunch with the big TV star Boomer to be with him. That's how hot Larry had become.

Cosmopolitan magazine had asked me to do a profile on Larry Hagman, to tell their readers what he was really like. What a chance, it seemed to me—to turn the Cosmo girl on to J.R. J.R. *is* the Cosmo man, the one all the Cosmo girls deserve. Mr. Nice Guy meets Ms. Nice Girl. The two of them deserved each other. Justice would triumph.

Personally, I never want to know what the actors who play characters are "really like"; in TV, it's irrelevant. The real people in TV *are* the characters of the shows, not the actors who play the characters. Fonzie is real; Henry Winkler is a fictitious character. Who cares about Henry Winkler? The characters in the weekly shows are so real, they are like beloved relatives who come to visit the house every week. They're even more beloved: They leave at the end of the hour.

But Hagman was a curiosity. I had never seen a character so similar to the actor. In the whole history of acting, nobody acted less. Not Gary Cooper hisself, who played one role all his life. J.R. and Hagman, I was sure, were exactly the same person. He appeared to be walking through the role.

One time, Hagman had to act like a man who had been shot. He was awful. I couldn't wait for him to throw away that cane. But in three or four weeks, as he regained his health, he was his old wonderful mean, malevolent, rotten self.

I kept thinking of all those Cosmo girls waiting with bated breath to find out who Larry Hagman really was. (What do you take for bated breath—Certs? Scope? Worms?)

I had met Hagman for lunch on the sidewalk outside Hisae's on the East Side. As he stepped out of another long-long Lincoln, a messenger passing by greeted him. "Kick ass, J.R.," he said. A man with a suitcase radio next to his ear said from the corner of his mouth, as he went by without looking at Hagman, "Okay, J.R., get the motherfuckers." Hagman was a man of the people.

"This is why nobody is going to spot me in New York," he explained, putting on his big white ten-gallon Stetson for the walk across the street to the restaurant. That's his camouflage.

God forbid, nobody should recognize him, I thought at the time.

Hisae's is normally a laid-back, blasé kind of place when it comes to celebrities. Ad-agency people, big-business executives, secretaries come up and kiss Hagman as he studies the menu. "What kind of restaurant is this?" he asks the waiter. "Japanese-western," the waiter explains. "In that case, I'll take chitlins tartare," Larry says with the insane J.R. grin.

A table of middle-management types are celebrating an engagement. The waiter whispers they are sending over a drink to honor him. "Well, now," Hagman says, "how many of them are there over yonder?" He whips out eleven postcards with his picture from the inside pocket of his creamy western suit, and autographs them. "At least I can spell the name right." Then he lopes over and hands each one a personally autographed postcard. Other times he hands out hundred-dollar bills; you can tell their authenticity by the motto, *In J.R. We Trust.*

He is not one of those shy actors who believes he should save acting for the stage. Hagman not only enjoys his privacy being invaded, he provides landing barges.

Hagman doesn't mind giving out autographs, but he does them as a deal. "I like to get something back. Normally, if it's only one person, I ask them to give me something in return, recite some verses from a poem, tell a story or a hundred Hail Marys." He watches the frenzy of his fans, getting all agitated in a restaurant or on the street, like an oceanologist. He says, "They remind me of a fish called Terhunes, a species which bites its tail off in the frenzy of excitement.

"I know this, too, is going to pass," Hagman says from the perspective of a man who had *I Dream of Jeannie* in the 1960's and then some lean years before getting to *Dallas*.

He is talking about how he has six thousand sweat shirts coming in from Hong Kong. He is going to open a sweat-shirt shop in the basement of his beach house in Malibu. "I autograph them now—you would be surprised where they want them autographed—and I don't get a dime out of it. I'll sell my *own* T-shirts, dammit. I've got some forty old scripts annotated with bullshit from a bunch of TV creeps at the network. I'm going to sell one for fifty or a hundred bucks, set the value for tax purposes. Then I'm going to donate the whole lot to a library and take a whopping tax-investment credit. What the hell, it only lasts about forty seconds."

Hagman was again with his wife, Maj Axelsson, a Swedish designer. He has been married to the same woman since 1954. He is sick that way; his is a radical alternative life-style in California. Maj, who is three years older than he, plays a very important part in his life. Larry's agent, Swifty Lazar, wanted him to do this character who is a real swine. Maj read it. "This is it," she told Larry about the J.R. role. "Git it." "And I did," he says. They can melt your earwax with the warm and wonderful stories about their private life. The Cosmo girl would love to hear about Mr. Malevolent's devotion to fidelity.

Soon I realized what we had here was the old rat-who-is-a-nice-guy story.

A popular rat has to be a really nice guy underneath it. He has to be likable. That's what the camera picks up. No way Bruce Dern would work as J.R. He's a fine actor, but just doesn't project likability. Humphrey Bogart as a gangster was your classic nice-guy rat underneath that hard-boiled exterior. Hagman could be the Bogie for this generation. A society fellow, yet accepted as a tough guy. The only other person who rings the changes, who has this magical quality, but in a more positive way, is Alan Alda. He is the nice guy who underneath it all *is* a nice guy. That's his *shtick*—and it works.

Later, I was invited to see the rat in California again. He wanted me to stop by his spread in Malibu, and, I suppose, take a hot tub with him and his wife and loved ones. But I have a little problem about California. I can't stand it. This is a disease that I'll explain later. We were supposed to meet again in New York—at an Indian-Jewish restaurant, the New Delhi, famous for their great pastrami-tandoori sandwiches.

The next time the rat came East, he said, he was going to be taking the boat to London—the *QE II*. But it was leaving from Philadelphia.

Whoever heard of a boat to Europe leaving from Philadelphia? He was afraid of me.

But I vowed to break him if it's the last thing I do.

Nobody in TV understood (at the time) what *Dallas* was really about and why it was so successful, certainly not the makers of the *Dallas* imitations, a leading growth industry in TV in the early 1980's. *Dallas* clones, as they called this programming genre, absurdly. They might just as well have called them Dickens clones.

Dallas was, first, a continuing story. And, as with Little Nell, you wanted to know what happened next week. You cared about these characters.

The imitations—*Flamingo Road, Secrets of Midland Heights, Yellow Rose of Texas, King's Crossing,* et al.—all featured large families and one bad guy. But they didn't work out. And the competitors will keep doing *Dallas* until they get it right, even if late. But they don't know. Not even Lorimar, which produces *Dallas,* knows why it really works, as evidenced by their *Midland Heights.* Here is the secret formula:

Southfork is the Garden of Eden. God is making each of them suffer for biting the apple. J.R. suffered worse when he was shot. The shooting was redemption. Everybody likes to see the bad guy get it. Except it wasn't one of the good guys who shot him; it was the bad girl (Kristin). Everybody in *Dallas,* you see, is a bad guy or bad girl.

Dallas also worked because the evil is easily perceived. All the rip-off *Dallas* clones had evil, but not so easily perceived as J.R.'s badness. The evil in *Dallas* is right out in the open. "I'm evil," J.R. says. This is what we can identify with.

Watching *Dallas,* then, offers comforts similar to *est,* or other "I'm okay, you're okay" groups. Follow your natural inclinations. Be bad and mean, knife your brothers, be happy being bad. I'm all right, Jack—or J.R.

There had never been a character in TV who went on, week after week, being continually evil, never getting his comeuppance, except in a temporary way to build up the drama of a plot. It's like real life, where the bad guys almost always never lose—where crime pays, and a lot better than minimum wage.

It used to be that no movie crime was allowed to go unpunished. The rules were quietly amended. First, they got away with crimes in the movies. And then, with *Dallas,* TV caught up.

Our heroes used to be the good guys, in the white hats, with the pure, simple souls. Now here was the meanest, most malevolent s.o.b. this side of the Pecos, or Malibu, idolized for all the wrong reasons. He was anti-everything America once stood for, except greed, avarice, and a nice home.

In Cairo, *Dallas* was on the air seven nights a week. It was the biggest hit of the century in Egyptian TV. I'm not surprised it was such a hit in Egypt. J.R. was not a secret hero, like in the United States, where we all know he is really a villain but we like his style. In Egypt, he was the *real* hero. In Egypt, he was the average businessman. Everybody is sneaky like him. J.R. is a national role model. They use the series as training films in all the Arab business schools.

But the idolization of J.R. in the United States was something unique, even for TV.

Dallas makes you identify with the rich and corrupt. The rich get richer in *Dallas*, and the poor don't exist. The meek are disinherited.

TV characters, as I've explained, are role models in our society, too. They have enormous influence on the young, the way uncles used to have in the pre-TV days. J.R. is the handsome, mysterious uncle of this generation, a cult figure in the nation's colleges.

Hagman is not helping at all with his visits to colleges, where he speaks to students *as* J.R. Someday he will be delivering commencement addresses to new M.B.A.'s. Joke? Raymond Burr did it at law schools, and Alan Alda at medical schools.

In his black robes, picking up his honorary degree in inhumane letters, J.R. will inspire the youth of the nation:

"Keep your back to the wall, your gun on the table, and your eyes on the door . . . Back those other bastards up against the far wall and keep your eye on the bottom line. . . .

"And the bottom line is this, graduates; Get them before they get you. Remember, your bright future is a setup—because it's a jungle out there. . . ."

His humility is preserved by the knowledge that under those black robes he is wearing his little B.V.D.'s*—because his daddy told him that there are two things he should be kind to . . .

You may laugh now. But the J.R. phenomenon is changing social history. The J.R. man will replace the other media-induced influences on human behavior, the Woody Allens, the Ollie Norths. The J.R. generation will be closer to the Humphrey Bogart style men affected in the 1950's and 1960's. But the J.R. man has no heart.

(* See his testimonial commercials for B.V.D. circa 1986.)

And if you think the number of amoral, self-centered narcissistic men is increasing now, wait until *Dallas* becomes a cult classic (after it goes off the prime-time schedule in 1998). Whole generations of snakes will crawl around at night. No more Mr. Nice Snakes.

There is an ominous quality to the *Dallas* revolution. Nobody talks about the show today (the way they did when J.R. was shot, for example). The show is already a classic. People don't talk about classics; they just watch them.

Dallas works because of J.R. Not one of the rip-offs (*Flamingo Road King's Crossing, Secrets of Midland Heights*) was successful. And J.R. works because of Larry Hagman. The other series have put in a bad guy. But they don't have that certain something, that gleeful evil.

"And you're the reason all of this is taking place," I told Larry Hagman.

"God, man, you're right," he said. "Shitfire, I couldn't have put it better myself."

"You're the reason all those kids are going to be so corrupt, immoral, can't be trusted with your girl friend. You are having more impact on Americans today than George Washington."

"Damn right," he said. "You're very perceptive."

Damn right he should agree with me. It was like somebody agreeing that the world is round.

"The whole country is going to be up to its ass in J.R.'s," Hagman said.

What does J.R. himself think of this development?

"I think it's wonderful. It's a lot better than folks just waiting around for something to happen. Kick ass. Get greedy. Stab your best friend in the back. Action. It's not just the coldheartedness they get out of the character—but the need for direct action. It's better than sitting around waiting for the federal government to do it for you."

I was speaking to Hagman about the J.R. phenomenon again shortly after he had returned from a European vacation in July 1982. The show then was number one in fifty countries. So every vacation turns into work. He had been on a *QE II* cruise from Philadelphia (the one that ended with the ship being converted into a troop ship for duty in the Falkland Islands). To Monte Carlo. And then on to Italy for an all-expenses-paid trip to Venice, Florence, Milan. *Dallas* was the smash hit of the season on Italy's Channel 5. He was having a cup of espresso in Piazza San Marco in Venice, when he was suddenly surrounded by three thousand *Dallas* fans. "Hey, J.R.," they called in Italian. "The Italian fans are so volatile," Hagman said. "They got to me."

"What's the matter with you, Larry," I goaded him. "Can't handle fame anymore?"

"Shitfire, you've got to understand the Italians. They pull on you. They want your hair, your pockets. And the photographers. There are always forty or fifty cameras. You walk out on the balcony in the morning to smell the air, ten guys with long lenses are taking pictures. I couldn't handle it. This guy who owns Channel Five is also in partnership with Fiat. He respected J.R. so much, he says he has this enormous yacht and how would we like to get away from it all? Can you imagine me on a boat like that? It was the largest privately owned ship under the Italian flag. It's two hundred feet long, sixteen in crew, two chefs, in case one gets sick. Just for four people."

He met trouble later on an all-expenses-paid trip to Sweden, where he crowned Miss Sweden for the Miss Universe contest, visited Maj's family in Eskilstuna, and ran into a controversy about *Dallas*. It had been taken off the air in protest because he (J.R.) treated women badly. "So I was on Swedish TV explaining to the people they didn't have to watch it; they could just change the channel.

"Of course they only have one station there, run by the government.

"The first day is okay when you travel," Hagman said. "Nobody knows you're coming. The second day is awful. The third day you move on. No, I'm not tired of it. Just a little scared of what happened in Italy."

As I gave Hagman my own theories about how he would last more than thirty minutes—perhaps even an hour, immortality in TV terms, living on through all the little J.R.'s running around in society into the 1990's—he was sitting in his new office, at the famous Hagman place on the beach at Malibu Colony, then being renovated. "You wouldn't believe what it used to look like," Hagman said proudly about the devastation, the saw-dust, the riveting in the background. "We're taking a nice, rustic forty-year-old house, and turning it into a nice, rustic hovel. Maj and I live in one room. The nearest bathroom is two hundred feet away. I have to pee in the sand at night, if I don't trip over a bulldozer or fall into a construction trench."

The Hagman place is called Malibu Mission, or Mission: Malibu (as in *Mission: Impossible*). Hagman also likes to call it Fort Malibu. The house then under construction with his *Dallas* money is twice as big as the old one.

It's the Alamo in Malibu or the hacienda Santa Fe look, white adobe. "But not real adobe," he explains. "You could have an earthquake here, and you'd be left with fifty million pieces."

Hagman's life is marked by reconstruction; his friends tell time by his renovations. "The first time I met him," explained Peter Fonda, "it looked like the bomb had hit. The only thing that worked was the Jacuzzi. When was that? 1969? 1973? I don't know."

Maj is always building the house. She is a designer by profession. It stabilizes their marriage, another friend says. "She builds and rebuilds the nest all the time, while he earns the material to feather the nest."

"Maj, get to work," he calls out. She is putting up hooks for cups, books in the shelves, crockery. "Doing women's work," Larry laughs in his ugliest J.R. way, "while I'm doing what a *man* should do, the more important work—talking to a writer."

Outside, the completed part of the house is huge, creamy, Navajo style, with flowers on different levels cascading, ivy crawling. Inside, the one completed room, Hagman's office, is thirty-five to forty feet long, with a twelve-foot ceiling and windows open to the ocean. The walls are genuine packing crate, "the cheapest, most beautiful wood in the world," Hagman says. The grains are light brown, tan, grays, faded red, all mill-edged at forty-five degrees, fitting together like a picture puzzle. Across from Larry's desk is a five-foot-long white couch, dwarfed by a seven-foot-long pair of Texas Longhorns on the wall. On each side is his bookcase filled with *National Geographics*. "I collect *National Geographics*," Larry explained. "I love them. Whenever I go to garage sales, and I love them, too, I see if there are any old *Geographics* for sale. Marvelous magazine. They record the political, economic, and geographic history of the world."

Do you actually read those things? "Hell, yes. My collection dates back to 1924."

Was he familiar, I asked, with the study in the respected scientific *Journal of Irreproducible Results*, which hypothesized: Since *National Geographic* began publishing continuously 148 years ago, 7 billion copies have been innocently, yet relentlessly, accumulated in basements, attics, garages, the Library of Congress, and Salvation Army stores—never discarded, always saved. Each issue weighs approximately two pounds. The relentless accumulation of this static mass approaches the disaster point. The geologic substructure of the country can no longer support the incredible loads. First will come foundation failures and the gradual sinking of residences. Then towns and cities will submerge. Areas of high-density affluence and magazine subscriptions will be the first to go. The island of Manhattan, for example, is doomed, has already sunk to a new low.

"God damn, I always knew New York would go first, not California!" Hagman whooped happily.

On one wall is a picture of Jim Davis painted on leather, which Hagman had made in Mexico. Davis played Jock Ewing, J.R.'s father in the series, who died in 1981. Over the fireplace is the bleached skull of a steer. It's a Taos-style big open fireplace. The house is going to have eight fireplaces. In the back of Hagman is a rustic granite-floored, huge-beamed balcony overlooking the parking lot of the California Highway Patrol (CHiPs), his next-door neighbor. On the other side, opposite the white couch, is Burgess Meredith's house.

"The only drawback having CHiPs as a neighbor," Hagman said, "is that they change the guard at four A.M. First thing they do every morning is check their radios." "Awk, eek. Roger, over . . ." (imitating static). "I get up at five-thirty A.M. to go to the studio. Four o'clock I'm in deep sleep. You don't say to the cops, 'Hey, cut that shit out.' "

To his left is the Minolta photocopying room. To his front left is his wife's drawing table, where she is drawing and redrawing the plans for the manor house, back at the road. There's another office, "a tiny priest hole," with an extra Murphy bed, a place for Larry to meditate, or for a secretary to work. On top of all of this is a massive hot-water solar-heating plant. "We've not spent a penny for gas so far," Larry says. "It gets the water up to one hundred twelve degrees, as hot as I want to shower in. It's going to pay itself off . . . by 2062."

The center of his world now is the huge TV video complex he is building into one wall as part of the new Hagman production company, Majlar Corporation, which is planning to do TV movies and pilots for TV. "I see all the other assholes doing it," he explained, "why not me? Got any scripts? Anything written can make a movie."

TV repairmen are continually working on the video center. "I have every system that is needed to be in the industry: three-quarter-inch video; two half-inch, so I can dub one from another; a quarter-inch Sony Betamax; a new Technicolor unit, like audio, very small, but it's video, really tiny, for going out scouting locations. The whole thing weighs seven pounds. Everything is on remote control. It fits into the wall like a chess game." His assistant, Marina, is trying to master it. Chip Korbin, the man who installed it, is looking wide-eyed. He can't understand why neither Larry nor his assistant can get it. There are twenty-seven variables, or modes. "We have to call him every night and ask how to turn on the TV set," Hagman says. "He's offered to stay here permanently. One button and we're in the wrong mode."

But you don't even watch TV, do you? "Well, shitfire, no. But I like to see old movies, though, and see where I've gone and been."

Have you seen yourself lately?

"Yup, and I was brilliant. I just watched my ad for *Filthy Rich* (a CBS sitcom of 1982–83). I thought it was very funny, funnier than the program, which I never saw. Just saw pieces of it. They brought it down to Texas when we were doing *Dallas*. Just the highlights. They wouldn't show me the whole thing." That didn't stop J.R. on the CBS promo from telling the people it was his kind of show, the reason it became number one (briefly). A lot of people, I told Hagman, got euchered out. Thought he would be on it. He should have gotten a piece of the show, since CBS used him as a come-on gimmick. "Shitfire, I couldn't agree with you more," he said.

What else have you seen that's brilliant on TV? "Well, I saw my new CBS film. It's now called *Deadly Encounter*. First it was called *Birds of Prey*. Then *American Eagle*. It's the story of two helicopters who fall in love. I don't play J.R. I play it straight—a nice-guy role."

One of the big enigmas of Hagman's success is why he hasn't done a big movie. The only thing he had done lately (at the time) was a bit part in *S.O.B.* "I have no idea why," he explains. But he is in the midst of ex-ing his agent, as he delicately puts it. "I liked him. He was a very nice person. Like all good agents, he looks after himself better than the clients. I'm going to take over my reins myself. If anyone is going to fuck up my career, I want to say I did it myself." His friend Carroll O'Connor manages himself.

While he is waiting for the good idea to come along to do his big movie-movie, Hagman has hired someone to collect all of the old *Jeannie*s, *Good Life*s and *Here We Go Again*s (the three series he made before *Dallas*). He wants a whole library of them. Why? "Hard to find anymore. How else am I going to get to see myself?" Then he is going to donate them all to the Hagman Memorial Library for a whopping tax-investment credit.

I asked if he had thought of turning the house into a museum; then he would be able to get a tax deduction for his while life. "Actually, I wanted to turn the house into a church," Larry says. "That's really a business. I had Reverend Ike's business manager come out here. He's about five feet three inches. 'You've got the stained-glass windows,' he says. 'Only one thing makes it possible to make as much as Reverend Ike does.' 'What's that?' I ask. 'God, tell me.' 'You've got to believe,' Reverend Ike's business manager says. 'Oh, shitfire, you just shot it down.' I hate paying taxes so some guy in Washington can ride around in fancy cars. Anyway, we're zoned against having churches in Malibu."

Hagman was contemplating museum status, though. The Hagman Museum of Eclectic Idiosyncrasies, he would call it. A central exhibit would be his hat-and-flag collection. "I've got five hundred hats and two hundred flags that Maj is unpacking. I have eighteen flagpoles on the beach. Somebody is in residence from England, I run up the Union Jack. From

Germany, Holland, you name it. Then I have personal flags. People make up special flags capturing my personality. I have one with two actors' masks, one smiling, one crying. David Wayne, a friend and neighbor, gave me one reading VITA CELEBRATIO EST ('Life Is a Party'), he thinks it represents me. I do, too. On the band sinister—the slash across—it says 'Lawrence Di Malibu.' I sometimes sign my letters that way. Also, 'the Mad Monk of Malibu.' That's my CB handle, too."

What is this perversion with the flags? "It started as a way to check the weather for the boat. [*The Hobie Cat*, an eighteen-foot catamaran is on the winch hanging off the bulkhead.] Flags show the prevailing wind. You can hear when the wind changes. Then I like to have flags around on the weekends. Maybe fifty or sixty of them are stuck in the beach. What's my favorite flag? I like the New Mexico [a yellow field and zunni sun]. I love the Korean Flag—Yin and Yang in pentagram. Sort of reminds me of I-ching. No, I'm not into I-ching. But I like the symbolism associated with Oriental religions. They've reduced it all to a bunch of symbols. Opposites, good and evil, black and white. I find it easier to accept this than virgin birth. What religion am I following now? Gol-lee. They haven't invented one yet for me."

What's with the hats? "I noticed that certain kinds of hats are accepted in some places, others not. Cowboy hats in the South are okay. But in New York they say, 'Hi, there, Tex.' Hats have different social values. A bowler in London, you're a distinguished person. But in New York, you're a snob. You can be the same person. You fit into different societies just by changing hats. It makes cruising easier."

You can wear no hats, too, I said, and get by. "Yah, but the sun gets in my eyes. Burns the nose."

How many hats Hagman takes with him depends on the mode of travel. "By plane, I take maybe only four or five. But when I go to Dallas, when I go by recreational vehicle—a thirty-three-foot RV job—I take thirty hatboxes stacked up in the back. Go up to the wine country to shop for wine, maybe I'll only take ten or twenty hats. Three or four good Resistol felts, two or three funny hats, Indian war bonnets, a police bobby hat."

"Every time I go to a foreign country," explained Peter Fonda, "I bring Larry back hats for his collection. Also, medals. Didn't he mention those? This guy is really into medals. I got him a rare one that only guys like Douglas MacArthur ever wore. The American Foreign Service Medal, given out by the governor of the Philippines to military commanders of the Philippines. He wears them on his jackets, coats, tuxedos, bathing suits, both formal occasions and beach parades."

The parade is a major activity at the Hagman house, around three o'clock on weekends. Most people on the beach in the Malibu colony participate in Hagman's parades. "But there are those who also serve by standing and watching," he explained. "Some can be in the audience. You need observers or it's not a parade." There will be up to five hundred people marching, but generally fifty, one hundred, two hundred. Maybe he will be wearing his Beefeater outfit or gorilla suit, karate outfit, Indian outfit with feathers, beads, and medals. He carries a flute and a drum, which he plays as the spirit moves him.

Hagman leads parades on the beach in honor of the Fourth of July, Ellsberg releasing his papers on the Pentagon to *The New York Times*, or for Labor Day. "It's more often for no special reason," Fonda, a loyal marcher, said. "The tradition started back in the 1960's. It was the heaviest period of protest against the government. Everybody was on their decks as we went by, wanting to know what we were protesting about. 'Shitfire,' Larry would call out, 'we're not protesting anything. Just get down here and march.' Larry would start playing the flute or bang the drum. He was demonstrating for life and parading for fun. There was no reason or purpose to parade. The purpose was to *do* it. To enjoy a walk along the beach was more fun as a parade."

Larry likes to go to what he calls pleasure fairs, or Renaissance Fairs, as the promoters in California call them: booths, medieval costumes, games. "There was one in Agura," Fonda recalled, "on the outskirts of L.A., you shoot up the Malibu Canyon. That was the time Larry dressed up as a bishop. 'Fuckfire,' he said, 'everybody else is getting dressed, otherwise you would go naked. I might as well get dressed up as a bishop.' He went around blessing everybody, having a ball. That's what's funny about Larry. He has the ability to take a commonplace thing and take it to the absurd conclusion. Like, we all have to dress, then why not dress as a bishop?"

Since he's become J.R., he dresses more conservatively. There was a big social event in the early 1970's at the Dorothy Chandler Pavilion. "Since you're not from L.A.," Fonda explained, "you don't know what a stuffy place that is. Everybody dresses very fancy. Everybody knows that. It's something you grow up with. But Larry is not a child of L.A. He is a child of Weatherford Shitfire Texas. Ravi Shankar was playing that night. This was the time of the hippie movement, remember. Maj is wearing a leather dress, feathers, beads. I'm in basic hippie jeans, with a beautiful shirt, clean. Larr gets dressed up as Engineer Bill. Instead of trainman's hat, he has on a ten-gallon white Stetson, not shaped, and a big mail pouch on the back. Larr takes us down to the first row. Very loud, he is calling out, 'Come on down here, Peter.' He takes these silver goblets from England and a champagne bottle out of the pouch and sets it all on the stage, and starts serving. My father would have killed me. Henry the Great would have said, 'You don't do that in the theater.' After it was over, Larry says, 'Now wasn't that something—aren't you glad we had the champagne and the goblets?' He has an irreverent sense of fun."

"Shitfire, that's what life is all about, having fun, isn't it?" Larry said about the incident.

This was on a day when Larry Hagman was talking. It doesn't always occur. "Oh, he doesn't talk on Sunday," Maj Hagman explained when I called to set up further interviews. "Not even to you?" I asked incredulously. "Not to anybody. From sunup to sundown. It's a blessing in disguise."

Hagman stopped talking on Sundays about fifteen years earlier. Why? 'Well, it's a nice way to have a little discipline in your life," he explained, "to just lie back. I don't answer the phone. Everything shuts down and I listen. It started when I was working on a show and during the week I had to scream a lot. My voice was gone. I had to shut up for a weekend. By Monday my voice was better. Silence was good for me."

He watches football games on Sundays, silently. (The silence doesn't stop the parade, however.) He reads the papers silently. He studies his lines during silent periods.

"You keep the sabbath in your way. That's nice," I said.

"*Shabbas*, you mean? It's not a religious thing. I'm not a Quaker, or anything, or Trappist monk. It's just that silence has a place in my life. It's not even every Sunday. Sometimes I'll be quiet on a Saturday or a Monday."

Sometimes when the phone rings on a silent day, he will whistle into it. Generally he doesn't get calls on Sunday, or doesn't answer. Whistling, he knows, will only confuse people. But if his mother calls, he whistles. She digs the code. "His family and close friends know the tone of his idiosyncrasies," Fonda said.

Peter Fonda was recalling the period of mourning for his father. Hagman had gone down to Shirley Fonda's house to pay his respects and suggested Peter come to the beach house for some fun the next day. "But I decided it was my duty to stay here with the family. I was sitting in a room with my sister's husband, Tom. Then I decided to call Hagman at the beach. It's a Sunday, and I figure the service will get it. Suddenly there is a whistle on the line. 'This is Peter. (Whistle) You know I really want to come down. (Whistle whistle.) Throw some Frisbee. (Whistle whistle whistle.) Spend some time in the Jacuzzi. (Whistle) But I can't.

(whistle, sadly this time.) Well, it's really good talking to you. (Whistle.) Kiss Maj. (Big whistle.) Good-bye. (Whistle.)

"He said hello to you, Tom," I told my brother-in-law.

"The whole conversation was right out of Edward R. Murrow's conversation on *Person to Person* with Harpo Marx and his son, both of whom answer questions by whistling, like Larry was doing. I knew exactly what he was saying by the whistle, like Harpo's. It has all shades of feeling.

"The thing was, everybody was weeping and wailing around the house. As far as Hayden or anybody knew, I was having this straight conversation with Larry. If my sister had heard it, she would have thought it was totally bad. Shitfire, I'm totally out of touch with reality, she'd say, talking to Larry like that. Crazy. But we're in touch with reality."

There was one time, when I talked with Larry—without whistles—and he was doing eight things at once. Larry was working on *Dallas* as well as *Knots Landing* this week. He was also getting ready to start directing *Dallas*. He was doing three episodes that season. "It's nothing new," he explained. "I am a director. Started sixteen years ago on *Jeannie*." Does he like being a director? "Well, it's one less actor to argue with. One big crazy actor. It's very tiring directing. They're always asking you, 'Is this spoon correct?' Everybody wants to know your opinion about the flowers. But I do it well."

What's his style?

"I say two basic things—'Do it faster or slower.' Or, 'What should I do here?' an actor asks. 'Do it better,' I tell him. 'What do you want with this scene?' I remember Linda Gray asking last time. 'Do it better,' I say. She says, 'Oh, I get it.' I also like to say, 'Let's do it the way you want to do it.'"

Which great director did you get that from? "I made it up. It's from wishing directors would say that to me. It's the ultimate wish fulfillment in a wish-fulfilling profession. What the fuck. We're not doing Shakespeare. We're making more money than Shakespeare. We must be doing something right."

Would they hire Shakespeare today? "They'd laugh at Shakespeare," Hagman said. "Not commercial. If Dostoyevsky came to us with *Crime and Punishment*, we'd say, 'Go back to your janitorial service. What's this with the obsession to kill somebody? Raskolnikov? What kind of name is that for a lead character?' Shitfire, he'd eventually adapt to TV, though. The system eats up writers and actors. I don't know how Tolstoy ever got anything published in the old days. Maybe they had to bribe, rape, pillage somebody, just to get published. Just getting recognized must have been a problem. Now all kind of shit is recognized."

I suggested he hire Mark Twain to do a sitcom pilot for his production company. "As a matter of fact, he could have done a good one. *Rolling Down the River* they'd call it, instead of *Huck Finn*. They'd get Tina Turner to sing the lead song. One of my favorite singers. Gol-lee, she is dynamite."

The double duty on *Knots Landing* two weeks in a row was unusual. They liked the first week so much they wrote him in again. "It pays for the office. Fuckfire," Larry says helpfully, "can't pay for an office, better not build an office." He had to wake up at 5:30 A.M. after the CHiPs radio check-ins, get to the *Dallas* set by 7:00, do four and a half pages of script, then lunch briefly with Maj, be at *Knots Landing* by 3:00 P.M., do five more pages, finish at 1:00 A.M.

He drives himself to the studio studying his lines on the tape recorder. "We're doing twelve *Dallas*es at the same time. We could be doing one scene from the twelfth show tomorrow and one scene from the seventh. What's difficult is I may have different attitudes. For instance, I'm marrying Sue Ellen in one episode. Don't tell anybody. Why are we getting married again? She has something I want. What? Sickness. It's crazy to marry her again. Lorimar is making a big deal out of it. Huge. Three hundred fifty people at the wedding. We did that in Dallas during the summer. It was a hundred twenty degrees, sweat-streaming-down-the-back weather. It's kind of fun doing all the shows at once. Like putting a broken stained-glass window back together."

On a normal, *Dallas*-only shooting day, Hagman gets home about six. "What I do is take a shower, take the makeup off, grease up the face to keep the pores clean; mix myself a drink, white wine spritzer; go through the mail, discarding anything that makes me unhappy; take a Jacuzzi; make a fire on the beach. By then, it's eight or nine. Maj has made a soup and a Japanese salad. We have light meals. In bed by nine-thirty and asleep."

Hey, that sounds exciting; when does he party, have orgies? Go to Beverly Hills? He doesn't. It takes an hour to get into town from the beach. By ten-thirty at night, even on a weekend, no matter how much fun you're having, you start to nod out. People they ask in for dinner usually know enough to go home by eleven.

His dinner guests are friends like Carroll O'Connor; Jerry Hellman, the director of *Coming Home*; Billy Hayward, Leland's son; Brooke Hayward. Then there are people like Ed Drier. He owns a meat market in Three Oaks, Michigan, Drier's Butcher Shop, a nineteenth-century-style market, famous for Drier's Bologna. Larry doesn't eat meat, or serve it. "I'm not against it. It just doesn't fit into my life-style." He sends it to the cast for Christmas. He met Eddie the butcher while doing stock during *Jeannie*. "He doesn't smoke either," Hagman said. "He collects old No Smoking signs from Victorian cottages in England and sends them to me. I have a lot of friends like that. People people." An investment banker from Wall Street, Phillip Mengel, who specializes in oil-and-gas-reserves limited partnerships for wealthy investors, and a well-known court-tennis player. That's who J.R.'s best friend is? Another, as noted, is Peter Fonda, the most un-Hollywood-like person in Hollywood, a hay rancher in Montana when he isn't in Malibu Colony.

At his dinners the nice guy in rat's clothing and his friends usually talk about family or the past. "They don't talk shop," Fonda says. "It tends to leave everybody else out when actors talk shop." The Hagmans talk about what happened in Dallas—the city, not the series. There was the time Maj saw the car rolling down the driveway in front of the house, after she had used it to go to the market. It went off the cliff. This was Larry's car, the three-hundred-turbo diesel Mercedes he said he bought for her. The car was one of the spoils of the show. He'd never had a luxury car before, except his mother's. He always had gas savers and the van. He really loved that Mercedes.

After the car made its own exit, Larry sent Maj a big bouquet of roses and a very small card reading, "It was the only object I ever loved." "It seemed like he was a spoiled child, almost chastising her," Peter Fonda said. " 'That was my favorite toy you have given away to the Goodwill, Mommy.' The brakes popped; the emergency didn't catch. Nobody knows what made the Mercedes drive away after Maj came back from the market."

What the Hagmans do for entertainment is sit in their combination hot-tub-Jacuzzi-pool. Maj designed it. It's kind of a grotto in the middle of the house. The Hagman bathing facility is deep enough to stand in, with your feet flat on the bottom; the water is just under Hagman's nose. Three or four people can fit in the main section; two or three at the other end. A Jacuzzi massages the body (Hagman's). "I had a bad shoulder and elbow at one time and a bad knee when she designed it." It's done in black plaster. About thirty have been made for friends. They measure them by lying down in wet cement in old clothes.

"Larry has a theory," Phillip Mengel explained. " 'The family that bathes together stays together.' For a show-business family, they have been remarkably close. That Jacuzzi thing is also great. It's the social center of the house, between the living room and the deck to the beach. After dinner or before breakfast coffee in the morning, it's a meeting place."

Saturday night at home, Hagman will sit in the tub with old friends.

"Boys take baths, then girls," Larry says. "Not too much mixing. No sense going in bathing suits. Carroll and Nancy O'Connor never do things like that, though."

Watching football in the bathtub on Monday nights is Hagman's idea of fun. "David Wayne, his brother-in-law, Shelly, a couple of carpenters or construction guys, come in to soak and talk about football. Carroll O'Connor doesn't talk about football."

What does he talk about with Carroll? "Almost always about the state of the nation and politics," Hagman says. "He's a fiend. I bland out on that. He's a shaker and mover. I'm a sitter and watcher. I talk about football, usually. But when you're with Carroll, you talk about what Carroll wants. He's very forceful.

"I also admire the hell out of Alan Alda's way of doing things. The way he works, his politics, the equal-rights thing. He is a role model. Ed Asner? It's okay if Ed speaks out. Still, when he talks, my eyes roll back into my head. I don't understand what he's talking about. That's my problem. He's one volatile guy. He puts his mind and heart where his body is. His stand on El Salvador is probably right. I don't know where the country stands, either. Alda is my idea of a soft, good-thinking person. Do I get involved in politics? Yah, I give a thousand dollars to the Democrats. I'm a member of the Peace and Freedom party, myself. During Vietnam, they were for getting them the heck out of there. I voted for Dr. Spock three times. Any man openly admits having fucked up two generations got my vote."

"Some nights we're sitting in the Jacuzzi," Fonda says, "it gets too hot. We run out and jump in the ocean to go bodysurfing in the middle of the night." It sounds dangerous. "Or suddenly Larry will say, 'Fuckfire, Frisbee!' We play cutthroat Frisbee on the beach. Punch it with your fingers, the works, every variation known on the Frisbee."

Larry Hagman's life is so wholesome it's positively revolting. You never hear talk of him fooling around, taking drugs. He must get it all out playing J.R.

"What Hagman does is called acting," Mengel explained. "In real life, he is the exact opposite of J.R. He's a delightful, irreverent person. He is kind, a super family man. But mainly a comedian who loves to have fun. He's playing a role. Nobody could be further away from J.R. than Hagman. He's my closest personal friend, the best man at my wedding. Believe me. I know."

They have the ten plagues in Hollywood—forest fires, mud slides, frogs, murrain, pestilence, herpes, cable TV, gold chains, and bad ratings. Oh, yes, broken marriages. The more successful they become, the harder and the faster they fall into the maw. Larry Hagman is the only one I know who is so rich who has resisted all the plagues.

He's been married, as noted earlier, to the same woman since 1954. Hagman met Maj Axelsson in London in 1951. The guy who introduced him to Maj was his best friend there, Henry Kleinman, the London furrier. Larry had run away from Bard College to get a job as a chorus boy in his mother's current show, *South Pacific*. Kleinman also got him a job as "the Shabbas goy." It was during rehearsals of *South Pacific* in London.

Hagman had been staying at the Savoy. He had a fight with his mom and said to hell with it, and just left. "I needed a place to stay. And Henry said, how would I like a job? Get two pounds a week and all you had to do is work one day a week from Friday night sundown to Saturday night sundown. You open the door, turn off the lights, light the stove . . . shitfire, easy work."

The families in the big house were Jews from Japan who had moved to England. "It was like being a butler goy," Hagman said. So Larry is one of the few in Malibu Beach who speaks Yiddish with a Japanese-English accent. In the six weeks he worked for them, he gained twenty pounds. "I was living up in the garret. They would feed me chicken, boiled dumplings, soup. They fed me like a son. Eat, goyem [sic], eat."

For all of his wealth now, and the house, Hagman avoids the wild indulgences associated with stars. He doesn't have six cars and limos (although everybody usually sends limos to pick them up). In times of renovation, or when they rent their Malibu beach house to pay the mortgage during the summers, they would load the Recreation Vehicle up with dogs (which they got from the pound) and kids (Heidi and Preston) and camp out at places like Fonda's funky office in downtown Hollywood, where Fonda found himself living, having lost his house in a divorce settlement. Michael Cimino was also living there. The Hagmans would subdivide the office with a parachute hung from the ceiling and move right in. Or they'd camp out on Fonda's tennis court, when he had one. "They're gypsies," Fonda said.

The Hagmans work hard at their marriage—and at friendship. They have had positive impact on the lives of their friends. "I learned a lot from watching Maj and Larry," Fonda said. "He's great with his mother. At first she didn't understand him, thought he had gone over the edge. But they were able to examine each other's life-styles, become part of it. Not as freeloading, filial duty. They were funny with each other. I'm not very comfortable with parents. Larry and his way with his mother made it possible to be with my father. By word and eye contacts my father said to me, 'I love you very much, son.' Larry inspired me to do it, to talk to my father. He said to me, 'You do it.' He is very direct. He would say about my kids: 'I saw your daughter. Fuckfire, she's beautiful, but she's got orange hair.' So few people allow that kind of direct friendship. I adore him. I'm hooked on Hagman. It's my habit."

Larry Hagman once went to a shrink, he told me on the day we met. We were sitting on the set of *Dallas* as everybody was waiting for Sue Ellen (Linda Gray) to find her second expression. It was after the first year of his success with *I Dream of Jeannie*. He began throwing up. "I was shitting, pissing, earwax was coming out of my ears, every orifice something was happening," he reminisced. "They had to throw me into a pickup and drive me to the shrink. I was a mess."

The shrink told him, "Don't worry. Be happy." The advice helped him cope. He put those two magic words up on his mirror in Malibu. They're etched. He added his own motto: FEEL GOOD. So every morning he sees them first thing. "Some days, I may skip over reading them. But I know they are there."

Hagman didn't worry. Then one day the shrink gathered all his clients together and told them he was leaving his practice. He was retiring and going off to Tahiti. "Don't worry," he told them. "What do you people have to worry about, anyway? You've got a lot of money, nice homes. You think you've got problems? Don't worry. There are people a lot worse off than you."

So after four years at sixty-thousand dollars a year, Hagman's analysis was ended. He wasn't worried. Everything was okay, the shrink said. And the Hagmans were.

"Of course, two of the patients committed suicide," Hagman explained. "And five marriages broke up. But we got by." What really happened to the shrink? "Oh, he just got depressed listening to all those assholes. He's doing okay, he made some good investments. He's still out there, traveling around the world visiting former patients—the survivors." He stops at Hagman's house, bathes with the Hagman family.

And Larry still isn't worried. Why not?

What was Hagman's problem? Obviously, his mother. Mary Martin, the famous musical-comedy star? She was briefly married to Ben Hagman when she was seventeen. Mary Martin, Peter Pan, who raises in private life—J.R.? Think about that for a moment. Her heart may have belonged to Daddy, not to her son. I hadn't been reading Joyce Brothers all these years for nothing.

Hagman, you may have noticed, never talked about his mother in the clips or in interviews, except to say they separated when he was a teenager (until an automobile accident almost took her life).

As rich as Mary Martin was, Larry always lived like a poor struggling actor. When he married Maj, and they had children, and he was trying to make it in the theater, they lived in New York above an off-Broadway Chinese restaurant named Pearl's. Pearl was a nice lady. She let the Hagmans use the toilet facilities downstairs in the restaurant. "You always saw Hagman," an old friend recalls, "on the way to the john."

Hagman, as Dr. Brothers might have explained, could also have thrown his mother out of his life. The son could have rejected the mother because she was an enormously successful actress. His whole life could have been spent trying to wash that woman out of his hair, of his life. Perhaps his success in *Jeannie* was too much for him to handle. He had finally shown his mother he could do it. And would, in one sense, far exceed her achievements. Such is the power of TV series. TV makes theater look like summer stock, at least in numbers.

J.R.'s being so mean and nasty is his way of getting revenge. But is it also a device to catch Miss Ellie's attention? She favored Gary (the other son, the one for whom she bought the house in *Knots Landing*). He was the apple of her eye. J.R. is the worm, always making trouble, a negative way of getting Miss Ellie's concern.

That the nation took J.R. to its bosom so warmly may indicate that the nation has a mother problem. Between those with a mother problem and those with a father problem, you have a real cross section of the population. You have, in fact, the population.

Our problem dates back to the Founding Mother of the country, Martha Washington. Her husband got the big billing. But she got hers, in the end. After all, who inherited Mt. Vernon?

Hagman, however, has become the new father of our country, suitable also for export to other countries, and its spawning generations. One day, his face will be on our ten-thousand-dollar bills (useful for tips to parking-lot attendants) and on Mt. Rushmore.

We have dwelt too long on sinister symbols of success like Larry Hagman, Mary Martin, and Martha Washington. Let us turn to more substantive matters, like the aforementioned subject of violence.

9

MIAMI NICE (*MIAMI VICE* IMPACT)

I am sitting around a fashionable Columbus Avenue restaurant on the glamorous Upper West Side, with the noted New York stockbroker Annie Navasky Strongin, stockbroker to the stars and media people. The Santa Fe, a Tex-Mex place on Columbus & Vine, as we call it, caters to Foodies. It's not exactly well lit. It's like a coal mine. But most of the other people are wearing their shades.

Everything in the restaurant is in pastel shades. The off-greens, the peaches, the melons, the lemons. The people are all sort of half-dressed. They are wearing expensive Giorgio Armani suits and cheap seven-dollar T-shirts. No ties. Some are also wearing stubble, fur on their faces ranging from five o'clock shadow to five-day growth.

"What is it with these people?" I ask, perplexed.

"Don't you know?" Strongin says.

"No."

"It's *Vice*," she explains.

Suddenly I knew what she meant.

Miami Vice—the story of two overdressed cops on NBC. Of course I had heard about it.

"Everybody dresses that way now," she explained. "I know and I don't even watch the show."

And they were all sitting around looking vaguely sinister, like Detective Sonny Crockett or Ricardo Tubbs. To me they looked like they were waiting for a waiter. But they were waiting for action, whatever that means.

Me, I was in my rumpled Sydney Greenstreet sack, a gray-white shirt with bespoke ring-around-the-collar, as I watched them waiting. When nothing happened, we left.

This new phenomenon persisted as we walked down Tofutti Avenue. Everybody was in designer T's and pastel suits and stubble.

I saw further evidence among the real people. In Fire Island over the July 4 weekend, I was visiting at the home of Jane Globus, when her son, the famous photographer, came in from the beach with his kid. He was wearing a white Panama hat and a tacky Hawaiian shirt. I was looking at Ron Globus, who had invented a 360-degree camera called the Globuscope, and his strange outfit.

Every place I went that summer I saw more and more *Vice*. TV is on the cutting edge, creating "life-styles" if not great drama.

People were all dressed up, or down, acting very rich and beautiful. It was high style. Not since Hemingway and Paris had there been a work of contemporary fiction that so affected the young. *The Sun Also Rises in Florida?*

I never thought that the show, much less the clothes, would catch on. The way the characters in *Miami Vice* dressed that first season reminded me of that tacky stuff that Harry Truman and his Cabinet members used to wear in the late 1940's, the rayon Panama hats and painful Hawaiian shirts. But, hey, I'm not one to complain about the cultural influence of TV detectives. My big influence sartorially was Lieutenant Columbo, for example. I dressed a lot like him, with the old permanent-wrinkle raincoat and the pockets used for ashes, the unmade-bed look.

There are two kinds of *Miami Vice* fans today:

1. Those who liked the show before it became popular.
2. And those who like the show *because* it became popular.

I'm in a third category, alone.

I discovered it, oddly enough, on the local news. Every week, it seemed, somebody from the NBC show was being interviewed by my local WNBC-TV news. News of *Miami Vice* was a regular segment on *Live at Five*, like the weather. They covered *Vice* news on local programs more thoroughly than the president's tax program or Star Wars. They know what's important. Interviews with the stars, directors, chief gaffer, and best boys took half the night.

Why was *Miami Vice* so successful?

I remember one night during my long summer of study and analysis hearing the producer, Michael Mann, explain his success formula. It was a stunning revelation.

"No earth tones," he said.

No earth tones? I recall at the time. What is this—some kind of Zen saying, like the sound of one hand clapping? No earth tones . . . Ommm . . . Ommm . . . It was the mantra, perhaps, of *Miami Vice* disciples.

As everyone else knew, this was a reference to the special look of the programs. The scenti (as I call the cognoscenti for short) know it is the pastel shades that make *Vice* different.

No earth tones! Absolutely. There were no dark colors on *Vice*, that first big season. Just punk colors. Miami colors. Lime greens. Drug-dealer oranges. Cocaine lemons. (You can see how much I like Florida.) The peaches, the melons, all the colors I always hated as pukey. Plus shades of white.

There were no reds, greens, browns, blues, mahoganies. Earth tones were what you saw on *MacGruder & Loud*. Or in family sitcoms—all the earth tones in those kitchens with the cheap cabinetry. Earth tones blend together. Joan Lunden on the heavily-biased-toward-earth-tones morning news show *Good Morning America*, for example, blended into the set. You could barely see David Hartman, the only morning-news-show anchorman on a life-support system.

Others said it was the special low-camera angles that made *Miami Vice* so successful. They shoot it from sewers. Not to mention the elliptical cuts and the special scissors they use for editing. Then there is also the music. They play hit rock songs in the background, instead of the usual boring bongo and synthesizer tracks.

Maybe all of those things are important.

What I loved about watching the show, though, was the clothes. What threads. Obviously the cops are all on the take. How could they be so fashionable, so well-dressed, at today's prices? The cost of cleaning those white suits alone could wipe a man out. My wife said the MPD cops either have a high clothing allowance or a prisoner doing dry cleaning in the basement.

I don't know what I like most about *Miami Vice*. Crockett's Ferrari? My sources tell me that the Daytona Ferrari Don Johnson drives costs $125,000.

Or the $150,000 boat he lives on.

Or his pet alligator, named Elvis.

I like that alligator. Elvis adds comic relief. His diet is macho macrobiotics. Eats everything not tied down. The first couple of weeks he ate alarm clocks, LSD evidence, Crockett's Buddy Holly record collection. Alligator or not, strictly kosher he's not. Elvis could have his own show, as far as I'm concerned. His own network. Anything he wants.

Some viewers told me that what they liked about the show was the bodies of the actors Don Johnson and Philip Michael Thomas. Indeed, Don Johnson was the most overexposed TV star of 1985. And I don't mean his being shirtless, which he has a propensity toward, as we always say. Only his co-star, Elvis, had been photographed more often without his shirt. I'm talking about the press.

The cover of *Time* . . . the cover of *People* . . . then the cover of *Rolling Stone*. All on one day in the last week of October 1985. And the same day an article on "Macho Men" in the *New York Post*. Jeffrey Lyons's review of *Cease Fire*. And a no-show as host of *Friday Night Videos*, leaving that tough job to Philip Michael Thomas, the other cop on *Miami Vice*, Detective Ricardo (Tubbs).

But the phenomenon was not all the press or the unpressed suits.

There are three plots in *Miami Vice*: drugs, smuggling, and drug smuggling. Forget the plots. If you want a more cogent plot, watch the nightly news. What *Miami Vice* is about is feeling the hot wind in your hair as you speed through the streets of Miami at ninety miles per hour. Shiver in the cool breeze, caressing your shoulders at a party on Sonny's boat.

The fourth plot, or subplot, as scholar Cheryl Blum explains, is showing us Johnson's body in as many ingenious ways as possible.

The first few times I saw the show in its premiere year (1984) I thought its distinctive feature was the lack of dialogue. You couldn't hear what the characters were saying. They had this state-of-the-art, hand-held audio sound equipment, which picked up all the street noises and explosions and violence.

That was a positive. You don't want to hear what most detective shows are saying.

The dialogue is the boring part of an action-adventure show. It's *shtick*, something the producers add perfunctorily, a vamping between car chases.

I also had trouble understanding what I could hear. I don't know a lot about drugs or drug paraphernalia, or how to do it, i.e., deal. So I was missing a lot to start with. Like since I don't speak Swedish, you can't expect me to get every nuance in a Bergman film.

This was another plus. I was always being surprised by occasional evidence of a plot.

They speak, or mumble, drug talk on the streets. And it's often in Hispanic-Yiddish slang. An obscure reference like *Panamanian schlepper* is mixed in with Nam talk (about violence from experience of the Vietnam War) and inside stuff about intra- and inter-police-departmental rivalries. Incomprehensible. Wow, was this deep! Most of the time it was like listening to a tape from the DeLorean trial.

TV is traditionally afraid of using words the general public doesn't understand. Like they're trying to protect you from coming down with Cosellitis, that mysterious disease that causes people to suddenly start breaking out in an enriched vocabulary. But when it comes to the arcane and obscure language of drugs, apparently anything goes. This is not fair to ordinary people, who aren't into drugs. They should use subtitles, or maybe Garrett Morris, who used to do the news-for-the-hard-of-hearing on the original *Saturday Night Live*, could spell it out for us not-with-its. "What they mean by *snorting* is . . ." he could yell.

The other unusual thing about *Miami Vice* is the use of music. Most police-show sound tracks are substitutes for plot: When they can't think of anything in the way of suspense or mystery to carry a drama, they play music.

Miami Vice, on the other hand, uses famous music in the background, like great paintings. It's a classical-music lesson. *Miami Vice* is the only place on prime-time TV you can hear the Stones' recording of "Miss You," which was on the charts the summer of 1978.

The only kind of music they play is in earth tones, of course. Sometimes, a whole show is based on one song, "Smuggler's Blues" by Glenn Frye and the Eagles.

Wow. Wonderful. It's MTV *and* a crime show. Even a teenager who can't count could count his blessings here.

Not only that—they do *Miami Vice* in four-track stereo sound. It's the sound wave of the future, they say. Maybe. But why anybody today would want to hear your average police-show dialogue in both ears is beyond me. Police shows in stereo give your brain freezer burn.

There was a personal side to my interest in the show. I used to watch *Vice* originally to see if any of my relatives down in the Big F were selling "smack." The leading outdoor sports in Florida used to be shuffleboard and buying prune juice at the local supermarket. Now I'm convinced they all sell dope. What the heck, it's better than surfing for my older uncles, saying "Hang ten?"

My father came up from Florida a few weeks ago for his great grandson's *brith*. In a lull of the weekend, of which there were forty-three, one of the other grandsons asked, "Gramps, what do you do down there?"

"Nothing," he said.

The grandson rolled his eyes. "Sure, baby. We know what you're into. Pills, drugs, what is it?"

"Drugs?" Gramps said. "Sure." Which was true enough. Between him and his wife they rank next to Colombia in the international drug market. "Lopressor . . . Corgard . . . nitroglycerin . . ." He started to list all the pills they take.

"Come on, Gramps, what do you think your friends are doing? They're all dealers."

"Deal? Nobody can see the cards," Gramps said.

"Horse? Flesh? What's moving on the street with your gang, Gramps?"

"Nobody can walk down the street," Gramps said.

All the grandchildren smiled. Sure. Who do you think is sitting in the back of those limos?

NEW TRENDS IN VIOLENCE

We must not avoid the big issue, the undercover appeal.

One of television's early leading thinkers, Lawrence Welk, was asked by a reporter, "Mr. Welk, what do you think of violence on TV?"

"Violence?" Mr. Welk said, "I got twenty-four violence in my orchestra."

And what do I think about violence? I'm against it. As with sin. And like sin, there are certain kinds of violence I'm against more than others.

First, we have to have *some* violence on TV. Otherwise we can't have Shakespeare. The final scene of *Hamlet* plays like *The Untouchables*. And what's a mystery without a corpse to start things off? And you need violence to make war stories work dramaturgically.

I'm against *meaningless* violence. The trouble is there is practically none of this on TV, according to TV-network minds. To them, it is always "so-called meaningless violence." Their violence is meaningful, as are their relationships. And what it means is this: When you don't know how to produce an interesting, involving story, shoot somebody. As a matter of fact, this kind of thinking is based on their most profound philosophical system:

Whenever a story drags, kill a person. This happens in the first two and a half minutes of an action-adventure show. Every few minutes after that, when there is a lull in the action, another person is killed. The duller the show, the higher the death rate.

A couple of seasons back, there was a show about life in small-town America in North Dakota called *The Manhunters*. Eight or nine a night were killed. The show soon had to leave the air. The scriptwriters realized everybody in town had been shot.

So, basically, what we have on TV today is all meaningful violence. Yes, the networks are very responsible today. For example, they don't *show* the actual killings as often as they used to. They talk about it.

In the old days, they stuck the knife in the body, and gave it a turn or a lift. Somebody got strangled, the eyes would pop a little. By 1986, they were showing a small hole the size of a pencil to indicate a bullet going through the head. Then the networks came up with the actual killing off camera. This raises the question, What is worse? I still remember when Charles Whitman, the crazed twenty-two-year-old Texas sniper in an NBC meaningfully violent TV movie, *Deadly Tower*, ran his mother through with a bayonet. Would it be better to have seen it or just to have thought about it? It depends on how powerful one's imagination is. Personally, I think it's worse to imagine it. I find it more sickening and disturbing to see a pool or bathtub with blood—the way they used to show violence without showing it—than to see the actual killing. But then, I have a vivid imagination, as my network foes suggest from time to time.

There are new trends in violence each year. In the 1983 season, for example, they played classical music while they were beating Lee Majors up in *The Fall Guy* (ABC), one of the more meaningful violent shows of the period. Meaningful Mozart or Vivaldi, I think. In 1984, the big trend was comedy-violence. All the new police and private-eye shows had their hilarious moments. *Hunter*, on NBC, for example, featured Fred Dryer, the ex-pro football star, playing an LAPD cop who yelled, "Stop—or I'll shoot" at an alleged criminal. He had already shot him.

They had jokes about the reading of Miranda rights. "You have the right to remain silent," Sergeant Hunter says to a guy he's already knocked out. Even the cars, which give and take a lot of violence on the police shows, were laugh riots in 1984. They did stunts—leaping canyons and tall buildings—in *Hawaiian Heat* and *Hunter*, which amused the audience. They were so wild and crazy and surrealistic they could make your *Mother the Car* laugh.

All of this came on the heels of an even bigger trend in violence in the 1980's—the trend away from killing. Take *The A-Team*. (With apologies to Duke Ellington.) No one ever gets killed. No one ever gets scratched. As Ronald Weinger, noted TV viewer, asked, "What kind of impression will this make on kids? That they can roll a car three or four times, or fly a helicopter into a mountain, and walk away without getting their hair mussed? It's totally dishonest."

Even hand grenades on TV today are no longer dangerous. This trend could undo everything *M*A*S*H* did to show that weapons kill. And hurt. "I'm surprised that the N.R.A. doesn't sponsor these things," Weinger said. "There is more killing on MTV ('Don't Shoot Me, I'm Only the Piano Player') than in some TV drama."

One of my favorite hobbies, next to watching TV, is reading the reports on TV violence. They are produced sporadically, attempting to measure impact on teenagers, young children, mothers, moths, motes of dust on the glass screen, and so forth. They always ask for more surveys and studies about violence by the social scientists. Studies about violence by social scientists, in fact, are a major growth industry.

Some of my best friends are social scientists. You can always tell a social scientist. He's the one who is asleep at a party. And I suppose I should be more impressed by social scientists' work. They do get bogged down a lot. Get five of them together on any issue. Two will say it's good. Two will say it's bad. One says, What time is it? Nobody can agree with the others' "methodology," much less what they're trying to prove.

Reports are tricky things. Networks put them out. Universities. Even ad agencies, who never lie. In the Middle Ages, they defended the castle by throwing boiling oil down on attackers of the keep. Now, they throw down reports.

Roughly, what I've come to believe from all the reports by social scientists is that television causes violence today. But I've also heard a rumor that there is some evidence of the violent nature of man for two hundred thousand years. They found these stone tablets in the subway that said so. I also seem to remember that everybody always blames other things for violent behavior. In the nineteenth century, the English blamed the novel for loosening morals. In the twentieth century, movies were blamed. Then comic books. Now TV is blamed for violence. They also blame TV for everything from cancer to commuter trains coming in late in the morning. It could be that reports about violence cause violence in society.

It may be that *anything* causes violence. Or in the words of social science: Any causative factor causes violence. A clothesline with black net stockings and a garter belt on Park Avenue could cause violence. Where I live in New Jersey, we think the air is causative. Breathing our air causes organized crime. A person can be driving along the Jersey Turnpike around Elizabeth and suddenly become corrupt. That's what happened to our last senator who was indicted. That's why we don't trust any air you can't see. Or anyone. But I digress.

TV may or may not be causative, but this much is certain: TV is convenient to blame.

And I think that the TV brass love it, secretly. To be blamed for causing a volcano of violence? It makes them seem very important, the medium all-powerful. If TV were that powerful, there would be much more violence on the streets.

I am, as this suggests, a confirmed skeptic about whether TV causes violence, or to what degree. But whether it does or not, I'm still against violence on TV shows. One thing is sure, it doesn't do any good. And more importantly, it is very boring. A real mystery is so much more deeply engaging. There are other aspects of human behavior more gripping. Sex, for example. I have never seen meaningless sex on TV, or anyplace else.

Violence should be regulated on TV. Crime is supposed to pay. Let it. If TV is going to persist in using violence for profit, that noted social scientist Art Buchwald once told me of a licensing plan:

Hunters need licenses before they can kill. They should also be required on TV.

- If you want to kill a cop on TV, for example, the license should cost about twenty thousand dollars.
- The license for an attempted rape should be eighteen thousand dollars.
- For killing a sane person, it will cost fifteen thousand dollars.
- For killing a psychopath, only ten thousand dollars. (Psychos come very cheap. The way they kill psychopaths on TV shows, they must be a dime a dozen. In some seasons, you practically never see anybody sane killed.)

The idea is that you won't be able to kill or commit any kind of a physical crime without a license. If a script calls for killing three cops, the producer might say, "WE CAN'T DO IT. The budget says we can afford only one cop." To save money, the producers will cut down on violence.

The Buchwald license plan, I firmly believe, is the only possible way violence can ever be reduced. The licensing fees collected could go to underwriting mental-health programs for writers and producers obsessed with violence. We can make them well again.

Or it could go to support public TV, the other leading open wound in society.

I hate to be so negative about such complex subjects. The most interesting contribution I've heard on television violence and crime in the streets was reported to me by a high-school student, Abigail F. Strichartz of Valley Stream (N.Y.), who came to a conclusion while walking home from school. TV violence is NOT the cause of crime in the streets, Strichartz hypothesizes. We need simple urban redevelopment. "The basic, most fundamental, in fact, the only cause of crime in the streets is . . . the streets. You get rid of the streets, you get rid of crime in the streets."

THE ELEVEN O'CLOCK MUSE

Crime is not all in the streets, however, or even on action-adventure cop shows.

Your average eleven o'clock news show in the New York market starts with a murder in Brownsville (Brooklyn), a murder in Jersey, a body in the Bronx. There might be a rape or two in Long Island, with one rape victim describing the ordeal in detail. A tenement fire in Newark. Possible arson.

And in between they show a few clips of World War III, or Ron and Nancy nude, etc. That's a joke. Still, I can't say for a fact that they would interrupt the local crime for the end of the world on my TV stations.

Some days they have to delay the crimes. There is an international incident, an important election, a summit conference, something that might precipitate nuclear warfare, which runs first. But I always have the feeling they are dashing through the boring stuff, the election results on a presidential-primary night, say, to get to the real news, the local crimes.

My anchorman is breathlessly reporting that a woman has been hacked to death somewhere in Bayonne or Maspeth (Queens). They didn't even have identification yet. And they had to rush to tell us.

Immediately this reminds my anchor of a case in Austin, Texas, where you must recall, he says, a couple of women were brutally butchered two days ago. Luckily, they happened to have footage of the dismembered bodies in Austin.

Will they find a link between the Bayonne and Austin killings?

No matter. Our news is a parody of early Peckinpah without all the cinematic blood and gore.

The night of March 11, 1984, the eleven o'clock edition of *News 4 New York* had an eight-crime show. By that I mean they had started out the news report with eight crimes in a row (if you count arson as a crime). It was a new high, or low, in TV journalism, a record that will be tough to beat, especially in news shows that only run twenty-three minutes.

Not all the crimes were first-rate news stories. And not all of them were new, either. At least one was six months old. Two had taken place the previous week. Three took place "early yesterday." Two of the eight crimes actually happened on the same day of the evening news show.

The blotter:

1. Fire in the Bronx. Abandoned building in the South Bronx. This was big news?
2. Fire in Harlem. Happened the day before. Police still searching for the alleged perpetrator.
3. Fire in Newark. Happened the day before.
4. Policeman shot in the hand. Manhattan.
5. Woman shot in the arm. In the Bronx. Yesterday. But she's recovering.
5–A. And then, in the classic Channel 4 fashion, they had reporter Jim Van Sickle recall three previous crimes. Van Sickle, who was also known as "the Voice of Doom" for his stentorian "March of Time" style, was the specialist in retracing murders, step by step, with an air that says, "I'm not being titillating; I'm trying to be analytical."
6. Woman shot in Whitestone. Last September.
7. Man shot in Penn Station. In February.
8. Boy shot on the West Side Highway, also in February.

There may have been more. I had stopped watching and counting after eight, for reasons I will soon describe. I should also point out this was a slow news day, a Sunday night, when not much happens in New York. Except on local TV, when eleven o'clock on a Sunday night is known as "crime time" or "slime time." There was no particularly important crime that night, darn it.

Eight in a row is a glaring example of TV avidity for crime, so I wrote them down. But top-loading the deck with crime is not unusual on *News 4 New York*.

Three nights earlier, a Thursday night (March 8), which was probably more typical, they had three murders and three rapes, with one rape victim giving all the details. Plus an exclusive report on a series of muggings in city housing project.

On March 23, they led with five crimes:

1. "Midtown Madness," as it was slugged when the graphics came up. Attempted stickup in Manhattan.
2. Reactions to a barroom rape in Massachusetts.
3. Barroom rape in New Jersey.
4. Beating and strangling of young Long Island girl. Suspect is in custody. They had already had the story (earlier in the week). Now they have a suspect. Now they can rerun tapes showing what he allegedly did.
5. Man arrested in murder of city marshal.

The sixth story that night was one all the newspapers and other TV news shows were leading with, a report on the new Board of Education commissioners' problem (the Anthony Alvarado case).

The same Channel 4 also had another "EXCLUSIVE" report in their series, titled "Fear on Ninety-fourth Street." Of course it was exclusive. Nobody else had it. Who else would do it but *News 4 New York*? It takes unmitigated gall to use "EXCLUSIVE" when nobody else will stoop to a story. The thing about Ninety-fourth Street spread further fear about mugging on a side street, not exactly a new anxiety in Manhattan. No wonder Channel 4 is called *News Fear New York*.

And this was the routine news. During the sweeps months, the local news shows pull out all the stops in applying scare tactics. On one New York station, WCBS-TV, Roland Smith did a report on how we can save ourselves in a nuclear holocaust. The usual procedures—how to load a gun, how to get your neighbor before he gets you, really useful stuff for scaredy-cats like me to know.

There was a special report on the underground peril by Arnold Diaz, which explored your chances of being burned to a crisp on the subway.

And then there was Jeanne Downey's report about the dangers of watching porn on cable TV. As if I didn't have enough to worry about.

Over on Channel 7, the famous *Eyewitless News*, Dr. Joyce Brothers was finding, in a special report, that reducing the amount of food one consumes can be effective in weight loss. Also, you should use smaller plates. That woman should win a Pulitzer Prize for reporting the unknown someday. Dr. Frank Field, then of Channel 4, was saying that cancer shouldn't be feared as much as it used to be. Good. Now if somebody can find a cure for fear of TV.

Enough with this highbrow stuff. I don't mind admitting my local news show was scaring the hell out of me. Murders and muggings and decapitations, not to mention the subway derailments and cranes falling on your head at building sites—the other stories they reported between the murders.

It's not just crime that bothers me. It is obsession. In that season, local TV news had been going through an obsession with bomb scares in Manhattan. Every day, it seemed, a new bomb was planted in one of the city's airports, or train stations or bus stations. Next to being murdered or mugged, one of my great fears is being murdered or mugged on the way to the airport. Or, worse, having survived the ordeal of traveling through the city to have my suitcase explode. Yes, a bomb or two had gone off in the terminals. And the TV news shows were making it sound like the U.S. Eighth Air Force visiting Dresden at night.

Then the bomb hoaxes started. Which wasn't too surprising. Who did they think was making all those calls? The people at home with nothing to do but watch late-night TV "news," and get a vicarious thrill out of planting bomb stories. People who work and have to go to sleep at night don't need that kind of thrill.

There are enough genuine problems in Manhattan without TV's obsessed exaggerations.

You know, sometimes I think the main purpose of the eleven o'clock news is to get us scared. Crime in the streets, crime off the streets. They don't really care what they report as long as it makes your hair stand up inside your head. It's a wonder anybody ever goes outside. Do you have any idea how many senior citizens in New York never leave the house anymore because of (1) crime, (2) TV news about crime?

FDR said we haven't got anything to fear but fear itself. Actually, that's quite a lot.

HELTER SKELTER

The teaser for *Helter Skelter*, which CBS presented as "entertainment" for the first time in April 1976, was itself a classic. The coming attractions for the movie about the Tate-LaBianca slaughter of 1969 opens with a scream in the night, shots, and rock music. The screen then fills with a blotch of living, or dying, color (red). Credits. More shots in the night. A voice is heard pleading for mercy.

It is the appetizer for the main meal itself. And unlike many of the teasers used with made-for-TV movies, it did not oversell the dinner.

Helter Skelter featured seven—count them, seven—of the most grisly murders in recent history, committed by the Manson "family." It also mentions, in passing, several murders that never made the headlines. "We cut him up in nine pieces," a family member explains about a missing person. "We chopped his head off, too."

With so much going for it, I knew *Helter Skelter* had to be a hit. Sharon Tate and her swinging friends, and Mr. and Mrs. LaBianca—victims of what seemed at the time meaningless crimes—would not have died in vain. They helped CBS get blockbuster ratings for two nights in April 1976. Their death stories, as told on TV, served also as evidence of what is surely sick about our society and the television network people who considered this suitable programming material.

The "star" of the movie is Charles Manson (played by Steve Railsback). I was especially fascinated by those eyes. He must have been wearing radioactive contact lenses to show such a marvelously crazed expression. Magnetic. It was said in the first part of the movie that he could stop the watch of the special prosecutor in a courtroom.

Manson, the Father Flanagan Boys Town dropout, was given ample time in the movie to do his version of Jesus Christ Superstar. One clearly saw the impact that his impersonation had on the "family," co-stars of the movie.

And what a family it was, perfect for the slime-time family hours (9:00 to 11:00 P.M.). There was Sadie-Mae Glutz (Susan Atkins) who described in great detail how she wanted to cut out Sharon Tate's unborn baby. And other family members who wouldn't talk to the special prosecutor until he gave them what they really wanted: candy.

The four-hour movie had plenty of time to explain the motivations of the Manson family; it had uncovered the truth: Charlie's love, that is, his girls would do anything for Charlie Manson. Because, they explain, he is Jesus Christ.

"As I understand it," my friend Jay Sharbutt, then of AP, said, "it's a kind of extended *All in the Family.*"

What the movie really seemed to be was what the networks have always dreamed of doing but didn't have the guns to do straight out—a made-for-TV "snuff movie," where one or more actors really die.

Curiously, the two-part Lorimar miniseries did not dwell on the sex orgies, another part of the Manson life-style. But the attention the scripts gave to the details of the murders was impressive. The Tate maid came to work on that bloody morning. On seeing the first body, she screamed and sobbed incoherently. The police arrived. "Hey, look it," a cop says. "There's even blood on the button" (which opens the front gate to the mansion grounds). And then the viewer was taken over the horrifying scene, like one of those Hollywood tours of the stars' homes: Here is one body, then another.

Much of this was shown through the eyes of the business manager of Mrs. Tate's husband (Roman Polanski). In his tennis whites, he went around making the identifications. Ah, but first he must interrupt this business to run out of the mansion and puke. This, incidentally, was a first in broadcast history.

What realism. It was the old mouthful of oatmeal spit-up trick. But it played—and captured the emotions of this sensitive TV critic.

Not all the details of the nauseating murders were presented. Just enough to make you puke. For instance, CBS didn't actually show the forty-one times Miss Tate was stabbed. The stabber just talked about doing it forty-one times.

And the dialogue:

Sadie Glutz (Susan Atkins) described how the eight-month-pregnant film actress pleaded with her, "I want to have my baby."

"Look, bitch, I don't care about your baby," she recalled saying to her. "I just kept stabbing her." It was heartwarming stuff.

The violence in *Helter Skelter* set a new high in what they call in TV "excessive." Not the traditional kind we see on television. CBS shows of that day, like *Cannon*, contained violence. But this was a kind of make-believe violence, the modern equivalent of the barroom fights in movie westerns, or on the cartoon shows, where the animals go around hitting each other on the head without damage (except, maybe, to the kids who watch them). An atomic device explodes over Roadrunner and it doesn't give him a headache.

Nor was the violence in *Helter Skelter* the kind you saw in the horror movies. That was sort of campy fun. *Helter Skelter* was real-fact violence, the kind that can turn on the few impressionable people who may in their sick minds envy the attention Manson got from the media. It was a bloodcurdling, frightening, and truly sickening television experience.

But, it took real courage for CBS to put the second part of *Helter Skelter* the following night, despite all the protests in the press about Part I. It makes one thankful for the First Amendment, which guarantees the freedom to air views regardless of how unpopular. Going ahead with *Helter Skelter* showed what a network was really made of: convictions of steel, a stomach of cast iron, and a conscience of pure oatmeal.

It was always assumed by television that the audience identifies with the good guy. And the healthy thing was to root for prosecutor Vincent Bugliosi (played by George DiCenzo), who does his best to be the Clarence Darrow of Los Angeles County. But there was something more unusual about the Manson character. Those eyes. That sexual magnetism, which turned on his so-called "family" (more discussed, of course, than portrayed).

It was not television's job to give good examples of behavior to follow, CBS could argue. Goodness is so undramatic, so boring.

It didn't seem to matter to CBS that there were people out there who could see again what a good mass killing does for one's reputation or recognition value. The media sure do go bananas over a good vicious killing. A good killing can give a drab person with no special skills instant celebrity status. It's not like in the old days of Attila the Hun, when you had to devote a lifetime to becoming feared and loathed. In the electronic age, it can happen overnight.

It didn't seem to matter to CBS that the message in the movie was not what a great special prosecutor Bugliosi was, or how senseless the killings were. The randomness and meaninglessness of it all—especially in the case of the noncelebrity LaBiancas—was so appalling. The Manson tribe could have killed anybody those bloody nights in 1969.

What did the CBS officials who allowed this movie to go on the air for two nights care? They lived nicely insulated, locked up safely at night in well-guarded luxury condos and estates. They went to work in limousines. They made their decisions about putting on *Helter Skelters* with carpeted walls all around them. They were safe from the nuts who may roll around the streets after two nights of studying the Manson case.

"Drive through Bel-Air some day," Bugliosi said in the concluding episode. "The fear is real, you can feel it." I wondered what this movie was going to do to the fear index in the homes of the CBS stars, as well as others, living in their deserted canyon mansions.

It didn't seem to matter to CBS that violence, not just sex, can be obscene.

It didn't matter to CBS that their movie gave a blueprint of how to commit a mass murder. And almost get away with it. Manson came close to not being convicted, even though, as Bugliosi points out before the trial, "he's guilty as Hitler." There was a lack of physical evidence, like the murder weapon. The police couldn't find the gun, even though it was literally under their noses.

The only socially redeeming value in *Helter Skelter* was that it showed what a bunch of dummies the Los Angeles Police Department were. The suspense angle in the first two and a half hours of the movie was: Will Special Prosecutor Bugliosi get the physical evidence needed to convict? A small boy had found the gun used to bludgeon the victims, but the police mislaid it in their property department.

This radical characterization of the LAPD was striking. The LAPD is usually very smart, on television. Since time immemorial, or when Jack Webb began ransacking their files for story ideas, the LAPD has always been vaunted by our medium for its astuteness. In the business of getting the man, their efficiency—on TV—was matched only be Efrem Zimbalist, Jr., and the FBI.

Was the compulsion to finally tell the truth about the LAPD the motivating factor in *Helter Skelter*? A triumph of honest journalism? Or did some CBS official get a parking ticket and want to get even? Nobody in the business could be that small, right?

And the movie didn't make the LAPD out to be nearly as dumb as did the original book by Bugliosi and Curt Gentry.

Why *Helter Skelter*? Well, there was television's traditional duty to society, their license to educate and inform. Presumably there were three people in the United States who had never heard of the Manson murders. Second, the story was true. But a lot of other true stories never get on the air. Truth may be the last refuge of TV scoundrels. Was it a desire to associate itself with great works of literature? Bugliosi-Gentry's book was a good job of its sort, but not quite *Crime and Punishment*; the show was a crime, the end result punishing. And it was not anywhere written that it was TV's duty to help sell books, even mine. Could it have been for commercial gain? O heinous accusation! Out, damned spot! And in spot after spot after spot.

It could, indeed, have been a psychotic episode—the flip-out of CBS itself. Such conduct is similar to a message scrawled in blood on our screens: STOP ME BEFORE I KILL SOMEBODY ELSE. (Or, Stop me before I show you the grisly details of somebody else killing somebody else.) Where was the FCC? Where was the Congress? Where, for that matter, was the public?

Watching, some of them, when it ran again on CBS five months later, in January 1977. This gave me time to think over my initial opinions, as expressed above, only at more length. Had I been too harsh, as some of my colleagues suggested? It was not nearly as appalling as, say, NBC's *Deadly Tower*, about how good ole boy Charles Whitman went berserk and used a rifle on people from a tower at the University of Texas, citadel of higher learning and shooting.

This was like saying the panther is less violent than the python. My overall, reasoned, balanced, judicial view remains unchanged. The show was the worst kind of garbage. Undumpable offshore in any decent environment.

Helter Skelter was a Lorimar production, the house that gave us *The Waltons*. And of CBS, which does many commendable things. For an explanation of such behavior, see Dr. Jekyll and Mr. Hyde.

CBS is a responsible public corporation. It is licensed by the federal government (at least the five TV stations it owned in 1977). Its executives answer summonses to appear before Congress, which periodically wants to find out why there is so much violence on TV.

CBS would probably argue, in effect, that it's all your fault, kiddies.

You want it. Here they will cite the Nielsen ratings on the first showing of *Helter Skelter*, which were a smidgen less than *Gone With the Wind*. Get it?

Furthermore, they might add, they had to do it. Something had to be done to stop *Roots* on ABC (the competition this night), which could become a runaway show in the ratings for eight nights (and did). *Helter Skelter* was the biggest knife up the CBS sleeve. They play rough in television.

To be sure, CBS was in a desperate position at the time. After all, they were running third in the ratings, and were really down at their heels. Let me tell you just how bad things were financially at CBS at that point of time. The network bought Fawcett Publications for $50 million. Cash.

How desperate is your financial position when you can lay out $50 million in cash?

Anyhow, things got worse.

I ran into "Charlie" Manson again in 1981—on a TV show. We were finally, as the song went, family.

There was something truly grotesque about putting Manson on network TV for ninety minutes the way Tom Snyder did the night of June 18, 1981, on a special edition of *Tomorrow Coast to Coast* (as the old Tom Snyder NBC show was called briefly, when Rona Barrett was the co-host or ghost-host).

Who *was* this anyway? Garbo? Schweitzer, back from the dead, for a last TV appearance? Manson was a killer, guilty of nine senseless, gruesome murders, a lunatic as far as the state of California is concerned, who had to be put away in a nut ward for society's good.

So many sane people cannot get on network TV today. Articulate, intelligent people with social ideas and ideals that need spreading, people with moral missions, Nobel laureates, missionaries, visionaries with possible solutions to problems that plague mankind can't get on. Vladimir Zworykin couldn't get prime time on the air today, and he only invented TV. Margaret Mead, if a young woman and just back from Samoa, couldn't get on.

You could argue that one man's Mead is another's poison. But there is something wrong about this lowlife, this cesspool, Manson, getting the ninety-minute blockbuster treatment from Snyder, the highest honor Western civilization at the time could bestow (next to a Barbara Walters Special).

NBC called a special press conference the morning before the show to announce its journalistic coup. This was so big, they were preempting *SCTV Network/90* to run it.

The flacks told the critics the good news, that after thirteen years, Manson was allowing himself to go on TV. That's funny. What else does a man serving nine life sentences have to do? His schedule is tight? Did he have other more pressing commitments? NBC actually paid someone ten thousand dollars to get the interview? I tell you, guys in jail will be hiring press agents: "Get me on Carson, Sammy . . . or else."

Was the Snyder interview with Manson to be a new program form— *Person to Person, from My House to the Big House*? Would we soon see Berkowitz, Chapman, Hinckley, Richard Speck, or Charles Whitman?

I hated the idea of making Manson a star again. At first I wasn't going to write about, or even watch, the show. But then I saw the impact the interview had on my teenage daughter Andrea and her high-school friends.

Everybody watched it. They thought it was cool. Manson was some kind of great historic figure to them, like FDR was for my generation. "He's interesting to us," she explained. "You saw the trial. All we saw was *Helter Skelter*. Was Charlie Manson in that, or an actor?"

Teenagers were a significant part of the audience for the first slammer special: those with the least perspective on what Manson was all about.

It could have been worse: The interviewer could have been Dick Clark.

Tom wasn't easy on him, the kids said. They were right. He was a veritable Tom (Tiger) Torquemada as he grilled the nine times guilty man about his life and times and crimes. He was absolutely fearless with Manson, who has the power to do what? Make a voodoo doll and give him the needle?

Oh, Tom really chewed him out for not confessing to him, Tom, about the murders. He accused him of being "evasive." This was some weird performance. Here was Tom talking to a crazy person—and expecting him to be sane.

Ultimately, Tom was mystified by Manson. That's because he sometimes actually listened to people. Tom expected straight answers. Manson would be plausible for four or five sentences—then veer off. (That's what it means to be crazy, Tom.) An angry and hurt Snyder accused Manson of "being on the space shuttle" for not playing the journalist game. I got news for you, Tom, you were both on it that night.

Manson is no Raskolnikov and Snyder certainly no Dostoyevsky. It was "Looney Tunes TV."

MY STATE (PUBLIC EXECUTIONS ON TV)

New Jersey, one of the leaders in both crime and enforcement (New Jersey first invented disorganized crime) is bringing back executions, the papers said. My state has thought of everything in adopting lethal injections as its new form of capital punishment. (Actually, Trenton is its own form of capital punishment.) They will be done behind one-way glass. The executioners are disguised. Three will be giving the injections, only one of which is fatal, firing-squad style, so nobody will ever know who did it. We are sensitive about feelings in New Jersey. The state is even bringing in executioners from out of state. Even with legal hit men from out of town, the state is missing a good thing. It could make money on the executions by selling the TV rights.

People are getting a little tired of watching the state's other big TV show, the Lotto drawings. Tickets could be sold in a lottery with the big prize being the chance to serve as state witness at an execution. The bigger the prize, the closer the seat.

"It would never work," explained Reuven Frank, a former president of NBC News. "The problem is—we couldn't sell repeats. It's the same thing wrong with baseball reruns. You know how it turns out."

TV hasn't had a good public execution since Gary Gilmore. And that was bungled, as far as I was concerned. It wasn't live—and in full color. To this day, I'm still not sure Gary Gilmore is dead. I don't think anything is true until I've seen it on TV.

I remember watching ABC's *Wide World of Sports* the weekend (in 1977) following Gilmore's execution on the chance that this was one of those events that might be a tape delay. But no, Howard Cosell didn't have his arm around the warden in Utah after the firing squad finished, saying, "Warden, that was the most boring execution I've ever seen. You're a disgrace to humanity." No, they just left Gilmore suspended, metaphorically, hanging up there in limbo.

I never understood TV's reluctance to show live executions. Capital punishment is supposed to be a deterrent. A variety of attitudes prevail about that. As the eloquent Mayor Rizzo of Philadelphia explained in 1972, "The electric chair might not be a deterrent for everybody, but it sure deters the hell out of the fellow sitting in the electric chair."

TV news is not so squeamish about showing me the murders themselves, or the aftermaths, which can lead to a death sentence. Local news shows every night keep me up-to-date on all the latest killings. This poor lady brutally hacked to death in Yonkers. This elderly man bludgeoned in Bushwick for three dollars. They show the bodies, the blood on the sidewalk. The weapons. They would show the killings, too, if they usually hadn't happened in a fit of passion or rage and with few killers having the presence of mind to call *Eyewitness News* before they do it. Only hostage takers, and rioting prisoners, so far, call the media while the act is in progress.

I used to see a lot of executions on TV. But that was called the Vietnam War, a source of exciting programming now dried up. The good guys were always shooting people in the head during the dinner hour in downtown Saigon. It had a deterrent effect. It deterred me from ever going to fight with or against the Viet Cong.

My guess is either TV is secretly against the death penalty as a matter of principle (unlikely), or they don't know how to do it. How anything new ever gets on TV is amazing. TV is like Oxford University, whose motto, I've been told, is (in Latin): "Nothing should ever be done for the first time."

I recently attended a seminar on capital punishment as a deterrent, conducted by W. H. Ferry, formerly of the Center for the Study of Democratic Institutions at Santa Barbara. At "the Center for the Destruction of Democratic Institutions," as the Ferry Foundation of Scarsdale, New York, is sometimes called, Ferry first asked, "If executions are supposed to be a deterrent, how come we can't watch?" As early as 1972, Ferry was arguing that executions should be televised in prime time, when the young people would be able to see them. The noted educator said, "What's the use of reaching a lot of fifty- or sixty-year-olds, who do very little murdering . . . ?"

Traditionally, this sort of thing is done at dawn. So what? If they can arrange football-game schedules for the convenience of TV, there is no reason why executions couldn't be scheduled at decent hours.

Preempt *Jake and the Fatman*, *Wiseguy*, *Miami Vice*, *Hunter*, or any violent program that attracts the young. Another good time would be during reruns of *Starsky & Hutch*. It has an audience deeply involved in law and order. On one episode, I saw the two young law-enforcement officers cornering a black drug dealer and beating him senseless with their fists, without reading him his rights under Miranda.

Any show that the family watches together would be okay, according to Ferry. "That way a father will be able to say to his sons, 'Boys, this is what happens if you kill anybody.' That's the heart of the matter."

But they could also pipe the shows directly into the high schools and grammar schools. Public executions instead of the dreary public educational TV they now force kids to watch, and there will be a marked increase in attention, attendance, and deterrence.

I would also run the executions at night out of doors. Put a big screen on street corners in the South Bronx. Open up Briggs Stadium in Detroit for free public executions, like a drive-in theater.

And while we're getting fancy about it, they could also increase the audience for the event by tying it in with a network superstars challenge, or a telethon, perhaps. The event could be underwritten by your local electric company, the American Gas Association, or your friendly pharmaceutical company.

Public hangings went out of style, but that was before we had sponsors ready to pay for big audiences. Why do our killings have to be done in secret? Let's make a buck out of them by bringing them out of the closet.

TV's major long-term reaction to the shooting of President Reagan was changing the name of Ralph Hinckley in a so-called comedy, *The Greatest American Hero*, on ABC. The schoolteacher, who could fly (not well: He had lost the flight manual) was thereafter known as "Mr. H." It would have been funny, if it wasn't so pathetic.

I say that was not enough of a contribution on TV's part.

Now, as I've explained often in my writing about violence, I was not saying that TV was guilty for the shooting or Hinckley. TV doesn't cause violence. Texas Tech could have caused Hinckley to turn violent. Hamburgers and vanilla ice cream can cause violence. God can cause violence. Even Jodie Foster. It's inexplicable.

Yet, it's really crazy, shooting at a president because you have a fantasy about a movie star. I always tried to explain to my teenage daughters, that's what "crazy" means. You don't understand it.

Violent shows on TV are like dumdum bullets. They go in small, and leave a big hole coming out. They consume certain individuals. Maybe no more than one in a million is affected adversely by contact with a violent show. But as we have seen, too often, it only takes one.

TV's role, if nothing else, is making violence seem commonplace. So somebody gets shot. What's the big deal? That's life. Heck, ninety-seven people get shot on TV in an average night on prime time.

The KPN (kills per night) should come down immediately in a sane society with a communication industry that is even remotely responsible. It is no help throwing a little oil on the fire that smolders in some of us like underground methane in the swamps.

The vigil, waiting for the results of the operation on the president, was an experience like sitting in a hospital waiting for the report on a relative who has just been mugged. Time after time, they showed us the incredibly chilling videotape, made by cameraman Herb Brown of ABC. Then in slo mo, with freeze frames and an instant replay. There was a sense of déjà vu, like being with a group of Kennedy-assassination freaks playing their films from Dallas on the big Advent screen, as if it were some kind of home movie. I liked the Reagan shooting better, where the plot to kill the president fails.

On this disturbing and awful day, I noticed again what a difficult job the crisis anchorman has. He must take the incoming information—little or too much, true, false, confusing, and contradictory—from field reporters, wire services, phones, and wherever, and somehow try to make it coherent and be reassuring at the same time. The last thing we need on TV is somebody wringing his hands and falling into a pit of despair, gnashing his teeth in rage and frustration, as I was doing at home.

Frank Reynolds met my needs most on that terrible day. He was authoritative and steady as a rock, sorting the pieces of the story on the air. I especially liked the human quality in Reynolds. He exploded during the confusion over James Brady's condition at about 4:00 P.M., obviously upset that he had been told, and had reported, Brady's death. "Let's get it straight," he told his people standing off camera, "and nail it down. We don't want to be first with the news. We want to get it straight." The emotion was appropriate. You saw that this was a human being, under enormous pressure, with voices talking into his three ears with conflicting reports.

And I was touched by the way Ted Koppel eased into the other chair, almost instinctively, openly explaining to viewers he had come to share the burden with Reynolds so one of them could be listening to the off camera reports while the others talked. Reynolds and Koppel made a good team, if you have to hear bad news.

Marvin Kalb of NBC also impressed me during that crisis. The State Department man on TV was very important in this administration, which had an American Strangelove eager to take over prematurely, judging by Alexander Haig's performance. And Kalb rose to the occasion, sitting in for John Chancellor until he finished putting on his makeup and other chores before *The NBC Nightly News* "took over the fort." Kalb is bright, articulate, one of those fortunate people who can talk without a script, the real test of a TV newsman.

But the star of the day, in my book, was the president. I was very impressed by the man in a crisis. You've got to give him credit for the way he handled himself.

The TV reports about the little jokes he made with his wife ("Honey,

I forgot to duck") and his hope that the surgeons were all Republicans made you love the guy. And his statement that on the whole, he would preferred to have been in Philadelphia—it really made me proud that he was president. Yes, it was like a movie script, and it was good.

I didn't think too much of NBC interrupting its coverage at eight o'clock. Bryant Gumbel made a long speech, explaining NBC's decision to leave the drama in progress. It's our duty, he explained, in effect. We gave it a lot of thought, and this is the way. The network then went to a basketball game. This was the sort of shoddy thing ABC used to do. Dump the news event, and go back to regular programming.

Don Ohlmeyer, the head of NBC Sports (at the time), is one of the great moral philosophers in TV sports. I believe he studied with Martin Buber. But I think he was traveling without the ball on this one.

So was ABC, which, a half hour later, went back to its original programming. They ran *Show Business*, a pilot for a series starring David Frost and Sandy Hill, which had to play right away. It was like keeping dead fish in the can—it couldn't wait another night?

The juxtaposition of the president being shot and that basketball game and John Travolta getting an award from Hasty Pudding at Harvard and the rock singer Pat What's-Her-Name in *Show Business* was surrealism for the viewer who was trying to cope with the real world.

They should have gone off the air for a while, possibly. Left the people thinking about what had just happened. Any gesture would have been better than nothing. The Oscars being delayed twenty-four hours was a step in the right direction.

LONG DAY'S NIGHT
(SHOOTING OF JOHN LENNON)

"Who is Mark David Chapman?" Chris Borgen of my local Channel 2 news was asking rhetorically on the street outside the Dakota the day after that more awful night when the music stopped.

I then watched a very long report on the man from Honolulu who had allegedly shot John Lennon. His childhood, yearbook pictures, where he lived and worked. There was also an hour-by-hour report on what he had been doing in New York before the horrible act was committed. Few tourists have had such coverage.

Meanwhile, the same kind of massive coverage of the who-what-when-where-how of the Mark David Chapman story was going on at Channel

7, Channel 4, Channel 5. Indeed, the TV stations were fighting to give the most complete portrait of Mark David Chapman in history. The reports were not analytical. They stayed with the straight facts of his life.

Still, Mark David Chapman was the man of the week on TV.

I had the sinking feeling I'd seen this all before, déjà-view-TV: *Schizo acts out his worst fantasy, winds up on television as a star.*

Still to come were the exclusive interviews with the best TV reporters about why he did it. And then the TV-movie-of-the-week: *The Mark David Chapman Story*—three hours on a Friday night so all the baby-sitters at home could measure their own violent fantasies with the reality of what happens when you actually act one out.

It is, as I've said, only a handful who are leading lives of such quiet desperation, for whom it would be better to be a notorious somebody for a couple of minutes than a nobody for the rest of their lives. They are the marginal, the fringe, the ones who do the damage.

TV itself is a medium with a screw loose. Its values are wrong. Entertainment shows glorify violence. And the news shows reward it.

The stars of TV news every week are people who have no known talents. How do they get their break? By shooting, stabbing, throwing lye in faces, taking hostages. Rape, murder, robbery, all the negative hostile acts against society are recompensed with valuable time on the news shows.

TV, of course, says, Well, what can we do? It's news. We've got to over-cover it this way. Or the other guys will do it.

It doesn't matter they don't cover much of the other news. I could list a hundred stories they are not covering on any day, for reasons ranging from the obscene to the too complex. It's a matter of priorities, moral judgments, and a sense of social responsibility.

What TV really needs today is a new, workable code of ethics, a Ten Commandments, which takes into account the way things are in the real world, and the new reality created in part by television.

Just as you don't show pictures of a man defecating on the street, so TV news should not show pictures of a man just because he has committed a crime. Murder is obscene. As a bare breast is not but is still considered to be today.

I'm not against TV news giving us the facts. But after the facts they should shut up about criminals. TV should take a lesson from the silent vigil that was conducted by young people outside the Dakota, the night a Beatle was killed.

John Lennon was a man of peace. He would have liked something good to come out of his death, perhaps an end to publicizing the sick nuts who do this sort of thing.

HOSTAGE HYPE

We had a fascinating hostage case on local TV news shows the week of October 20, 1982, starring a fellow who broke away from his guards at a Brooklyn hospital, then locked himself in with six hospital employees who had been playing cards in the basement. Soon, he had many nonnegotiable demands. First, this lunatic in the locker room at Kings County Hospital wanted a print reporter, his own Boswell. Then he demanded radio coverage. Then an appearance on *Eyewitness News* on WABC-TV. By the third day he was asking for not just news of his activities but the time for full statements. Five minutes on prison conditions in New York state prisons.

Hey, man, the end of the world will get only ninety seconds on our TV news. Film at eleven.

Another day or two in the bunker, and he would have been asking for his own weekly show. Or at least a guest shot, so to speak, on Johnny or with Barbara, or Merv, who would ask the only question that he ever really asked anyone: "How does it feel to be a celebrity?"

The escalation of demands by the lunatic, and his intuitive knowledge of the media, were bizarre and frightening. Especially the way they gave in to everything he wanted. What if he had asked for a chair in crime-news reporting at the Columbia School of Journalism?

When he didn't like the way they were covering the story on the air, the guy almost went berserk. He didn't like the use of certain nouns in descriptions of him, such as *informer* and *snitch*. Everybody is a critic these days.

The guy was a real media freak. Not only did he want to be on radio and TV, he wanted to see it himself. He had them send a radio and a TV down into the bunker so he could see and hear all about himself. What's the point of being a superstar if you can't see the big show? I was reminded of the classic question raised by Bishop Berkeley, long before the electronic age: If a tree falls in the forest and nobody hears it, did it really fall?

Well, in the New York TV market, we heard about this guy's rise and fall.

After the story itself, there were the discussions. Was TV wrong in granting all the requests? It was presented as a dilemma. Our local WABC-TV station (Channel 7) gave the hostage the most live coverage. That's what he said he wanted. It was the only major network (ABC) affiliate station he could see in his locker room. Stations on the lower end of the spectrum were unreceivable in the basement. "What is a little station to do," asked, in effect, the news director of WABC-TV, especially if lives can be saved? Channel 7 thought it saved a life by giving him time. I've got to say this: At best, I don't believe it was the most important consideration. If anything, it was a passing thought.

A guy in a hostage situation can ask for anything. He can demand to see or to be Roone Arledge, president of ABC News. But it's wrong for TV and radio to honor these requests. If you ask me, it's wrong to even cover the hostage stories in progress at all. I don't believe these nuts should get any publicity. (No names, let alone aliases.)

Haven't the TV news officials who order the coverage and air time noticed how contagious these reports are? A few days earlier there was massive coverage of a hostage taken on the train in North Carolina. Then the Kings County basement story. And twenty minutes later, it seems, there was another hostage case in the Bronx.

The hostage story is becoming a regular feature on the TV news, like the weather or sports.

"The sparks jump," as Dr. Erika Freeman, a psychoanalyst, noted on the WPIX-TV news in the only examination of the psychopathological impact of media coverage I heard during the hostage circus. "The criminal mind is most open to this kind of story." What is even worse, as Dr. Freeman pointed out, massive coverage by media gives the criminal knowledge of the latest in hostage-intervention techniques. It shows them the cards before the game starts.

The public wants nudity and sexual intercourse. But they don't show it on the news. In the coverage of crime, TV news uses discretion in, say, showing the contents of body bags. They don't show heads blown apart in the nightly killings. Blood and gore are, largely, exorcised, except for the spot on the street.

The free-press issue here makes a civil libertarian's heart beat faster, but it is something of a joke in the realities of local TV news. The bottom line in the covering of hostage taking is that it gives them a chance to cover something "live," a welcome relief from all those silly "live" remotes. ("Here we are standing at this bus stop, Morris. A bus went by five minutes ago. Another is due in five minutes. Now back to you, Morris.") On a hostage story, they get to use all the mini-cams, micro-dishes, and other expensive toys. A hostage story is *visual*, a triumph of technology over the common good of society. The local TV news station doesn't give a damn who gets hurt from the coverage or how it perpetuates the thing. It's the ratings.

The way our WABC-TV played up the hostage taker in the Kings County Hospital case, you would think he was a member of the *Eyewitness News* team. They made it their story, their exclusive. ("Your Official Hostage Station. Try us first.") In the next hostage case I won't be surprised if he asks for bids to rights to the siege, as they sell off the rights to Olympic coverage. It was blatant exploitation of the worst kind on the hostage story, on WABC-TV's part.

Hostage stories have, in effect, taken the media hostage. The TV news shows must report them because they say it's news. And it's only news because they are covering it.

Are people not going to watch the TV news because it didn't have the hostage story? What are viewers going to do—stop watching the news because they didn't have a hostage story? They won't even know what they are missing without first watching the whole show.

I suggest it is the unpredictability—the not knowing what you are going to see on a news program that is the governing principle behind audience involvement, not the predictability of any one kind of story. If you already know what's on the news, then it's not news, it's olds.

Okay, that's how I feel about it. Others say that once you start controlling or curtailing the public's inalienable right to know the minutest details about hostage taking, hijackings, and other similar antisocial behavior, we're in trouble. As Ted Koppel of ABC News's *Nightline* argues eloquently, if some government agency banned news about hostages, hijackings, and the like, what would prevent the same group from claiming a news-information blackout on protests (which helped end the Vietnam War), the Bay of Pigs Invasion, the Pentagon Papers?

Well, I have an open mind on most issues. Maybe a solution would be banning the reportage of these events on the local news shows—at five, six, and eleven o'clock. At the same time they could be required to be shown on public TV. Why?

Public TV is an underutilized resource. It is significantly involved in few socially useful functions, other than reruns of British "programmes" and old Hollywood movies.

Public TV has an audience of some intelligence, perhaps better able to cope with violence. A similar criterion is used in the showing of sex, banned from commercial TV. For years they have been able to show for example, frontal nudity on public TV. As long as they took off costumes from the eighteenth century or nineteenth century in drama, it was thought to be less likely to drive TV viewers mad with desire.

Can you imagine any psycho-media freak turning himself in on *The MacNeil/Lehrer NewsHour*? Can you imagine any crazed gunman calling up and saying, "If you don't get Big Bird over here, I'm going to kill these hostages"?

Public-TV viewers read books. People who read books are less likely to take hostages or need to fulfill themselves on a local news show. Call it snobbery, elitism on my part. I believe it anyway.

Thus we would be satisfying Ted Koppel and other civil libertarians' need for reporting all the news a democracy needs to grow, including every bizarre aspect of human behavior, while improving public TV's ratings at the same time.

Another way to resolve the public's need to know all about the day's violence in a noninflammatory manner could be as follows: Use commercial TV news shows, but require that they tell the news in print, or flat and factually. For example, a slide on the *Eyewitness News* could read:

ANOTHER HIJACKING TOOK PLACE TODAY.
Period.
or:
THE FOLLOWING PEOPLE WERE MURDERED IN NEW YORK DURING
THE LAST 24 HOURS.

Then run the list on the screen. No elaboration.

Are the gruesome details really necessary? TV news is a headline service. They seldom explain why inflation is rising, why an energy crisis, why anything?

A third solution is to show still pictures of the crime.

A fourth solution is to show the moving picture but without sound.

The reporting package currently used consists of superstar anchorperson, news reporter on the scene, and camera coverage, and is incendiary. By manipulating the medium, perhaps the bomb can be defused.

The message from TV when you do something bad should be: Drop dead, get lost. You will be thrown in jail, ignored until you get your fair trial, etc. This would be much more consistent with due process. I wouldn't have a single picture on TV of the alleged worm who allegedly took a hostage or shot a president. Maybe when he got out of prison after serving his time, and was going to devote his life to working in a leper colony or otherwise serving mankind, I'd finally give him a little publicity. TV is, oddly, one of society's biggest awards. It should not be squandered on the lowlifes.

None of this is likely to happen by itself.

Now I'm not going to ask you to write letters to the networks and ask them or tell them to stop with the killing and hostages already. Forget forming organizations, boycotts, and crusades. Forget the petitions—which are time-consuming and seldom work.

The only way television will change is for the broadcasters to do it themselves. You can't legislate these things, just as you can't control guns totally through laws. It's time TV as an industry got control of itself.

Society has gone berserk. Everybody feels they have no control over what happens, or responsibility for making it happen. We feel powerless and, increasingly, hopeless.

I am reminded of how complex and mind-boggling warfare became after World War I. The major powers held a meeting among themselves and outlawed certain practices as inhumane. At the Geneva Convention, they agreed not to use poison gas, for example. In a similar way the TV networks should unite to ban certain practices that they all know in their heart of hearts are bad for society. Ignore that phony-baloney First Amendment stuff about free press, which is invoked by TV when the government through the FCC tries to influence the content of programs. And the Justice Department should ignore antitrust conspiracy laws this once. Let the networks lock themselves in a hotel room, or a closet, and conspire for the common good.

Certain "conspiracies" just happen. All three networks will run documentaries at the same hour, accidentally, or they will have their one culture show of the season on against the other networks' cultural hour. That's serendipity!

Let TV do what comes naturally. Make rules about what can be done and can't be done. What I'm asking for is the establishment of an unwritten code of ethics, a mind-blasting concept in a business that has some ethical people but no ethics collectively.

The three networks should declare unequivocally their opposition to certain unethical, socially irresponsible, potentially harmful practices.

For example, no more explicit shows depicting violent crimes. You know, the kind of TV movie like Sally Struthers in *A Gun in the House* (CBS), which showed step by step how to rob a house in the suburbs, attack housewives, and so forth. No more shows like *Texas Tower* (NBC), which step by step depicted how you go about climbing up tall buildings with a lot of ammo, and kill twenty-two.

When a cop gets blown away, his killer should not get more coverage than the cop and his funeral.

The vacuum in TV should be filled with stories that glorify the real heroes in society, the ones who save lives, the ones who work in a university, laboratory, courthouse, or hospital. There is no such thing as a boring situation, only boring writers who can't make it come alive without killing or bombing.

Commercial TV can afford an ethics code now. This is not some struggling, starving art form like the theater or public TV, with its ribs sticking out. This is a hog-fat business, with zillions of dollars from commercials, which they run too many of.

FUN CONTROL (ANTIGUN CAMPAIGN)

Guns have an attraction for the young, Ed Bradley said several times in a CBS Reports documentary, *Murder: Teenage Style*, one night in 1981.

Wouldn't it be great if Madison Avenue came up with an ad campaign aimed at kids that made them think that guns are stupid, gross, sick, immature, yecchy, or for nerds and wimps?

ONLY CREEPS CARRY GUNS. Anybody who uses a gun is a sitz, a lowlife, or whatever the term of derogation is today for the lowest of the low.

I'm not talking about another one of those tacky public-service ads they throw into programs nobody else will buy time on, run righteously in the intellectual-ghetto shows. I'm talking about Bruce Springsteen. Madonna. Michael Jackson. Sting. Brooke Shields and Richard Avedon, Cosby. Kid class. Aimed at young teenage girls, the real movers and shakers in this society today. They control young boys who think guns are cool.

I'm not talking about messages from adults, doctors discussing in an intelligent manner how guns may be harmful or hazardous to the health. I'm not talking about testimonials from distinguished Americans who have been shot. None of this stuff from the Oval Office with your president saying, "All things considered, I'd rather have been in Philadelphia." Or messages from the families of victims, urging a laying down of weapons. Or any of this junk about Hey, it could happen to anybody.

I'm talking about peer-group stuff, MTV mindless mode. Blow smoke up their elbows, as all successful ads do.

They can sell almost anything on TV. Jeans . . . work clothes at forty dollars a pop. Kids who cry because they don't have a Jordache behind. Oh, oh, Sergio . . . Junk foods. Teenagers are turned into walking laboratory rats, as if testing to see how many chemicals they can take into their bodies before turning into Willard . . .

Shampoos and bleach. Beautiful girls at home who think they are unattractive because the color of their hair is different from Christie Brinkley's or Cheryl Tiegs's.

I'm talking about a TV ad saturation campaign, a blitz, a million times a day, and in prime time, on the indy stations where all the reruns that kids like are. With a saturation campaign, in three months guns would have a bad image. If you *hocked* at them day after day that guns are not hip, guns would be on the way out. *Persona non gunna*.

AUTO-DA-L.A.

A thing of beauty on TV is car driving. The chases and the crashes are done with consummate movement and grace, choreographed and performed by the Auto Ballet Company de Detroit, and brought to us by a grant from the Used Car Foundation.

It is a marvel to see such supple cars negotiating a leap off a San Francisco hill, never blowing tires, never breaking suspensions or the necks of the drivers. Masterly! You just don't do that without training, discipline, and special high-duty shocks.

Who will ever forget the greatest moments in car dancing, the immortal car chases in *Starsky & Hutch*, the Baryshnikov and Fonteyn of the car-ballet field. The way they took the corner on two wheels (the *pas de deux*), it made you want to stand up and applaud, "Bravo!" Or was it "Brava?" What is the sex of Starsky's '75 Ford Gran Torino (a.k.a. "the Tomato") or Hutch's '73 Galaxy sedan?

That was car chaseography at its finest. For *Starsky & Hutch* they would write the car chases first, then the rest of the show. What detectives Starsky and Hutchinson used to do with cars made *The Dukes of Hazzard* look like a high-school student-driver educational film.

Have you ever noticed in TV drama that a hell of a lot of time is spent getting into cars, not to mention chasing? That's because TV and cars go together, are made for each other, symbiotic, like books and sex. Car demolishing is something we learned at our mother's knee. (And I don't mean *My Mother the Car*.)

The way a TV show deals with cars is a sign of artistic integrity. It's the way you can tell, for instance, a low-budget show from a high-budget show. In low-budget shows only people get killed. Demolishing a car is the mark of a big-spending producer.

Eva Reuben, kindergarten schoolteacher, was telling me one day that the favorite game of her children was *The Dukes of Hazzard*. The class wagon is "the General Lee." The children call each other "cuz" and fight over which of the cousins get to drive the make-believe General Lee that can leap rivers without bridges and hurdle barns as if they were potholes. Next to the children (five to six years old) shooting, stabbing, and blowing each other up with dynamite, besides the usual beating with fists, what they like to do most is drive. The toy cars and trucks are for crashing and rolling over. "Whatever happened to dolls and playing doctor?" Eva asked sadly.

Those kids sure have an advantage over me. They will know how to drive, should they live long enough to get their driver's licenses, in a style I'll never learn.

To this day I can't get my car to go on two wheels without tipping over. I see that basic little driving technique on every TV drama, even serious ones like *Hardcastle and McCormick*. I have trouble sliding around corners without making a mess.

The Dukes of Hazzard set such a high standard for driving. All TV, in fact, is a regular driver's-ed course. It teaches you everything you have to know. What they do on TV is technically known as "Hollywood driving." This is a form of passage in which the driver spends 90 percent of his time staring at the passenger sitting next to him, and looks only occasionally at the road. One of the great car drivers when I was a kid growing up was "the Saint," Roger Moore. He *never* looked at the front of the road, except maybe in passing. Another one of the big drivers of my youth, Joe Mannix, used to drive on the wrong side of the road without looking at the road . . . AND at excess speeds.

The stars don't look in their rearview mirrors very often, either. That's because TV cars don't *have* rearview mirrors.

Driving on TV shows is usually done in one of two types of cars: the "street cars" and the "rear-projection cars" in the studios, without rearview mirrors. The rear-projection cars are the interesting ones, the ones where the stars can do their best Hollywood driving. Not having rearview mirrors is not much of a problem for them. People like Magnum can just look at that small dot on their windshield (where the mirror should be), and say they're being followed.

I've never figured out how to get tailed, though. I've been driving for thirty-five years and have never been followed once. On TV they can't get in a car without someone following them. It's like pinning the car on the donkey.

It was amazing how those early heroes drove so well, too, usually with one hand, tooling in and out of complex traffic at high speeds.

From TV you learn that you never have to leave any time to find a parking space. They always find a beautiful spot in the big cities. They never have to worry about alternate-side-of-the-street regulations. Or meters. They never drive around a half hour like I do, and park six blocks from the scene of the crime. Or come back and find their cars towed away.

And have you ever heard of one of the TV cars' engines not turning over immediately? It's a dream world of instant ignition, like battery commercials.

They never have to roll up the windows, either, when they park. They just let everything hang out. They don't seem to take their keys out of the ignition, do they?

Can you imagine what would happen if they left KITT from *Knight Rider* on the street, say, in Manhattan or L.A. for five minutes? Unattended, with the keys in the ignition?

The most important thing you learn in the TV Car Driving School is never to worry about crashes. Not the cars but "the drivers of those cars," my friend Mickey Redican told me the other day, "must be indestructible. They miraculously survive car crashes on *The A-Team*. No seat belts, either."

What seat belt? A recent scientific study titled "The Portrayal of Driving on Television," by Bradley Greenberg and Charles Atkins for the *Journal of Communications*, found "fewer than 2 percent of all drivers on television are shown buckling their seat belts." If they had them. If they didn't have rearview mirrors, you're really not into automobile safety in a big way.

"Would you please find out the dealer who sells the heroes their cars?" asks Joseph G. Shannon. "They can go through fire, famine, pestilence, and war, and keep going. My two cars have seizures when it's cloudy. Are these special cars made in Detroit? Tokyo? or Tibet?"

These cars, Mr. Shannon, are specially trained. They go to a school of autobatics, where they learn how to do rolls, slides, and leaps, and be generally indestructible. They are cars that leave the ground more often than most airplanes. They can perform what in autoerotical engineering is called "irregular tracking": immoral driving acts between consenting adults, screeching but not complaining tires, etc. Safe driving, which is like safe sex, is practiced by cars that never go off the cliffs, explode, and otherwise make fools of themselves.

More seriously, I'm troubled that the kids who watch TV don't know this. TV car chases/crashes and new-car ads are bad because they imply to kids and adults that high-speed, high-risk TV driving is okay, even if a little dangerous.

It might be useful if every time there was a driving scene in a drama, an authority figure like Mr. T would explain (voice-over or in print) that these are stuntmen in specially balanced cars, with brand-new tires and roll bars, and padded interiors. (Stuntmen are not optional equipment.) Some automobile manufacturers and ad people make an effort—in small type. And, someday, somebody will be able to read it.

LIFE IN THE FAST LANE I: (DRIVING IN NYC)

One of the advantages of all the more recent shooting on location in New York—a trend hailed in 1985 as the hottest thing to happen since sauerkraut on a frank—is that you get to see different kinds of scenery in the police shows. Just when you have tired of those helicopter shots of State Highway 101 along the Pacific, now you get a chance to tire of seeing the glamorous FDR Drive between Houston and South Streets, and the Brooklyn Bridge ramp from a helicopter.

It's all because of Tartikoff's Theorem. "Chasing up La Cienga Boulevard is not enough," our Brandon, the legendary programming genius and president of NBC Entertainment, explained that January.

And suddenly even *Miami Vice* was doing location scenes in New York. They had already broken new ground by moving their chases from the Norman Lear Freeway to Miami and the Everglades. Every show, with the possible exception of *Dallas* and *Mr. Rogers' Neighborhood* has been using New York streets and highways and byways for chase scenes.

As I have explained, chase scenes have long been a staple of the TV arts and sciences, the chase itself named after Salmon Chase, banker and former secretary of the treasury during the Civil War. The first chase took place during a run on the bank during the Bank Panic of 1876. No, wait a minute, that was actually another Chase, I discovered, for an essay I'm doing on runway inflation (or anchorperson's contracts).

I am a student of chase scenes, with a special interest in surveillance—those scenes when the good car tails a bad car. Observations:

1. NBC's *Hunter* has the best surveillance scenes. Sergeant Hunter, played by Fred Dryer, who drives some of the most incredible junkers (cars with inoperable doors, cars that often fail to start just when most needed to become a pursuit car). It's one of the few realistic touches in the car-chase field. Hunter, meanwhile,

is a master of surveillance. On one episode, he successfully tailed a motorcycle using a suspicious wreck of a car with fenders of mismatching colors and wasn't detected. Of course, the scene was shot in L.A., where anything unrealistic is likely.

2. The tail inevitably leads to the chase.

3. There is an unwritten law—until now—about car chases. My nephew, Dr. William Blank of Costa Mesa, California has observed, "If it's an old car driven by a bad guy (not Hunter), you know it will crash and explode."

    Watching *Hunter* one time—shows you how tired I was—I saw an old Camaro. Before I remembered Blank's Law, it was goodbye!

4. "This is not true in the case of old Pintos," Dr. Blank explains further. "It won't explode. All the suits against it. They don't want to pour oil on the fires. They have more suits than you have hanging in your closet."

5. Cars and their chases always have the same movements, swerves, two-wheel turns, flying leaps, and so forth, as in formal classical ballet. So its always exciting to see a car chase conducted outside of L.A., or Miami, like watching a new production of *Swan Lake*. I was especially impressed with both the new scenery and the moves of the cars in *The Equalizer*, a CBS show starring Edward Woodward and his Jaguar XJ-6. Did you see the chase across the Brooklyn Bridge in the premiere (September 18, 1985)? Wow.

I was just getting over the way the Equalizer—who is a combination of Bronson and David Horowitz, helping poor people fight the system—was telling his clients they had nothing to fear. All they had to do was call him every hour on a pay-phone. Did you ever try to find a phone that had a receiver on it in Manhattan? Or the circuits are not busy? Suddenly there are these two cars screaming through the traffic on the Brooklyn Bridge at 120 miles an hour. At about four o'clock in the afternoon. Are they kidding? This has to be the funniest thing seen in the name of realism in the 1980's.

First of all, the roadway is made with threads or ribbons of metal. You could slide across at 120 miles faster than you can drive.

And the road in real life is always being repaired. It hasn't been finished since 1897, and it never will be.

None of this should trouble people in Middle America, many of whom are hereditary owners of the Brooklyn Bridge.

What a dangerous thing this is to show New Yorkers. Subliminally motivated, they're going to accelerate going into the Brooklyn Bridge. They saw it on TV. Life follows art. In the name of verisimilitude, as well as common decency and common sense, I wish they would put an ID on pictures of car chases across the Brooklyn Bridge saying SIMULATION.

THE CAR AS STAR

I grew up in the decade of cars as inanimate objects. Lately, the cars have become, as suggested above, stars on TV. Today, cars, not the U.S.A. or U.S.S.R., are the superpowers. They can fly like KITT, the Firebird on *Knight Rider*. "They think they are helicopters," Bill Luciani, a careful student of the subject, says.

It is when TV cars start talking that I get nervous. The anthropomorphic process began with the early orange Dodge Charger (the General Lee) in *The Dukes of Hazzard*." Even Boss Hoggs's white Cadillac convertible has more cosmic intelligence than the police in Hazzard County. I wouldn't want to get in an argument with KITT, who knows everything.

Incidentally, for collectors of KITT trivia, Simon Nathan of New York informs me that KITT did not attend high school with David Letterman.

TV cars are on cocaine. It's in their contract, along with an oil change, a five-thousand-mile checkup, and a garage.

"A sixth-generation computer may be an accetible suspension of belief," explained the noted TV viewer Ronald Weinger. "But KITT's acting is getting to be as bad as co-star Michael Hasselhoffer's."

There is another side to the esthetics of the car chase-race TV has institutionalized. It is, to some, a crashing bore. And it's inhumane. I recently got a letter from the Society for the Prevention of Cruelty to Cars.

"As recent patrons of HBO we have sat through some movies," explained the chairman of the SPCC, Joseph G. Shannon, "where they would have about thirty seconds of plots without car mishaps." He mentioned *Smokey/Bandit*, *Blues Brothers*, *Grand Theft Auto*. "In those car chases, hundreds of cars get smashed, wiped out, destroyed, blown up. Now really. We are not car nuts (nine-year-old VW and an eleven-year-old converted telephone truck). But let's show some respect and reverence for the automobile. If these TV shows and movies continue to destroy cars we will have an economic depression . . . cars may replace the alligator as an endangered species."

Now I don't know where Shannon studied, but contrary to his fears, the opposite has happened. TV helps the automobile business. The broadcasters single-handedly may have been responsible for pulling Detroit out of its last slump, helping the Reaganomics turnaround in the 1980's.

"The automobile industry, whose health reflects the state of the national economy, is being given an immense financial shot in the arm from the TV industry," explains the noted economist and letter writer C. Grimes. "These broadcasters nightly struggle to revive a sagging economy by wrecking, at their own expense I might add, dozens of brand new cars. They burn them in accidents, shoot them to bits, and dump them off the cliffs. Just the past evening I saw two shiny models tossed into the rivers. What more can Hollywood do to spur Detroit's production?"

I am a Grimesian—TV car drama is doing more than Lee Iacocca for the business, bottom line-wise. Southern California was invented by Detroit in the 1920's and 1930's to supply cars to fill that space. All that land and no transportation was a natural. It's an irony, now that they have five million Mercedes in California, the largest per-capita Mercedes rate in the world. Mercedes is the Volkswagen of Beverly Hills. They'll give student loans to buy Mercedes. It's no accident that you never see a Mercedes going off a cliff out there. It's only the cars without agents that go off the cliff or explode. Superstar cars like KITT live charmed lives.

Middle America loves Jesus, pickups, and car wrecks. Somebody who is afraid to get a scratch on his car loves to see others demolished on TV, as in real life. Why do you think rubbernecking at a fender-bender (to use the special language broadcast traffic reporting has given us) is such a major outdoor sport? We like to see other people do unto others with their cars.

The cause of the car in American arts and sciences could be further advanced, as I have propounded earlier, if next Memorial Day at the Indianapolis 500 Speedway they would stage a special match race between Starsky's '75 Ford Gran Torino; Hutch's '73 Galaxy Sedan; KITT, the Firebird Pontiac; the Trans Am in *Hardcastle and McCormick*; the General Lee of *The Dukes of Hazzard*; throw in the *Blue Thunder* helicopter, if you want—all against Mr. T. dragging Freddie Silverman's *Supertrain* around his neck, like a piece of junk jewelry.

BOX VOBISCUM (*HILL STREET BLUES* BOXES)

And while we're on aids to industry, and lost causes, what about the boxes? Have you ever noticed how in *Hill Street Blues* and *Hunter* and all the great car-chase shows they're speeding down an alley, bad guy followed by good guy, and the cars crash into boxes? And they're always empty. Who makes them? And why are they always empty?

The boxes seem to have no function, except to be piled up in alleys where car chases go. Do they have a special empty-box factory in L.A. that grinds out big boxes that never get used except on TV shows? Are these the boxes that originally contained all the stuff certain salespeople told us "fell off the truck"?

Of course, these may not be regular boxes. They have special cinematic—in fact, aerodynamic—qualities. TV boxes fly higher and farther than most boxes you and I know.

They are attractive, as boxes go. Visually arresting. They don't explode—they just go flying all over the place, like chickens.

All I know is TV has been a boon to the box business.

Someday there's going to be something in the boxes, and won't the car chasers be surprised?

PALE FACE, PALE RIDER
(LAUGHING AT VIOLENCE)

The in-flight movie on American Airlines Flight 1 winging its way out to L.A. one morning was *Pale Rider*, a memorable Clint Eastwood item based on Katherine Anne Porter's novelette *Pale Horse, Pale Rider*.

Although the film version is a joke as far as Katherine Anne Porter's fans are concerned, it's not a comedy. As seen on a plane, the movie looked like a religious allegory-western, kind of a Jesus-on-horseback morality story, with old Clint playing a religious mystery man, a padre-podner who rides into town with four or five unexplained bullet holes in his back. Usually, as you know, the homesteaders are being driven off their land by greedy cattle ranchers who want the land for grazing the herd. This time it's greedy mining interests who are trying to run the good people, the homebodies, off the land.

Now Clint Eastwood doesn't smile, much less tell one-liners. But suddenly American Airlines Flight 1 started to shake with laughter. There were bursts of chuckles and guffaws, as if a canned-laughter machine had run amuck briefly in the DC-10.

I looked up at the screen in disbelief. I hadn't rented the three-dollar earphones, having seen it originally in the movie-house version. I also saw the book.

What was making the travelers laugh hysterically at that moment was an act of violence. Twelve hoods, a gang in the hire of the greedy mill owners, were being plugged out of their saddles by Clint. In a flick of the eye, pow . . . pow . . . pow . . . they were all being dispatched.

I'm not sure how reliable a body of air travelers is for a study of human behavior. I still remember seeing a group standing around in LAX terminal watching a TV set showing a free episode of *Three's Company* (they do that in Los Angeles). It was a rerun, but the group was laughing their heads off. Of course, being in L.A., with all the smog and murders and bad air and sprouts, gallows humor prevails.

But this seemed very interesting behavior on the plane. I noticed then that whenever the violence worsened, the laughter increased.

It was almost as if the people on the plane had been reading the newspapers that day, which contained statements from network TV officials about violence. The network execs were saying that while movies like *Rambo* and *Commando* were very violent, people didn't take violence seriously anymore.

The TV industry was doing its usual dance—the atomic chicken at the Roxy Disco—on the moral issues. It's always fascinating to watch their fancy footwork, the way they reach a high moral stance on any issue, usually based on principle. The principle is: It may look like we're doing the best for ourselves, but we're actually saving the world, or at least giving it what it wants.

So, for example, they were explaining their stand on vigilante issues, like *Rambo*, in TV movies. Vigilanteism (by the good guys) is "out," no way. So in a TV movie like NBC's *Hostage Flight* (1986), they spent two hours showing step by step how terrorists can take over a plane, in case there were still some groups who didn't know how to smuggle the grenades and Uzis aboard. But as long as they don't have the passengers overthrow the hostages and hang them—as the producers' (Frank von Zerneck and Robert M. Sertner) original idea went—the network thinks it deserves the Nobel Prize in Humanity.

The producers changed their minds after taking a meeting or two with the NBC Standards and Practices Department. Funny, the way producers give in to the censors. Otherwise they will be labeled as troublemakers and never work again. It's very humiliating. But nothing harmful. In southern California humiliation is like jogging.

If you like to laugh, read the networks' rules on violence.

Tony Geary once explained after leaving *General Hospital* to work on TV movies: "They sit there counting the number of *hells* and *damns* in the script. If there is violence, they make sure no guns are pointed at the heads, no knives to the throats. They have safe target areas. You can shoot, maim, or kill. But be careful where you aim that gun. It's okay to shoot at the toes."

I was talking to Van Gordon Sauter, the ex-president of CBS News, about the days when he was the CBS censor, in 1976. One of the hit shows he was in charge of censoring was *Young Dan'l Boone*. A big issue internally in 1976 was the *amount* of violence in TV dramas. They were allowed to have three overt acts of violence per episode, so many threats of violence, and so forth. It was enough to age Young Dan'l. How can you have a show about the frontier without, for example, killing a few Indians, or a whole parcel of them? People expect it. And it was historically accurate.

But, it was decided, only three killings per episode. Thirty-nine in thirteen episodes, Van recalled. Sometimes, they could have six in one show, if the plot warranted: Then they would have to deduct them from the bank (base). In one show they were out of killings: Dan'l was fighting an Indian, but they couldn't kill him.

Van Sauter said, "He was a real bad one, too, one who deserved to die. They built up his character that way." So they had him fall off a cliff.

Maybe he was drunk on a motorcycle. Or firewater. They had rules about everything at CBS, including stereotypes. The Indian had to be physically inferior in dexterity to the white man, of course.

But I digress. The bursts of laughter on the airplane at the violence, which would not be censored when *Pale Horse*, etc., played on a commercial network, were understandable. Cathartic release, the experts say. People are so frustrated much of the time, all they can do is laugh.

And it's nothing to worry about. Everybody knows it's absurd. The violence is so violent, you must laugh. Why, it's ridiculous. Hysterical. Unreal!

I was reminded of the line about reality: "Reality is so real, sometimes I feel like I can reach out and almost touch it."

But, again, what about those who can't touch reality? What about those who don't realize it's funny, or at least supposed to be? And who take it seriously.

Why don't they, I started thinking, use a laugh track to go with the violence, then?

Laugh tracks in comedy were once considered as wild and crazy as what I'm proposing. Canned laughter is a device to tell people what they just heard was a joke, and is funny. Otherwise they presumably wouldn't know. It's also for people who are afraid to laugh alone; the man who thinks he's gone completely crazy if he's the only one in the empty room laughing. It's saner to be in a company of laughers *inside the set*.

All of these principles should work with violence, too. The violence laugh track tells you when to laugh, and how hysterically.

A possible scale: (a) A man getting his head blown off by a six-shooter would rate, say, a titter; (b) three men killed in a jeep, blown apart by a land mine, is a guffaw; (c) a serial killer is a rib-tickler; (d) a maniac raping, maiming, threatening a community is a belly laugh; (e) a country nuked, but only a Communist country, a roll in the aisle.

You can't tell me this is too obvious. *The A-Team*—the most violent show of the 1980's—is in the minds of NBC a comedy. I've seen a lot of kids watching this program very seriously. You can't tell me it wouldn't work better with a laugh track.

Of course, there is another problem: The laugh track makes people lose their sense of humor. The funny bone is a vestigial organ in TV viewers, like the appendix. TV viewers could also become violence-impaired. It's an experiment worth trying for thirty or forty years to see what would happen—an attempt to deal with another aspect of television. The powers-that-be in communication have no idea what they're doing or what its impact will be, beyond this season's ratings and audience-advertiser response.

I'd feel better about all of this, incidentally, if the network censors in charge of violence were the Three Stooges. This is not an epithet I'm hurling here. But Moe, Shemp, and Larry, as vice-presidents for Standards and Practices, would take out their violent impulses on each other and spare the rest of us.

A SYNTHESIS ON SYNTHETIC VIOLENCE

They haven't tried so far to show the impact of violence. I mean, the impact of an act of violence on you or me. How is anyone to know TV violence can be harmful to health?

There is no way to eliminate violence from TV. We wouldn't be able to see *King Lear*, not to mention my other favorite violent shows, *Macbeth*, *Hamlet*, and *Richard III*. Violence has to be in some shows. Don't take it away, but make it grisly. As in *King Lear*, the remarkable production with Olivier (1983). After Gloucester's (Leo McKern) eyes were taken out, he wandered about with rags covering bleeding sockets, a festering wound. They didn't go so far as to show maggots geting into the wounds or anything messy like that. But those bloody rags said something special about the enormity of the violence wrought.

The most effective and fascinating use of violence I've seen in a police-type show was in *Philip Marlowe—Private Eye*, the HBO series based on Raymond Chandler's detective stories (1983). "Are you Marlowe?" a hood asks the detective in his office in one scene. "No, P. Marlowe . . . Philip," the star (Powers Boothe) says.

"Wise guy," the hood says, and starts twisting Marlowe's arm. P. Marlowe begins screaming in pain.

Mr. Big beats up Marlowe. And when it's over, Marlowe's lip is split. He is in obvious agony. His face is twisted and marked. He can't talk afterward. Nice going.

The reverse is the problem with violence as portrayed on the TV screen. It never hurts. There is no impact. It's unreal. It's not a deterrent.

Violence on a typical show like *Hunter* doesn't look too bad. It makes me feel more confident about having to take a bullet in, say, the head. And it certainly doesn't sound very bad on *Miami Vice*. Hey, with that music in the background, Rolling Stones in golden oldies from the 1970's, when a car explodes in a fiery ball—well, it beats "Open Up Those Pearly Gates" or the lack of a sound track when one dies in real life.

We still don't know the whole story about the impact of TV violence. For instance, Gary Gilmore didn't watch TV. He went out and killed while he could have been home watching violence shows.

If TV doesn't help, fear is a good deterrent. I don't fight because I wear glasses and I'm phobic about getting pieces of glasses in my eyes. When was the last time anybody saw glasses smashed or contact lenses rammed down the ear canal, in a TV action show?

When a chair hits somebody in real life, half the time it kills them. And doesn't break.

Punches are the most misleading. Boxers slip punches; they turn, twist, catch it on the arms. And they have padded hands. You can punch a wall and put your hand through sheetrock. But when you hit a jaw, you first break your knuckles, chances are.

I don't like the synthetic violence of the private-eye shows. They are beyond belief. I have watched Jim Rockford receive six or eight blows to the stomach, and within seconds he's on his feet, not even breathing hard, and coming back at his assailant. If you've ever been in a serious fight, you know that wouldn't be possible. He'd lie there and hold on to his belly for a while, and the bad guy would kick his face in. That's reality, even in fiction.

If violence is of any redeeming value, it is to make you think badly of it.

Also missing is the emotion. The fear of getting killed is not a factor in most stories, nor is the fear of others getting killed or concern for oneself. But let's start with just *showing* the impact of being hit in the face, the broken teeth or hands. Don Johnson can win the next slugfest. Let him have broken caps after a fight. Let his hands be in a cast.

Why are they afraid to show the effects of violence on the screen, anyway? It will mess up the pretty faces of the actors? "Live by the sword, be defenestrated by the sword," Dumas said in *The Three Musketeers*.

TV should say, "Kids, this is what happens to somebody who punches and gets punched, hit with a bat, or chair."

Feature movies in theaters have gotten gory. Seeing Philip Michael Thomas, Tom Selleck, Fred Dryer, or a gang of outlaws riding away from a barroom brawl with their arms in splints, their mashed knuckles in plaster of Paris, their teeth hanging by the roots and hurting like hell, would do more for the subject than one more report.

A GUIDE TO YOUR BASIC FEARS

Gatophobia is the scientific word for fear of cats. (Don't confuse this with *Katzophobia*, or the fear of Katz, who lives next door.) Television is such a relatively new development that psychiatrists have not yet even gotten around to giving the fear of it a proper name. Obviously, *videophobia* is all wrong.

Names of fears are very important. I believe it was Freud who first said, "Tell me a man's phobia, and I'll tell you what he's afraid of." (See *Eine Kleine Golden Bucher*, by Shlomo Freud, M.S.G., F.C.C., A.T.T.) Leipzig: 1912.

Even though they haven't named it yet, that doesn't mean that people are fearless re: TV. As a pioneer researcher in this field, I have so far isolated and named forty-seven basic fears connected with TV viewing.

None of them may be as basic as staple fears of life, such as the fear of biting down on a piece of aluminum foil, of being knocked down by a taxicab in the street when you don't have clean panties on. (If you're a man and have this fear, you have another problem, I'm afraid.) But they are pretty bad, anyway.

One warning before I go any further: Some people are more susceptible to phobias than others. The saddest cases are those who suffer from *phobophobia*, which has been defined as the fear of getting a phobia even though you may not have one at the moment, the fear of fear itself. As Jung wrote, "This takes the form of a patient sitting in terror and saying to himself, 'Suppose I should be afraid of food. I would starve to death.' Not a very pretty picture, you will agree." (See *Cymbals*, by David Jung, Iowa City: 1988.)

Please stop reading here if you are fear-ridden, or unduly prone to phobias, your own or other people's.

The Forty-Seven Basic Fears of Television Viewing (Digest Version):

- Fear that people are talking about how much TV you are watching lately.
- Fear of falling passionately in love with Barbara Walters.
- Fear of documentaries.
- Fear that the weather report by Willard Scott is *wrong*.
- Fear of Mike Wallace wanting to ask you a question about your last year's income-tax return.
- Fear of not finding the Emmy show to be exciting television.
- Fear of feeling that you have wasted another evening in front of the TV set.
- Fear that you *don't* feel you've wasted an evening.
- Fear of not knowing what happened in last week's installment of *Knots Landing* when your best friends discuss it at a literary cocktail party.
- Fear of not getting the point of the dirty jokes the studio laughs at on Johnny Carson's show.
- Fear of not knowing who Joan Rivers is making fun of, or what's funny about it.
- Fear of standing up in the middle of an episode of *The Jewel in the Crown* on *Masterpiece Theatre* and shouting, "It's BORING." And you couldn't care less that the British lost India.
- Fear that you will overdose on your Anacin, despite using as directed.
- Fear of not understanding what Eric Sevareid was saying in the 1960's, but remembering that it was profound anyway.
- Fear of going into advertising.
- Fear of kissing your TV repairman.
- Fear of being kissed by a TV repairman.
- Fear that Dr. Ruth won't know the answer to your sex question.
- Fear that Dr. Ruth will never have heard of your sexual preference.
- (For academics only) Fear of being asked to appear on a panel-discussion show on public TV.
- Fear of not being asked (also known as "panel envy").
- Fear that the tablet you took is not really working fast, fast, fast.
- Fear that you will see your wife on *The Newlywed Game* with another man.

- (For orphans only) Fear that Joan Collins on *Dynasty* will turn out to be your mother.
- Fear that Martina Navratilova will turn out to be your father.
- Fear that you will never get enough soap operas during the week.
- (For TV producers only) Fear of being asked to make a magazine show at NBC.
- Fear of not remembering any single plot from an Aaron Spelling show.
- Fear of thinking Vanna White is very intellectual.
- Fear of TV networks running out of new ideas for police shows.
- (For New York market only) Fear of being on the train on a cold winter morning, when they've turned on the air conditioning, and you're sitting next to Lloyd Lindsay Young, and he's calling out the stations as you go, "Hello, Rockville Center . . . Hello, Lynbrook . . ."
- Fear that Walter Cronkite will grow long hair and tie it back with a bow.
- Fear that *Simon & Simon* is a Communist show, with Marxist plots.
- Fear of preferring *Wheel of Fortune* to *The MacNeil/Lehrer NewsHour*.
- Fear of falling into a hole in the fourth dimension while watching *Star Trek*, and being lost forever inside the picture tube.
- Fear of having your life story done in a miniseries, with Jack Scalia cast as you.
- Fear of not being a member of a typical American family (as defined by the sociologist Milton Berle: "She makes lousy coffee, and he has deodorant problems.")
- Fear of returning home one night to find your house burned to the ground with the Allstate man standing on the porch with badly burned hands.
- Fear of laughing at homosexual "in"-jokes on the Carson show.
- Fear that the Visitors will seek reprisals after *V*, the series, failed on NBC, starting with a plague of frogs and winding up with President Reagan ripping off his mask during the State of the Union message to reveal that it was Kermit the Frog we elected.
- Fear of the number 13, as in Channel 13, and of becoming unduly fond of pledge drives.
- Fear of making an obscene phone call to Jeane Kirkpatrick one night while she is on the Ted Koppel show.
- Fear of finding the articles about TV celebrities in *People* magazine too heavy.
- Carol Kitman's Special Fear: "That TV is what's real and my life is a fantasy."
- Fear of Fred the Furrier using your wife's name in a TV commercial.
- Fear of an overhead picture falling off the wall and knocking you further unconscious when you've fallen asleep on the couch while watching a rerun of *Brideshead Revisited*.
- Fear your whole life is an episode of *The Twilight Zone*.

And these are only the fears I can write about now. Others are so frightening I can't even think of them.

THE Z-TEAM

Everybody has their own secret favorite rotten show, the one opinion they don't go around broadcasting to the world. They're not especially proud of liking it. I was a closet *A-Team* watcher in the early 1980s. Nobody's perfect.

Was the (rat-tat-tat) *A-Team* violent (boom)? What are you (crash) talking (smash) about? (crashsmashboom)

Once it was a problem. It was on at the same time as *Vietnam*, the multipart, megadocumentary series on public TV. So, it was either *The A-Team* or history. *Vietnam* was a good series. It had a lot of new footage in it I hadn't seen when the war was running on our local news shows. But often when I'd be tired, from a hard day at the office, I found myself picking *The A-Team*.

Violent? It was a hilarious show.

The idea that these five guys—a group of high-tech vigilantes—could be living underground—in L.A.? What a concept. Mr. T taught welding. I never missed Mr. T's weekly welding. I thought he was funny.

I was into Mr. T-ism from the time the show began (February 1983). We had so many things in common. Aside from our good looks, and flair for dress, we shared a fear of flying.

What I tried to do was rationalize it. Look, I'd say to myself, what's the worst thing that can happen when you fly? The plane will crash. I also dwell on the things that can happen to go wrong without a crash. You can get into an auto accident on the way to the airport. You can get mugged in the waiting room. You can trip while boarding the plane. You can starve to death—or worse, overeat that airplane food. or be sterilized by the microwaves from the plane's galley. You can burn your retina by looking at the sun through your window. You can insult a guy bigger than you waiting for a taxi when you get off the plane.

What they used to do for Mr. T's flying problem in the early days of *The A-Team* was hit him with a hammer, shoot him up with tranquilizer darts, and use other psychoanalytically crude methods of dealing with his fear of flying.

But they got more sophisticated. One Tuesday night I noticed they had a new woman member of *The A-Team* who, before they went off on one of their emergency missions, was hypnotizing him. Swinging a watch in front of his eyes. Tick, tock, tick. I'm sure it's effective. It put me to sleep that night. Later, I woke up and thought *The A-Team* was an educational TV show. (More on this in a moment.)

I still remember the first time I saw him, an unadvertised feature on NBC's Super Bowl coverage—the show was premiering immediately afterward—on-camera almost as often as the Washington Redskins. The cameras kept accidentally picking him out of the crowd in the stands. Who could avoid him?

Mr. T, who played Bosco "B. A." (short for Bad Attitude) Baracus, was a remarkable character. He talked tough. He had everybody terrorized. Underneath it all, he was, of course, a pussycat.

Mr. T was garish and in bad taste. He wore too many chains and necklaces: six, when five would do. He had too many rings. But he pulled it off anyway.

His shorts looked ludicrous. Too-long chinos cut at above-the-knee length and untapered. But Mr. T could wear panty hose if he wanted, and it would be okay. By me.

His hairdo was ridiculous. What did he think he was—a British skinhead? How affected can you get?

But Mr. T could do anything he wanted. He was a fashion leader, a style-setter. The man had charisma. Four tons of it.

He was pure TV, a man who did nothing. He had no real talent or entertainment value, except being himself. He was not a singer, juggler, dancer, actor, or newsman. Mr. T became a superstar without a motorcycle. He was, in TV terms, big with no reason for being big. He was Mt. Everest. Great because he was there.

The A-Team—to return to my earlier note—was always an educational program for American youth. It taught them a lot of things about life in its first year. Lewis Deaton, noted TV viewer, was very impressed with the economics lesson in the episode of April 7, 1983.

"The plot centered on the need of the good guys to get their watermelon crop to market through a blockade of bad guys," explained Deaton. "At one point during the show the character on *The A-Team* who used to be Starbuck on *Battlestar Galactica* (Dirk Benedick) called up the watermelon market to find out how much the good guys could expect to rake in for their first crop. The quoted price was, and I'm not kidding: forty dollars a bushel.

"Do they sell watermelons by the bushel in Hollywood and Burbank now? If they do, do those people really pay forty dollars?"

You wouldn't believe the cost of living in Beverly Hills, Mr. Deaton. The gold-chain polish alone would break most of us.

I'm not saying that, as education, *The A-Team* was good or bad. It was just educational, and we had to face it. A whole generation grew up learning something from *Combat*. They learned there was a World War II. And in *Hogan's Heroes* they learned that there were only good or bumbling Nazis, and how it was kind of fun being a prisoner.

I think what *The A-Team* taught this generation is that you can't get hurt from explosives, unless you are involved in contract negotiations and not on the good side of the producers. This is the first of life's valuable lessons: Always be on the producers' side.

The show was morally corrupt, a bad influence on American youth, totally stupid and brainless, and I enjoyed it. It was fun. With some shows, you just put away your brains and turn off your other faculties, and turn it on.

The A-Team was successful in part because a lot of people thought they were watching the news. With all those explosions, people don't know if they are watching news or entertainment. "People think Mr. T is in Beirut," Roger Ailes, media consultant to the stars (Richard Nixon, George Bush, et al.), explained to me. "It makes liberals mad—showing how horrible violence is. Conservatives love it. That's great, they're blasting the hell out of them [whoever 'them' is]." The show probably would have done better if they ran it immediately after the evening news ended at seven-thirty.

Also, it appealed to a sense of decency. "Every so often," a lawyer once told me, "there is a case so clearly unjust, a guy is so clearly a public enemy, the crime so against the public, you don't want to see Miranda, etc., etc., you just want to take a hammer and hit the guy's hands. Like what they did to Paul Newman in *The Hustler*. That's what *The A-Team* does."

Our heroes, the Magnificent Five, were basically criminals. They had broken some law in Nam, vaguely alluded to, having to do with a bank. They were sent to prison for a crime they insisted they didn't commit, broke out, and were now living in the L.A. underground. (L.A. has only an underground, foreground, long shot, close-up, and Glendale.) They made a mockery of justice by eluding the military authorities, who were portrayed as bunglers and nincompoops, bozos who bumped into each other in the pursuit of law and order. A-Team members were flimflam artists and conmen. They lied and cheated, connived, deceived everybody from rental companies (to get airplanes for their adventures) to Third World government officials. All in a good cause.

Basically what you had was the bad good guys (the A-Team) vs. the bad bad guys. What a choice. So, every week, the immoral, corrupt, lawless Nam veterans were heroes for young people watching. As education, it teaches kids that being crooked can be fun and glamorous.

The Lone Ranger! Red Ryder! Come back!

The A-Team had real paragons—a lunatic pilot, for example, an angry black man with a Mohawk hairdo. His major function was to go around scaring white people. Just what black kids need as inspiration.

The A-Team solved its cases. With maximum violence. There was more shooting in the program each week than in the entire Spanish-American War (a show that ran briefly in 1898).

Their specialty in the beginning was making weapons from odds and ends. In the two-hour movie premiere, back in 1983, they converted a school bus into an armored car. This is what I mean by educational.

In the second episode they taught shop: How to make flamethrowers, rockets, and missiles with acetylene tanks and old mattress springs.

In a week or two, I wouldn't have been surprised if the A-Team had demonstrated how to make hydrogen bombs from spare parts in your basement.

The amazing thing about the violence, naturally, is that—again—nobody on the team ever got hurt. They survived thousands of rounds of machine-gun bullets. Their enemies are the worst marksmen since the invention of gunpowder.

A second confession: I'm a nut about violence. I inveigh against Type B. Love Type A. There are different kinds of violence around. Type B is *real violence*, like you see on the TV movies where they show people how to go about committing violent acts, ax murders, hijackings, rapes, step-by-step re-creations, blueprints for the acts they deplore, lest some psycho might not know how to do it. You got this in series like *T. J. Hooker* or *Strike Force*.

And then there is Type A, not serious violence, like the barroom fights in westerns. As with cars, they are kind of a ballet, a choreographed ritual. *The A-Team* often plays in this make-believe category. It's like the violence in video games. Or the Blues Brothers with Jeeps, satirical mayhem, fantasies of little kids exploding toys at F.A.O. Schwarz.

Also characteristic of Type A violence is, as I've said, nobody on the good side (of the producers) is ever hurt in *The A-Team*. NBC *should* win the Nobel Prize—for inventing explosives without pain. Nobel himself, Mr. TNT, would have loved *The A-Team*.

Another point to the show seems to be the destruction of stocks of old Jeeps. They went down like pins in a bowling alley. Does AMC own stock in the show?

I would like to see NBC do *The B-Team, The C-Team*, and so forth. It could be a new way to learn the alphabet, and overtake *Sesame Street*. All starring Mr. T, of course. Until we get to *The T-Team*.

Okay, maybe it's not Shakespeare. But, look, if Grant Tinker, then quality maven at NBC, the quality network, could make his peace with *The A-Team* as quality, who am I to say *dreck*?

Mr. T. did not promise me his used jewelry to write this glowing testimonial. It had more to do with his saying "Be there!"

OTHER LOVES

What I used to love about the old *Mickey Spillane's Mike Hammer*—starring Stacy Keach as a leading example of the detective *policier* in American TV fiction—were the babes. The twenty-four hour-long episodes that ran on CBS in 1984–85 were lavishly decorated. The women were pieces of art who hung around like minor masterpieces in the museum; often, they served no plot purpose other than bending over.

There was an old-fashioned look about the art, too, with their endowments popping out of deep-cut dresses, well-filled blouses, and sweaters. I hadn't seen so much creamy flesh since the Edwardian epics on *Masterpiece Breastworks* on PBS. But this was on *commercial* TV. It was really intense.

Once, you would tune into CBS for the usual action—adventure-escape. The actress-models who dominated TV art were the thin, the scarecrows, the Shelly Hacks and Kim Basingers who preoccupied TV of the early 1980's, the walking ads for anorexia.

And suddenly Mike Hammer had brought back the standards set by Marilyn Monroe. The poor old guys who accidentally tuned into the show for the first time must have thought they had died—and gone to heaven. They had so many different ways to bare their chests in *Mike Hammer*, you had to laugh after a while. But I'm one of those guys who will laugh at anything.

Mike's Angels were what used to be called "a bevy of beauties." The bevy was led by Velda, his secretary, and leg woman. Velda was played by Lindsay (get this name) Bloom, who must have studied acting on *The Dean Martin Show*, and became a member of the noted TV repertory company the Ding-a-Ling Sisters. Velda was a very competent assistant, besides wearing low-cut work clothes of the sort you don't see too much around the office anymore. The setting was the 1950's, remember.

The scripts called for all the women to (as noted) wear low-cut gowns and bend over a lot. "The lady with the torch," as Mike called the Statue of Liberty, was the only one who didn't have her décolletage exposed and remained erect.

You had to love the way they threw themselves at Mike. One even climbed the side of his apartment house in downtown Manhattan to get in to see him. She was a mountain climber. Talk about fantasy. With that chest.

"You poor dear," my wife explained. "You have to watch all that tit-illating stuff."

"All in a day's work," I said, reaching for my cigarette. And I don't even smoke.

I was a sucker for that hard-boiled dialogue. "Now I know why you're so thin, Barrington," he told his nemesis (head of detectives at the NYPD). "You have no heart."

And he did great interior monologues, which every classic detective story features. I'm a sucker for them. "It was raining dead bodies," Keach said one night.

This was Stacy Keach, his mustache and his hat against the criminal element. None of this high-tech, futuristic cars and helicopters-with-computers junk. He was a hard-hitting private eye. He used old-fashioned fists.

Mike Hammer was also a very violent show in other ways—with all the killings. It must be like this on the six o'clock news in El Salvador. After 32.7 people were killed in the premiere, I stopped counting. As Mike himself said, it rained bodies.

They killed them faster than others would kill the lights to watch TV.

And he *was* a violent person. He kicked in doors with his foot. He fought with a cigarette in his mouth. The man was a little light on the social graces. There was an almost-hostile manner about Hammer, which came across when he questioned people, holding them out the window by their throats. But there is violence, and there is Mickey Spillane. His doesn't seem like real violence. One feels, Oh, that's Mickey Spillane. There is a detective-story feel to the violence that does not cross the line. It's fiction. We know it. It's not like the other violence, the illiterate kind.

In the spring of 1980, Aaron Spelling produced a classic example of criminal illiteracy, called *Waikiki*, on ABC. Disco music. High heels running down the streets of Waikiki. Flashing thighs and breasts. Two weirdos in hot pursuit. Sickies. Laughing. Slaps. Screams. The next morning Oahu Police Department cruisers, lights twirling, are in the cane fields. "Was the battered, beautiful body raped before or after she was killed?" one cop asks another. Yes, the Cane-Field Killer had struck again. Cut to waves pounding, dolls in the bikinis parading, stars sailing around the island, palm trees waving in the wind generated by Spelling's flacks.

Waikiki looked like a pilot for a new *Hawaii Five-O*, the most sadistic of TV series. One vicious crime would have been sufficient for the night. But *Waikiki* had five.

Or was it *Starsky & Hutch Go Hawaiian with Gidget*? The two-hour made-for-TV movie starred a pair of p.i.'s (private investigators), played by Dack Rambo and Steve Marachuk. One rode a jeep, the other a motorcycle. That, in TV movies, is character development. Both of them were out-acted by the palm trees, who stole the show.

Or was it *Daughter of Police Woman*? Beautiful cop Cassie Howard, played by Donna Mills, was the pride of the Oahu Police Department. As a cop, she came across as Sergeant Pepper Anderson, as interpreted by Shelly Hack, which made Cheryl Ladd look like Sherlock Holmes. Mills got to dress up in one scene as a hooker, and then to play attempted-rape-in-the-cane-field-with-a-chopper-hovering-over,* a dream role for all TV actresses.

No, it was *Hawaii Five-O* crossbred with *Charlie's Angels, Hawaiian Eye, Surfside Six, 77 Sunset Strip*, and seven other series, all of them combined in one big luau.

At first *Waikiki* seemed like just another night of tie-up-the-blonde at ABC. But this pilot was important, something of significance, pivotal. *Waikiki* was the first of the new wave of violent programming now that ABC was (in 1980) in ratings trouble.

After four years as number one, ABC had been stung and bewildered by the incredible CBS comeback. There was a sense of betrayal by the perfidious public. Dazed and in trouble, the stumbling giant reverted to its roots. It was going to be Ollie Treyz time at ABC again.

Treyz had been chief executive at ABC in the early 1960's, when ABC won its first definable character as the low one. There's cash in trash, Treyz discovered. It was said of him that he made only one hundred thousand dollars a year (in 1962), but he did more to lower the standards of television than many other, higher-paid executives.

Treyz became the sultan of slaughter, the mogul of mayhem. He coined the words *action-adventure* for shows that beatified brutality. His blood and guts spilled out into shows like *Surfside Six, Hawaiian Eye, 77 Sunset*

---

* Like the symbolism?

Strip, *The Roaring Twenties*, and *The Untouchables*. He took the drabness out of TV, as dominated then by the drama and information series like *Omnibus* and *Studio One*, and the various playhouse TV theaters the new guns killed dead.

Sex, violence, and bad acting—the legacy of Ollie Treyz and the 1960's—it was all whacked back again in *Waikiki*.

The latest Spelling "original" for TV was not just your usual repetitive, boring police show. This was the really sadistic stuff. The two rapist-killers were brothers, you see, genuine psychotics, with a . . . well, sibling relationship that of course went unexplored. It turned out that they were chasing girls down the streets to videotape sex acts. Then one of the brothers chokes the girl with a lei.* In case you ever wondered what special function those traditional Hawaiian flower arrangements were to serve.

Spelling, courageously, showed us the choking part. There was also a much shorter clip of the early sex acts (preforeplay).

Porno snuff. Sex creeps and perverts. No more Mr. Quality-TV Nice Guy for ABC. They were playing hardball now.

Waikiki was not vintage Spelling. It made his *Vegas* of the previous year (1979) into Tolstoy. I never loved Spelling. But he had never done anything more gruesome than *Waikiki*. I predicted in my column that it would probably be a big hit.

I was wrong.

---

* Like the pronunciation?

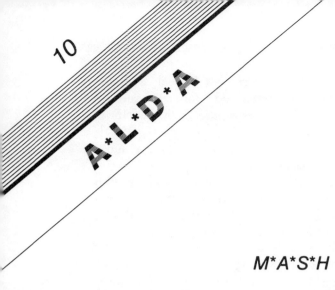

10

M*A*S*H

We're all old soldiers by now, veterans of *M*A*S*H*, the 4077th Mobile Army Surgical Hospital, located somewhere on the Pusan Perimeter, Korea (circa 1949–52). Also located on your dial at CBS (1971–83). We have put in our time in what was really the first "living-room war." It was also the longest war in TV history, eleven years, almost three times as long as the real Korean War. With reruns, it will be right up there with the War of the Roses (the so-called Hundred Years' War) for the title of longest-running (or in this case, longest-sitting) war.

We're noncombatants, of course, private people, first class. They also serve who sit at home and watch. *M*A*S*H* was, for instance, Diana Trilling's favorite show. Also mine. I was especially fond of Captain Benjamin Franklin Pierce, chief surgeon at the 4077th, Hawkeye to millions of us at home. "Dedicated, talented surgeon, court jester, passionate advocate of justice, instigator of endless mischief and puncturer of pomposity," says his official military record. "Part D'Artagnan, part Peter Pan, part Don Juan."

He is also Alan Alda, a beloved actor, a symbol of all that is good in America, the perfect husband, father, handsome, funny, warm, ingratiating, and a great doctor. "If I had to have my gallbladder or something taken out," Mary Schilling, a foundation executive, once explained, "I'd feel a lot better about it if Alan Alda in his bathrobe showed up in the operating room."

Alda, like all the characters in *M*A*S*H*, is a member of our family, everybody's family. TV shows coming into the house every week make of the characters an extended family. Even more than beloved. They leave at the end of the half hour.

Alan Alda, as it happens, is also my friend and neighbor. I've known him since 1964, when he was like the rest of us, a nobody. It's hard to believe that he was ever a struggling actor in New York with a gift for political satire, a Second City comic-actor-type guy, who could do a William F. Buckley, Jr., that was withering and much funnier than the original. Before that, he was into odd jobs. He used to tell us about his career, in which he eventually rose to the rank of doorman at the Forum of the Twelve Caesars, before being promoted to driving one of the cabs he used to summon. He must have been one of the most charming cabbies in New York, not that it's much of a contest.

I never let his success in Hollywood go to my head.

In the beginning of *M*A*S*H*, he used to fly home every weekend from the Coast. It was his way of keeping his feats on the ground, touching home base, being with real people. Hawkeye would fly in on the Red Eye on Saturday mornings and fly back Sunday nights. Jet lag was his middle name.

My wife and I, who lived a couple of blocks away, were in the inner circle when he came back East. It consisted of the town doctor, a population expert at the UN, a psychiatrist, a painter, a couple of musicians and photographers (Arlene Alda, his wife, had been a clarinetist with the Houston Symphony and is a fine photographer). They had live chamber-music recitals in their living room. Or we would sit around in the suburbs talking about which kid was sick, who fixed roofs well, how bad the schools were, my super backhand. We never discussed the really important things in life, such as what Hot Lips was really like.

None of his friends traded wisecracks with Alan. He seemed to get enough of that on the other coast. Alan loved to discuss feelings. When he asked, "How are you?" *he really wanted to know.* He was that sort of person. "Sick," I used to say privately to my wife. "That's his *shtick*— being nice."

He was, of course, a serious person inside. That's why he never understood why editors always wanted pictures of him smiling. "I can laugh because I allow myself to be serious," he once said. He enjoyed most talking about what he feels strongly about, which is most things he talked about. He had a personal antipathy to war, which wouldn't surprise anyone who ever saw *M*A*S*H*, which he came to write and direct. He talked about women's rights, science and metaphysics, religion, diets, vital signs. Alda had all the theories he had read in books and magazines on the airplane. He was well flown. Smart, articulate, compassionate, the antithesis of the actor who is only "into" himself.

We never talked much about *M*A*S*H*, either, which was just as well. It would have created problems in my work as the nation's number-one TV critic. (At that time, I was only number thirty-four.) Knowing me was probably a strain on him, too. He didn't talk about my newspaper, or its editorial policy. We had sort of an unwritten rule: "You don't talk about M*A*S*H, and I won't talk about how great you are."

I just never brought it up. Maybe I should have asked what Hot Lips was really like. Maybe he was dying to tell me. You never know. But that's what friends are for.

When the show began in 1971, I wrote something noncommittal like "It will never last. It is too good, too honest, too real, and too funny for TV." So, I was off by eleven seasons . . .

Every time I wrote about Hawkeye, or, as he was known familiarly around the paper, "your friend Alan Alda," I had to explain my special relationship as a disclaimer. As if it were my brother, Lucky Luciano. It was resolved by not writing about his many achievements. As I say, he managed to succeed anyway.

But I watched his show quietly over the years, like an ordinary viewer.

M*A*S*H was a wonderful program, less about war than about loving people who care for each other. It was an amazing piece of artistry. Week after week, it told about men dying or maimed in a far-off place in a war with issues unclear. It cut close to the bone, often too close. You'd come for laughs, get them, and get something to think about. It raised issues of morality and the insanity of living and dying. Whatever happened to good, old-fashioned, mindless entertainment? I used to think.

M*A*S*H was an unusual experience for the viewing audience: You'd keep watching it week after week to have a good time, share a laugh with these people you loved. And then, often you'd wind up feeling kind of down. M*A*S*H night was kind of a secret national downer. We hear a lot about the Nielsen ratings. But what about the suicide rates on the nights M*A*S*H was on? I'll bet they increased, too.

But we didn't complain about the quiet, secret depression that went with the joys of M*A*S*H. You had to be a traitor to say a bad word about it. (In all the years I think I received only one letter, from a doctor, which discussed M*A*S*H in negative terms.) If you felt a little bad— hell, this was war.

M*A*S*H was also a kind of us and them situation. We watched other sitcoms and thought, What does this fluff, this contrived scene or that, have to do with us? That's sitcom. That's them. In M*A*S*H, it was always us. All of us—writers, performers, viewers, society—we're all together looking to laugh about war. You couldn't do much else about the insanity of the situation, about the way governments do things. The Korean War still lay unresolved in the national conscience. What was THAT all about, anyway? All the issues we (or our brothers and fathers) fought and died for in Korea, what did they resolve? It didn't stop Vietnam. The real purpose of the war may have been to make possible a TV show called M*A*S*H. That was something, at least.

The series used to upset me psychologically. "We don't show the wounded screaming in pain," I remember Alda saying on the TV documentary *The Making of M*A*S*H*. Right. Underneath the show I always felt I was not hearing something, as if one part of reality were turned down, as if there were a reality knob on the TV set.

"You have to be willing to be funny and let the pain come through," Alda said. "But the pain came through after the laughs. It's hard enough to write good jokes, hard to get them to feel something. You risk failure by trying to capture the ambiguity of war."

But there were ambiguities, artful ones. On the one hand, M*A*S*H was very funny . . . Alan cracked me up doing his Groucho Marx on the Pusan Perimeter . . . and the next minute he could have me on the point of tears. This was something different for TV. It was the ambiguity of the situation. We were used to simpleminded war comedies. Being a prisoner in a POW camp in Germany in World War II (*Hogan's Heroes*) was slapstick.

It was fascinating to see how M*A*S*H dealt with the ambiguity week after week—the things that demanded answers, when there were none. The show always grappled with the ambiguities of right and wrong. It was great not because it gave answers, but because it acknowledged the problems.

Nobody was entirely heroic in M*A*S*H, even though they were all heroes in their way, sometimes stupidly heroic. They all had their flaws. The ambiguity of the characters and issues made M*A*S*H.

Alan Alda later told me, "It takes a lot of trouble, dealing with ambiguity. You can't go home at six. It's hard to write jokes that make you laugh and feel pain at the end."

The thing about M*A*S*H is that it was fatalistic and hopeful at the same time. "Nihilism is not realistic," Alan said. "We wouldn't have survived this long if we didn't have hope in it for people. It's the hope that made us last so long."

For eleven years M*A*S*H picked its way through the minefields of human emotions. Miraculously, it survived and flourished and became part of the national consciousness. "There are people enjoying and understanding M*A*S*H," Alan once said, "who weren't even *born* when it started. It was a show that grew in importance all the time." "It was to TV," my friend Michael Bouton, seventeen, once explained, "what the Beatles were to music."

And on February 28, 1983, a memorable event was to take place. *M*A*S*H* was ending. They were going to bring the conflict to a conclusion on TV, finally. You had to be careful about how you ended *M*A*S*H*. You could make people sorry the Korean War was over.

It occurred to me then that with the war about to become ancient history, I could scrap the nonintervention pact with its star. I could talk about the *M*A*S*H* experience we had both been having without compromising the friendship. Alan hadn't been back East much lately. In the last few years he had been going directly from the *M*A*S*H* shootings to work on his movies (*The Four Seasons*). I decided to fly out to visit him for the first time in his other life in California.

I found him sitting in the trenches at 20th Century-Fox two days before the final episode of *M*A*S*H* was to begin. This was it, what it had all been leading up to, quintessential *M*A*S*H*, the *1812 Overture* by Tchaikovsky, the "Ode to Joy" of Beethoven's Ninth Symphony (maybe both), four times as long as the usual episode, a two-hour TV movie. It would cost four times as much to produce, have more production values, which in California means being outdoors more. They would be making, in effect, a whole movie in four weeks in November: Usually they do a feature in nine weeks. The script, which was to answer all the questions, tie up all the loose ends of eleven years, was written by Alan (in conjunction with Burt Metcalfe, John Rappaport, Thad Mumford and Dan Wilcox, David Pollock and Elias Davis, and Karen Hall). He was also to direct the movie.

Alan is one of the leading hyphenates, as multifaceted people in TV are called. He is an actor-writer-director, with Emmy nominations in all three categories. That's like a newspaperman getting Pulitzer Prizes as editor, writer, and delivery-truck driver. Up against the best talent in Hollywood, he wins as writer and director as well as actor. And he's a nice person, yet. "With all that talent," a Fox executive explained, "he could be the meanest sonofabitch."

Alan was delighted with the pressure of doing the final movie while working on the *M*A*S*H* episodes for the current season. "It's like doing a high-wire act," he explained, "before the other end of the wire is tied down." He was excited about directing. He is the one who orders the actors and moves the equipment and makes the decisions. It's a chance to cause something to emerge from scratch. Literally. "I draw it on paper with stick figures. Here's the way I want it. Then the storyboards come back my way." He is thinking of setups all the time. There are 7 takes per page, 128 pages; it could take 6 months to shoot. He is dreaming of

ways to speed things up. The hundreds of details are like organizing a
military invasion. He loves to organize things. It's like playing a game or
running an army. It's a chance to be a general. This is the serious side
of my friend Alan. He has two serious sides, at least.

I wasn't allowed to talk about, or sit in on production meetings for, the
big final-episode movie itself. This was for my own good. Speculation
about what was to happen in the last episode was rife. Already, in September, offers for a copy of the script were at twenty-five-hundred dollars—the opening bid and asked price in the attempt to break security.
Script distribution was tightly limited and controlled.

A veil of secrecy had been imposed on the movie production, a press
embargo. Alan had insisted on the no-press rule himself. It wouldn't look
good if he had a friend snooping around.

"We are being extremely careful about the story, taking a whole month
to shoot it," Alan explained. "Everybody wants to know what's in the last
show. Viewers are sending in advice about what should be in." Alan said
about one letter, " 'First of all, there should be lots of crying.' Everybody
is taking the whole thing out of proportion, like *Dallas*. We don't have
any big secrets to tell, like 'We didn't shoot J.R.' It's a simple story. It's
just that we don't want it to be out all over. We don't want the actual
episode, when it gets on the air, to play like a rerun. We want it to be
fresh for the audience. So we're going incommunicado for a month."

The secrecy didn't hurt the cost of commercials. Advertisers were paying a record rate to be in the final show. The audience was expected to
be close to 100 percent. Many groups were using the final show as fund-
raising events/screenings, Red Cross blood drives, and the like. "I'm
scared," Alan said. "I can see hundreds of Nielsen families will be out at
fund-raisers for *M*A*S*H*. Who'll be home to watch?"

"Can't they say," remarked Burt Metcalfe, the producer, "they gave
at the office?"

It would be the biggest thing since V-J Day. I was happy to be in
California before the rice curtain came down.

The 20th Century-Fox lot, where *M*A*S*H* was made, is a very unreal
place. You drive into the studio gate past the Third Avenue El, a section
of which is standing. You expect to encounter Joan Blondell waiting for
a train. You look down the old streets around the El and think that you
see your parents as young people, walking out of movies long past.

Alan told Carol and me to meet him at 8:00 A.M. in Dressing Room A,
the corner of Tennessee Avenue between Avenues B and C, Aldaville at
Fox. It's got a terrific view of the parking lot. Carol and I are early,
drinking up the atmosphere like coffee-to-go. Sitting on the steps in front

of parking spaces 2018: A ALDA; 2017: M FARRELL; 2016: L SWIT. Mike Farrell drives up in his VW van. We tell him we're waiting for Alan. "Is he making the newspapers again?" Farrell says. "Oh, boy." Switt's Mercedes bumper sticker reads HAND GUNS: WE CAN LIVE WITHOUT THEM. Parking space 2015: W CHRISTOPHER. Mercedes diesel. Alan drives up in his Mercedes, blue to match his eyes (my wife explained). They also have a brown one (to match Arlene's). He turned off the radio. "This is nice. They're playing Scarlatti all morning." He listens regularly to classical music on the radio. He is smiling early in his fashionable unpressed fatigues.

Alan looks thinner than the last time I saw him at home. Dieting for the big movie. "I don't want to look fat for the reruns." He is on some cockamamie diet: no salt, pepper, bioflavins, food. The rules seem silly. Like BT and mayo—hold the B and T and mayo, serve the bread—which he doesn't eat because it's fattening. He doesn't drink coffee or tea, but hot water. Caffeine? The coffee makes him nervous. But the tea has tannin, and stains his teeth. That's show biz.

Alan's dressing room was formerly the child actors' classroom on the Fox lot. He has a lot of books on the table. *Traumatic War Neurosis. Medical Studies U.S. Merchant Marine, Jan. 28, 1943. Gray's Anatomy. Korea: The Untold Story* by Joseph H. Gordon. *Abnormal Psychology: Experiences, Origins, and Interpretations*, Goldstein, Baker, Johnson. There are bird pictures on the wall, English sparrows, by Arlene. Otherwise the room hasn't changed since 1929. The end of the tenth year, Alan asked if they'd take down one wall. "We were all standing up for conferences." He is not one of the stars who asks for things.

We start to talk about war experiences in the real Korean War. I had been in college for six years (1947–53), I explained. "Majoring in draft dodging."

"One of the Brooklyn Dodgers?" Alan asked.

A draft notice after the peace talks started at Panmunjom finally arrived: a graduation present. They would never draft me, I thought. I wore glasses, was very nearsighted. The sergeant told me, "Don't worry, you'll be able to see everything, even with your eyes. We need people at the front this week."

Alan had been in the ROTC at Fordham. He served for six months as an officer. The peace talks were in their fifth year by the time he got into the army. He served with more distinction than I did: They didn't drag him in kicking and screaming.

With Alan in his *M*A*S*H* fatigues, looking as if he had just walked out of a TV set, we were like two old soldiers, chewing over what we did in the TV war.

"Do you realize I've spent one quarter of my life already doing *M*A*S*H*? That's incredible. How have I changed? I'll tell you how I've changed. When it began, I could read the dog tags at the length of this chain. Now I have to bring them closer to my eyes, like this." He pulls the dog tags nervously as he talks, the way we used to do reflexively in the army.

I look at the names. "They're real dog tags," he says. "Hersie Davenport, Texarkana, Arkansas . . . Morriss D. Levine, Brooklyn, New York." From the first day of the show he has worn the same ones. "Mike Farrell gave us new dog tags with our own names on it. Wanted me to wear them, but I wouldn't. This is the real thing. Do you know what that notch is? Yep. When you're dead they put the tags between your teeth."

Your lucky dog tags? "Don't be ridiculous," he says. "I'm not superstitious. I just don't want to change them." He wonders how the next of kin (Marcie Levine, 545 Riverside Avenue, Brooklyn, N.Y.) would feel knowing their loved ones' dog tags have been on TV all these years. He doesn't know whether he should try to tell them. I think they would be proud. They hadn't died in vain.

"*H* is for what?" Alan muses. "*Hebrew*? *P* is for *pothead*? No, *Protestant*." That's the irreverent side of Alan, the side he doesn't let out much in public. He subdues his barbed, satirical, Swiftian side.

He is putting on his combat boots, lacing them up to go out to the set. "Worn the same pair for eleven years," he explains. "The tongue is falling out."

It's a good thing he's not superstitious. "They're not my lucky boots," he explains. "It's just that I didn't want to change them."

"I didn't have any milk this morning," he tells my wife. He had had a frog in his throat for the past month. She thought it could be mucus formed from milk. They always exchange mumbo-jumbo theories. They were born in the same quarter or house of the moon. They both have the same cold pinkie (Raynaud's disease) and poor blood circulation. He is an incredible hypochon—I mean, scientifically minded person, about physiology and food and biorhythms, always taking his own pulse.

We are walking across the lot to the set, and a car pulls up. A few words are exchanged. "Just before you said your name I knew it was you, Tom." He is such a nice guy he won't admit he doesn't remember a name. Tom is an actor reading for a part in the movie. It's either Truman or MacArthur. I try not to hear.

"I remember driving along this street at this corner eleven years ago," he says, "thinking I'd like to be able to come here every day to work. It would be like an artist coming to the studio. I'd be able to invent new things for a part. Wouldn't it be fun, I remember thinking, the joy of being able to get better at a job."

We cross over to Stage 9, where the *M*A*S*H* set is located. "They gave us one of the smallest sets on the lot. They expected us to fail. The show was always out of kilter because of this. We had a stepchild feeling. We had to shoot the larger scenes at the 20th Century-Fox ranch. No room for us here. They gave the big studio to *Anna and the King of Siam*. That was Fox's big show that year on CBS. Old school Thai.

"Here we are in the mess hall," he explains as we enter the darkened studio and he picks up the day's script changes in the mailbox. The mess hall. I knew it right away. I recognized it from the pictures on TV. It took me about five seconds to accept the reality of this fake place.

Alan is like the stage manager in *Our Town* as he walks me through the 4077th, our unit in our war. It's a weird experience, like being in and out of a dream, out of TV programs, bits and pieces of sets, coming to life with the stars as characters coming into and out of focus, like a cross section of the TV viewer's mind.

The officers' mess tent. The swamp. Pre-op. O.R. The showers. The colonel's office where Radar had cranked the phone to get on the horn to I-Corps to make those deals. The generator that was always breaking down in the middle of operations. The street post with all the distances (TOLEDO, 8,765 MI.) The nurses' tent. They were three-sided rooms so the cameras could get in. But it didn't matter. I had operated, fought, laughed, loved, and died with these people . . . characters. It meant something. And I was just a relatively casual observer, a dilettante. I mean, I wasn't one of those viewers who watched *M*A*S*H* three times a night (five if you had cable in your market).

The *M*A*S*H* set was like visiting a shrine, like visiting the real battlefield at Gettysburg. It occurred to me that instead of striking the set in February, Fox should run tours through the battlefield. Or turn it over to the national parks people at the Department of the Interior and run it like Gettysburg. People would pay four, five, six dollars, whatever they pay for a movie these days, to see all of this—live.

An amazing thing happens on this set. You don't even have to shut your eyes to think you are really in Korea. Any minute I expected to see Radar or Klinger walking along with his clipboard. This *is* Korea. Such is the power of TV, realer than reality. And the best thing about the tour is that nobody gets hurt. Nobody is screaming from the pain of stepping on land mines, nobody is being hit by shrapnel from mortars, nobody wakes up terrified by the Chinese bugles before having their throats slit in sleeping bags. And we all get to go home, not in a box, but when the tour is over.

It's about 9:00 A.M. But it's nighttime in this Korea. The yellow street-light is burning. As we're walking along the street, Hawkeye in his bathrobe, I'm pinching myself. A few minutes ago, it was the Third Avenue El in the 1930's, and a hundred yards away there are palm trees on Pico Boulevard, Los Angeles, 1983, now I'm in Korea, 1952. Circles of reality within reality. It's like Alan in Wonderland, falling into the hole with him.

We are trudging down the road, the two old soldiers ransacking our memories, each in his own way. I kick at the dirt. "We used to have real dirt on the ground," Alan explains. "It made it seem realistic. There were always clouds of dust in the studio. Gene Reynolds [the first producer] had a dust allergy. There was dirt in the nose all the time. Gene said, 'I can't breathe. Build a special rubber road that looks like the real thing.' Now it's shiny all the time. It looks like mud and photographs better."

You could almost feel it squish in your boots as we walked over to makeup, on the fringe of the set, talking about how Fox is reacting to the end of the war, this war, the televised war. "They're going to make me change my name after the show is over. They get the rights to *Alda*. But they let me keep the clothes," he chuckles. "They think Alda is a character. They want to merchandise the name."

He warns the makeup man, "Don't say anything, he's writing an article." Alan looks over the three or four pages of script as the fellow makes him up to look haggard and drawn. They have to paint in his beard with pencil. He is such a nice guy, even his beard will not grow in stubbly-looking for the cameras. It's like pointillism as the makeup man applies dots to the face, black measles, giving him that drawn look we see every Monday night.

"These are my friends," Alan says as he watches Mike Farrell approach from the corner of his eye, past the crow's-foot. "Be careful. You're going to do my chin like *that*?" Alan says to the makeup man. "Wait a minute," Mike says, "I'll fix that." He winds up as if to punch Alan out.

"He's writing down every stupid thing you say," Alan says.

Sitting in the makeup chair while talking, Alan hears with a third ear. He is also a creative consultant on the show, to go with his other hyphenates. He hears the scene Klinger and Father Mulcahy are doing in Colonel Potter's office. It's about a race that Klinger is staging illicitly and betting on. Alan is talking to us, memorizing his script, and listening to the other scene anyway. Like an Indian in the forest. He can hear a twig break at a hundred yards. Or a line.

"It needs something at the end," he calls out to Mulcahy and Klinger. "It stops dead." Klinger's last line on the phone to the bookmaker at I-Corps is "All bets are off." They're going to freeze-frame. Alan says, "Say instead, 'What do you mean? It's too late?' " They do it that way. It gets a laugh. And Alan is listening, smiling, and still has time to explain to me, "I'm functioning in my other capacity, as a 'creative consultant.' If I was to suggest a real change in the dialogue, I'd call the writers and tell them." They have respect here for writers, unlike other TV situations. That started with scripts by Larry Gelbart, the legendary co-creator and major writer of the show in the early years. "We never changed a syllable of Gelbart's. I remember watching the rushes with Gelbart once in the first year. 'What did you say that for?' Gelbart asked one of the actors. 'It was written that way,' the actor explained. 'But that was a *typo* in the script,' Gelbart said."

Chuck Panama, the Fox P.R. man, is nervously following us around. "Alan never spends more than ten minutes with anybody anymore," he explains. "We've got a sheaf of requests for interviews, everybody from *Sixty Minutes* to the *Daily Bruin*." "That's my alma mater," Metcalfe says.

Alan and I continue slogging our way through the rubber mud on the set. "The thing I remember most, the best moment in the last eleven years?" Alan says. "I'm sorry. There weren't any. Is it too late for you to get a plane back? It's not easy answering seven thousand questions the same way.

"Let me tell you what this place really means to me. The experiences in the show were very similar to life. We didn't have actual blood, we had psychic blood. There actually were rats in the studio, like at the front. The mattresses have lice in them. In the summer it's sweltering here. Air conditioning is not effective. The light eats up the oxygen. We had to think in some of the same emotional conditions as a MASH unit. In the same way we had to learn to live together. . . . It was like a Pirandello play, doing these shows. You don't really know what's real and what isn't.

"Every square inch of this place has a meaning attached to it. This is the motor pool," Alan says, extending our tour back into time, down the hole. "This is where I learn my lines. Somebody seems to have stolen my chair." There is a series of six yellow director's chairs, with names of the stars stenciled on back. It's a ritual sitting in your own chair. He doesn't want to sit down in another chair. "It's our meditation center. Once they took our names off. It was terrible, a real identity crisis. Marty," he calls out, "where's my chair?"

Father Mulcahy comes and whispers something. "Do something from the distant past," Alan says. "Oh, that means last week," Christopher says. He spills coffee on his hand. "Are you supposed to call for a medic?" I ask. "Or a priest," he says.

Marty Lowenstein, whom Alan calls "Mr. Lowenbrau," has found the chair, and Alan is underlining his script. "That's my internal peak. Why don't you be Loretta," he says offering me her chair. It's like the three little bears.

"Hi, I'm Mike Farrell," Farrell says, walking past.

"No, it won't work," Alan says. "This says you're B. J. Hunnicut.

"I hear you're running for the Politburo," Alan calls after him. "I kid him all the time," he says of Mike's penchant for social-action causes. It must have been like this with the Three Stooges. B.J. and Hawkeye lurk behind them as they walk from scene to scene, each ready to trip the other while he is deeply absorbed in learning lines.

I wander over to the swamp, the home of the famous martini still, where Alan has done some of his best acting as a man who is truly dedicated to the grape or the potato. The truth is Alan is not what I would call a real drinker. When he comes over for cocktails at home, I ask what he wants to drink. "Oh, anything that will slur my tongue," he says. At the height of the madness while making *The Four Seasons* and *M*A*S*H* simultaneously, he was, I noticed, hitting the bottle heavily, having two glasses of wine instead of one. Such an irony. You would think his real family name was Martini instead of D'Abruzzo. They're even selling 4077th *M*A*S*H* vodka, the bedside stand, twenty-five dollars a bottle, because Alan's endorsement on the shows makes those lab-still martinis sound so luscious.

We walk along past the painted mountains on the horizon. I've seen the sun setting on that horizon a hundred times on the show. "When I get tired [in the show]," Alan says, "I like to come out here and look at the view. It cheers me up. The funny thing is I get so tired sometimes it *really* cheers me up.

"We've done two hundred fifty shows," he says. "Two hundred sixty-seven," Metcalfe, the producer, interrupts. That is amazing, seventeen shows missing in his mind.

"He's brain damaged," B.J. says. "We're running a benefit for him."

The names of the shows, the titles, aren't clear to Alan, either, or the seasons. Like TV viewers' remembrances, too, they all run together on one tape, 250 or 267 shows long. All three periods of the show merge in and out of the consciousness: the old (with Alda, Wayne Rogers, McLean Stevenson, Larry Linville, and Loretta Swit as a sex symbol), the in-between (Alda, Farrell, Morgan) and the new (David Ogden Stiers and the new, improved, serious Major Houlihan).

"I remember the small things about the eleven years. By this bed here." We're standing in post-op. "I remember shooting a scene from 'Point of View.' I was trying to get a four o'clock plane out to go home. One of the kids was having a birthday party in New Jersey. I was so concerned getting the scene right, yet it was closer and closer to flight time . . . I'm not even aware of the story anymore. Just the rushing to get the plane.

"This is where we did the tray scam on Loretta. It was based on something that really happened when I was in the army. You had to sign for trays. But nobody ever had the number of trays they signed for. You pass on the shortage to the next guy who signs. The creativity is in the counting. Major Houlihan is a stickler. She wanted us to have the exact number. So we're passing them around and under and over as Loretta is counting."

"Which show was that?" I ask.

"It's best known here as 'The One About the Trays.' "

We're tramping along between the swamp, the showers, and the mess hall. In the road I keep my eyes out for jeeps. I don't want to get a purple heart.

We're outside the swamp, near the showers. "I remember the day after wrapping up production of the pilot of We'll Get By [a CBS series he did for one season—1975—moonlighting from M*A*S*H], I was so happy. I remember drinking a bottle of champagne all by myself way into the night. Next morning, fortunately, I was playing Pierce hung over in the swamp. I went over here in the bushes during a scene and really threw up.

"Here, I remember the time I got a brand-new bike. I used to ride around in the road to get some fresh air. Oxygen from all the trees painted on the set. You look at the false bushes for buds and signs of spring. It was a nice blue Schwinn, three-speed. I was really attached to it.

"And here is where Mike Farrell hung it in the rafters once."

A new woman working on the set once said, after spending a day observing all of the weird things the cast does to each other in such a rapid-fire parade, "These people are crazy, what are they doing?"

"We keep a level of looniness," Burt Metcalfe said. "The pressure of the show, doing it week after week, builds. After one season, it's something. Can you imagine what it's like after eleven years?" Alan says that on movie sets it's always quiet. Here it sounds crazy and chaotic. People are lying on the floor, everything.

The tour stops. Alan has to appear in a short scene: He trips over a sandbag. "You deliberately put it there so you'd trip yourself," Loretta, Christopher, and Farrell all charge.

"The premise of M*A*S*H is the crazy behavior of the people in crazy situations. They had to let it out in some way," Metcalfe says. "As . . . in Korea, when the job had to be done, it was done. They stop horsing around to make the show."

We're standing in the road near the Red Cross box, which reminds Alan of a scene he played with Alan Arbus, Colonel Friedman, the psychiatrist. He was always good.

"I remember when this place was covered with snow, covering the windshield of the jeep." We're standing in the area between the mess hall and the swamp. "I was directing. They thought I was dead. It was the show 'The Late Captain Pierce.' My best friend had died on the operating table. He was the first one to die in the show, a sad moment.

"And this is where we first heard about the death of Henry." ("Abyssinia, Henry.")

"That was also very upsetting at home," I said. It was as if a real person had died. They could have had a funeral for Colonel Blake at Arlington National Cemetery, and the nation would have attended.

"The problem with that was the way it happened," Alan said, "in the final scene. It was the last show of the season. They weren't able to talk about it on the show until the next season. It hit you at the very end. Even in the most harrowing Greek tragedies, at the end they give the audience something to relax the tensions, the sense of tragedy. Henry's death was so explosive because it came at the end and was so unexpected.

"People reacted so deeply to Blake's death. It stayed with them. If he had a sickness and died, it would have been a moment of mourning, and let it go. This was like the end that would come in war. It's almost as hard for the audience to take in TV as in life."

We sat on a box along the road. Hallowed ground. "That was Gelbart's idea. He told me ahead of time that Henry was going to die. I was the only one in the cast who knew. Everybody was stunned, nobody more than McLean. The others found out a few minutes before they did the scene."

People said at the time, I reminded Alan, that somebody wanted to get even with Stevenson. He wanted to leave the series, as he kept saying on all the talk shows, he wanted to further his own career. Well, then they would show him, make sure he could never come back to M*A*S*H. That was good-bye—with a vengeance!

"It didn't seem he would want to come back," Alan says. "NBC was committed to a million-dollar series for him. Blake come back? We wouldn't ever have done that. They also said that when Radar went home. Have Radar re-up? It wouldn't be realistic. When you leave in a war, you don't see them again. It's not real. And you certainly don't come back to the same outfit, anyway . . . it's not summer camp, where you return as a junior counselor after putting in your time as a camper."

Then we were in the mess tent. "Did you ever really eat anything here?" "No," he laughs, "I'm remembering now how Wayne and I used to send out for Chinese food. We loved Szechuan. We'd run out sometimes for an hour or send in. Then I started gaining weight. I'm filtering out a million memories here. In the sneezing show it wasn't going right. I remember Alan Arbus and I stayed over three hours after the others left. We made changes till I had the scenes constructed right."

We were standing in the corner in back of the swamp. "This reminds me of the time Mike jumped out of the tent just before the tank crashed into it. It was back at the ranch. A tank was bearing down on us. The rest of us ran out of the swamp early, as planned. Mike waits until the tank is three feet away before catapulting out. Gene Reynolds was a little upset. 'Another few seconds, you'd have been a toad in the road!' he was yelling. Mike is an athlete, likes to show off. I'm kidding. But the tank coming down and Mike going out the screen door in one shot, it really was a great scene.

"And here is where I got my first Emmy. You know, it sometimes looks like the only thing I remember or liked are things that I wrote or directed or won an award for. I apologize." We were standing by Radar's bed (now Klinger's) in Colonel Potter's office. "I remember sitting on the floor here with Mike in the show that Radar goes home. Mike gets drunk, hates the war. He was wonderful . . . He should have gotten an Emmy for *that*.

"I was the officer of the day in one show, stayed in Potter's office at night. Radar has to pull his pants down to get into his pajamas for bed. The only thing is, Radar *really* got embarrassed. He got the giggly fits. Had to do twenty takes. It was a very funny show.

"And over here is where I watched the rat come out of this vent and go into that one. I'm there keeping my feet off the floor. The little rat used to eat the flowers in the bushes, round the edges, and after lunch, would run back in.

"Over here I always remember David Hawkes's [the assistant director] voice. I was directing, I think, Mulcahy. See, we have three pages of script left, and that usually takes an hour. Only we have a half hour left. When you have to get it, everything goes fast, the lighting, the acting. Otherwise in the morning you can take an hour to get to one page.

"And this is where the old stage floor used to squeak outside the O.R. whenever I tried to get a beautiful, tricky dolly shot. The scene plays great, but the floor squeaks.

"That's the scrub room." We were walking past a space filled with boxes and storage crates. Empty spaces are dressed up for shots. "Now you have to imagine." I can. "This is the hallway outside the O.R. This is the O.R. The first time in the operating room I can still remember I was learning, making bad mistakes. Like I was going from one wound to another without changing gloves. But now I know. I would never do that. We have a nurse on the set, doctors reading scripts so we are always authentic, changing diagnosis or treatment.

"We just lost Connie Izzay, a nurse who was advising us on everything that affected nursing. She wanted to show nursing presented accurately, a very nice woman. We're going to dedicate one of the shows to her this season. We never did that before. It's a very touching show in which a nurse dies. We got the idea from looking at the photos in her belongings, going through Connie's effects after she died. Just like in war. She was in very bad health, in her seventies. She didn't have any family. It was amazing looking into the box. She had been an actress in the 1920's. I think this was Jamie's idea. Wouldn't it be interesting going over the effects of a nurse who died? We realize we have touched her in life, and her death touched all of us."

Standing in the O.R., I found myself dreading the PA system announcing "incoming wounded," the chopper landing, everybody running toward the stretchers. I'd have to operate.

"By and large, the show was praised by medical journals," Alan was saying. "We tried to be accurate to the period of medicine. Some tricky procedures were very difficult to do, like chest massages on live persons without cracking their ribs or stopping their heart circulation."

"What do you use for blood?"

"That was a shame," Alan said. I had opened a wound. "The blood used to be good in the beginning. Now, it's lousy."

"Not ketchup?"

"No, in the first place, it smells like garbage. Under the hot light for eight or ten hours. We do use something made out of food now, Karo syrup and something else. But it's terrible. Our fingers stick together. The instruments stick to the gauze. But it's washable when it gets on the uniforms. That's the big thing. We keep trying to get the right new blood. 3-M used to make good blood. But they stopped making it. Can't find their formula. We keep experimenting, shampoos, hand lotions, hair conditioner. And they keep foaming up."

We are moving around the operating tables in the O.R. "And this is where we did the first show without the laugh track."

"It's one of the worst things about the show," I told Alan. You can be watching a show, and all of sudden there is a burst of laughter. Are the North Koreans supposed to be in the bushes outside laughing?

"The laugh track is an example of the prehistoric thinking of the network," Alan says. "They believe in laugh tracks. We had an agreement with networks. There would be no laugh track in the O.R. So Gelbart cleverly got the idea to do a show totally in the O.R. I think it was 'Mail Call.' No, 'Bulletin Board.' "

The most famous *M*A*S*H* show of all was "The Interview." An Ed Murrowlike reporter interviews soldiers. That was the one in which Hawkeye is asked what is the worst thing about the war. "Everything painted green," he says, the clothes, the sky, the food. "Everything is green except the blood, which is red." There was no laugh track in "The Interview." As in the actual war, Gelbart explained.

*M*A*S*H*'s laugh track was a close second to a show called *Ripping Yarns* (with Michael Palin) as the worst. Subdued, like the recorded voice from a funeral parlor laughing over the death of some dear friend.

"And this is the famous rehearsal table," Alan explains, "where we read the scripts and make suggestions starting at twelve-thirty on rehearsal days. We rehearse one day and shoot three or four. Fox didn't like that. 'Nanny and the Professor used to shoot two days without rehearsal,' they said. 'Well?' I said.

"Then on Fridays we use the table for a party. I send out for drinks and pizza for the cast and crew. I added the pizza after a couple of years.

"Starting with the first show, we'd sit here for hours, from seven to ten P.M., bellyaching about what's wrong with the show, the network, each other, what we're expecting and not getting. It helped us to respect each other, even though we're very different personalities. If people had disgruntlements, they could always find an hour to talk about it. It saved us. It made it possible to work under these conditions.

"I remember the time we were doing a story that had really happened. It was very well written, very special, but I can't remember the name. The doctors were dealing with a guy responsible for a lot of deaths. The doctors want to keep him out of battle, so they take out his appendix.

"Mike got upset. 'That's mutilation. I don't think the doctor I play would mutilate, even if it was for a good cause.' I took the other position. We were desperate. It was the only way to keep the guy off the front, saving lives.

"We argued heartily for a couple of hours. After a while we realized it would make a wonderful scene, real drama, with totally conflicting views. I stayed up late with the writers till one in the morning. I had to come in at eight to shoot.

"B.J. had a point. I had a point. I hate this place. But I hate myself a little less if I did this. Hawkeye is not proud when he comes from O.R. Even as he is talking, more casualties are coming in. So he held back the ocean a little.

"Hey, Marty, remember the name of the show where we took the guy's appendix out? Ask Metcalfe. He remembers all the names." Metcalfe says, " 'Preventive Medicine.' "

That scene in the changing room, one of the strongest in the show, condensed a couple of hours of fighting to two or three minutes. "What I loved about it is there was no preaching. It dealt with the ambiguity of what's right. It was not totally pleasing to me or B.J. The ending was wonderful. A very nice moment. B.J. put his hand on the shoulder of Hawkeye to comfort him. Even though he's stepped on his conscience, both realize what a mess they're in and both feel self-conscious.

"And this is where I have to do a scene with Loretta and B.J., and the Father." Alan goes to work again, into Mulcahy's tent. Loretta flubs her line. "Take back her Emmy," Mike yells. "Good, I could use two," Alan says, in his Groucho voice.

Loretta says, "I just got the line. If it was one of mine, I would know it."

She takes Alan aside while they change the lights and camera angles. She is concerned, I overhear her say, about an interview with *Good Housekeeping* last night. The writer is coming on to her. It's a sexist thing. He doesn't mean it, he's just doing his macho number. Alan is very concerned, patient. People come to him with their media problems and others. He is quiet, thoughtful, patient; he listens closely, like a Father taking confession from his flock.

The bell rings, and the scene starts again. "Mumbles in protestation," Alan says, reading from the script. "I don't know what *protestation* is." Dr. B. J. Hunnicut says, "It's like a prostate. I took out a protestation last week." "There are too many crucifixes in this tent," Metcalfe says. One of the production assistants says this will be offensive to some viewers. Farrell takes one and puts it in his belt, as if that would do.

Liz Alda, one of Alan's three daughters, arrives on the set with friends from acting school. She has been auditioning for a part. "I have the feeling she is going to be famous in fifteen minutes," Alan says. He stops everything to talk to her about the audition, with the same intensity shutting out the rest of the world. "She is going to be the star of the family," he says to everybody. "The family needs a comedian," she says. "Did you tell Marvin about the time you threw the sandbags down at Mike from the catwalk at the end of the O.R. and then you started to throw tape and mattresses at each other?"

We were sitting on the bed in post-op. "I was sitting here when I learned I won an Emmy for the first show I wrote, 'Longjohn Flap.' After that, I directed everything I wrote.

"And over on this phone is where I learned I had been swindled. I walked in a daze from the wall here to the bed. It was right after I had learned I won the Emmy. A reporter from the Walter Cronkite show called up from New York and asked what I thought about losing all that money. 'What are you talking about?' " I said. "My business manager has invested in oil wells. One hundred forty-five thousand dollars.' "

I remembered seeing Alan's name among the swindled in the *New York Post* one night, and whistling. Then I began to suspect he was doing very well.

"It was disconcerting, to say the least, is how it felt. Funny. I had just been talking about what an incredible year it had been for me. I felt like I was one of those lucky guys who are about to be sacrificed in an Aztec temple. They wine and dine him, give him vestal-virgin persons, then a few hours later cut out his heart. I was writing, co-producing *We'll Get By*, and winning Emmys. And then I hear I've lost all that money.

"A lot of other people in the crew thought it was very funny. But Wayne told them to stop joking about it. Wayne was very nice. He told them to cut it out; it wasn't that funny. It was a lot of money compared to what we had at the time.

"Wayne does a lot of financial advising for other actors. He explained it could have happened to anybody. He managed money for other actors and was always buying apartment buildings in L.A. I liked Wayne. I would drive him out to the ranch. He didn't like to drive. He would tell me his dreams, and I would tell him mine, and we'd look for signs. It was a way to have fun and to encourage each other not to give into the merchants, not to budge an inch on aesthetics. Wayne was even invited to lecture on accounting at UCLA. He asked me to think of some jokes. I could never think of any."

We are sitting at the long table in the mess tent. "I'm remembering a whole scene here, the time when we had a choral group singing 'Dona Nobis Pacem.' The extras, the stars, we were all crying. It was beautiful."

A stagehand throws over two *Star Wars* theater-program books. "For your kids," he says.

Liz is back with her friends from acting school. "This is Daddy," she says, introducing her father. "We don't say much about him. He wears makeup." Alan and Liz sit down at the mess table and read the *Star Wars* book together.

He is whistling "Fascinating Rhythm" as he leaves the set.

We are back in the dressing room. Alan offers me a drink. "In California they drink Perrier as if it was water," he explains. "And they drive on different sides of the road."

I ask him one of the fan questions I've always been too embarrassed to ask: What did he think was the best *M*A*S*H* show? And the worst?

"Our best shows took a moment of truth and made it real," he explains. "We have had some shows that were silly . . . We try to do the best all the time. We were proud of the stories originally, but they didn't turn out right. An idea may seem good. Then it gets too many steps away from what could happen. There are shows I cried at. We had an unusually high percentage of good shows that worked out right. Two or more really special shows every season."

Do you have a list of the best?

"I think I could make two lists—the ones I hate, too. 'Edwina' (1971). Can I have a third category?" He is looking over a printed list of the first 265 shows to refresh his memory. "The top layer is very special. The pilot is in the middle. By middle I mean very good. 'Tuttle' was very good. 'Longjohn Flap' was very good, not one of the absolute best. 'Carry On, Hawkeye,' which I won the first Emmy for acting in, was very good. There are a lot of shows I really liked." He is still reading through the list. "This brings back memories. It's wonderful."

Picking the best *M*A*S*H* becomes a major indoor sport. And here is Hawkeye himself playing the game.

" 'The Late Captain Pierce' is one of my favorites. 'The Kids.' 'Hawkeye: The Monologue,' I wrote. But I didn't take a credit on it. 'The More I See You.' Very interesting. 'The Interview' was one of our very best. That was the one in black and white I told you about. 'Dear Sigmund' is one of our best. I won an Emmy for directing it. 'Fallen Idol' I was fond of. I wrote it. That was the one where Radar sees me get drunk. 'In Love and War,' when I fall in love, that was just nice. I had to cut it down to thirty minutes from forty-five minutes. I had too much to say. It would have been one of the very best at forty-five. 'Showtimes' was very good, from the first season. So was 'Yankee Doodle Doctor.' 'The Major Fred C. Dobb,' the one where I almost talk Frank into staying. Why would I want him to stay? Can't imagine why we did that now. We told him oil and gold were in this area." Alan obviously didn't like the way that one turned out by the face he was making.

"Henry Please Come Home" was my least favorite, I explained. What bothered me was the way they had a chopper carrying Colonel Blake's desk out. It was illogical, dishonest, sitcommy. "What bothered me afterwards," Alan said, "was how we used a surgical saw to cut a wall.

" 'Point of View' was one of the very best. 'Dear Sis,' terrific. 'Ingrid,' one of the very best. I won an award for writing it. I loved 'The Party.' Burt and I wrote it. 'Dreams' was one of the best. 'Dear Dad,' one of the best. A very unusual way to tell a story.

" 'Guerrilla of My Dreams' I liked. It was the first time *sonofabitch* was used on TV. They were going to censor it before we did the show.

"In TV," Alan explains, "we say, 'You can't say that? Why? Why not let us do it?' What happens in television is unintentional censoring. They teach you to censor yourself. It's one of the insidious things of TV.

"Can't you change it?' they asked about 'Guerrilla.' When that Southern Korean secret police takes the woman patient off to shoot her as soon as she recovered [from an operation performed by Hawkeye], I was not interested in saying anything else. That was a powerful show.

"I would put 'Follies of the Living, Concerns of the Dead' as a special show. 'Sometimes I Hear Bullets.' That was the first time a patient died on an operating-room table. It may have been the first time somebody died in a comedy. That was the show which made somebody at the network say, 'What is this thing—a comedy or a tragedy?' Little by little the audience, then the network, gave us permission to do what we wanted to do or what we thought we wanted to do or what we thought we thought we wanted to do. We didn't say anything about what we wanted to do in advance. We just did it."

"What couldn't you do because of the censors?" I asked.

"I can't think of anything I wanted to do I couldn't do. There were things I couldn't do, but not because of the network. I couldn't get other people's enthusiasm. I couldn't sell it to the producers. Most of the best shows I've written, I couldn't get the enthusiasm for at first. 'Dreams.' Two or three seasons I brought it up before I finally made them do it. Problem was it shouldn't look like sitcom dream fulfillment. Bob Denver dreams of escaping from the desert island, things like that. After a certain period of time, all sitcoms want to escape from a desert island." ("Dreams" won another Emmy for Alan as a writer.)

"I had to sell them the two-parter on 'Hot Lips Loves Hawkeye.' They have an affair. Gene Reynolds didn't like the idea. Two disparate personalities: How could they have a relationship? That's the basis of the stories—that they are so unlikely. I had to organize it into two halves. They are thrown into each other's arms by the shelling in one episode.

The next morning [second part] when they wake, they wonder how they had gotten together. It was wonderful, to be able to take the reason you can't do it and turn it into the reason you can do it. I never lost anything from resistance to an idea. It always got stronger.

"Sometimes it came in five minutes. Like 'Radar's Fallen Idol.' Sometimes we couldn't do something because we had developed taboos. We couldn't have doctors drinking before they go into the O.R. Then we'd look like bad doctors. But what happens if we broke the taboo? Hawkeye gets sick in the operating room and throws up. He was also guilty about sending Radar out to get laid. Radar lets him know how disappointed he is. He berates him, calls him a ninny. One of the best stories we ever figured out, and it only took five minutes. It all just kept tumbling out. And it came from something we couldn't do.

" 'Margaret's Marriages' had some very funny stuff in it. I only remember the funny stuff, not the rest. I like 'Hepatitis' very much. There was no show like it. I wrote it to be done as improv: a series of two-person scenes. Hawkeye went around checking for hepatitis. I wanted everyone to improvise their scenes. But we couldn't get the cast to agree. 'Interviews' was largely improvised the same way, with Larry (Gelbart) coming in, taking the improvs, and polishing them. It's the best of both worlds.

"A small handful of the shows were not done right. I have regrets. But that's like life. The only one who doesn't regret something is in the insane asylum."

He reads the list over. " 'Dreams' I said I wrote. Be sure to say it's from a story by James J. Rubinfier." That's nice. He goes out of his way to say that. He's scrupulous. "One more I know you should put on the list is the final movie. I know that's going to be special."

"Why are you stopping *M*A*S*H* now?" I ask. Another one of my fan questions.

"Not because we're arrogant," Alan says. "We get a lot of letters accusing us of being arrogant, not caring for the feelings of viewers. They are very warm letters, in some cases, heated. Also despondent. People are crestfallen. There is a sense of betrayal. They don't understand why.

"The reason we're doing it is only that we love it so much. We want to finish at a point where we can still say we're proud. We don't want to wish we had stopped six months before."

Producer Metcalfe, who has joined us, says, "We're like boxers who want to quit while we're still ahead. We don't want to lose the crown. Retire as champs."

"It isn't that the ratings have gone down," Alan says. "This summer's ratings were higher than ever; this fall, too. It's a fear that we wouldn't be able to do our best for a whole season, for twenty-two to twenty-five episodes. We don't want to put ourselves through the agony of running dry. It's always been a special show. We didn't want people to say this year they took the money and ran—well, what do you expect?

"All of which is not a call for more stories, ideas from your readers. Every time we said we were considering stopping in the past, that's what happened."

What I as a critic never understood is why all the other shows that tried to duplicate *M*A*S*H* always failed.

"No other show had the concept," Alan says. "Ours was unique. The others may have tried to be real, but they didn't have the whole concept. Here we had one, people who didn't want to be where they were; two, people dedicated to saving lives; three, people in a pressure cooker, learning how to co-exist; four, in a war situation, which automatically is dangerous; five, having to have a sense of humor to prevent themselves from going insane; six, and the Korean War really happened."

Even the show's creators, Gelbart and Reynolds, couldn't do it again. They tried with *Roll Out*, a 1973 series about the 5050th Trucking Company (the "Red Ball Express"). "It didn't have the concept," Alan recalls. "That was just a service comedy. *M*A*S*H* was not a service comedy. It was never just fun and hijinks at the front. They didn't have the anger and bitterness as the basis for reality. *M*A*S*H* doesn't take its own bitterness seriously. And none of them mastered the ambiguity.

"You have to credit the ambiguity of the characters. Heroes, yes, but everybody has commonly found traits that are not ideal. Also, we have a lucky combination of actors. They are all such lovely people as actors and characters. They're all tuned in on the affection we have for each other, even when they are impatient with the others' personalities. It allows scenes to pass through them, resonating, loose.

"All the casting changes over the years worked out. When Frank Burns reached a dead end, as a character, we replaced him with a multidimensional B.J.

"Everybody who left the show knew how to do another *M*A*S*H*. But they never had the concept, only half the equation. We were lucky."

To this day nobody seems to understand why it works. Even 20th Century-Fox and CBS. "They're always copying the externals," Alan said. "They can't do it again. I have to give CBS a lot of credit. They stuck with us a whole season, even though the show was in the bottom fifty the first season. It wasn't until reruns the first spring that it started to make the top twenty. That's what saved *M*A*S*H*." Nowadays they take shows off in the first few minutes.

"If you took the six 'best' shows on your list, you wouldn't get *M*A*S*H* on the air today," I said. Alan agreed. Why?

"It's something Radar used to call the stupidities. They wouldn't believe audiences would go for it. It's really amazing about audiences. Some weeks the number-one shows are *60 Minutes* and *M*A*S*H*, and the others, *Three's Company* and *Dukes of Hazzard*. The fact is, audiences have a wide range of tastes. If TV has decided an audience only likes simple-minded, childish humor, it is shortsighted and shortchanging them."

"*The Mary Tyler Moore Show* was about to be canceled," Alan recalls. "*All in the Family* had to make three pilots before it was bought. Most shows that have anything fresh take time to develop. The networks don't really know how to put out shows. I'm not trying to denigrate them. That's what their business is. But TV is like a supermarket. Wait a minute, where are the Wheatenas—or whatever is the big health food today. It should be self-evident that you have to stock all kind of things in the store, not just the most popular foods.

"What has happened in the last eleven years of TV? There is an increasing interference from networks. They are constantly telling producers how to write shows, cast them. It's a little like Coca-Cola drivers of the trucks changing the recipe. They're getting an even trashier grade of crap on TV, although that didn't seem possible."

He's only seen a minute or two of the new shows. Maybe that's why the interest in *M*A*S*H* has grown as the years go by. It gets more valuable as the new shows get worse.

Liz Alda and her acting-school friends come into Dressing Room A. "Who's acting this afternoon?" she asks her father. "Just David [Ogden Stiers]," Alan says. "How boring," Liz says. "But he gets so emotional in this one."

Alan talks to one of Liz's friends about his schoolwork. "Are you an actor?"

"Who isn't, out here?"

He's a chubby, funny-looking fellow. He doesn't like acting school. "They're always asking 'What's your motivation?' You're a flower, you're a lamp. They never ask me to be a motel room, a twin bed. I'm big enough."

"Be a tree," Alan says, as he gets ready to do the scene with Stiers.

"You're not nervous, are you?" the fat guy asks. "Is your hair okay? Break a leg."

Alan goes off to the set. The fat guy, Mark Goldstein from Nanuet, New York, rubs his eyes. "I'm talking to Alan Alda, not to another person. Wait a minute, I have to adjust my horizontal hold."

The one question I didn't ask Alan is what really happens in the last episode. So I figure Klinger goes home to Toledo, where he goes into the dress business. Big deal. So B.J. and Emerson Charles Winchester III and their spouses take the Love Boat cruise to Fantasy Island. So Hawkeye Pierce goes off his rocker, flips out, cracks up after all the emotional *Sturm und Drang*. He's been on the brink for a decade. And you could see it happening. That would be the kind of ambiguity Alan would love. It would be honest and true, the punishment to fit the crime, the final insanity after eleven years of making us laugh when we wanted to cry, the most incredible attainment in the history of TV sitcoms, an achievement that may never be matched again.

I agree with Alan when he says discussion of the show in advance is like a magician explaining the trick before he does it. He didn't even want to talk about the fire that burned out the famous *M*A*S*H* set. (Not the Stage 9 set on the Fox lot, but the ranch.) Is somebody up there trying to tell them not to stop or this will make sure you'll stop?

Sight unseen, I predict the final episode of *M*A*S*H* is going to make more people laugh and cry at one time than in the history of TV.

For eleven years *M*A*S*H* had been crossing the minefield of emotions. It broke all the rules of TV sitcom—including mindlessness. It was increasingly well written, well acted, daring, gutsy (for network TV).

For months they were talking in the press about the final two-and-a-half-hour movie that was going to bring to a conclusion the Korean War on TV, finally.

Everybody was telling me what happens in the last episode. Those scholarly journals, the *National Enquirer* and the *Star*, had the accounts. My son Jamie at law school in Boston called me with all the details. He had overheard it from somebody on the subway near Fenway Park. I even heard from a group of North Koreans, the people in the bushes outside the 4077th Mobile Army Surgical Hospital.

Heck, I even told Alan Alda how I thought it should end:

"The real war hasn't ended yet," I explained while lunching with him at the 20th Century-Fox commissary. "Nobody really knows the two sides have been meeting regularly at the peace table in Panmunjom since 1954. Wouldn't it be great in the final episode, if *M*A*S*H* unilaterally ended the war? Declared it over. The U.S. wins, of course. It's a great victory. In Asia, Europe, everywhere they watch *M*A*S*H*, everybody believes what they see on TV. Peace breaks out. V-K Day. 'I saw it on *M*A*S*H* on TV,' they say. All wars could be ended this way, on TV. 'The reality on TV,' McLuhan or Ching Chow in the *Daily News* first said, 'is greater than real life.' "

Alan smiled. "We want the show to follow history."

But frankly, I didn't want to know. I could wait to find out on M-N*I*G*H*T. I didn't agree with my colleagues in the press who felt they had to lie, cheat, go through wastebaskets, to get the secret about a TV show. Why don't they break big stories about corruption in high places? TV viewers had so little to look forward to. Why ruin it?

So Klinger didn't go home to Toledo, where he opened a dress shop. So Winchester didn't become the team physician for the Boston Red Sox.

The final episode turned out instead to be a long good-bye, perhaps the longest in TV history. Everybody has trouble saying good-bye to loved ones. We drag out the farewells as long as possible, standing at the door with our coats on. But this was ridiculous. They milked it so much you could hear the cows mooing all the way from Panmunjom. Two and a half hours—five times as long as a regular episode—was too much. Gibbon's last five chapters seemed short by comparison.

Some of it *was* moving. The last fifteen or twenty minutes had me in tears. I loved the long kiss between Hot Lips and Hawkeye. Loretta Swit will have me disbarred for not appreciating the professionalism she has brought to nursing after she dumped Frank, but I still think Major Houlihan is Hot Lips and a delicious dish. Hawkeye and Hot Lips should get married in the postwar period, if you ask me.

But most of the time the finale was soporific, not terrific.

Everybody but Rizzo, the motor-pool Sergeant, got to say what they would be doing after the war was over. It was a high-school class-yearbook night of writing by Alda and the seven other writers. It went on maybe two hours too long.

I know, too, that this was just a case of network greed. They blew the whole thing up so they could add all the extra commercials. The poor CBS guys. As Larry Gelbart explained to TV reporters the night before, "CBS had already earned $340 million from *M*A*S*H*. You don't understand how anybody wouldn't be satisfied with that from a little half-hour sitcom? Well, that's what greed means.

The thing they should have done is a miniseries on the farewell, a five-night, five-movie good-bye. Heck, they had taken eighteen hours on ABC earlier in the month for *The Winds of War*, and that only had to do with the *start* of World War II.

Or why not another farewell next year? It could be a tradition, like the

Bob Hope farewells on NBC. Jack Benny used to do his Third Annual Farewell Special. Maybe you can't get too much of a sad thing.

They took themselves too seriously in the final episode. Where was the black comedy? They didn't even have any gray. It was so sweet it hurt the teeth, as well as the heart.

The best part of the show was when Hawkeye went crazy. Something had happened in the bus to make him snap. Sidney Friedman saved him, though. I never realized that they had such great shrinks in the army, right up there with military dentists.

Hawkeye didn't sound too insane when he was in the loony bin with General MacArthur and Harry Truman (two other G.I.'s). And, in fact, he didn't look much different when he came back to the M*A*S*H unit in the second half, except he wasn't wisecracking so much. This was one of those miracles of modern medicine, dating back to the pioneering early work on mental illness done on *Major Lionel Newman, M.D.*

My kids in the audience at home said it was not unique, they had seen a case just like it in the psychoanalysis of Tippi Hedren in Hitchcock's *The Birds*. The depth of scholarship among the young is frightening sometimes.

It was so smart of Alan Alda not to let his character stay crazy. It would have invalidated everything he had been saying for the last eleven years. He would have been saying the war wasn't crazy—he was. Can you just imagine what a bummer it would have been to the American people if everybody's beloved Hawkeye Pierce ended up insane from all that bloodshed and senseless violence?

But his cure, I knew, was just the beginning of the trauma. What Sidney did was only lance the boil. I sure hoped Hawkeye continued seeing a shrink at the VA hospital in Maine.

After *M*A*S*H* ended, a lot of us would go through separation anxiety and other problems. I talked about the future with Alan in his dressing room at 20th Century-Fox.

"Hawkeye is going to be president of the United States by the time he is seventy," I said. "We don't have to worry about him. But I'm worried about your future."

The best part of being a powerful critic is that you can advise actors on what they should be doing with their lives. They are usually too busy living them to have a masterly overview.

"Now here's my plan," I whispered to him.

"First of all, you should make a new movie called *M*A*S*H*. You were never *in* a movie called *M*A*S*H*. Then you should do . . . a series based on the new *M*A*S*H* movie."

He looked at me suspiciously, as if I had been nosing around.

"They already wanted me to do it at Fox. They were going to call it: *M*A*S*H: A Movie.*"

"A genius figured it out," I explained. "He got paid big money to think of that idea. It would be a blockbuster. Then they'd make a sequel. There would be *M*A*S*H the Second* and *M*A*S*H the Third.*"

"Now here's my next plan. You become a host on a morning show. Like the *Today* show. You know—a David Hartman with brains."

The *CBS Morning News* has Diane Sawyer in her basic black dress with pearls. "You could do it in your bathrobe," I explained. Alan Alda could do anything in his bathrobe, even operate, as far as the American people were concerned. A morning-show host in a bathrobe would be a major advance in communications. Why dress up so nattily for people at home who are in their curlers? Diane Sawyer and her pearls on *The CBS Morning News* looked like she was throwing a dinner party. Put a lot of people off.

"Now I'm sure you'd say you don't want to do it," I explained. "I'm sure you would say you don't want to be prime minister of England, either."

"As a matter of fact," he said, "I was asked about that, too."

But I went on anyway. He would be great as a morning-show host. He had once hosted *Good Morning New York* for a week in the early 1970's. I was a guest on his *Good Morning* show. The amazing thing about him was that he asked questions, and listened to the answers. Something magical, known as conversation, happened.

He has an air of certainty and relaxation about him that comes from being able to say, "I'm Alan Alda, and you're not." And it never gets to be too much. He's the only person I know who can't be overexposed on TV.

However, there was one period when he came close. It was during the promotion for his movie *The Four Seasons*. "I'm being over-Aldaed to death with the magazine articles, and appearances," my friend Monica Williams said. "Can't he have a six-month pass from the media, a furlough?

"But," she added, "the pain threshold created by too much Alda is different."

This is what was happening, I explained to him. Everybody knows that what they see on TV is not the real person. Underneath, the real person is a rat. But underneath Alan, they see a good guy.

"As a matter of fact, they have approached me to be the pope," Alan said. Then he was, briefly, serious. "I'm not saying which one, but they have approached me to be host of a morning show."

"It just goes to show how smart they are," I said.

The great thing about the job, I explained, is that he could get his ideas across to the American people—directly, not hidden in messages in sitcoms. "Look at what you could have done for the ERA. You've got decent ideas. You're not a radical. I never saw you come out for anything really wild, like closing down nuclear-power plants. You're a force for good, if you're into that. You could be a true God-figure. Of course, the networks have despaired of ever getting you. But I know how they can."

"How?"

"All they have to do is offer the co-host job to Arlene. Have Arlene Alda as Mrs. CBS Morning News. TV hasn't had a husband-and-wife team since Tex and Jinx."

He laughed that insane laugh you'd recognize from Hawkeye on *M*A*S*H*. I knew then I was right about everything.

"I want to do movies," he said. "Shut up."

"Yes, I know. But I'm talking down the road, after you've won Oscars as best actor, writer, director, and producer of the century by 1990. And the best thing about being a morning-show host is you can't be too old for it. Later, later."

Like I said, Alan Alda will be running for president by the time he is seventy. And his opposition will be Joan Lunden. They will offer a real choice, the two major parties, ABC vs. NBC or CBS.

THE *M*A*S*H* TEST

So, we are now into reruns; a number of people are hopelessly addicted. They watch it two to three times a day—four times on Monday. "On Sundays," as two *M*A*S*H* junkies, Sue and Rich Ferrara of Islip, New York, explained, "we go through withdrawal—because it's not on at all. We recite lines from the old shows like Scripture, and serve our families chipped beef on toast." The only known antidote is a *M*A*S*H* test. Judging by the numbers sent to me at the paper, making *M*A*S*H* tests is a leading cottage industry. Such exercises are usually called "trivia," which makes them sound trivial. Baloney. It's like calling geology or physics "trivia." You have to be smart to pass these tests. It's a special area of knowledge that could baffle the great brains of our time, like Professor Carl Sagan and Dr. Joyce Brothers. As an example of what I mean, here is a typical *M*A*S*H* test that even a devotee like myself failed. It's the dreaded M.A.T., or *M*A*S*H* Aptitude Test, invented by a leading scholar, Michael Huppert of North Babylon, New York.

WARNING: The Agitant General has determined this test may agitate and be hazardous to your health. Before going farther, take the following pop quiz:

1. What is Hawkeye's real name?
2. If you got two of the three names (Benjamin or Franklin or Pierce) correct, proceed to the true test ahead.

Some of the questions are easy. Some are hard. Some are what you might call truly trivial. If you have what it takes—upstairs—you should get a passing grade.

THE M. A. T.

1. What is the motto of the 4077th?
2. Who wrote the theme song to *M*A*S*H*? (a) Henry Mancini (b) Johnny Mandel (c) Simon and Garfunkel (d) Robert Groundfield
3. How many helicopters are shown during the opening of the show?
4. From the earlier episodes, who was the black doctor and star

football player? (a) Sergeant Zale (b) Spearchucker Jones (c) James Earl Jones (d) Alias Smith and Jones

5. Which character tries to get out of the army by getting a Section 8? (a) Rizzo (b) Igor (c) Klinger (d) Radar
6. What is Father Mulcahy's full name?
7. Name B. J. Hunnicut's wife and child.
8. In what profession is Hawkeye's father? (a) librarian (b) fisherman (c) doctor (d) farmer
9. Who is Corporal Cupcake? (a) a horse (b) a CIA agent (c) a dog (d) the helicopter pilot
10. Why did Frank Burns get his Purple Heart?
11. The army wanted to make a film about the 4077th to send home. What was its title?
12. What was the inscription on Major Houlihan's wedding ring?
13. Who was chosen to box the champion boxer of all the M*A*S*H outfits? (a) Trapper John (b) Hawkeye (c) Rizzo (d) the Cowboy
14. What was the name of Radar's champion mouse? (a) Spike (b) Sarge (c) Daisy (d) Mickey
15. Klinger's ex-wife's name is (a) Peg (b) Laverne (c) Blanche (d) Lorraine
16. In one of the Christmas shows, what "saves" Charles Emerson Winchester from a long stretch of holiday depression?
17. Who comes up with the suggestion that it would help?
18. What is odd about Dr. Sidney Friedman, the psychiatrist?
19. Trapper John had a pinstriped suit made by a local Korean tailor. What was wrong with it?
20. What is the name of Colonel Potter's horse? (a) Rosie (b) Cupid (c) Sophie (d) Sea Biscuit
21. For what is Father Mulcahy's sister (the sister) noted?
22. What type of gun did Frank Burns steal from the gun bin?
23. What is the name of Radar's valiant rabbit? (a) Hoppy (b) Daisy (c) Bugs (d) Fluffy
24. Hawkeye and B. J. outfit Lieutenant Colonel Donald Penabscot in a special "suit" on the eve of his wedding. What type of suit was it?
25. What was the name of the Chicago spareribs restaurant that Hawkeye called for a takeout order? (a) The Rib Cage (b) Adam's Ribs (c) Ribs 'R Us (d) Rib 'n' Run
26. What did he forget to order? (a) coleslaw (b) napkins (c) extra salt (d) sauce
27. Who organizes the gathering of the 4077th loved ones in New York City? (a) B.J. (b) Hawkeye (c) Father Mulcahy (d) Trapper John
28. During the preparations for this event, Klinger announces that his family can't go because he never told his mother that he went to Korea. In what post did he tell his mother he was in? (a) Fort Lewis (b) Fort Dix (c) Fort Apache (d) Fort Carson
29. At this gathering, who takes a fancy to Mrs. Potter?

30. Whose team won the M*A*S*H Olympics? (a) Hawkeye's (b) B.J.'s (c) Lieutenant Colonel Penabscot's
31. What is the name of Colonel Potter's favorite western movie? (a) *High Noon* (b) *Calamity Jane* (c) *My Darling Clementine* (d) *Thunder Over the Plains*
32. What famous general came to commend the 4077th on its fine work?
33. Klinger's favorite baseball team is the (a) Cleveland Indians (b) Toledo Roosters (c) Toledo Redskins (d) Toledo Mudhens
34. When he is sent to Korea, how much money is owed to Winchester by Colonel Baldwin? (a) $50.17 (b) $623.45 (c) $1341.23 (d) $5.53
35–37. Name at least three of Colonel Potter's models for his paintings.
38. The character played by Marcia Strassman before "Welcome Back, Kotter" was (a) Nurse Kelly (b) Nurse Able (c) Nurse Drewes (d) Nurse Cutler
39. Whose unexploded bomb lands in the compound? (a) the navy's (b) China's (c) the CIA's (d) the Soviets'
40. Which two doctors were asked by a leading surgical publication to write an article about an operation they performed? (a) B.J. and Colonel Potter (b) Charles and Hawkeye (c) Colonel Blake and Trapper John (d) B.J. and Charles

B*O*N*U*S Question:

41. According to B.J., why does Frank Burns love his wife?

ANSWERS

The ETVTS (Educational Television Testing Service), which puts out this test, rules that scoring for the test consists of one point for each correct answer, minus a quarter-point for a wrong answer, plus the derivative of the square number of the test questions, times y, plus the limit of the number correct times by .74198. Using this procedure, you probably will not be able to understand your final score. So, take the number correct (add 3 points if you got the bonus correct), divide by 40 and multiply by 100.

1. "Best Care Anywhere"
2. b
3. Two
4. b
5. c
6. Father John Patrick Francis Mulcahy
7. Peg and Erin

8. c
9. c
10. shell fragments in the eye (eggshell fragments)
11. *Yankee Doodle Doctor*
12. "Over hill, over dale, our love will never fail."
13. a
14. c
15. b
16. his toboggan hat from home
17. Father Mulcahy
18. He writes letters to the late Sigmund Freud.
19. horizontal instead of vertical stripes
20. c
21. She plays a mean sax and has a great hook shot.
22. pearl-handled Colt 45
23. d
24. a body cast from the waist down
25. b
26. a
27. a
28. b
29. Hawkeye's father
30. a
31. c
32. MacArthur
33. d
34. b
35, 36, 37. his own thumb, a gaping Winchester, Hawkeye (glass in hand), Radar, Klinger as the greek God
38. d
39. c
40. d
41. B*O*N*U*S (3 pts.) because she owns real estate

11

THE IMMORAL MAJORITY

The campaign by the Moral Majority against television—the so-called Cleaning of America—which swept the country in the early 1980's, left me the leader of the Moral Quandary.

On the one hand, I remember thinking about the most awesome wave of reform to threaten TV in its first half century, the networks are bad guys. They are immoral. What is worse, they are amoral. They have a scant sense of social responsibility. A TV license is a license to take the money and run. It's also a license to take the money and stay. Why run?

A network has no soul. They can do anything irresponsible without pain or a sense of guilt. They do not feel bad about antisocial acts such as showing, in detail, how to shoot somebody, or in glorifying killers and criminals. They lack the conscience that differentiates us from worms.

The networks say that when the Reverend Jerry Falwell and other Moral Majorityniks examine the networks' program content they are threatening the networks' civil liberties. They are right. Free speech is being impeded.

I'm not too thrilled at having to defend the rights of the networks any more than those of the Nazis. I'm one of those liberals who is just not going to go to the barricades to defend the rights of those who want me killed. Let other guys do it.

For the networks, in their way, are the fascists of the arts. They wrap themselves in the First Amendment. But when it suits them, they discard it. CBS News gave in on some First Amendment issue regarding outtakes, after years of having made such a strong argument for not doing so. The network code regarding principles is that the governing principle is expediency.

The networks' appreciation of intellectual freedom within their organizations is even more murky. The reasoning about what can or cannot be said on entertainment programs is convoluted, filled with contradictions, obscure, ever-changing. TV is a medium that in less than a generation went from not allowing writers to use the word *pregnant* in a sitcom to a two-hour prime-time movie on CBS called *Fallen Angel*, the step-by-step story of how a pedophile got a twelve-year-old nymphet to pose for dirty pictures. TV's moral code? They make it up as they go along, whatever they are saying on any given day.

TV, the bastion of free speech, defender of intellectual freedom? Have you ever tried to get an opposing point of view on the air?

Forget the lofty issues. Have you ever tried protesting a piddling matter—say, the cancellation of a show? The only time they heed a protest, i.e., *Cagney & Lacey*, they have already decided the cancellation notice was premature. Conversely, you can write letters until your fingers are blue, and it won't save Linda Ellerbee [*Our World*]. Totalitarian nations' broadcast systems are not much less responsive. There are other similarities.

Have you noticed how all three networks' evening shows are alike in content? How is that possible with three different news staffs, each presumably studying the incredibly extensive, complex, boiling world at large, then boiling it all down in such a way that they can all say, "And that's the way it is . . ." It's a "miracle" of coincidence we all accept. Anybody who grows up watching TV should be aware that free speech involves a lot of lip service.

The same miracle is found in entertainment programming. Year after year, working in absolute secrecy, the three networks manage to come up with almost identical programming: the same sorts of shows about the same professions (police, law, medicine), the same sitcoms about the same situations. They each discovered sex at the same time. The joys of unlimited liberty and freedom of expression on TV are numbing.

So, one has a secret sense of pleasure at seeing the networks under the pressure of the Moral Majority groups. Let them be fearful. Let them be concerned, lie awake at night. Let them sweat it.

The only trouble is that the Moral Majority forces are not such good guys, either. The Reverend Mr. Clean and his people couldn't tell the difference between *Three's Company* and *Soap*. Both of which were on their very, very bad, or very, very evil list. Like all vigilantes and censors, they lump everything together indiscriminately in such an intellectually bizarre fashion that it's scary. Sometimes I think they have not only closed minds, but closed eyes and ears.

There was the famous Wildmon vs. Mater debate (June 1980), which will live in the annals. It featured the Reverend Donald Wildmon, of the Coalition for Better Television, against Gene Mater, then a CBS vice-president in charge of explaining moral standards. They were debating the filth in TV drama issue before a group of TV critics, many of whom were on a junket (paid for by CBS).

"You had that terrible filthy show—*Gorgon*," the Reverend Mr. Wildmon said, as I heard it secondhand.

"What show was that?" asked Mater.

"You know," the reverend said, "the one with the Polynesian girl. She was topless."

Mater stared blankly.

"He was a painter."

"He means," one of the critics called out, "*Gauguin.*"

David Carradine playing the French impressionist was an example of what they are trying to cleanse TV of? They're against anything they can't pronounce.

The Moral Majority folks can't seem to differentiate between sex and violence. They lump the two so-called evils together, treating them as if they are the same. I suggested to them a test: Have somebody make love to you and shoot you and see which does more damage.

They are lumpers. They like to lump things together in catagories. And if you don't like it, you can go lump it.

The worst thing about them is that they are also blacklisters, people who draw up lists. Once the networks give in on any particular point, they want somebody to pay for the confessed sins.

Thus, the major struggle that took place in broadcasting in the 1980's was a case of the bad guys (the networks) against the worse guys (the Moral Majority). As I said, a dilemma. You can't know whom to root for without good guys.

These were some preliminary thoughts on the eve of the first important fight—the boycott against sponsors of TV's most violent and sexiest shows, the first tactic proposed by the Reverend Mr. Clean and the Reverend Mr. Well-Done in the Cleansing of American TV. The battle was to begin on June 29, 1981, with the release of the Reverend Mr. Well-Done's Coalition for Better Television list of offending advertisers.

It was a plan of the same strategic genius as using Raid to fight bubonic plague. First of all, boycotts never work in TV. Viewers are too apathetic. Most viewers don't know which program is on which network. The notion that they could name (or remember) the names of the producers of products such as Warner-Lambert (Listerine, Rolaids, Trident), Beecham (Aqua-fresh, Brylcream, Jovan), Smith Kline, Procter & Gamble, or General Foods is laughable.

Now that the sponsors simply buy spots on programs, the way advertisers buy pages in magazines, it's even harder to scare them. Their sense of responsibility for the programs' content has been reduced. It was a lot different when Jell-O presented Jack Benny or G.E. presented *The Ronald Reagan Theatre*. Sponsors care only in a general way when they are indicted by groups like the Moral Majority 400. When you count on the moral sensitivity of sponsors, you're in trouble. With such allies, you don't need enemies.

Still, advertisers came crawling privately and publicly to meet with the Reverend Mr. Clean.

The man who most needed cleaning that June had to be the chairman of the board of Procter & Gamble, who rode out to battle and immediately surrendered. He said yes, there was too much sex and violence on the air, and he was just as disturbed as everybody else.

Procter & Gamble is the largest advertiser on TV today, in the multi-megabucks. If it wanted reform, P & G had means. Don't let P & G kid you with public-relations malarkey about its helplessness.

The advertisers managed to snatch defeat from the jaws of victory by crawling to the Reverend Mr. Clean's consciousness-raising sessions. This went on for weeks. It gave the reverends a way out of certain disaster. When the day came (June 29) for the list and the boycott to be announced, the Coalition for Better Television, the Reverend Mr. Wildmon's group, canceled the whole thing. The reverend instead encouraged members to purchase products of the Hershey Foods Corporation, "because in our opinion Hershey made the best effort of sponsorship based on the programs available during a three-month monitoring period this spring." Chocolate kisses to you, too.

In August the Moral Majority next turned on Phil Donahue. Phil Donahue, Mr. Middle America, the Saint of Blands, the Notre Dame Boy who does no wrong. They actually considered him a menace? They accused our Phil of being a sex activist of the worst order. They counted up the number of so-called "sex" subjects in a four-week period, and he broke their record. They made Donahue sound like a sex maniac.

As I said, such people are sinister and dangerous. The TV industry is still vulnerable to blacklisting. They do it themselves with the TvQs (lists of actors, rated by "popularity"; those with low TvQ scores are not employed). The Moral Majority will make lists of people who are in favor of putting pants on animals. Anyone who has heard the reverend and his cleaning men and women know they are not for diversity of expression. The milk of human kindness in them is skimmed and powdered. They could make the Joseph McCarthy/Red Channels period of broadcasting seem like the good old days. And anyone who had witnessed the debate between the CBS executive and the Reverend Mr. Wildmon would have been particularly unnerved. Half the TV press seemed to agree with the reverend, yet. Today, TV; tomorrow, the print medium.

In all the talk about boycotts for sex or violence, none of them dealt with punishments for bad programming—the junk, garbage, trash that is a staple of TV today, and punishing in itself. Does an advertiser ever pull its commercials out of a program because it is of poor quality? Lots of luck. Not if the ratings seem to signify approval. When P & G stands up against *The Love Boat*, I'll sign a petition supporting them.

The Moral Majority is a frightening movement. But I don't think the networks, Norman Lear, and other concerned civil libertarians aligned against them are on the right track, either. They should stop giving them so much publicity. Ignore them, as they largely ignored other groups in the past, such as Nick Johnson's National Council for Better Broadcasting, which campaigned against violence and bad TV in the 1970's. The public will not support any group against television. In the electronic age, the positive power of apathy is freedom's strongest weapon.

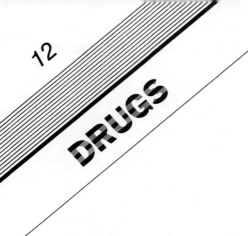

12

WHO'S DOPEY?

I was reading our leading professional journal, *TV Guide*. It had this amazing story by Frank Swertlow, which said that producers, actors, writers, and almost everybody else in the TV business is on coke.

I always knew it had to be something.

Now this wasn't a story in my other leading source of information, the *National Enquirer* or *Star*, a well-known bunch of troublemakers. *TV Guide* was not exactly on the cutting edge of industry criticism. For years it had been a leader in the Mary Poppins school of journalism; its reporting saw everything in the most wonderful light. So things must have been really bad out there in Lotusland if *TV Guide* was finally blowing the whistle.

Industry leaders denied it. I immediately figured it must be true. They always deny the use of cocaine. Deans of the industry, like Grant Tinker, are always saying, "Not us. Oh, sure, some people out here may shoot Maalox." ("They mainline it," a young producer told me once.) The establishment gets some kind of perverse high out of denying reality in California.

The *TV Guide* report was a turning point in my work as a critic. It was the critical connection, the synthesizing of everything that was wrong; dope was the missing link. And it had been as plain as the burned-out noses on their faces.

I used to think maybe the reason TV shows made in California were so bad was the three-hour time difference. Chronological cultural lag. Time warp. They are out-of-synch, like register color in the newspaper comics.

TV Guide's explanation was more plausible. It had the ring of truth. It explained, for example, the inexplicables, like the appallingly unfunny quality of sitcoms. How else could you possibly put together such contrived inanity in one century as *Lobo, Harper Valley P.T.A.*, *The Brady Girls Get Married, Aloha Paradise*? As the character Woody Allen played in his movie *Manhattan* said, "Of course you think that's funny! All you guys do all day is drop ludes and do coke. You should open a pharmaceutical company on the side."

(Didn't he also, in *Annie Hall*, sneeze in the living room, solving the problem of what to do about cocaine by blowing it away?)

The fact that so many peole in TV are on drugs, as Swertlow claimed, would explain everything. Before I suspected that something was eating the gray matter of the so-called creative minds in Hollynose, I couldn't understand how they did those things. Neither could they. They were out of their heads. TV was on the Drug Boat.

The *New York Times* told the same story on the front page one Sunday in November 1982. It was a rerun of Swertlow's story. But the front page of the *New York Times* on a Sunday made it official. Cocaine, the *Times* report said, is used by agents and producers pitching properties to studio and network executives. A studio executive said, "You snort in the car as you're parking it in the studio lot to get yourself up for the meeting. Meetings in Hollywood tend to last thirty minutes, but a snort of coke is only good for twenty minutes. When it wears off there's always a trip to the bathroom in the middle of the meeting."

This is fine, except for the poor people who actually have to use the bathroom. They are assumed in the TV industry to be on coke.

The use of cocaine explained why comedy shows aren't actually funny. Everything seems funny when you're on coke. It explained why certain actors get all the jobs, despite their lack of talent. Everybody seems talented on coke. It explained why certain producers got to do so many of the shows on the schedule, despite track records of proven failure. How bad could he be if he was rich enough to have bags of coke to give to his friends and associates? It even explained the lack of morality, the lack of concern about the human impact of what you are doing. On drugs you don't have to say you're sorry.

I was watching a rerun of *Laverne & Shirley* one night. Laverne and Shirley were on pot. It was really stupid and strange. That had to be a show that was done on Ovaltine.

The fact that just about everybody out there in La La Land was on drugs was in a perverse way wonderful news. It meant that I was not crazy. I had been looking at the stuff that came out of Hollyweird, not laughing at the "comedies," bored by the endless, essentially the same "action-adventure" show. I had gradually begun to feel there was something wrong with me. The laugh track on a sitcom was laughing. Why wasn't I? Because I wasn't putting anything into my nose, except my finger.

Swertlow's article said that it was all paid for by the big money from TV itself, by producers who would add the costs of coke as a below-the-bottom-line cost, along with other basic necessities, like limos and hookers. Every time we saw an extra commercial, we should remember: Somebody has to pay for the powder.

Soon, I had the solution: The people who made the shows were on coke. The people who bought the shows were on coke. The only thing missing from the creative process was the viewer at home.

The system would work perfectly if *everybody* in the audience also was on coke. The poor viewer was the only one left out of the delivery system. The person at home was the missing link in the distribution chain.

If it was such a wonderful, desirable thing to do, why shouldn't the viewers receive packets along with the programs? So we could all laugh and laugh like those tracks?

There should be socialized stuff, too. The government should give coke stamps, for those who can't afford it, like food stamps. Or it could be pumped into your nostril from the TV set. There would be a control on the set, like Volume or Hue or Color tint, with which you'd turn on as necessary. There are a few technical wrinkles I haven't worked out even yet.

Then, too, the free coke plan would put a crimp in organized crime, while at the same time improving TV programming.*

Of course, TV viewers are drugged already. On TV itself. That's how we can sit and watch all those comedies that are not comic and mysteries that are not mysterious.

Everything about TV is so coke. Even the bad reception is called snow.

What a relief to know it hadn't been me, after all. It was them, flying up there. Swertlow and *TV Guide* had seen the bare facts. They should build a statue for him and his magazine on Rodeo Drive. Or maybe a new store, which would sell only emperor's clothes.

---

* When I first mentioned this plan on Tom Synder's *Tomorrow* show, I added that I was just joking—for those TV executives in the censor's office watching the show who were probably on drugs.

THE REAL THING

"CALIFORNIA IS THE ONLY PLACE WHERE THE STATE LINE IS DRAWN
IN COCAINE."

—Rick Moranis on *SCTV*

The congressional hearings on cocaine usage in Hollywood opened in Los
Angeles in April 1982 before a sellout audience of dealers and users. It
was the most important cultural-political event since the 1950's, when
the Communists were accused of subverting minds in the movies. Noted
TV network moguls, studio heads, producers, and others of that ilk tes-
tified. In fact, a whole herd of ilk were there to show that their noses
were clean. It was a convention of the Benevolent Order of Ilk.

Was cocaine widespread in TV? In New York, the only impact of Swertlow's articles was that they stopped serving saccharine in the cafeteria at
NBC. But in California, industry leaders led by Grant Tinker of MTM
Enterprises attacked Swertlow with a ferociousness that was quite surprising. Normally, a grapefruit makes more noise than some of those
people.

Tinker, for one, told a luncheon meeting of the International Radio &
Television Society that reports of rampant drug usage were ridiculous.
He said, in effect, when all the people he knew in TV felt the need for
kicks, they played tennis. He told the congressional delegation substantially the same thing.

Some people can't see what's going on under their own noses. So Tinker
is not the Wizard of Nod. Nobody's perfect.

There were two sides to the issue of cocaine usage, apparently: (1) those
who thought cocaine was rampant, and (2) those who said it was normal.
Tom Brokaw of the *Today* show joined the argument one morning by
asking Swertlow accusatorily why he hadn't named names, and used so
many anonymous quotes? It was surprising that an experienced, perceptive journalist like Brokaw didn't know how the media works, that *TV
Guide* is even more timid than NBC. Swertlow was known as the best
reporter on the TV beat. He didn't use names because nervous Philadelphia lawyers made him take them out. His editors were aware that
every quote had a name, a job, a studio, behind it.

Given all this, I was dismayed. I didn't see anyone using cocaine when
I was in California on my first visit. I was never offered coke. (What does

that prove? "Was I carrying a spoon?" one insider asked. "Was your chest bare? Were you wearing any gold chains?") I didn't see any sex, either. Nobody offered me a starlet for breakfast. Or lunch.

Well, of course. The people I was with in Los Angeles were trying to protect me from decadence. They were a group of intellectuals who happened to live in Brentwood, and Orthodox Jewish people who lived on the Lower East Side of Beverly Hills.

On my first visit to Sodom and Gomorrah West, I had to fall into the hands of religious fanatics. What rotten luck! The cult was led by Shimon Wincelberg, the TV writer and novelist, who is so serious about his religion that he doesn't answer the telephone from sundown Friday to sundown Saturday evening. Not even a call from Aaron Spelling. Instead of coke, the Wincelbergs served bagels and cream cheese. The Wincelbergs didn't even have a hot tub in their house. For their crowd, religion was a high.

But back to cocaine. "I hear a lot of blue-collar workers are using it," explained Don Segall, a producer. "Instead of lanes at the bowling alley, they are laying down lines. They're also developing a new kind of coke for the L.A. market. It keeps you low instead of high. No-coke it's called. I'm on coke right now," he said, ridiculing the rampant-usage theory as if it were some kind of propaganda spread by effete easterners.

So not everybody was walking around with straws in their noses. Not everybody was living in the fast lane. "A big night for me and my friends," explained Stanley Ralph Ross, the producer who did the jungle classic *The Gold of the Amazon Women*, "is a cup of Sanka. Or a second cup, when I want kicks. The worst thing I do is maybe an extra banana on my ice cream late at night.

"It's the movie people who do drugs," Ross said. "TV writers can't afford it. Coke was put on earth by show-business people to show that you are important. Cocaine is God's way of saying you have too much money."

I began to think that coke usage might not be the right problem for Congress to investigate. They don't need coke to get high in the land of bilk and sunny. California is drug-prone because everything is a drug there, everything leads to addiction. Salads are a drug. The good weather is a drug. The surf is a drug. Nuts and berries are drugs. Sex is a drug. There is a famous network executive who used to fly out to California just to *shtup* a woman executive in purple toreador pants. Her position in the company was vice-president in charge of purple toreador pants.

Cowardice is the biggest drug. It's the most potent downer. There are so many good ideas for shows that never get past the script stage. "The

networks see them and decide the shows are good," explained my friend
Glenn Rabney, who has been trying to make a name for himself (other
than Glenn Rabney) as a sitcom writer. "But they are not the type of
show that is currently on TV. So they don't take a chance. Give them a
story about two female mud wrestlers who have a pet aardvark they hide
in their apartment, and they'll probably go nuts."

Of course, it soon developed that nobody in TV uses cocaine. The
reports, as Grant Tinker explained, were exaggerated.

Van Gordon Sauter, then president of CBS News, was telling me,
though, that his brother-in-law, the governor of California, Jerry Brown,
couldn't meet him for dinner in any L.A. restaurant. The state police first
warned him, then forbade him. "You couldn't go into a restaurant bathroom without hearing all this snort-snort in the booths." Ed Joyce, then
the number-two executive at CBS News, said at Dar Magreb everybody
kept leaving the table. "I thought they had kidney problems induced by
the food."

Grant Tinker may be right. Or he may have a problem. He is high on
tennis, or life, the biggest drug of all. I remember Mary Tyler Moore,
who used to live with him, saying she got a kick out of collecting driftwood
at the beach and making sculpture. Try putting that in your nose and
smoking it.

"The doctors' offices in L.A.," Dr. Donald Kaplan, the New York
psychotherapist, told me, "are filled with patients on Percodan highs,
getting prescriptions for more Percodan. No drugs? They're a bunch of
mushrooms with brains the size of green peas because of drugs."

The kinds of kids who used to be hard-core drug users ten years ago
are doing drugs. The big thing was fruit cocktail. L.A. teenagers dumped
all the pills into a bowl, gobbled the handful. Whether they counteracted
each other didn't matter. No concern about contrary usage, uppers and
downers. It's all one high—and for the few who live, one big low.

TV became so bad that it raised another question: Are people taking
drugs to write for TV or because they write for TV?

I don't want to give drugs all the credit for the mediocrity of TV. There
are mediocre peole who could do mediocre work unaided by drugs.

But maybe cocaine explained the lack of perception about the *dreck*.
There hasn't been a new idea in sitcom since *M*A*S*H* in 1972. There
hasn't been a satire since *Soap*. *Filthy Rich* was the big satirical hit the
summer of 1982 at CBS, the comedy network. It was hard to believe that
incredibly awful show, which demeaned southerners *and* the rich, was
created by Linda Bloodworth, famous in TV for funny, warm, sensitive
scripts done earlier for *M*A*S*H*. Or to compare *The New Odd Couple*

(1982–83) by the legendary Gary Marshall—the old *Odd Couple* (1970–75) in blackface—with the original. What a downer.

The cocaine connection is the nose dive TV has taken since the late 1970's. Just when it seemed they finally figured out how to make dramas of some quality after *Roots* and good comedies after *The Mary Tyler Moore Show*, *M*A*S*H*, and *Barney Miller*. They had it for a while, and they lost it. It all got so druggy.

You especially saw this druggy, draggy effect in hip new comedy shows aimed at young people. A New York producer was hired to save a pilot for a new satirical series being made in L.A., called something like *Flakes*. (They always give the young people's shows names like *Off-the-Wall*, *Bizarre*, *Loony Bin*, *Crazy*. Self-fulfilling prophecies.) The show was really in trouble.

The producer went out to the Big Grapefruit and found almost everybody on drugs. Performers, writers, technicians were constantly coking. He wanted to put up a sign reading NO COKE ON SET. Everybody was doing it except him. What's wrong with him? A spoilsport. And he couldn't stop it. Everybody had contracts. If he hired somebody else, he would have two people for each job. He wanted to put fans in every room so nobody could lay out lines on the tables (the Woody Allen solution, automated). He couldn't fire anybody. Drugs are not a breach of contract in L.A. And the final show was funny only to druggies.

There are famous writers and performers with *Saturday Night Live* who had as many as three different personalities. They could be up, down, and in-between all in the same day, even the same hour.

"You look at the original screen test of Belushi and Company," an *SNL* writer-alumnus said. "Really depressing. He was so good. Incredible. He went to the word and the concept. I walked out. I couldn't stand seeing how much he lost over the years."

Where did they go wrong? Why did the show stop being funny? Because they stopped being funny. They were the only ones who were high. Eight potheads sitting around the table can only be funny to each other.

I remember the shock of the first meeting with one of my comedy heroes, an author of classically funny books. It was also the first time I had been at a party when they were passing around pot, a masterblaster, a carburetor, grease gun, Uzi, whatever it was called. I had come to hear the master guru be funny. He laughed. His co-smokers laughed. But there was nothing funny being said.

In the beginning there were writers. The process of creating comedy was simple. They would sit around a table saying that's funny, that's not funny. There were no drugs.

Comedy writing developed a mystique. Young people picked up the idea. You have to be on something to be funny. Writing comedy is not a religious experience. "It's a job," as Roger Ailes, the producer, once explained. "You come in at nine o'clock and look at life awry, and go home at five." You don't have to hang around Studio 54 and take drugs and hang from the ceiling to be funny.

The old *Saturday Night Live* cast had a lot of talent and ego problems. Drugs reinforced them. If junked up, it's easy to think you're great. The decline of the show in its final years could not be blamed totally on drugs. The new cast was mostly mediocre to begin with. A few were desperate people with junkie mentalities.

In English comedy, they don't do drugs, I'm told. As Michael Palin of *Monty Python* explained, "We couldn't afford it. Also, our audience people can't find identification with druggy performers. It's not like in L.A., where they are totally fixated on drugs."

LIFE IN THE FAST LANE II: ABOUT SPEED

California TV dramas are characterized by speed. Not the drug—the tempo. The pace is bang-bang, chop-chop, boom-boom, biff-bop, bop-biff, pow-wow. The shows have the kind of twitchy impatience of people on drugs. Give it to me fast; don't bore me with the whole megillah. Don't semaphore it, or send it by Addis Lamp. Telegraph it. Everything about the show must be fast-fast, speed-speed. TV drama is a course at the Evelyn Woods School of Speed Television Viewing. The shows are written by moths for people with the attention span of a gnat. What our standard California drama seems to lack most is story. By story, I mean *Tinker, Tailor* or *Smiley's People*, a show you can't put down. Understand it or not, you hang on every word of John Le Carré's story. It's involving.

A number of the people who make the shows don't know what you're talking about when you say there is no story. Sure, there's a story, they say. So-and-so is driving his new Trans Am, black, down the Coast Highway. That's a story. So-and-so is walking into his beautiful house with the glass doors overlooking the beach at Malibu . . . So-and-so is making a phone call . . . So-and-so is slamming a door and getting back into the car and heading up a highway again . . . All of those are stories. You might as well explain to an armadillo.

There is no exposition, no interesting detail. The only development is on the actress's chest. What you saw last week was what you got. Action and movement. Speed is the story.

It's the sound of TV they substitute for stories. The audio track. The explosive screech, tires going around corners. Sirens, gunfire, the synthesizers and bongo drums denoting dramatic action in the absence of drama.

My wife doesn't even have to watch the TV to know when a police show is on. She hears the bongos.

If you turn off the sound on TV drama, there is no story.

Many a show is saved by the sound people. "In the absence of drama," explained George L. Vales, of the Video Center at New York Institute of Technology, "they make the explosions louder. Soup them up. No real drama in the script? Don't worry. We'll fix it up in the 'post' (the editing room). No continuity in the script, or logic? Don't worry. The music will supply the continuity."

Music is a form of language in movies as well as TV drama. But it sometimes has to be the whole "story" in television. A woman is walking down a street. You know she is in potential danger. The music tells you. You know the bad guy is entering the room. The music tells you. TV music is story for illiterates, stories for the dramatically impaired.

The sound track is as excited as hell by the drama it accompanies—but there is no involvement by the brain. Something a human mind might be curious about? Sitting on the edge of the seat of consciousness to find out? No, there is none of the breathless anticipation of the classical story. "And then what happened? Tell me. I'm dying to know." On TV, the music tells you, and the show is dying.

The background music has become the program itself. Something to have on, to fill space, while you do other things, eating, sewing, schoolwork, phoning, or writing legal briefs.

In the BBC's *Smiley's People*, which is one good example of how to tell a story on TV, there is almost no music on the sound track. Just words and pictures and acting that is enthralling. The silences (especially) are gripping, taut. Silence commands more attention than noise. What is this silence? For anyone brought up on American TV, it's deafening.

California dramas can be cited for noise pollution.

In the absence of genuine story, they also use that previously mentioned art form, violence. And to keep you hooked, they escalate the violence from scene to scene. A mindless show like *Gavillan* on NBC (1983) started off with a bang (car crashes), and by the end of the hour it was as if they were staging World War II.

This hyperactive, twitchy, impatient random violence is not enough to occupy the human mind. It captures the attention, yes, like watching an accident on a superhighway. But TV's crashing and thrashing ultimately becomes ennui. The conveyor-belt monotony of movement without involvement in TV drama is what bores you out of your gourd.

It was always assumed, or suggested, that TV shows are the fault of the viewers. The public *wants* all the fast pacing, movement, noise. Our fingers are on the dial, ready to switch to any show that will give it to us fast. We don't want plot, exposition, character development, information, or story. The public is getting what it wants.

Certain developments dispute that widely held industry belief. There were the huge audiences for miniseries like *Shogun*, James Clavell's novel of sixteenth-century feudal Japanese history, a twelve-hour movie, half in Japanese, without subtitles, yet. This was perplexing to those who knew better. But they largely ignored its significance.

Other factors, as I've been explaining, have been at work in the making of TV dramas. The twitchiness and impatience of the shows can be understood partly in terms of the Cocaine Connection.

A friend of mine, an indy producer who regularly pitches at the studios, noticed this.

"Originally, they asked you to submit a three-page treatment. Then it was a page. Then they wanted a paragraph. Then they nodded off at a line. Now, if you can't tell them what a show is going to be in a syllable or two, they don't want to hear. If an idea can't be told in a syllable, it can't be good."

That's why shows are so predictable. Somebody said, "Hawaii . . . Selleck . . ." That's it.

It's not that they don't want to hear new things. It's that they want them fast. "First of all," my producer friend explained, "they'll only be in the job for two weeks. They have to hear as much as possible in as short a time." After a line, a word, or a syllable, the executive will say, "So what?" Or, "Next."

There is a dichotomy here. On the one hand, they don't want to miss any ideas. Warhol said that everybody is going to be a celebrity for fifteen minutes; they want to hear every idea in the history of the world in fifteen minutes. Time is short for them, too.

You see the same executives at parties. They are the men with no eyes. You talk to them, they talk to you. But the guys are scanning the room to see who is important. You're important, true, in TV terms. You write a column. But fifteen or twenty others are just as important, or more so. They don't look at you while you talk. You never see their eyes.

They've heard in thirty seconds all the great ideas. But they can't dwell on them. They can't concentrate. And they have no history.

Hollywood's definition of history is last week's grosses. People buying TV programs have even less of a sense of the past.

For storytelling you need a feeling for history. Stories are history. TV has destroyed history. History, to such people, goes back all the way to last week's Nielsens. Films? Nothing existed in Hollywood before 1948, or 1968. They don't know anything about the past. They only care for the instant, what is absolutely current. They are not students of anything, except the moment. They don't even believe in the scientific principle of cause and effect. They invented themselves and the job, they think. It all begins with them.

The situation is further aggravated by the fact that network execs buying shows are, for the most part, kids, i.e., people without much history. History consists of the pursuit of information, over a distance in time. TV people can't remember yesterday morning. Network executives are, in effect, well-paid kids.

It's in films, too. Many TV shows and films today are about sensation, like amusement-park rides. Heightened consciousness, in brief bursts. It has little to do with reality. It doesn't reflect the real world substantially. Video games have that quality. There is no reference point to them, no history or background, only motor stimulation—exciting for thirty seconds.

The dramas play like a cocaine experience, a series of highs, short bursts of action, euphoria of a car going over a cliff or bursting into flames. The euphoria of action, then followed by dysphoria, the being let down by the nothing of the experience. The cycle continues endlessly, always the same, except when you escalate the power of the drugs (free basing). Euphoria, dysphoria, then paranoia. The commercial-TV drama is a drugged narrative of discontinuity and disbelief.

Conversely, the Cocaine Connection also explains such growing phenomena as the three-hour prime-time movies. Take a fairly good one-hour drama and drag it out all night. A thin drama becomes tedious when stretched. With enough outside help, chemically, you can get through six hours of TV.

Cocaine might also explain such things as why American TV has resisted running commercials at the beginning or ending of TV dramas, as other civilized countries do, thus not breaking the continuity or suspense of the dramas. But how could people have time to go to the bathroom to snort?

I am not saying, of course, that all the TV executives in California are on cocaine. Studio executives are among the hardest-working people in California. They work long hours and are well paid—by the hour they do better than at McDonald's. That's also why they may make so many wrong decisions. Working eighty or ninety hours a week, they can goof without drugs.

It is overly simple to say drugs alone make TV bad. It's also contracts. Deals that tie up the network schedules for years. In order to get one show, a piece of junk, they've had to buy six or seven pieces of other junk for future years. We are still paying for ABC's desire to keep *Bewitched* in the late 1960's. All the smart executives who have jumped or fallen from power have deals to make series: former NBC program chiefs Marvin Antonowski (known as "the Universal Connection" because he bought so many programs from Universal when he was at NBC), Larry White, Freddie Silverman, et al. There are so many "golden parachutes" that the business of supplying programs is like the 82nd Airborne veterans' reunion.

The men who didn't have the judgment to buy the good shows when they were in power. And now they are making them.

The Cocaine Connection also opens the TV art to a new form of critical examination. If a program one week is not up to snuff, so to speak, or is better than usual, the critic must ask: Was there a shortage that week? Had there been a bust that cut off the show's supply?

THE SNOW JOB CONTINUES—THE SNOW MUST GO ON

The battle raged on over the *TV Guide* article. I happened to think Swertlow was performing a public service by raising the issue. Yet industry leaders were trying to get him fired. Said "industry leaders" are a group of about thirty guys, kind of a club or lodge, who do virtually all the work in TV. They'd chattered about cocaine all the time, privately. But as soon as Swertlow had the nerve to mention it, they drew the wagons around to defend against this Indian. Not against the users and dealers, the bad guys, against the good guy. Swertlow had shot a flaming arrow into the camp. Now, he was the savage.

It's puzzling why the club members should have cared. Why was the club so overwrought about Swertlow?

They were running scared in California in the early 1980's, worried sick about Jerry Falwell, about Congress, about how so many of the town's dealers were disappearing into Bolivia.

I soon felt very positive about all of this. It meant that TV could be better. It gave me hope. If they didn't do drugs, they could dry out in ten or fifteen years.

Maybe now that coke usage was official on the front page of *The New York Times*, the industry could go beyond the denials and do something about it.

My two-point plan for improved programming:

1. Sure, nobody uses drugs in TV. Let's ban them anyway. No drugs. Period. Just like no drinking while driving; they don't mix. No drugs while buying, selling, making, or even describing shows.

2. Hire better executives. Not all should be under twenty-seven. A friend of mine was pitching a show at a woman who was the comedy head at a big cable system. He had an idea for a show starring Stan Freberg and Mort Sahl. She had never heard of either of them.

Redistribute the power. A young agent told me a story that may be apocryphal. He went with a producer to pitch a new idea to Ricky Schroder, who was twelve at the time. The producer was a fairly distinguished "old" guy, fifty, silver hair, with a long track record in the golden age of TV. He tells Schroder the idea for the show, the story, plot, secondary development of character. The kid yawns. When they are outside, the agent says to the producer, "Didn't it bother you talking to that twelve-year-old?"

"You don't understand," the producer says. "They are all twelve years old. This one is a little shorter than the others."

Use natural resources. Instead of boy wonders from Harvard Business, Wharton, and Stanford with M.B.A.'s in business, sales, and drugs, use experienced talent, with a sense of history and showmanship. A sample executive team that could help TV out of the depression of the 1980's: Martin Mull, in charge of late-night and talk shows; Alan King for prime time; and Uncle Floyd for news and public affairs.

THE DYING OF BELUSHI

John Belushi is still dead, as they used to say about General Franco on *Saturday Night Live*'s "Weekend Update." He died on March 5, 1982. It was a very upsetting experience for me, as it was for Belushi, I'm sure. The fat slob. Why did he have to do it?

Like a million others, I was very upset when the news came that Friday afternoon that John Belushi was dead at thirty-three. It was as if a brother had died. And the way I was on the telephone all the time that Friday night my wife said it was as if I had to make the funeral arrangements. It's not as if some relative died, she said. Why are you carrying on so? It was not the same as when John Lennon died.

He ruined my dinner by dying. I was getting ready to go out with Alan Alda that night. He had flown in from the Coast on the Red Eye, taking a weekend off from *M*A*S*H*. We were going to go to an Indian restaurant on lower Lexington Avenue.

But then they started calling from *The Sandi Freeman Show* on the Cable News Network. They were putting together a panel to pay tribute to Belushi. Would I appear?

What's dinner with a friend? Where were my values, my journalistic principles? I could have the mulligatawny soup and the ghoti balls, jump into a limo, speed over to the CNN studios down at the World Trade Center faster than you can say tandoori chicken, and still have time left over for the mango-chutney ice cream with the silver foil on it.

I should have told the truth: I was too choked up to talk about it. That John would have done the same thing for me—eaten a good meal in honor of the dead. And burped loudly. And then maybe he would have eaten everybody else's meal, too. That's why Laraine Newman and Gilda Radner were able to keep their weight down while they were on the show. Belushi used to eat all their food during rehearsals. It was like a miracle diet having him around—the Wild Boar, or the Pig of Studio 8-H, Diet.

But I went to the cable TV show, anyway. It was a good thing, too. Everybody else they'd said would be on the panel with me had canceled. Chevy Chase, who knew the departed well, was supposed to be there. Childhood friends, industry leaders, all canceled. It turned out, I was it for the whole hour. Me and some clips. For an hour I had to do my Samurai TV Critic act.

The Sandi Freeman Show, then a prizewinning talk show on cable, was a weird media experience. The gorgeous blond hostess is in Atlanta. And her guests are in the World Trade Center, eleven hundred miles away. Her voice is beamed up to a satellite, over India someplace. And so was I. We mix on the satellite, and it all comes back neatly sandwiched. In the studio, I am supposed to watch her on the monitor. But her voice from the satellite arrives six seconds later. Her lips say one thing, and her voice says another. It soon gave me a headache. And as if that weren't bad enough, the hostess didn't seem to understand what I was trying to say about Belushi and the meaning of his death.

I didn't know him personally, I explained. Oh, I had seen him on the set of *Saturday Night Live*, which I liked to hang around, like a reporter on the police beat. We were two ships passing in the night. I never wanted to meet him, either. He wasn't likable in some ways, you know. I didn't want to go to lunch with him, for example. He ate without tools. He was the only man I knew of who ate chef salads with his hands. The mayo, too. He put the dressing on with his fingers. John loved to eat, as they say. He was, too, very sensitive about his weight.

I used to love to hear those stories about him. Do you remember the time he was at the fat farm with William Holden? And they were both in the swimming pool. They were buddies. He asked Bill Holden if he would do one favor for him, one that he would be eternally grateful for. In all seriousness, Belushi asked Holden if he would float like he did in *Sunset Boulevard* (facedown).

I tried to say that it was the system that killed Belushi. Hollywood. Life in the speed lane. Look at his many bad movies, all of which compared unfavorably with his work on *Saturday Night Live*. She didn't know what I was talking about. This is no time to speak ill of the dead, she seemed to be thinking [with the six-second delay]. What better time, I argued, when it's fresh in everybody's minds? *Sic transit Belushi.* There was something sacrilegious to her about discussing his career in any terms short of unstinting praise.

What a disaster, I thought afterward, as the limo raced back to the Indian restaurant and my dinner with the Aldas. "How did it go?" "Fabulous," I explained. And I was right, in a way. The great thing about cable is that nobody sees these things. The programs go off into the airwaves and are stored up there in the ozone, along with all the other great talk-show appearances. You really have to know what to ask for in trying to retrieve an old *Sandi Freeman Show*.

I was angry about John Belushi dying. I was mad at John for not respecting his body and his talent, for depriving us of the chance to see him develop an extraordinary gift. There was no way you can get all of this out about a person who is really nothing in your life, just a few dots on a screen, at best a symbol, a metaphor; it gets all repressed, and makes you even sadder than the events warrant.

John Belushi, I used to say, was my favorite Albanian-American. He represented the flowering of Albanian humor in TV. He was also one of the ten best of the younger comics developed since the mid-1970's on TV—a list that included Dan Aykroyd, Chevy Chase, Rick Moranis, Dave Thomas, Harold Ramis, David Letterman, Robert Klein, Billy Crystal,

Richard Pryor before his accident. "Accident"? Look at how we describe that unfortunate event today.

Belushi was, dammit, a major comic actor, a man who could roll on the floor imitating a frenzied Joe Cocker singing while drinking a can of beer and then capture the calm of a Henry Kissinger or the charm of a Ray Charles. His Elizabeth Taylor, munching on a chicken bone, was better than the original. I used to tune in on *Saturday Night Live* wondering what disguise Belushi would be wearing this time. What a talent. He used to give everything, it seemed. He'd kill himself in a part. He was the readiest, it seemed at the time, of the not-quite-ready-for-prime-time players, the one who could always make me fall down laughing.

I admired his work, raved about him in my column all the time. I wanted NBC to know he was brilliant, a major achievement in TV comedy. NBC should encourage Belushi and others of his persuasion.

And what did it get us fanatics? Success. We helped to make a superstar out of him on *SNL*. And the first thing Belushi did was abandon the show. Praise had apparently gone to his fat head. It goes to nearly everybody's head in TV. And they immediately stop doing what made them so great. It's the catch-22 of the TV arts.

John did not fulfill his promise. Seven pictures in three years? Talk about your fast lane . . . and head-on collisions.

I still remember *1941*—the movie, not the year. The movie, which told the story about what happened the day the Japanese invaded California in 1941, was absolutely stupefying. The best part was the credits. Half the state of California, it seemed, was employed by Steven Spielberg to produce this enormous gumball. They even had three best boys listed (shouldn't they have been better boys?).

1941 was a stupid, slobbish, sluggish, slimy, disgusting, awful comedy—and not only that, it wasn't funny, either. It had toilet jokes—on a Japanese submarine, yet. It made *Animal House*, a dumb movie that I thought was funny anyway, a comedy classic, up there with *Animal Crackers*, or anything written by Aristophanes. Belushi had gotten his career off to a flying crash dive. Belushi as the fighter-pilot ace had two lines of dialogue: his name, rank, and serial number, which he repeated continually, while sucking on a cigar, with grunts, slobberings, drooling, and sputtering spits. The samurai Flying Tiger ace. What he was doing, I think, would probably make even a Japanese audience laugh. Occidentally.

This "blockbuster" movie gave new meaning to self-indulgence. Belushi was a guy starting to slip on his own banana peel and heading straight for the manhole, and if he didn't go in immediately, it was only because he was too big for his britches.

Where were the people, the pros, the friends, to tell Belushi that what he was doing wasn't funny in *1941*? Did Spielberg and his staff, and accountants, actually think the movie was funny at any time? They must have. Nobody spends 30 million bucks on a comedy without hearing, "Hey, that's really funny." The film *1941* was an example of what you get in comedy when people start putting coke, Coke bottles, Mars bars, pencils, and whatever else they use for inspiration in their noses.

There were many other self-indulgent people out there in Hollysnort when Belushi began his movie career. They brought out the worst in John's instincts. *The Blues Brothers* may live in the annals of music, but not of comedy. So much of it was stupid, especially in the business of the police cars. It was the full-size fantasy of a little kid (with a big budget), throwing Tonka cars out of the apartment window to see just how many cars you can destroy before your mother comes in and yells at you. For all the speed, there didn't seem to be a great rush to catch Belushi's latest films, like *Neighbors*. That was his final statement as an artist.

Under the discipline of *Saturday Night Live* in New York, he had seemed to be growing comedically. He was the samurai sketch-show actor doing a kamikaze act that got funnier and funnier. If only he had stayed where he would have continued to develop his craft, someplace where he could have grown up, matured. . . . Instead, he went to the real-life, or unreal-life, kamikaze situation, with no comedy at the end.

I'm not saying that *Saturday Night Live* was the ultimate in TV comedy. What was that show, anyway? Ernie Kovacs revisited—but in Living Color. Have you ever watched a rerun of *The Honeymooners* late at night, forgotten to change the channel, and wound up sitting in front of a Belushi, Radner & Company second-rate skit about piles? "It's like eating a dinner in a fine French bistro," my friend Buddy Zech once explained, "and then running to Burger King for a sundae dessert."

All the greats coming out of *Saturday Night Live* needed more work. Remember the great Chevy Chase, who rushed out to Hollywood before Belushi? Remember his *Chevy Chase's National Humor Test* on NBC (1979)? Why should you? I get paid to remember things like that. It was the start of a new genre of watching TV by peeking through fingers with your eyes cupped by hands. You couldn't believe it. You didn't want to see what was happening; it was so incredibly bad.

Scotch has to age slowly. So does great wine. Even beer. Bread has to rise and bake in time. Seeds need their required months to grow. Look at how long George Burns and Bob Hope have worked at their craft. I couldn't help but think the day I heard John Belushi was dead how he would have been at eighty.

No way he ever would have made it. We put our talent in the microwave ovens. It starts early in TV. A kid has five good lines on a talk show one night. The next day casting agents from both coasts are after him. He gets a three-series deal from Universal. Or he gets a holding deal for one hundred thousand dollars from one of the studios. Then he sits around with other writers for six months or so, thinking of a concept. If the idea is picked up, he lands another hefty chunk of money. He starts giving interviews on what it's all about. Then he is too busy to write the material that he was signed for. They hire other writers to work with him. He does one script. The pilot comes out. And then you don't hear from him again. The sun in L.A. blinds him, the golden vacuum cleaner sucks him up.

The other problem is that children are not equipped to live with success. They find an eleven-year-old kid in a Little League in Wisconsin. The kid can throw a fastball at ninety miles per hour. But he is still eleven years old. The kid is in danger.

When the light hits them, it doesn't cause them to flower, it stunts their growth. They can't benefit from modest failure, as in the vaudeville, radio, local live TV, or little theater. What's their hurry, anyway?

It still makes me mad thinking about the day Belushi died. Too early. He could have been somebody someday. He was too big for TV, and too small for posterity.

BELUSHI II

Live at Five was the first to tell me, that Black Friday, that John Belushi was dead. Jack Cafferty explained on the WNBC-TV local news show: Belushi had died in a car accident. He said it twice, in case you missed it the first time. The first bulletin said it was a car accident; the second time an automobile accident. He later said it was something John ate. He also said there were unconfirmed reports of a drug overdose. This way, no matter what had actually transpired, the Channel 4 news had covered all the bases.

And then the tributes started. We were soon attending a video wake. "He really enjoyed life," Robert Klein was saying. Sure. And maybe he did. Like the kid who says after a wild party, "I must have had a wonderful time. I can't remember a thing.

There were other bizarre events in the coverage that strange first week of Belushi, dead. For example, the natural-causes theory being advanced by the Los Angeles medical examiner. A civil servant named Noguchi, himself something of a superstar, on TV a great deal explaining the causes of the William Holden and Natalie Wood cases, and who already had his own TV show—they say he was the model for *Quincy*—was reporting Belushi's death "from natural causes." Natural that a thirty-three-year-old guy dies in bed. Later, I understood: Cocaine and heroin are natural causes of death in L.A.

But at that moment, I had the crazy feeling as the confusion and fog settled over the cause of Belushi's death the first couple of days that somebody was trying to cover something up, and I couldn't figure out who or why. It was odd that it took so long to find out the cause of death, I remember thinking. The existence of these substances in the body is usually found very, very fast in lab tests, at least on *Quincy*.

A peculiarity of the reporting of this tragic death was that everybody seemed to be waiting for more on the story. Nobody I knew thought they had heard the last of it. Nor has it been told. Someday, somebody will write fiction loosely based on the Belushi case, and the factual story will be told.

So it turned out a week or so later that it was drugs that killed him. He overdosed on whatever they overdosed on in L.A. It was one of the longest-drawn-out overdoses in recent entertainment history. *Orchestrated* is the word I'm searching for. Everything seemed orchestrated about Belushi's going.

It had begun with the way his death was announced to the press by a P.R. woman from the L.A. office of Solters/Roskin/Friedman on Sunset Boulevard. And it continued with the orchestrating of a small funeral in Martha's Vineyard. Lee Solters himself seemed to be conducting the service, at least for the eighty-two members of the press at the cemetery. It seemed strange that Dan Aykroyd should arrive at the church in the old Dodge from *The Blues Brothers*. And that he had a covenient motorcycle to hop on to lead the parade to the gravesite.

Was there a reissue of *The Blues Brothers* being planned in two thousand theaters the next week? And a memorial record album? So Belushi's death wouldn't be a total loss, as they say in California. But, hey, that is show biz.

One becomes cynical. Who was surprised to learn that the private ceremony in New York drew such an SRO crowd it must have been listed in *Celebrity Register* or *TV Guide*. Will they be selling Belushi souvenirs next, a recording of the eulogies, you know, T-shirts, beer cans (crushed), posters, used spoons, mirrors, tacky record offers (*Slim Whitman Sings the Best of Belushi*)? Nothing like dying to boost sales. Look what we've done with the Elvis phenomenon, almost better dead than alive.

Ten days after John Belushi died, I was still searching for the meaning of it all, wondering what that whole thing was about.

What, for example, would the effect of his death be on TV comedy (then almost a contradiction in terms)? What is his legacy?

He made it possible for fat young guys to work on TV. Every off-the-wall, flaky, bizarre young contemporary repertory TV company now had a Belushi-type comedian (short, pudgy, fat, slobby). Well, there had been these types before: Costello, Hardy, Gleason, Bendix. What else did he leave behind culturally? Eating food with his hands? Was Belushi stuffing Jell-O in his mouth as funny as Harpo eating an entire dinner with his hands in *Room Service*? Who was John Belushi, anyway? A George Burns? A Sid Caesar? A Bob Hope? An obscure genius like Milt Kamen? A Lenny Bruce? One possibility occurred to me: He could have no impact. Zero. He could be degaussed in our own time!

The death of Belushi, I soon saw, was a metaphor for what was wrong with TV. Or maybe a megaphor. There was a big truth behind it somewhere, if only I could find it. It was like the old joke: With all the horseshit in the box, there must be a pony in there somewhere.

Who was to blame for what happened to John Belushi? The system killed him, I was one of those quick to say. I am convinced of that. For I always blame the system. Dylan Thomas was killed by "Those Sons of Bitches in their Brooks Brothers suits," as Alan Ginsberg reported. Here was this poor, fat, young comic slob, who does good work for a while on a TV show. The youth of the nation idolize him. He is swept away by the star-making machinery, landing on California's golden shore. In his world, there is no other way to go.

If Belushi had been born in England, he might, after his early success as a comic actor on *Saturday Night Live*, have gone into serious drama on TV, or onstage, work in repertory developing his skills. Like Cleese or Palin or Simon Jones. In the United States, there was only one thing a successful young person like Belushi could do—go into the movies, go Hollywood. If he wanted to try repertory theater in Yorkshire, "Wise up," his agents would have said, like Mephistopheles. "Don't be a big fat dope—go for the bread."

In England, perhaps Belushi might have developed along lines that were not cocaine lines. In England, they don't take as many drugs. Self-control? Self-assurance? As Michael Palin of *Monty Python* explained, "We can't afford it."

Cocaine is very expensive. So is designer bread. Everything is expensive. But the insane sums of money the entertainment industry pays out to young performers who have yet to establish themselves beyond an initial success, before they have built the proper foundations on which a career grows, makes it all possible. It's like keeping the bars open to 4:00 A.M. You close them at 10:30, as they do in saner societies like England, you drink less. Belushi was one of those who didn't go home till the bars closed or after.

Indeed, the bar never closed for John Belushi. When you have enough money to do what your weakest instincts dictate, you do it. The bar was another sort and just came down across his chest and broke him.

If I had a kid who wanted to be an actor, I'd tell him, "Do something useful with your life. Become a waiter. And don't go to California. If you are an orange or a grapefruit, go to California."

Will there be one young comedian who stops, or doesn't start, using cocaine because of Belushi's death? I doubt it. Cocaine is comedy, according to one of my spies, a kind of social, chemical, cultural necessity. They say.

The prevailing attitude seems to be one of, "Well, he was just doing drugs to excess, and it can't happen to me, pass the coke." I read one report that 90 percent of the stand-up comics perform on drugs of some type. I can't see how you can do drugs and know if you're funny or not. How does one perfect his trade when his perception of what's going on is impaired? Glenn Rabney, a young comedian, told me, "Needless to say, my parents read articles about drugs in Hollywood and about Belushi and the like, and start worrying about me. I just prefer to remain straight." He added, "When I perform, some of the common comments to me after are, 'You're really a sick person.' I take it as a compliment. I'm not sure drugs would have a helpful effect. I'd probably become a middle-class accountant at Price Waterhouse." Glenn Rabney, as a performer, is a cross between David Letterman and Martin Mull. Not a bad cross. He does kind of bizarre observations. Very hard to describe. Unfortunately, most of the people who go to comedy clubs these days jokes about sex and drugs.

And the young comedians think they need drugs to do comedy. This is no time to give up drinking and smoking glue, they say. The reason Richard Pryor is so successful is because of "the accident."

Baloney. He would be more successful artistically today without drugs.

W. C. Fields used to drink all the time. Without it, he might have lived to be on TV, like George Burns. He could have had a second career, like Groucho Marx. Look at Edgar Allan Poe and Oscar Wilde, great talents who also died drug-related deaths, incidentally (coke and absinthe). That was the nineteenth century. And they didn't have as much money. And they were geniuses. I also think Edgar Allan Poe and Oscar Wilde would have been better writers without drugs.

I grew up in a period when a newspaperman assumed he had to keep a bottle of whiskey in the desk drawer next to the typewriter. But whatever they accomplished on alcohol was minimal compared to what they could have done without it.

The Marx Brothers and Fred Allen and Jack Benny weren't on drugs. The greats today, like Woody Allen, Steve Allen, Alan King, and Jean Shepherd, aren't on drugs. Drugs necessary to be creative and funny? Salami.

Maybe I was wrong about making it too young. There are people in California who make it young and don't destroy themselves by injecting poison into their veins. The ones who ruin their lives have characteristics in common—they are not the brightest people in the world, and they are of weak character. Character and common sense. If you're together, you survive; if you're not, you don't.

So what am I making such a fuss about? Belushi's death was not a tragedy, like that of John Lennon, who was trying to do something about himself when he was cut down by an assassin. Belushi was just another fast, funny young guy who made it too fast too young, and brought himself to his own end too soon.

I know gluttony is "in." We are all supposed to live to the hilt, or admire those who do. But Freddie Prinze and then John Belushi? What's so great about death in the fast lane?

"Don't mourn John Belushi," an anonymous postcard explained after I wrote my obituaries in the papers. "He has gone to the great animal house in the sky (with a smile, and a coke)."

"If John Belushi is the American people's embodiment of success," Jim Mattimore, an English professor at Suffolk Community College, explained, "I'll pass on it, and gladly accept the sterility of suburbia, life with one loving and giving woman, three children no one could replace, and a debt load that exceeds my income: because I won't be dead at thirty-three."

And, yes, I know that all rock-and-rollers die tragically in plane crashes, metaphorically, when they are too young. But it isn't fair. And it still makes me sad thinking about John and what he could have been, and all of TV.

DOPES DOING DRUGS

In the goodness of its heart, and with compassion and understanding for the personal plight and suffering of those involved—the star, the supporting cast, not to mention the technicians and others—CBS, two days before Christmas, 1984, announced it was dropping *Mickey Spillane's Mike Hammer*, starring Stacy Keach, from its schedule.

At the time Keach was having a slight problem with his own schedule. He was in prison in Reading, England.

He had been jailed two weeks before the CBS decision, after being tried and found guilty of possession of 1.3 ounces of cocaine. His appeal was turned down (a day before the decision to cancel *Mike Hammer*). He was to be in the slammer for nine months.

Anybody else probably would have gotten nine years for such a stash of cocaine. I saw *Midnight Express*. I know what can happen to Americans in foreign countries when it comes to drugs. The card says, "Go directly to jail." It does not say, "Come out and do episodes of a TV show."

But canceling a show because a star was paying his debt to society? That seemed a high price for the *Mike Hammer* TV show fans to pay. Canceling a show for a mere jail sentence? Why, earlier that season, Jon-Erik Hexum had shot himself, accidentally, and that didn't stop CBS from keeping his show, *Cover Up*, on.

As a matter of fact, there was an even more valid reason for *Mike Hammer* to go on, with its central character in the pokey. All the good guys in private-eye and other law-enforcement shows regularly violate laws in the pursuit of law and order. I hadn't counted the number of violations in a regular *Mike Hammer* hour, then running on Saturday nights. But a friend of mine, the lawyer Alan Levine, then of the New York Civil Liberties Union, once counted fourteen abuses of law in an average episode of *Mannix*. Indictable offenses by Joe Mannix went from speeding, to driving on the wrong side of the road, to trespassing, breaking and entering, bribing a public official, and obstructing justice. And that's when he was not doing anything illegally. It could have been very educational for viewers to see a hero like Hammer in the slammer. To get his thoughts on what it's like inside a British gaol, as they call it.

The Keach case was fascinating. It was so stupid of him to have carried cocaine in his suitcase to start with. The Brits were super antidrug in those days, anyone could have told him. It used to be that only the upper classes did drugs in the U.K., the only ones who could afford it. Now, kids were being hooked on heroin, as in New York. It's become a working-class problem: drugs in the council estates (public-housing projects). The BBC has documentaries showing school kids doing heroin; they now had dealers in the school yards. The American way! The police were on a drug crusade.

As a young British director, Joanna Proctor, explained, "Everybody knows they have dogs sniffing the baggage these days. You really have to be out of it to try to smuggle it in." Besides, she added helpfully, "It's so cheap on the streets, anyway."

Then, it was a shock to me—and probably more so to Keach—that he actually went to jail. Heavy duty! as the cultural British say.

Keach made an impassioned speech before the court. From the clips in the papers, it ranked with Nathan Hale's, a kind of "I regret that I have only one nose to give to my country" speech. His oration was filled with contrition and apology and new paths to be followed. He obviously thought they would let him off because he's a well-known and good actor. At worst he'd have to do community service, a reading or two of "The Ballad of Reading Gaol" in the grammar schools, or he'd be assigned to gardening on weekends in Hyde Park. In the United States celebrities like Robert Evans have been similarly severely punished.

Britain, too, is a land of free speech, and after his wonderful talk, they threw him into the slammer right away. "Thank you very much. Well said. Nine months."

Mr. Keach was deluding himself. Our country must sometimes seem like a kindergarten, a Garden of Eden where anything is possible, where you can break the laws and get off with a tap on the wrist if you're rich and famous enough.

Or maybe the court had not enjoyed his recent work, as in *Mistral's Daughter*, a jailable offense in itself.

Actually, the greatest good to the community—"his public," as CBS calls it—might have been his going to jail. Possibly it taught the kids a lesson. Stars are up there and they always get away with it, or so it seems. Not so, the Reading decision says, they are not above the law.

The case helped explain some of the mysteries about Keach's career. His performance on TV, for example, had always been erratic.

He was first arrested in May 1984, on the cocaine charge, on his way to Paris, where he was filming the curiously awful *Mistral* miniseries. He was very strange as the passionate painter, Mistral, who, as I explained, painted like a madman for eight hours. He even ate paint while in the throes of creativity. Somebody told him Van Gogh did that. Good thing nobody told him about the ear.

It reminded me of what Margot Kidder said in *Glitter Dome*, the great HBO movie based on Joseph Wambaugh's novel exposing life in Holly-snort. Kidder, playing an actress in the fast lane, tells James Garner, the police detective, "The reason we take so many drugs is the material."

It was doubly unfortunate that Keach was caught with coke in his shaving-cream can. With Coca-Cola running Columbia Pictures, the makers of his *Mike Hammer* series thus had to reduce their passionate interest in rehabilitation for the man. Had Keach been involved with some other chemical substance, Percodan, or even caffeine, it would have been less of a problem.

Or maybe it was just the disappearing audience. There is nothing like bad ratings to turn a network's small heart into a lump of coal in a Christmas stocking.

As with the sad death of John Belushi, there was more here than meets the nose.

I thought of Stacy Keach's fall again during an antidrug campaign conducted by CBS in September of 1986. It was part of a massive antidrug crusade on TV called *Stop the Madness*, featuring a lot of big stars like Michelle Lee, Kate Jackson, Pat Summerall, Linda Gray, and Stacy Keach delivering ten-second messages about the drug epidemic sweeping the nation. Also, at CBS Dan Rather was doing a major documentary called *Forty-eight Hours on Crack Street*, which featured Dan in Times Square without his tie on. It ran forty-seven hours too long. Sophia Loren was playing a drug buster, an undercover woman from the DEA, in a TV movie called *Courage*. Potsie (Anson Williams) from *Happy Days* and Dave Toma from *Toma* were telling kids the way it was on *The Drug Knot*. And that was one network alone (CBS). Everyone was antidrug on TV.

This was not like the 1970's, when we were all pro drugs. Oh sure, they never came out and said Support Your Local Drug Dealers. The programs, when they dealt with the subject head on, explained that drugs could burn your brain out. But the message on TV was that drugs were cool. But they did not, in the main, deal head on in a way any fourteen-year-old could understand.

I frankly hated the way they made jokes about drug use. Some notable talk-show hosts, including Johnny Carson, along with their guests, thought it hysterically funny to talk about a "laid-back society," with a wink, that being stoned was an admirable way of life. They made allusions to the studio orchestra getting its shipment from Colombia, ad nauseam.

In his opening monologue one night, Johnny Carson talked about the unusual weather—there was snow in Brentwood and Beverly Hills—and a little kid said, "Daddy, somebody dropped SHIT." But what was originally a reference to cocaine was turned by the censor into garbled gibberish on the audio.

And it was worse on cable. You could get a high just turning on the TV. Robin Williams, one of the leading drug jokers, was a major talent and a leading role model. And I appreciate that drugs can make you see little mice in Frederick's of Hollywood lingerie. But kids are impressionable. It became a national joke, which famous person was on what stuff, and who wasn't.

Billy Crystal said, "When it snows in southern California, half the population is out there snorting the driveway." With cocaine having such a debilitating effect on the young, one would have thought those many people would not find the use of a controlled substance a source of humor. The dramas were worse. They portrayed the drug scene as glamorous. Dealers on *Miami Vice* always had good clothes, good cars, and good music behind them. Sure they got caught in the end. But doesn't everybody?

And I disliked the way TV turned over its air time to a guy like Timothy Leary, high priest of altered consciousness in the 1960's. It made me want to throw up at the way TV idolized him on *Live at Five* and other shows, when he was making the rounds in the early 1980's plugging his new dog-and-pony act with Gordon Liddy. He did incalculable damage to the youth of America, and now he was back as a hero.

"Pleasure drugs," they were calling them. And the front-page stories were saying three out of two people were on cocaine. Everybody seemed to be in it or on it. Word was out that Lassie was putting stuff in her nose.

But no more. TV has declared war on drugs now. They're in the fight to the end, or until the first commercial break, whichever comes faster.

It reminded me of the "Get High with Yourself" campaign of 1981, one of the major social achievements of the Grant Tinker regime at NBC—a whole week of programming with an antidrug theme. Of course, Tinker had long insisted that drug use was not a problem in Hollywood's TV community.

Brandon Tartikoff, who first thought of the idea after Robert Evans suggested it, had been high on his idea for weeks. You would think it the greatest thing since the invention of the orthicon tube. But you've

got to understand this about Brandon, who was to be the head of programming at NBC. Everything he did was monumental. When he gets
a call through to New York from the Coast, he gets a high.

Get High with Yourself was supposed to give young viewers an alternative to drugs. It featured a special made by the noted film producer
and drug user Robert Evans, and a series of jingles starring America's
drug-free heroes, like Ted Nugent, singing "Get High with Yourself."
The jingles, which varied in length from a minute to a minute and a half,
were running sort of like Bicentennial minutes.

The cast featured the Getting High Chorus, sort of the Vienna Boys'
Choir of California, with kids from eight to eighteen jumping up and down
like at revival meetings. Each spot was basically the same. But when you
stared at them, you suddenly saw other stars in the group, Cheryl Tiegs,
Linda Gray, Muhammad Ali, Bob Hope, Magic Johnson, and so forth.

But the main thing you heard was the message in the song (written by
Steven Karman of "I Love New York"), asking you to get high with
yourself. Find your own thing.

Easy for them to say. The trouble is that many of us who view TV don't
have much of a self to work with. We are burned out inside—from watching TV all the time.

"You can make yourself higher," the jingle said, "than you have ever
known/When you're making up your own mind." A nice plea for being
an individual, for marching to your own drummer, making up your own
mind. Right after the jingle one night, I heard a laugh track. TV won't
even let kids decide a simple little thing like when to laugh.

I was surprised by how many people did not use drugs. According to
the special. (Didn't Tattoo in *Fantasy Island* ever take any growth pills?
Didn't Cheryl Tiegs ever take any weight-reducing pills?) Oh—there was
a misconception about the entertainment world. Olivia Newton-John explained that most people in show business don't really use drugs. And
people in Australia never do.

The best part of the show was when Burt Reynolds told kids how useless
drugs are. Kids could identify with Burt because they love his movies,
like *Cannonball Run, Hooper,* and *Smokey and the Bandit I* and *II.* The
message was, I guess: Kids, kill yourselves behind the wheel, not behind
the needle.

"I was so depressed by the special that halfway through the show I
went out to get high," explained my pen pal Andrew J. Rossi. It was an
incredibly dopey campaign, weird seeing Ted Nugent standing up and
calling himself drug free on national TV. And the big hit song never was,
either.

There were, too, all those social-issue TV movies. I remember Doug McKeon in the 1982 classic *Desperate Lives*. It ended on an upbeat note, with everybody in the high school throwing their illegal substances on a bonfire in the high-school gym.

"I think that was the most pathetic waste of time I've ever seen," explained Howie Abrams, Queens Village TV critic, age fourteen (at the time). "They should have run the cameras about twenty minutes longer to see how many people flew out of the room after being in a closed gym with about ten pounds of burning pot in front of them."

TV movies were often so juvenile that only adults who didn't know what was going down liked them. The kids laughed.

Will massive publicity help stop drug usage? It might. It could have a reverse effect. People not on drugs could conceivably wonder, given all the heavy message shows, what they are missing.

Impossible? Kids are not too smart. You know what happened with cigarettes. Kids know cigarettes are bad for them. It says on every pack that it's dangerous to their health. But kids also know they are going to live forever. The ads are getting more and more specific, listing exact diseases. And young women are smoking more. They could put messages on the models' foreheads, and they still wouldn't listen.

And you always wonder if the drug specials on TV ever get to the right people in the first place. The ones who need it most are on the streets, smoking and holding up people to pay for their drugs. Those watching the messages and documentaries are the good and convinced, like you and me. Bad people aren't watching TV. They're out there making trouble or hurting themselves.

I started worrying about this problem when David Begelman did his famous TV documentary about angel dust. He was sick, you remember. The famous movie-industry executive (Columbia Studios president) had a rare disease later diagnosed as *forgitis*. It made his hand write checks in exactly the same signature as other famous people. So they let him serve his sentence by doing a little TV special on a social problem. He could have done it on morality in show biz, but he chose angel dust. Did the punishment fit the crime?

Begelman was a fucking common forger. What did that have to do with angel dust? Why didn't the courts make him do a documentary on penmanship? That's the point. Or confess in public: Tell kids his life story, where he went wrong, and why he won't do it again. Why didn't they just throw Robert Evans in jail instead of letting him off with a TV work project? Why send anybody to jail? If they arrest some poor slobs in the Bronx for doing what Begelman or Evans did, why not tell them they can go home if they can get their friends to make a video special?

Now it's no fun going to jail. I'm reminded of the judge who recently refused to send somebody away to the slammer because he'd mix in with a bad element.

Doing a TV special can be hell, and it is difficult work. But it's not going to jail.

I would respect this campaign more had Evans gone to jail, then come out, contrite, reformed, rehabilitated, and voluntarily offered to conduct a crusade against drugs. "I did a bad thing, I paid my dues, debt to society, etc."

The real message in the "Get High" campaign is society's double standard. In these inflated times, it's almost a triple standard. If you're a big enough big shot, it says, you can get away with anything.

And so, suddenly, four years later, the TV industry was against drugs again. It's holier-than-thou time again.

These moral-fervor fevers last about thirty minutes (as in government). I remember the ZPG crusade in the 1960's, when the networks were all supposed to cut down on large families in shows like *The Brady Bunch*, thus reducing, like electronic Malthusians, overcrowding on Earth. And the anticigarette campaign! After years of fighting the idea, claiming they would be committing economic suicide if they had to stop cigarette commercials (talk about blowing smoke in our eyes), they stopped. The bankruptcy rate of networks did not increase.

And then, perhaps most important, actors were no longer to smoke. Kids were so easily led, and actors looked so suave and socially secure.

Notice how many cigarettes Joan Collins refuses in *Dynasty* (cough-cough) these nights? Of course, they are imported. When Don Johnson smokes on *Miami Vice*, what's that—chicken liver?

They get bored in TV, restless, always needing the high of a new campaign, a new cause.

Will *Miami Vice* now fight hookers, the squalid, unglamorous work Vice traditionally does in police organizations? Moving Crockett and Tubbs out of the glamorous drug scene alone would do more to deglamorize drugs for TV viewers than Tom Brokaw looking around for crack in the streets.

The thing about drug shows like *Miami Vice* is that much of the audience is rooting for the dope dealers to get away, not be busted.

On the one hand, they had all the antidrug shows on NBC for a month (in September 1986). And then Willie Nelson was playing a dope dealer on the *Miami Vice* premiere. How many users did likable old Willie turn away from drugs?

The trouble with TV and its big causes is that the problems don't go away after thirty minutes, like the shows.

THE DRUG OF (MY) CHOICE

Religion used to be the opiate of the masses. Then, it was TV. Today, opium is the opiate of the masses.

The big news I learned from an NBC white paper called *Pleasure Drugs: The Great American High*, reported by Edwin Newman, is that cocaine is growing in popularity for consciousness-altering. Marijuana is still popular. So are Quaaludes, sleeping pills, uppers, and downers.

I didn't mean to suggest that cocaine was only TV's problem. I was driving past the City College School of Business (now the Bernard Baruch School) on the corner of Lexington Avenue and East Twenty-third Street in Manhattan one night. In 1948–49, I went to night school there. We worked all day, and studied all night. What a shock it was to see those who had followed in my Thom McAn's. The now generation was standing on the corner outside the school with the radios on, buying and selling, a new generation of accountants, accounting for the economics of drugs.

I don't like marijuana. The smell of it in movie theaters doesn't make me tranquil; it gets me angry. In Loew's State, watching *Reds*, they were lighting up. Even with an exciting movie like that, the ten days that shook the world, the Russian Revolution wasn't enough to occupy their minds. I deplore the way the advocates keep saying it's like drinking. Well, I don't like drinking that much, either. I keep hearing users say marijuana doesn't affect them. Then they would have no objection to their neurosurgeon, on the way into the O.R., stopping off for a few joints? I've seen famous humorists sitting around laughing at their own jokes while under the influence; believe me, it does affect them—and leaves us cold.

I don't like cocaine, either. As a matter of fact, I hate all drugs. All arguments to the contrary, I prefer being conscious. There's a lot of stuff going on I'm afraid I'll miss.

People, the *National Enquirer*, and the *Star* are filled with stories of actors who are confessing they have abused drugs—during the years I used to watch their shows, too. What does that say about me? And the abuse of the audience?

If I read another confession by a druggy superstar, I'm going to scream. Or start taking drugs.

I have little tolerance for comedians or actors or writers who say they need drugs to create. The drug of my choice, I guess, is TV. It does enough damage to any one mind.

TELEVISION ABUSE

The greatest drug of all in television is money. Under the influence of money, even I have been known to do or say or write anything. Money is a drug of choice.

I was paying my bills late one morning in the summer of 1982, when I saw an item in the paper about David's Hartman's new contract.

In his previous contract, the host of *Good Morning America* had been paid $850,000 a year. I don't know how he could get by on that money.

In the new ABC contract, Hartman was to make $2,076,776 a year, or just a little more than Dan Rather. Even more epochal, David Hartman was making not only more than Rather. He was making more than Johnny Carson, who makes only a tad less than God! Even in an era of staggering salaries, this made the mind reel.

$2.1 million! No wonder ABC was trying to add extra commercials. They had to pay for David's salary. This is right out of the Weimar Republic. That's $39,998 a week. Most people I know would be overjoyed at earning that in a year. I'd be happy just to have the taxes David must pay.

MORE ABOUT MONEY

Imagine David Hartman getting $2.1 million a year for doing what he did, whatever it was. What was a David Hartman, anyway? A failed actor (name his last series—and you win $2.1 million) on a morning show that had failed five or six times. And even with Hartman as host, not many people watched his show, or any of the rival early-morning shows. In the 1980's, more people *read* about David Hartman and his salary, or his feuds with his co-hosts and producers, than watched *Good Morning America*. In the early A.M. drive-time, we watch radio.

Once a washed-up baseball-pitcher-turned-teacher, in *Lucas Tanner*—also Dr. Paul Hunter of the *Bold Ones*—the $2.1 million bionic newsman? Every time he went to lunch back in 1982, with an agent, a lawyer, or another network's executive, his bosses at ABC sweated dollar signs.

In the eleven or more years after David Hartman began as host of *Good Morning America*, many changes had taken place. For example, in 1981, he started to believe he was Henry Kissinger, talking about momentous things. Instead of saying "gosh" or "gee," his original contributions to the show, he began analyzing the budget and giving his views on enforcing the gold standard. He had met enough congressmen and senators. Informed people still didn't know what it was all about, but David was able to explain the complex mechanism not in supply-side but in slide-side economics. He was talking about missile systems, giving their code names. He had become the most authoritative TV person since Merv Griffin was solving the Vietnam War in the late 1960's.

A major, seismic change for television. I had always assumed David was hired by ABC as their morning-news anchorman because of the puzzled look on his face, as if what was coming through on his earphone was another program. His initial success was in asking questions while looking quizzical, as in "huh?"

And the nice thing about David was he was the same way off camera. In person, he seemed a profoundly stupid person. And arrogant about it, too. He approached all subjects with the same serious and self-important air. The subjects themselves were serious and important, but he wasn't. My fear at cocktail parties that both David and I attended was of getting trampled in the stampede of people who were trying to get away from one of his private discussions of national or world affairs.

$2.1 million—five times as much as the president of the United States earns. Or gets, anyhow. Where are our priorities?

I had experienced a similar bewilderment a few months earlier during the exciting negotiations contingent on the signing of Tom Brokaw as the new co-anchorman of *The NBC Evening News*, with Tom Brokaw and Roger Mudd, and/or *The NBC Evening News*, with Roger Mudd and Tom Brokaw (whose name was to go first was one of the bargaining points). NBC was offering him the whole city of Minneapolis to keep him from going to ABC.

ABC's first offer to Brokaw, I learned, was two square blocks of Manhattan (Sixth Avenue—from West Fifty-Seventh to Fifty-ninth); four Leonard Goldenson paintings (originals); plus Suzanne Somers's option, or Suzanne, whichever was larger. And a trillion dollars in petty cash.

Meanwhile, CBS was saying they were "interested" in Brokaw. CBS wants Brokaw, my sources were saying. My sources were the newspapers. They'd like to have Barbara Walters, and Prince Charles, too. Sometimes I thought CBS's "interest" was malicious. It kept driving the star's prices up. CBS might have been hoping to bankrupt the other networks with its "interest," if you ask me. It's solid business practice in today's TV-news journalism, not to get the story first, or correctly, but to bust the competition.

What Brokaw had going for him in the negotiations, it turned out, was RCA Chairman Thornton Bradshaw, a longtime admirer and friend of Brokaw who maintained executive distance and objectivity. "Give him what he wants," he told NBC's negotiators. Under no circumstances was NBC going to let Brokaw go to ABC or the disinterested CBS.

Of course, the actual figures TV anchors get are never official. They are not listed in the annual reports. I knew for a fact (as a stockholder at the time Hartman's contract was negotiated) that Elton Rule, the president of ABC, was earning in cash and cash-equivalent forms of remuneration: $720,000 in "salaries, directors' fees, and bonuses"; $73,067 from "securities and insurance benefits"; and $211,180 from "the aggregate of contingent forms of remuneration."

The last figure I heard on Tom's contract was $1.9 million per year. But my brain, or VCR, starts to short out at the numbers $1.75 million. Anyway, the contracts escalate all the time. As with the Congress, when you see a figure in the papers, you have to know which phase of the deal you're talking about. Only the IRS, like the Shadow, knows.

There is no doubt, however, that Tom got a nice piece of change, more even than I may make from this book, difficult as that may be to believe. This is what I love about TV. As his reward for failing in the morning— and how else could you characterize the way the *Today* show went from first to no-longer-first under his anchormanship (1976–82) in this most bottom-line of the commercial arts—and now they were deluging him with offers. It was an example of what the philosopher-novelist Harold Robbins once called "the Theory of Ostentatious Failure." Every time you fail, have your agents ask for more. Failing up, it's called. Brokaw is a source of inspiration to all of us potential failures out there, I thought, paying my bills that month.

I later learned of another reason to admire Brokaw's contract more than his work. Apparently it was written into his deal that he wouldn't have to appear on the *Today* show, no matter what. In case its ratings dropped without him, they couldn't bring him back to beef up the show. Or beef down. He couldn't be made to visit the scene of the crime; it had something to do with constitutional guarantees against self-incrimination. The

Brokaw emperor's clothes provision should be a lesson to agents. It will live in the annals of great TV-journalism contracts, a course I would like to see given at J-schools for fledgling newspeople. When your contract makes more news than the latest summit conference, you are the summit.

But seriously, folks, the stories about Hartman's, Brokaw's, Rather's, and Barbara Walters's contracts all violate another of Kitman's Laws: *Something is wrong when news makers make the news.*

There was so much news about TV newsmen that I began to think that newsmen were the cause of inflation. Anchormen were an economic index, like the prime interest rate, freight-train loadings, the price of hog bellies and corn futures. Along with the Dow Jones and Amex figures, I heard one day, "Gold was up in Zurich, and in anchormen trading the price was up in Boston and down in Dayton and Fort Lauderdale . . ." It was getting to be a new commodity market.

As, indeed, a source soon confirmed. One morning my breakfast was disturbed by a story in *TV Guide*, which asked the question, "$500,000 + [Plus] a Year For Reading the Local News? Are They Worth It?"

But, of course, explained Bill Fyffe, "dapper and mellow-voiced," as *TV Guide* described the then-general-manager of WABC-TV, my favorite local TV station, the figures were not outlandish. "My God," he explained in his mellow, dapper voice, which I could recognize even in print, "their price is established in the free market place, and they are worth every cent that we're willing to pay. People who are electric, commanding, compelling, believable, real intelligent, are rare commodities."

("He neglected to add 'informed,'" the *TV Guide* reporter said. A smart-ass.)

That was easy for Fyffe to say. He should know. More than any one man, he created the boom market in New York's local anchors. They didn't call him the Bank of Fyffe for nothing. And to understand this pace-setting, you'll have to allow me a report on New York.

Fyffe's financial coup in March 1983 was signing that electric, commanding, compelling, believable, real intelligent commodity Ernie Anastos, for $750,000 a year. But nobody should be expected to work for a flat three quarters of a million dollars a year anymore. His salary would be escalating to a million dollars a year in the course of a five-year deal. With such an escalator, who needs an elevator?

Yet Fyffe hadn't created New York's inflation. The dapper mellifluous general manager had only thrown oil on the fire. Or oil on the oily.

The great bull market in local anchormen began in 1981, under Fyffe's predecessor at Channel 7, with the "discovery" of the electric personality Storm Field. At the time there was a lawyer-agent named Dweck (honest) who was going around trying to peddle Field, then a minor weather guy, at Channel 7 whose expertise was in prescribing eyeglasses. (He is also an ordained optometrist.) Dweck was asking for triple Field's old salary. Nobody was interested. But fate waved its wand at Storm and Dweck— creating *Sturm und Drang*. Why the turmoil? Channel 7 had just lost their most popular sportscaster, Warner Wolf, who earlier had asked a logical question: "Are you going to rehire me? If so, can we renegotiate my contract?" Channel 7 pretended he was speaking a foreign language. They made him feel like dirt. By the time Wolf said he was leaving Channel 7, they were willing to pay anything to keep him. But he went to Channel 2 for even less money than Channel 7 would have paid him.

Reeling under the blow of the loss of the Big W, Channel 7 didn't want to lose its weather guy at the same time. It could have created a transitional feeling, as in the rats leaving the sinking show. Rather than laughing in Dweck's face when he made his incredible demand, Channel 7 said sure. So they paid three times what anyone else might have paid for Storm, with a salary, bonus, options. Imagine: five hundred thousand dollars a year for a weather forecaster (who was right half the time. Maybe.) To be an anchorman?

Field went on to a career as an anchorman filled, as in a weather report, with highs and lows. A high was the night when he revealed he didn't know the difference between Tennessee Ernie Williams, or was it Tennessee Williams Ford? He referred to the famous playwright who died as "Tennessee Ernie (sic) Williams."

At least he didn't call him "Jerry Lee Williams."

A low was his suspension for accepting a free trip out West, despite his half-million-a-year salary. He was also suspended for not doing a promo for *Eyewitness News*. I thought this might have been a burst of good taste or principle. But we found out he didn't want to do it because he wasn't getting paid. Stormy, the weatherman gone to anchor, was often under a cloud during his reign.

Storm Field used to make people think. Here was a guy earning five hundred thousand dollars a year who sometimes appeared as if he wouldn't know a story if it ran up and bit him on the leg. TV people started thinking: If this guy is worth half a mil a year, I can imagine what I'm worth. Fyffe usually agreed.

Fyffe's first big move was the opportunity to hire Tom Snyder as an anchorman for $750,000. Fyffe jumped at the opportunity. He discarded the station's Ernie Anastos like a three-day-old newspaper with coffee stains.

Then Snyder proved to be a ratings bomb. The station went from first to third. Not good. So Fyffe went back to his checkbook.

He said to Ernie, approximately, "I concede we were a little bit hasty in getting rid of you. How would you like to come back to work for us at twice your original salary from a few months ago?"

Anastos, who had been thrown overboard like an old anchor to make way for Storm Field, used to impress station executives when he sat in temporarily for Field on the five o'clock show. Of course he impressed people. Station executives at Channel 7 would have been impressed by Mr. Rogers as anchorman. The Cookie Monster or Yogi Bear would have been still more impressive. Field was not your toughest act to follow.

Anastos a millionaire anchorman? Frightening. But that was the developing financial mentality under Fyffe. If *Eyewitness News* wasn't the best news show, it was the highest-priced in history. Under Fyffe, the anchor team looked to make more than the Knicks or the starting backfield of the L.A. Rams. Commercials on the newscast were going to cost as much as the Super Bowl.

It was an ironic footnote, or bank note, to a situation: *Eyewitness News* had become popular because it appealed to blue-collar audiences. And now it had all these semimillionaires in the chairs.

Maybe what Channel 7 should do, I thought, is change its orientation. Why not a news show for rich people only? No more stories about the poor, nobody living under bridges, no more homeless, starving, huddled masses. These things depress rich people. Have commercials for yachts and polo-pony food.

Meanwhile, all this was not lost on blond, handsome Chuck Scarborough, crack anchorman at WNBC-TV, the home of three news shows we thought of as *Live at Five, Dead at Six, Buried at Eleven*. At one time he had been the most highly paid local anchorman in New York, and thus the free world. Now, he saw himself slipping into fourth place, behind Anastos, Snyder, Field.

Scarborough was not precisely a pauper. Between him and his wife of the time (Henry's daughter, Anne Ford), they could buy NBC. Before his last contract renegotiation, he was getting half a million. Chicken feed. Maybe food stamps were thrown in. But Scarborough once said that any major anchorman is worth seven hundred thousand dollars. As a minimum, Scarborough would consider working for a million. He also wanted other concessions, such as appearances on the *Today* show. Clearly, a two-million-dollar man of the future.

Sue Simmons, his co-anchor at six and eleven, Chuckette to his Chuck, was earning $475,000 a year (1981–82).

Dr. Frank Field (Storm's dad) was then earning $370,000 doing weather and science, etc. But he'd been around for a century.

Even a college dropout, a former DJ from Reno, Jack Cafferty, was getting $230,000 to co-anchor the *Live at Five* show, and he didn't even know how to pronounce "DeKalb Avenue" (a main street in Brooklyn). The station had a champagne celebration in honor of his new contract. Although it's hard to know what they were celebrating. Cafferty reportedly had been appalled that everybody was making more than him.

Warner Wolf, my favorite sportscaster at WCBS/2 who coined the phrase "Let's go to the videotape," the son of a stand-in for one of the Three Stooges, was then making close to five hundred thousand dollars.

The weakest sister in the *Eyewitness News* team makes more than Babe Ruth.

Babe Ruth—as a TV viewer once asked, "Who was she?"

Bill Fyffe says that anyone who questions the salaries of TV newspersons is jealous. He couldn't be referring to me. I think anchormen may not be worth it, but most station executive are. Base pay for local station executives should be a mil a year, with stock options, plus 2 percent of the station's gross. Then, if they actually make a correct decision from time to time, they should get merit raises and bonuses. Anything less would be silly. I mean, what is broadcasting—a slave-labor camp?

Any question about anchorpeople's salaries always brings to mind: for doing what?

1. For coming in an hour ahead of time, to scan something written by another person?

2. Reading the TelePrompTer? Some don't even do that well. Have you ever watched my favorite brunette, and my ex-dentist's, Sue Simmons, whose salary was approaching half a million a year, trying to read a word like *Tylenol*? On one show she pronounced it three ways in one half-hour period. Hardly a night goes by without a new assault on the English language. One night she tried to read a story about William Musto, a New Jersey state senator who had run into problems. "Last week," she explained, "he was sentenced to seven years in prisoners in 'rackinteering.' " Then she added, "We'll have further on this reporter at six." She might have meant "more" on the report.

Then, when she did the Musto story again, on the theory of doing the thing till you get it right, it came out: "The State Supreme Court ruled that sate (sic) Senator William Musto must step down because of a racketeering convention (sic)." One could see people coming to the ballroom with badges, BIG MOE FROM CHICAGO, etc., balloons, banners at the door. She must have meant State Senator Musto and his racketeering *conviction*. The news with Sue Simmons is like Burns and Allen, only without George Burns.

There was the night Sue said it would cost "sixteen hundred dollars" to renew a driver's license in New York. It was sixteen dollars.

A real-estate man once told me he could live with 10 percent inflation a year. It was good for the real-estate business. But the rate of inflation in TV journalism is unreal; it's *Monopoly* money talk. We all remember when Barbara Walters got a million dollars a year, and made headlines. If anybody is worth it, Barbara is. But nobody in the news business is. They're all overpaid.

It could be that salaries in baseball are inflated, too. Remember DiMaggio getting twenty-five thousand dollars in 1939, and trying to strike as an individual? All the players are overpaid. It could be everybody is overpaid today, except you and me.

The good side of the incredibly large salaries is that they could make TV newsmen honest. Who could afford to "buy," for argument's sake, Tom Brokaw, have Tom in his hip pocket, because poor Tom has to send the kids to private school? Tom will be able to buy his kid's school by the time the child reaches the right age.

Such salaries could improve journalistic ethics. Nobody would dare suggest, for example, that Morley or Harry or Ed do commercials on *60 Minutes*. Can you imagine how effective Mike would be, say, selling watches? I suppose we should be thankful none of our superstar high-paid journalists have to earn money underneath the table, or take payoffs from P.R. firms, as was once common in newspapers.

Big salaries, however, are tough on journalists, too. Bryant Gumbel was lamenting one morning (during the first week after he took over Brokaw's chair on the *Today* show) how he couldn't find anything decent in the way of a condo to live in for under eight hundred thousand dollars. And it would cost another quarter of a million to renovate. That was Gumbel's way of relating to the audience as a new person on that show? His way of making friends? The problem probably grabbed the Detroit guy who hadn't bolted on a fender in a long time.

You lose touch with the real people.

Big money also affects judgment in news management. When you pay somebody five hundred thousand dollars a year, or more, all you can see when you look at their work on the tube is zeroes. You see everything through what you have paid for it. What do you *mean* they're not good? Look at how much we're paying them. They must be good. Something is omitted from the syllogism.

Money, in TV news, blinds. Money is like opaque sunglasses. The more you pay, the less you see. There are many Stevie Wonders in TV news.

Cut it out. These people will appear on TV anyway. The real perks in TV don't come from money. Fame is the biggest perk of all. Even if you're a no-talent, being on TV validates you. People recognize you, many admire you. Mere money can't buy that. TV fame, as virtue once was, should be its own reward.

THE COLOR OF MONEY

The little fellow who plays Arnold in the NBC comedy about the Park Avenue millionaire who adopts two kids from Harlem refused to come to work when production started on the show's second season. He was dissatisfied with his contract. It shut the show down on July 16, 1979. Apparently Gary Coleman was only getting sixteen hundred dollars a week for his work in *Diff'rent Strokes*. Another case of the workers being exploited and the need for stricter child-labor laws.

He had a point. By Hollywood standards, sixteen hundred dollars a week was allowance money. There were kids in Beverly Hills who ran up that kind of phone bill for the month.

It's hard for us to comprehend such things. But sixteen hundred dollars was really taking advantage of a ten-year-old kid. Probably because he was black.

"He is the highest-paid performer per inch on TV," an NBC executive said angrily when I accused him of being unfair to labor, blacks, etc.

The kid is still underpaid. Gary Coleman was the funniest thing NBC had (at the time), if you didn't count Freddie Silverman.

Laverne and Shirley, I heard that summer, had threatened to quit their show unless ABC gave them a few treasures from the King Tut exhibit. As far as NBC was concerned, Gary Coleman *was* King Tut, the boy prince of television, a superstar who could bring the people out. The network and the production house, Norman Lear's Tandem Productions, had treated this child meanly.

I didn't think much of *Diff'rent Strokes* when it opened on November 3, 1978. But that was before I saw *Hello, Larry*. The situation-comedy department at NBC was specializing in grimly unfunny programs.

Against this background, Gary Coleman was a giant of comedy and worth his weight (fifty pounds) in gold. I first noticed him in 1977, when he was but a boy of nine, playing a miniature Martin Mull on an episode of *America 2-Nite*. The spoof of the spoof was called "America After Lunch." You could tell the kid was a star from the start.

A basic function of programming in the 1980's became finding another Gary Coleman. One wasn't enough.

The Gary (an award I gave each year for the Best Coleman Clone) was won in 1983 by Emmanuel Lewis, the precious little orphan who was so cute everybody could just eat him, playing Webster in ABC's . . . well, *Webster*.

This phenomenon is not a racial issue. Garys can be of any color. Ricky Schroder, for example, was the 1982 Gary Coleman clone. The child actor, who got his start in show biz as the Ivory Snow baby, starred in an NBC series, *Silver Spoons* (which I improved by calling *Gag Me with a Silver Spoon*).

The development of a new Gary Coleman is a difficult process. It's a synthesis of many elements, like making a new artificial sweetener in the laboratory. You want it to be just sweet enough, not kill you.

It's delicate. Coleman clones have a cumulative effect. They build up in the bloodstream, like whipped cream, chocolate, and Carvel's birthday cakes. I knew Schroder was overworking when my daughter Andrea called him "Ricky *Yeccch*." He was too sweet. Tests by an independent research laboratory found that mice, when forced to watch *Silver Spoons* weekly, got the saccharin blues.

The producers and casting directors of our warm TV sitcoms are not perfect. Aiming at the heart, they often hit the gallbladder or the pancreas.

All of this is before Michael J. Fox in *Family Ties*. An exception to the rules is proclaimed here. He was different, a conservative politically.

What Gary Coleman and his clones in the earlier (pre-*Family Ties*) experiments in TV genetic engineering came to symbolize is a whole new breed of child. This race of super-shrimps share certain characteristics. For example, they tend to look old for their age. Webster, in a plot concocted by some Fanny Farmer for ABC, was said to be six years old, but in real life was actually twelve. Usually, the reverse is true.

Gary Coleman has always acted old for his age. "He is a forty-year-old vaudevillian locked in the body of a twelve-year-old and trying to get out," explained Steve Allen. "That's what's so creepy about him."

All the super-shrimps today are smart, very smart. They speak only in wisecracks, flecked with the wisdom of the ages.

Fred Silverman, as president of NBC, once denied that if somebody brought him *Hamlet*, he would put a dog in it. "I wouldn't do that," he said. "But I might put Gary Coleman in."

Superkids are an acquired taste. I haven't been able to watch them too often. But I'm sick and tired of smart kids on TV. They make me feel inferior. They remind me of a wasted childhood. I feel like a failure watching these kids resolve family crises. In my day, I used to *cause* family crises.

TV kids also have a tendency to make kids at home feel secretly inadequate. Belinda Carlisle, formerly the lead singer of the all-female rock band the Go-Go's, recently confessed that her role model as a preteen was Marcia Brady (in *The Brady Bunch*). "I used to wear my hair parted on the side with two pigtails, take toothpaste and rub it on my lips, and smear a paste of blue Comet on my eyelids. It was really sick."

And Marcia Brady was a nobody, compared to Gary Coleman.

But I digress. When I first became interested in his financial battles with NBC, Gary was a little on the obnoxious side. All know-it-all kids seem to run that risk. Still, even in a weak comedy like *Diff'rent Strokes*, Gary Coleman's brilliance stood out. He had presence, a sense of timing, a way with a line. And if he doesn't lose it by the time he is older, say, thirteen, he could be a serious comedian.

Tandem Productions, I later learned, had offered Gary Coleman a new contract for the 1979 season: sixteen thousand dollars a week. It was then that the walkout took place.

That's sixteen thousand dollars a week, not a year.

"Never sell yourself short," my broker always used to say. Gary the Short was right to quit the show, if they were still talking jelly beans instead of real bucks.

The doors on the *Diff'rent Strokes* set stayed closed during the next week, while teams of lawyers hammered out a new financial arrangement. On Thursday, an agreement in principle was reached, the details reportedly ironed out on Friday. The wonders of collective bargaining were demonstrated once more.

Sources suggest that Gary or his people probably settled for something in excess of sixteen thousand a week. It may actually have been closer to twenty thousand dollars. That's a week, not a year.

It's so wonderfully decadent when an eleven-year-old kid gets from sixteen thousand dollars to twenty thousand dollars for appearing in a limp, infrequently amusing, trite, embarrassing, contrived, plastic show. On the other hand, it's also depressing. I'm too old and too tall.

A SMALL STORY

It was a small story, perhaps. But in 1983, I read with dismay what they were doing to Herve Villechaize, the distinguished actor, co-star of *Fantasy Island,* in his fight against management (Aaron Spelling and Columbia Pictures TV). It was the old big bosses vs. the little guy story, a classic that will live in the annals of labor-management injustices, right up there with the Suzanne Somers case. (Suzanne was so poorly paid she had to wear all those shorty-pajama outfits in *Three's Company;* in the subsequent wage dispute, the buxom employee was laid off, so to speak, or lucked out.)

After years of fighting for betterment of economic conditions, Villechaize managed to talk himself off *Fantasy Island.* Spellingbee, as I liked to call him, announced that they were getting a butler to replace him the next season. He'd had it, he bought the farm. Him and his little mouth. It was final as anything can be in TV.

Villechaize played "Tattoo" on the multiple-adventure-suspense comedy-drama series, a hit on ABC's Saturday-night schedule for the previous five years. It was appalling to read the details of this poor little fellow's working conditions.

Tattoo was the one on the show who was always saying, "Zee plane, boss . . . zee plane." That's television acting today. Under his old contract he was getting approximately twenty thousand dollars a word. Now, no one should have to work for such wages, certainly not a small person with a foreign accent. It's sickening.

He had started at poverty level, seventy-five hundred dollars an episode in the 1978–79 season. And he wasn't even in the original script of *Fantasy Island.* By the end of the fifth season he was earning forty-five thousand dollars an episode, or about $1 million a year (with all figures rounded off). The problem: He wanted $2 million a year.

It may be a little hard for many TV viewers to relate to the man's plight, but you have to understand the cost of living in California. Do you know what a pair of elevator shoes cost out there? Sky high. In some of those classy gourmet restaurants in L.A., a salad costs eighty dollars.

Second, it's a dangerous job. Tattoo ran the risk of being snorted up a bull's nose in one script. And as an actor, Villechaize had to put up with all those leggy, kinky starlets running after him. He even married one of the Amazons.

Now, I confess, *Fantasy Island* was not my favorite show. Despite my height, it was over my head. For years I kept thinking Fernando Lamas and Ricardo Montalban were the same guy. But some intellectuals I know never missed *Fantasy Island*.

"It gets me away from my easel," explained the artist Jon Neroff, Jr. "Escapism. It is totally unreal. But I love it. Ricardo Mendelbaum (sic) is grandiose, and unlike most talk shows, he has good guests."

Nevertheless, I kept being drawn back to the economic struggle that seemed to endanger the program. The negotiations went back and forth, with both sides trading charges. Villechaize's side was eloquent about the inhumane, sweatshop conditions. It was right out of Upton Sinclair's *The Jungle*.

There was no doubt that Villechaize was underpaid. That's because everybody starring in TV entertainment, as in news, is overpaid.

Was Gable worth the money they paid him? Chaplin? Bogart? Shirley? (Temple, not Laverne & . . .)

Indeed, the excitement of contract negotiations is the major dramatic excitement in TV today. We are always counting other people's paychecks, measuring ourselves against them, and finding ourselves being vastly . . . ah, um . . . short-changed.

Herve is the same way. It's all relative. Gary Marshall once said, "I'm not rich compared to Aaron Spelling." Marshall, who produced (at the time) half of the shows on ABC that Spelling didn't produce, probably earned a mllion dollars a week from *Joanie Loves Chachi*. But he was poor by Spelling's standards. And I daresay Spelling considers himself pinched, by the dimensions of Armand Hammer or Malcolm Forbes.

Herve Villechaize undoubtedly *believes* he is being taken advantage of.

So that's why it seems strange to us that Herve complains of forty-five thousand dollars an episode.

I'm worried. As the economic situation worsens, the people at home could become more surly about these contract disputes. They are already on the back burners, simmering unhealthily. A new economic royalty is being established in this country, the new aristocracy of TV money. One day, when the revolution comes, the TV audience could boil over. The people, sir, being an unthinking beast, could turn irrationally on the TV stars. Some King Aaron or Prince Gary may make a mistake and say, "Let them eat TV dinners." And the peasants will storm the gates of Malibu Beach.

As I believe it was Donne who said, at one farthing a page, "No man is a fantasy island unto himself."

BUT ENOUGH OF MONEY—LET'S
TALK COMMERCIALS

My secret ambition is to be one of those real people in commercials.
You know, the average person in the street or at the laundromat who
gets to star in the tests. They are the real superstars of TV today, on the
screen more often than many of the stars on the programs in between
the commercials. How often do you see such luminaries as Beauty and
the Beast (Linda Hamilton and Ron Perlman) or Alan Thicke on TV?—I
mean, compared to Joan Baranowski, the real person on the Final Touch
fabric-softener commercial?

This sounds immodest, I know, but I think I have what it takes to be
a real person. I mean if I rehearse a little. There is not a man or woman
alive who couldn't do it, with practice.

I'd even be willing to go to acting school to be a real person.

There are schools to help people become supermarket checkers, truck
drivers, and air-conditioning repairmen, and I'm sure there must be a
place to learn how to become a real person. I want to be able to give one
of those sincere, touching performances in the "hidden camera" commercials. Where do they hide the mikes, by the way? In the interviewer's
lapels? In Alan Funt's nostrils?

It's hard for me to be sincere, as you may have noticed. But how sincere
are those commercials, anyway, which whisper, "Mrs. Sevastapol doesn't
know it, but we are filming her with a hidden camera . . ." As Charles
Mountain, of the New York chapter of the National Academy of Television
Arts and Sciences, once explained to me, yes, great secrecy. "Mrs. Sevastapol has been ministered to by a hairdresser, a makeup artist, and a
wardrobe mistress. And Mrs. Sevastapol has submitted to auditions,
screenings, run-throughs, and all the mundane matters actors go through
as part of the job."

I know that with my face, gender, and complexion, I will never get to
do the Oil of Olay commercials. But I'm a natural for headaches. (Bayer,
Anacin, Bufferin, Tylenol, Excedrin, please note). My face is often twisted
in pain of one sort or another, given my line of work.

I could be the poor slob who bought the wrong dog chow or something
that is equal in nutrition but costs more than six cans of dog food. I can
be the person who finds out the bleach is only second, the embarrassed
wretch who has to admit to being a stupid twit, who doesn't do anything

right. I can be the goofy husband in the stuffing-mix test who can't tell
the difference between mashed potatoes and stuffing. I once flunked the
wine test (which is the red and which is the white?). I might even be
able to flunk the Pepsi Challenge, if blindfolded.

But I'd better stop blowing my own horn here.

Real people in the commercials, of course, do these things better than
the stars: They do them for money, not just for the fame. It's a chance
to augment your income. With three kids in college, or on the way to or
out of college, my income needs as much augmenting as it can get. I'm
especially average that way.

But, naturally, I'd also want to be a real person in a worthwhile commercial. I'd like to become rich and help mankind by being in a commercial for a product with the unique position in the market that saves
millions of housewives (or whatever their current new title) hours of
drudgery. I'd like to be the man whose wife shows him how the
new detergent works, the one that not only makes clothes cleaner and
brighter but also folds and irons them at the same time. Please, detergent industry, develop this soon. My wife is a very busy woman, to
whom housewifery is only a part-time occupation. I'm sure you *have*
such a product—it's shown all the time in your commercials for deter-
gents.

My idol in the real-person-commercial-star field is the aforementioned
Joan Baranowski, the woman in the early 1980's who was so crushed and
depressed by dingy gray T-shirts in the Final Touch spots she was ready
to commit suicide when the announcers told her they'd taken out the
bluing. A good thing she didn't take the cyanide pill (hidden in her purse),
because at the last moment the announcer said, "We're kidding, Mrs.
Baranowski." I've studied all her movements and gestures, as earlier
generations studied Olivier, Helen Hayes, the Barrymores, or Bernhardt.

Other stars of real-people commercials have their followings. Sy Syms,
Tom Carvel, Fred the Furrier, Crazy Eddie, Frank Perdue . . . Some
night there should be a variety special starring these luminaries, sort of
a real persons' *Real People.*

Gene Shalit once suggested that he, Joel Siegel (the bushy-haired lu-
minary on *Good Morning America*), and I do a hair commercial that asks:
"Guess which one has his finger in the electric socket?" But so far, the
real thing hasn't come along.

Meanwhile, I have started having grosser fantasies, dreaming about
the true ultimate fulfillment of my life as a critic—doing a commercial

endorsing a TV set. "The reason I like so many TV shows," I can hear myself saying on camera, "is my three Sonys. . . . Shows look three times as good on my Sonys." What an honor it would be, standing around autographing TV sets in the appliance department at Bloomie's or Crazy Eddie's someday.

13

CALIFORNIA, HERE I STAY

THE TEN PLAGUES OF CALIFORNIA, PART II

- Rain (or no rain)
- Fires
- Quakes
- Not just mud slides but career slides
- High interest rates
- Low interest ratings, i.e., Nielsens
- VCR copies
- Unbroken marriages
- *The National Enquirer* writing about you
- *The National Enquirer not* writing about you
- Valley girls
- Valley boys
- Valley others

For years I'd been criticizing the quality of the TV shows. Yet the people in southern California who make the shows must have thought they were good. Maybe the reason I didn't find the sitcoms funny or the dramas dramatic was that my perception was faulty. It could be a point of view.

I tend to see everything as an easterner. Maybe by going out West one could get "the western point of view," that of the TV production community in southern California. Or what the academics call "insight."

It's hard to believe, I know, but in all my years as a critic, I had never once been to Los Angeles.

I'd be sitting in a network executive's office on Sixth Avenue, in New York, and he would say, "Sorry. I'll have to take this call. It's the Coast." And I'd think, What coast is that? Rockaway? The Jersey shore? That's the kind of guy I was—aggressively blind about the realities.

A decade as a TV critic without once making the pilgrimage to the

Coast, something my colleagues do twice a year? "Decadent," an NBC
vice-president of public relations said with disgust.

I had never once faced the beauties throwing themselves at you, or
the girls, either; the producers kissing the typewriters of the critics; the
free Perrier, the drugs, the hot tubs, the hot sun. How could I have
managed to write so much about television while knowing so little of its
origin?

My first ten years of essays about TV had been comparable to Kafka
writing *Amerika*, his novel about life in the United States, without ever
leaving his bunker in Prague.

In January 1980, it seemed time to turn from romanticism to naturalism,
or writing about how things really are. It was time to finally go to the
salt mines, to visit the sweatshops, so to speak, the boredom factories,
to see where all the "product" is made.

Could you stick a palm tree in the ground, in, say, Massapequa Park
or Hohokus, and call it California? Or was there something about the
environment, the combination of soil, air, and weather, that makes for
such programs? These and other questions were on my mind as I flew to
Los Angeles to begin maturing as a TV critic.

I felt like a foreign correspondent, as I arrived in California, which is
a Spanish word for land of the gold chains and 450-SL powder-blue
Mercedes.

My plan was to see how the people lived. I rented a room at the Beverly
Hills Hotel. They gave me the Liz Taylor-Richard Burton Memorial Bun-
galow (No. 5), then at $220 a night. But I wanted something less preten-
tious. The Sophia Loren (No. 9-S) at $140, or the famous No. 21: *Freddie
Silverman slept there.* Dolly Parton slept in two bungalows.

I spent seven days soaking up the local customs and culture at the
Beverly Hills pool. It only rained five days. This is the place, I knew,
where Miss Piggy was sitting in *The Muppets Go Hollywood* special. She
wasn't there. But Sue Mengers, the agent, was. So were Roy Cohn, the
then-notorious celebrity-lawyer, Bruce Jay Friedman, Tom Wolfe—I tend
to treat writers as celebrities—and a lot of intelligent starlets. Intelligent
starlets are the ones carrying the scripts.

I soon learned how to talk California, or Mellowspeak. In California,
as you know, we all say "taking a meeting" instead of just "having a
meeting" or "interviewing." A fellow easterner, Roger Youman, then
editor of *TV Guide*, swears he heard a network executive apologize for
not being able to meet one day by saying he had "to take a funeral."

I went to all the great restaurants, such as Dar Magreb and Ma Maison,
in several of which I actually ate. It was very difficult to get into Ma. You

had to really be someone to be able to call up the owner of Ma Maison, and say, "Reserve ma table for ma lunch."

I heard all the gossip. I interviewed all the important stars. My biggest thrill was ignoring Loni Anderson on the set of *WKRP in Cincinnati*. The poor girl must have had a back injury. It made her lean forward all the time. There she was leaning over expectantly with her low-cut gown waiting to discuss, say, OPEC with another journalist from the East, and I went right past her to talk to Mr. Big, newsman Les Nessman, Richard Sanders, my idol. I especially loved his "Eyewitness Weatherman" segment, which he did from a helicopter, the sound simulated by beating hands on chest. Not Loni's.

I saw all the landmarks, like Rodeo Drive; Bel-Air; a real person walking; Irwin Allen's office; Flippers (the roller-disco place where an episode of *CHiPS* with Erik Estrada on skates was filmed), and the Lew Wasserman Memorial.

I heard about all the best parties in Beverly Hills. (They're held now in Malibu. But tradition dies hard, as my friend Broadway Jay Sharbutt explains.) I was also mistaken for John Houseman by a tourist with extremely poor vision.

My adventures were exciting. It was a very educational experience.

A few foreign expressions, translated, helped me get through the anthropological study of native and plant life in Los Angeles.

Ma Maison, as in, "This calls for a celebration at . . ." Once, an exclusive French-Los Angeles restaurant in West Hollywood, run by the nephew of a famous Paris restaurateur, with genuine French waiters, ma favorite *place*, where all the people ate *la lunch*. Then a TV shrine. Danny Melnick, the TV producer turned top movie mogul, was said to have had sex with Cheryl Tiegs on one of the tables. This is just Hollywood talk—a slang expression for making a deal. It's also the sort of place Arlene and Alda take my Carol to lunch—to show her how the real people live in L.A. Easterners sometimes thought of it as *plastique*. But that's only because genuine Frenchmen in L.A. look so phony.

Ma Maison is no longer "in," anyway, any more than the word "in." My spies tell me it has been closed for years. The new "in" place is in Burbank—at the Balkan House . . . There you get the finest cuisine, Grant Tinker, and a group of strolling gypsy tuba players led by Broadway Jay Sharbutt.

Rodeo Drive (pronounced RoDAYo, as in the Belafonte song; cowboys have it all wrong).

A rich shopping street in Beverly Hills. Capitol of materialism. Fifth Avenue is nothing; the Miracle Mile in Manhasset is a dirt roadway in some Eastern European *shtetl*. "The ultimate shopping experience," say the ads. "Whatever you need, whatever you've dreamed of, from small pleasures to great treasures." And something undreamt of in Beverly Hills: validated valet parking for only a dollar-fifty, in front of Van Cleef & Arpels and Fred Joaillier.

The average little shop down this mean street is Gucci's. Prices tend to be . . . oh, high. One shop owner tells you things cost twenty dollars less a block away. People come to Rodeo Drive *because* it's twenty dollars more.

Shimon Wincelberg, TV writer, has a friend who went into a Rodeo Drive men's shop to buy a raincoat. He kept trying on different styles until the right one came along. It was fourteen hundred dollars. "By this time he was too embarrassed to say it cost too much," Wincelberg explained. "He took it."

My wife, the shopper, says "that is excuse number sixty-seven, the last refuge of scoundrels. Why didn't he just say he loved the coat?"

The majority of the purchases are made here by TV people. To say *rich* is redundant. Say you have produced one mediocre TV series, which goes into syndication. Your agent is in for a piece. Your lawyer is in for a piece. Your hairdresser has points. One hit show and—five millionaires.

Rodeo Drive is the marketplace where the native chieftains trade. It's so—Beverly Hills.

Beverly Hills—"I settled in Beverly Hills," explained Louis Jourdan, "because it is like a little fishing village by the sea." It isn't. It is the new capitol of Iran, a tribute to the number of new emigrés here. The Iranians now call themselves "Romanians."

By some, Beverly Hills is called "Paradise." What else can you say about a town with twenty-two thousand people and eighty-six thousand phones? Eight-year-old kids come home from school and say to their servants, "I have homework, hold my calls."

Beverly Hills is more like Zurich. Rich movie people seem to live there. A lot of newly rich TV people also live in Beverly Hills. Would you say they're a little nouveau riche? "A *little*," explained Lewis Chesler, the indy producer. "There are guys here who made their money LAST NIGHT."

Beverly Hills is in part pretty, in part a synonym for ostentation. "You haven't seen bad taste until you've been to Beverly Hills" is a common folk expression elsewhere in Los Angeles, the mecca of bad taste. Tacky ostentation is a leading cottage industry, displayed by most $3.5 million cottages.

"You drive through a middle-class neighborhood in Beverly Hills,"

Shimon Wincelberg explained, "and homes cost a million two. A lot of old retired people live in them." And a typical house will have only two small bedrooms. As the classic Beverly Hills expression goes, "What do you expect for a million two?"

You can be earning fifty thousand dollars a year, and the life TV executives lead makes you feel like an entry-level Puerto Rican houseboy. Ben Halpern, a public-relations executive for Universal TV, apologized for a half hour about the smallness of his house in Beverly Hills. He is making $80,000–$90,000 a year, and he has to rent. He can't afford to buy it. But his family does have five cars.

Car, as in "Bring my car." Usually a Rolls-Royce Corniche convertible, with the top down. Right-hand drive is the best.

A number of Beverly Hills residents lease their Rollses by the month. They also lease their houses and furniture, if they have any. Behind the drawn curtains at many a manse, those who may be really rich any day soon may only have a mattress. It's their security mattresses. Which may be why there is so much sleeping around in the TV business. The show of material things in southern California is the real show biz.

The workers' car in L.A. is the Mercedes, blue or beige, equipped with a twenty-six-year-old blond wife, very commonplace. The "in" car is the Jensen Interceptor. How much does it cost? The downpayment is a TR-7.

You must see *Scruples* country with the cars. You can pull into a parking lot, having had a little too much to drink, hit five cars, and wipe out half a million dollars (three of them are leased and one is a demo on trial), and still have a good time at the party that night.

Party, as in "We're having a little party in West Hollywood."

Hollywood parties are full of tall, blond actors, tall, blond actresses, and small, swarthy men with chest toupees, who have always just closed a deal at Universal. *West* Hollywood parties have all the fun people, the shorter, dark-haired, handsome, serious actors, working as gas-station attendants, waiting to be discovered.

The parties in Beverly Hills and Bel-Air are, as advertised, wild. Alan Alda went to a famous person's birthday party. When one friend couldn't attend, he sent a dancing girl. Everybody had to stop talking about Martin Buber (the philosopher, not the actor) and Kierkegaard to watch this poor dancer shake her navel for an hour. Then the bell rang again, and the gift girl from another friend who couldn't make it had arrived. It must have been this way in Caligula's day, too.

Lewis Chesler told me he went to a party where everyone was dressed up as their favorite vitamin. His host, who was supposed to be calcium nitrate, asked if there was anything she could do for him? After looking around, he said, "Yes, could you tell me where I can find planet Earth?"

At L.A. parties, there is sometimes sex.

Sex in L.A. A very short act repeated many times during the first two hours of the affair or miniseries. It consists of long, hard looks, with one or two kisses, followed, as noted, by a door shutting, a wave pounding, a blackout, or, most frequently, a commercial. All these sublimating and interfering images may be the reason for the frantic quality of the people. *Commercialus interruptus* is L.A.'s prescription for safe sex.

AT PLAY AT THE POLO

Every writer's second home, somebody once said, is Paris. For me, it is the Polo Lounge at the Beverly Hills Hotel.

It's such an old-fashioned-looking place, in pea green and pink (maybe it's salmon or flamingo). But that's the point. It's supposed to look the same way it did in the 1940's, when Darryl Zanuck used to stop in for a few brewskis with his Polo-playing movie-boss cronies.

There are five main tables, for the top Polo players (today, the big boys are TV industry executives), and about fifteen little tables, all to the left of the entrance, guarded by Walter. The right of the lounge is Guatemala, where the tourists, sightseers, and nobodies are seated. There, you can catch a fungus from a plant and die, and nobody will notice.

Some years back, the gold chains around the necks of the big California TV executives rattled so much in the lounge you couldn't hear yourself think. Small loss. Nobody thinks too much in the Polo Lounge, or in all of southern California. The Polo Lounge is the place to catch somebody's eye, or ear. Everybody there has a three-picture deal. Robert Evans, it was said, was discovered by Norma Shearer there. Women discovering men. Hmmm. Myrna Loy, who had checked into the Beverly Hills Hotel a day earlier, looked at me in a funny way. I didn't even know what I wanted to be discovered for.

The first few days in Los Angeles had been hard times, a little like Ray Bradbury visiting Mars for the first time after writing about it for so many years. I was disoriented, with a vague sense of disappointment, anger, and angst, a clear case of culture shock, a mild one, of course, there not being too much of that stuff around.

Everything was so laid-back. "The only trouble," as Alan Alda of

M*A*S*H explained, "is that I'm a laid-forward person." I had difficulty adjusting to the California style.

"What's there to adjust to?" asked Jay Thomas, the New York radio DJ (who at the time was playing Remo in *Mork & Mindy*). "There's nothing here. All they will say to you is 'Hey, you're beautiful. We love your column.' You can say it to yourself in the mirror. It's the same thing."

Thomas said he couldn't talk on the phone anymore, and not to worry. Living in L.A. hadn't affected him any. "Love you from the bottom of my chains," he said, hanging up.

Well, the lounge was my womb the first few days. It was like being in a movie with Joan Crawford and Robert Taylor. "Is that somebody?" I would ask any friend from the East who took pity on me and had a drink.

Bernie Sofronski is your average television superstar at the Polo Lounge these years. He was at the time a programming executive at CBS, a mogulette, the head of special dramatic projects, the man who is credited with putting it all together on Arthur Miller's production of Fania Fenelon's *Playing for Time*, which starred Vanessa Redgrave as the little twenty-two-year-old Auschwitz survivor, the controversial smash hit of 1980. Sofronski is one of those lucky people who always look as if there is a spotlight on them, even in a darkened cocktail lounge. He has just come back from a hundred-dollar haircut. His curly silver hair gleams in the gloom. His shirt is open, barely revealing his jewelry. He is thin, lithe, and in marvelous shape, a glow around him. The minute you see him you know he is on his way to stardom, and to becoming Susan Dey's husband.

But my first big thrill on the planet of Los Angeles was seeing Freddie Silverman, Himself, at one of the Polo Lounge tables. Three booths away at breakfast. It's a small world.

Freddie, then the big boss at NBC, who worked out of 30 Rock in New York, was a legend in California. They were still talking about his last visit, four months earlier, when he wore Gucci loafers with socks, those black ones with the little clocks on them, at the pool.

That is the sort of thing a hick, a rube, or any easterner would do, almost as bad as casting off your chains.

The first thing TV executives from New York do, as soon as they land in L.A., I've been told, is decide to go on a diet. That's because all the California executives are so trim and lithe, like Sofronski. They work hard at it. Most executives are clearly more concerned about their physique than their programs.

Freddie, on the other hand, was really flabby, built like a bowling pin.

He was my kind of guy. He had come to L.A. this time possibly to find out what NBC's peacock was so proud of. It must have been some sideline, certainly not the programming all his slender executives were turning out. There was talk he had a new miracle crash program for saving the network. And he had flown out to take personal charge. Heads, not cameras, were going to roll.

He sat there grimly listening to some big shot possibly outlining a new NBC comedy series. Freddie ignored me in New York, but I went over and said something in New Yorkese to him. It was amazing. He embraced me and dragged me into the empty seat, explaining to the other big TV mogul that all his relatives live in Long Island, and how they keep sending him all the flattering columns I write about him.

It was puzzling why he had been so friendly. "You're the only one here who was not trying to sell him a show," explained my friend Shimon Wincelberg.

"And," my wife explained, "he can tell you also wear short socks."

I read in the papers the next day that Freddie had just fired the head of programming at NBC, Mike Weinblatt. And hired a new young genius, a thirty-one-year-old rookie phenom, Brandon Tartikoff, whom they were calling "the new Freddie Silverman."

Everybody in the papers was saying that Freddie had been grooming Brandon for his big day, having hired him at ABC, where he had worked on such hits as *The Hardy Boys* and *The Nancy Drew Mysteries*. But Freddie had fired him, or not promoted him, at ABC. And when Freddie came to NBC, Brandon thought it would be curtains.

"Freddie's some cool cat, as an executive," I told a source. "He always seems to have a master plan."

"There is no master plan," my source said. "He fired Weinblatt because he happened to see him around at a bad time. Hiring Brandon was another whim. There is only one head of programming at NBC, Freddie Silverman. He does everything, even the pencils. It was a random thing making Brandon Tartikoff the boss. He could have just as likely hired you as head of programming. And if you sat there long enough, he would have."

By my third day in Paradise—La-Ca, as the "in"-people call it, the Big Grapefruit—I was able to say, with awe, outside the Beverly Wilshire Hotel, "Scotty Baio . . . Oh, God, I can't believe it's you." I was becoming quite an airhead.

It was a thrill to talk to all the fine actresses, such as Erin Gray. Colonel Wilma Deering of *Buck Rogers in the 25th Century* and I took a meeting in the hall of the Century Plaza Hotel during an NBC press tour. I told her I admired her work in the Bloomingdale's commercials. She confided she thought the Bloomie's spots were her best work on TV. Her full name, incidentally, is better than the short form. It is Erin Gray Schwartz.

If you don't like L.A., there is always . . .

Venice, California (pop. 39,491; roller skates, pairs, 38,019). The town of Venice is unique and distrusted by the rest of southern California. It has energy. It's a dream town. It's a place where the guy from Allstate Insurance Company gets in costume Sunday afternoon, roller skates away, then comes back to his house in the valley, gets out of costume, and goes back on Monday to Allstate. It's the place where disco roller-skating and dancing on skates started. Everybody is on skates, except for the weight lifters in the Muscle Beach area.

Everybody is doing something—skating, jogging, pumping iron on skates, handing out leaflets, buying health foods, eating salads at the restaurants. The shops have cute names like "United Skates" or "Cheap Skates." It is real theater, the closest thing to a stimulating experience for a flaccid eastern mind. It is well worth driving out to Venice from L.A. on the Joan Didion Memorial Freeway, or whatever it's called.

The day I made the 4.5-mile trip to Venice with Jay Thomas from *Mork & Mindy*, a Canadian TV crew was shooting what looked like an MG commercial using a parking lot as a glamorous studio. Two bimbos with blond hair were driving a stationary car in a parking lot, smiling their airheads off with a fan blowing their blond hair back. Two technicians were standing on the bumper (off camera) gently rocking the back bumper, simulating the romance of the open road touring. Nobody bothered looking at them.

ABC was also making a movie called *The Hustler of Muscle Beach*, starring those two stars you can just die actually seeing in person, Kay Lenz and Richard Hatch, who had starred in *Battlestar Ex-Laxia*, okay, *Galactica*. It was one of those superficial California TV movies written by a sea gull.

"Practically everybody I know at the beach," explained Jay Thomas, "is in the business. There isn't a girl who hasn't optioned some part of her body to a network or commercials. She's got a deal for her nails at Revlon. Or NBC wants her eyes. You're the only one here who isn't about to ink a multipicture pact."

People at the beach say a lot of cute and witty things, explained indy producer Lewis Chesler, originally from Shaker Heights, Ohio, and New York. "You mean your girlfriend?" I asked. "Like *Surf's up?*"

"Okay, so she ain't Margaret Mead. But she's got a better tan."

If you want stimulation at a beach town, you can always go to the library.

You meet individualists in Venice. ("Like the first person to rollerskate the Appalachian Trail," Jay said.)

The town is much more intellectually stimulating than certain other spots. In Hermosa, another beach town, everybody has a surfboard. Jay said, "The two main topics of conversation at my beach are: (1) Hey, I've got some wild new stuff you can try, and (2) Do you want to see my board?"

Venice is a terrific place to be poor. All you need is a set of T-shirts for different seasons and formal occasions.

It's a dreamland, its own fantasy island, the escapists' junk-community world that much of TV is about.

THE PRODUCER (IRWIN ALLEN)

One of the ten natural wonders of the United States is Irwin Allen's office. Another is Irwin Allen, producer of *The Towering Inferno* and such.

In any group of TV executives, Allen can usually be recognized by his Texas outfit, made out of purest polyester. Or his $79.95 knit-tweed leisure suit, also poly. That's Allen. He's 100 percent polyester. No blends for him. Even his rug is said to be polyessir.

Irwin Allen's office was located then (1980) at the Warner Brothers Studio in Burbank. It used to be a park, where they did *Barefoot in the Park*. Warner Brothers built the office for Irwin Allen in gratitude for his *Towering Inferno*, one of the biggest of the disasters in the genre, meaning a success, perhaps the biggest disaster of all time, until I saw Irwin Allen's office.

As I entered the office, I could just hear the decorator saying, "Irwin, it's you."

Earthquake Allen's office is this side of the Taj Mahal. The tacky side.

"You don't know the meaning of bad taste," Chesler had said, "until you've been to Beverly Hills." Irwin Allen's office is five miles farther out.

It costs money to decorate the office of Cave-in Allen. That's one of the first aesthetic matters Allen clears up. A quarter of a million dollars is the figure I heard mentioned. But I'm not sure whether that is the total cost or just the floors. Eight hundred square feet of marble, Florentine, flown in from Italy especially for Irwin Allen. It rivals Benito Mussolini's office.

The doors were flown in from Arizona. The walls from the Klondike. The standard tour of Irwin Allen's office is led by the producer himself. "You see this," he explains of the custom-built door made exclusively of knotholes. "Cost forty-four thousand dollars. The hinges alone cost fourteen thousand dollars. The doorknobs cost thirty-six hundred dollars . . ."

"Let me show you this desk," he says, directing the attention to the eight-foot oak with leather inlay tooled, hobnailed job. "Let me show you this phone. I could have it on top of the desk, like anybody." But he put it inside the desk. That's Irwin Allen. It costs nine thousand dollars extra to do that. But it doesn't collect all that dust.

And then there is the upstairs. It's a balcony overlooking the executive's desk. The "think tank," he calls the place where he and his assistants plan their disasters. It reminded me a little of the atrium in the Ford Foundation.

I missed hearing a lot of the rich details because we were having the quick tour. Getting in was no problem. "I understand you're the single greatest TV movie-maker in Hollywood," I'd said, "and I wondered if you could spare me ten minutes?" He made room in his schedule. I kept the motor running in the limo on my way to the airport.

Other executives' descriptions of Swarm Allen's office capture it rather well. It looks, said one, like a combination sauna and the largest executive john in America. It could have cost anywhere from $11 million to $42 million according to various estimates, but it was done so cheaply because they hired slaves.

The usual visitor, a network executive looking for one of Irwin Allen's disasters, as a made-for-TV movie, might ask, "What's your next film, Irwin?"

"Ten million," Irwin answers.

"What about the one after that?"

"Could go to twelve million."

"Are you doing—?"

"It's fourteen million. We have to go on location."

"He has no idea of art," says a leading network executive, "or even of what the film is about. He knows that it's about fifteen million or seventeen million dollars."

Allen was subdued the day I toured his office. He wasn't even calling his new projects "disaster films." *The Night the Bridge Fell Down*, a made-for-TV movie that NBC was running in March 1980, was not to be a composite story of six bridges that fell down. It was a people story, an adventure. That's because disaster movies are failing at the box office, since *Swarm*. Allen is now into his introspective period, a regular brooding, Camusian sort of guy. His new films are all about miasma murkily rising from the meadows.

Touring the offices can be a joke, but lunch? That's no joke. A network executive told me he had gone there for lunch and had been served Kentucky Fried Chicken—in a box.

"Anything to drink?" Allen asked.

"White wine," the executive said, keeping his cool.

"Ralph, bring him a glass of white wine." There was this guy dressed up like a waiter.

Ralph brought a giant highball glass with seven gallons of white wine.

When the executive, a bit of a snob and a Yale man, made an unconscious moue, Irwin said, "Ralph, Ralph, that's wrong." He didn't know exactly what was wrong, either.

Lunch with Irwin Allen at his office would make a disaster film. I hadn't been invited to lunch, which was just as well.

Irwin Allen's office changes from time to time, like the movies playing in theaters. The day I came to visit, the only new thing Irwin Allen seemed to want to talk about was the wallpaper. He went all the way to New Jersey to acquire it for his walls. "Did you know that New Jersey has the best wallpaper?" he asked. "The wallpaper capital of the world," I said amiably. "So you know that, too," Allen said. "You're smart."

The wallpaper was white-on-white damask, or, more precisely, gray-on-gray, like a clear day on the New Jersey Turnpike, near the Cartaret-Elizabeth interchanges, along Refinery Row.

Reviewing Allen's office is apropos. The same creative urge that goes into decoration he exercises on scripts. He is an active producer, a floor producer, who doesn't hide in his bunker, fancy as it may be. He re-does every page of a script written for him. At least one well-known writer I spoke to had demanded that Irwin remove that writer's name from the script. Irwin was very hurt.

Still, he sees himself as the Michelangelo of the made-for-TV movie genre, and he is right. The writers just hold the ladder for him as he *potchkehs*. He is the last and among the best of the breed.

RETURN TO CALIFORNIA

Every year now, I get invited to the junkets the networks throw for the critics in California in June. And every year, I don't go.

I always find an excuse. In 1983, for example, it was "I have to watch TV." Last year it was "I saw California once already." Once is enough. Once was more than enough.

Junkets. Ah, the romance of travel, the magic of television. And I treat it like a trip to the dentist for root-canal surgery.

The term itself fascinates me. Is it any coincidence the trip is called a *junket*? It's when they let the critics see early the junk they call TV shows. They have a lot of key words in TV terminology ending that way, like *starlet* or *racket*.

It's a chance to see the starlets of tomorrow, the ones they discovered a few minutes ago, on the casting stool, or couch, at Schwab's drugstore fountain. Imagine the thrill of being able to talk to some vacuous blonde about her ambition to become the new Lydia Cornell, the new Audrey Landers.

It's also the chance to see next season's shows ahead of time.

Frankly, I can wait. I never understood why the critics want to see the new shows so far in advance. Then there is nothing to look forward to all summer. It's the loss of innocence. I'm like a little kid at Christmas. I like to wait for surprises. I like surprises. Maybe the other critics need time to think about what they have seen. Thinking is not my style.

My colleagues just can't wait to get out there to the Coast every summer. It's one of the perks. The TV industry treats them like royalty. But have you ever actually met Aaron Spelling? He's from Texas. He's also from hunger.

Some companies give their key people a new car every year. Newspapers let their TV critics go out to L.A. and get *lagniappes* from the industry. It's hard to put a price tag on the love and lavishment heaped on them. It's a real ego trip for a guy from Charlotte or Chicago to be treated like a sheik from Kuwait.

An all-expense-account-paid trip to L.A., Lotusland—and I for ten years in a row don't go? A no-cost visit to Dreamsville?

Kids in small towns don't think about coming to New York anymore. L.A. is the new mecca, headquarters. And I'm dragging my Gucci heels. What's wrong with me, anyway?

At first I thought, I'm just not bicoastal.

Year after year the siren songs from the networks beckoned. Finally I realized I must really be sick.

You've heard of fear of flying? I've got something worse. What I fear is getting there, if it's California.

The place scares me. It's like Louis XIV time. All these guys with their marcelled curls. Everybody looks so tanned, healthy, wonderfully relaxed and happy. It's the only place I know where everybody is important. I never met anybody who wasn't. But why? Writer Herb Sargent of *Saturday Night Live* once told me, "As the plane lands, you can feel your IQ going down with it."

The first thing I saw at the airport (LAX) on my first visit was a lady carrying a Vuitton pet box. The dog in it looked like Pia Zadora's stand-in.

And everybody on the streets has those dopey grins on their faces. That's because they are all looking forward to another salad. They also consume a lot of wine in California, thirty-three gallons per man, woman, and child. L.A. is a place where nobody touches ground very often. Even the light is different. Everybody has this glazed look in their eyes. I had trouble breathing the first time.

Moving to California is like going to a permanent summer camp. It's not serious. It's like having all the Twinkies you want. It's like 80 degrees on New Year's Day. What can you say about life in Condo Heaven?

The real people in California are always asking, "Hi, how are you taking the day? . . . Isn't this a lovely day?" It's been like this four months in a row, and they're still asking? A weird bunch, these smilies. You know why the gas lines were so long during the shortage? First, they shut down the self-serve pumps. One pump is open, and the guy giving out the gas says, "How are you?" and they discuss the day. And then the motorist asks if it's okay to write a check for two dollars. Sure. They buy a tube of toothpaste out there and write a check.

The real people there form instant friendships. They meet somebody at a cocktail party and immediately they're best friends, like they had known each other for a month . . . All the work of TV is done at parties. They go to the office to rest up for the next party. They're all getting some kind of vitamins shot into them from a doctor. And you know what?— they're not unhappy.

They do drugs, or they don't do drugs, depending on whose view of the world you go by, Kathy Lee Crosby's or the house Subcommittee on Drug Abuse.

Oh, maybe some of the guys, like John Davidson, may put chocolate in their milk sometimes. It doesn't matter, though. Life itself is a big turn-on. The thing about California is this:

Creative people wake up and say, "Gee, what a wonderful morning. I think I'll make a salad." And that takes them a whole day.

They do sex. They do tennis. They do staying fit and thin. They do tanning. But they don't do reality as we know it.

They also don't do originality. It's not their thing. Nobody in TV wants anything new. Nobody wants to be the Ponce de Leon, or Lew Wasserman, or whoever discovered California.

I used to cringe inwardly whenever a friend told me he was going to "the Coast."

Lewis Chesler was a promising novelist (*Amusement Park*) and off-Broadway producer. I first met him when he approached me about writing a musical comedy version of *George Washington's Expense Account*.

Lewis and I shared roots. We were both midwestern, Lithuanian. He was from Cleveland (Shaker Heights), I from Pittsburgh (Squirrel Hill) and Finleyville, Pennsylvania. Our families were originally out of Vilna, the capital of Lithuania. Vilna was sometimes referred to as the Boston of the Baltic. My mother's family (the Grodzniks) lived slightly out of town, in the country, on a truck farm. I never liked to talk about it, but we may have been distantly related to the Royal Family of Lithuania, through my great-great grandmother, a ballerina in the Royal Lithuanian Dance Company. Or so it was said. Lewis and I were secret members of the FLNM (Free Lithuania Now Movement), same as Puerto Rico. We didn't like to use the initials, fearing the press will make the mistake and confuse us with the Puerto Rican movement.

Chesler had majored in American civilization at Amherst, winning honors for his graduate dissertation on "Turner's Thesis of Western Expansion and Its Impact on the Johnny Carson Show." He was the sort of person who relaxed with Fenichel's *Psychoanalytic Theory of Neurosis*, which he described as a wonderful guide to what the world means. He was in therapy, something he was open about in a closed sort of way. He would tell me about his problems, which included the idea that life seemed like a big abyss. "What kind of abyss is that, Lewis?" his therapist asked. "I don't know," Lewis said. "A little abyss, a little of that."

Shortly before he told me the news of his going West, Lewis called one day to say his psychiatrist had left for the Los Angeles area. "Why?" I asked. "I don't know," Chesler said. "I think he said something about wanting to be a grapefruit."

Chesler had been hired to produce shows for the Long Beach Exhibition and Convention Center, a kind of miniature Lincoln Center the town was developing around the *Queen Mary*, now moored to a dock. Long Beach is a suburb of L.A. close to the network production centers. As a start, he was working on a tribute for Abe Vigoda, which was supposed to get on NBC.

"If you are ever out that way," Lewis said, "please call. I can arrange the Churchill Suite for you on the *Queen Mary*, including the original ashes."

Chesler's first letters from Beverly Hills, his first new home, were excited. "Buddy Hackett told me he would sponsor me for membership in his *shul* [synagogue], B'nai Mercedes."

A couple of weeks later I received a form with a covering note that read: "Now that I have moved to Hollywood I have retained these people. Lewis." The form was on the stationery of an organization called the Hollywood Showtime Opinion Research Group, and began:

> Dear Occupant:
> Lewis Chesler has asked me to forward to you the enclosed questionnaire in order to assist him in planning his continuing friendships.
> Please answer the following queries 'yes' or 'no.'
> 1. Do you live next door to a movie star and/or someone with a continuing series?
> 2. Do you drive a Ferrari?
> 3. Do you carry charge accounts at Gucci's, Mr. Chow's ("Takeout to the Stars"), the Bel-Air Hotel, or Frederick's of Hollywood?
> 4. For men only . . .
> Do you wear a minimum of three gold necklaces, exclusive of religious ornamentation?
> 5. Are you rich?
> If you have answered positively to three out of five, or very positively to number 5, Lewis will continue to be in touch.
> Thank you for your consideration.

Quite a while later I received another letter: "Well, it's been six months since I emigrated and I've become total California. My mind has turned into liquid Prell. If you ever come out, please do not communicate in ideas, as I find they now overwhelm me. The only thing I've read since I've been here have been menus, and even then I prefer the kind with pictures of food.

"My body, however, what with the running and tennis and scuba diving in my whirlpool, is brown and gorgeous. But I'm not sure what century it is."

After some bad jokes about doing volunteer community work as a guidance counselor at the Roman Polanski Memorial Junior High School, Lewis went on to explain that he was writing a horror flick for TV, *The Flying Piranhas*. It's a story about a pack of flying piranhas who soar from Jacuzzi to Jacuzzi in Beverly Hills and devour unsuspecting producers when they wade in after a hard day at Universal.

His other Hollywood TV idea is *Beverly Hills Emergency*. The premise of the series is that there is only one emergency truck in Beverly Hills. It's staffed by out-of-work actors. "We see two separate vignettes to open the first episode," Lewis wrote. "One is Michael Eisner at the office just suffering a stroke. The other is Barry Diller on the tennis court and his heart stops."

The emergency crew has to decide whom to save—head of a studio or network chief?

It's probably just another one of Lewis Chesler's million-dollar ideas that won't sell. Now. But wait until he gets the power.

"I'm having a tremendous problem presenting works of quality to this audience," he explained about his then-temporary job as the Mike Todd of the Long Beach Convention Center. "It seems to me the country is divided into New York and the rest is Parma, Ohio. The only message these people care about is 'Please remember the number and section of your parking space.' "

It's a race to see who will win out regarding Lewis Chesler, his heritage from New York or the new influences of California. I think we are starting to lose Lewis. He called me for the first time since he went to California. And while we were having an argument about aesthetics and TV, he said, to clinch a point, "Do you know who you are talking to?—a personal friend of Sammy Davis, Sr."

Soon we will ask, Whatever became of Lewis Chesler? When last heard from, he was working for cable. He had produced a topless *Swan Lake* for HBO and a topless magic show. Also, *The Hitchhiker* for HBO. And he was living in Palos Verdes, where he was able to drive seven hundred miles a week to buy a bottle of milk.

Several weeks before the 1984 Olympic Games in Los Angeles, I read that the British polo team was thinking of sending over oxygen masks for its ponies. This was an alarming note. The British, who are famous for their reserve and understatement, feared that their horses would not be able to run at maximum efficiency because of the smog. Oxygen deprivation has a bad effect on animals. Also, by the way, on people. Marathon runners, for example, have to take iron pills to add oxygen to their blood so they can think and run at the same time.

I wasn't terribly concerned about the British horses, who probably had other problems, such as being slow to begin with. But I worried all summer that some pony or its rider was using up the vital stuff that a TV scriptwriter, or the associate producer who rewrites the script, might need. What's more important to you, a bunch of horses running around a lake, or the people who make TV shows? It's a matter of priorities.

Officials in L.A., and the Olympic Committee, and the press, all made light of the smog problem. It was nothing, we were told—a sure sign in itself of oxygen deprivation at work.

Upon arriving in L.A., the city where the future happens first, as they are fond of saying, I have always noticed a certain disorientation takes place first. It starts at LAX, where they meet visitors in private golf carts, a feeling like the plague, a combination of jet lag and future shock.

The famous laid-back quality of the residents, always assumed to be the result of controlled substances, may be merely due to the lack of oxygen. Ditto the strange way they have of talking and using words like *bitchin'* and *rad*.

On a slightly ugly day they all get into their cars and go driving. They're not going anywhere. They're just driving around aimlessly, free on the freeway. That's why the roads are crowded at 3:00 P.M. This in turn produces more smog, further reducing the oxygen level. They never see the connection.

Industry produces smog, too. But the main industry they have out there, as noted, besides TV, aerospace, and agriculture, is cocaine. Maybe white grains rise into the atmosphere when the coke is cut. Although I don't want to alarm anyone, the lack of oxygen is what did in the planets of Venus, Pluto, Mars, and Battlestar Galactica. Interstellar history could be repeating itself on the planet of Los Angeles.

Anybody who grew up in the Monongahela River Valley would not get sniffish or hold his nose at an air problem. I *know* bad air, having spent my childhood in the Monongahela Basin, between Pittsburgh and the environs of Monongahela City, Pennsylvania. You could smell Donora, Pennsylvania, and Monessen, Pennsylvania, neither of which was the fresh-air capital of the world. In my childhood, we didn't trust any air we couldn't see.

The valley itself was beautiful, what little you could make out. Nevertheless, it failed to become a center of motion-picture production or anything else. Name one outstanding creative person to come out of the valley, besides Andy Warhol of East McKeesport, Stan Musial of Donora, and Marvin Kitman of Finleyville?

On a clear day you can't see very far in L.A., either. The first afternoon of my initial junket to the TV studios in 1980 the sky had been filled with a purplish chrome-green cloud, real poison. The same colors, incidentally, show up on the lung X rays of television executives. Without taking any credit away from bad writing, or bad acting, I would say that whatever is in La La land's air strongly affects what we get on the air. You can chart the downhill course as the air quality has steadily declined.

Remember the golden age of network comedy [*All in the Family, Mary Tyler Moore*]? Back then, in the early seventies, a modest pool of oxygen was still around, stimulating those white cells. With the supply dropping almost continually through the eighties, the best they could turn up with by the 1983–84 season was *Mr. Smith*. For all the network hype and stories in the papers, he wasn't very memorable. Mention him now and people think you're talking about the guy who went to Washington. The briefly famous NBC scientist and government consultant has become the forgotten orangutan. Actually, Mr. Smith was a chimpanzee who delivered the most urbane and wittiest dialogue to be heard on the tube all season. It was ironic but indicative of the atmosphere that the only intelligent voice on the screen all season that year came from a monkey.

I think the TV industry should be sent away to a fresh-air camp immediately. Or move the whole business to the Monongahela River Valley. The mills are empty, anyway. TV or L.A.—which will end first? It's a real horse race. And I knew they were losing it the year they came up with "high-concept programming."

HIGH CONCEPT

In 1983, high-concept programming was the hottest, most pervasive intellectual movement out there since pesto (definitely *vieux chapeau* now among the latest West Coast brain-softeners). "High concept" was a phrase used to sell a show to a producer. A "high-concept" program is one you can describe in ten words or less.

To use an illustration from the movies, imagine that you, seller of the concept, go to a studio big, or bigette, and say:

"*Jaws IV*."

Or maybe, if you wanted to be excessively wordy and run off at the mouth, you'd say "I want to make *Jaws IV*."

They say, "Great. Make it."

Or, if they're in a hurry and have a few appointments later in the day, they might just say, "You got it."

"Low-concept programming" means it takes more than ten words to describe. Your chances of ever selling an old-fashioned low-concept show are as slim as a gnat's waist. So I won't go to the trouble of describing the dialogue of such a negotiation. But I'll tell you the difference in using the high-concept method:

High concept is below the belt. Low concept is above the belt. High concept is below the neck. Low concept is above the neck. High concept is poor quality. Low concept is high quality.

Everything in TV, as you know, is not what it seems. "We'll be back in a moment" means "we'll be away for what seems like three or four hours." A "pause" for a message is actually a full stop, turning the key off, and giving the car a grease job. You can launch a missile against the Soviet Union or Libya in some of the pauses they take in TV. Trash is good. Quality is bad, and so forth.

The Dukes of Hazzard was a high-concept show. *The A-Team* was a high-concept show. Low-concept shows were *The Waltons* and *Paper Chase*. Also, *Hill Street Blues, St. Elsewhere*.

Here is an example from a prestigious ABC-TV movie-of-the-week (1983) department:

Voyeurs and *International Male Model* are high concept.

Low-concept movies are *Streetcar Named Desire* and Jane Fonda in *The Dollmaker*.

The goal in the TV business is to think of high-concept programs. You can go into any production house, studio, or network and sell the show without a script, if it's well conceptualized. For example, to sell *The A-Team*, today, you would go in and say:

"*Dukes of Hazzard.* Violence. Car crashes. But it's not in the South."

"You got it!"

Of course, that's been done already. Here is a fresher idea. According to my spies, one network's idea of a high-concept series these days is *I Dream of Jeannie* crossed with a Mean Joe Green commercial. Another winner: *E.T.* meets *The Fugitive*.

A miniseries: *Noah's Ark*. It's *Roots*—with animals.

This is life in the fast lane conceptually, and is in marked contrast to the old style of program decision making. The young executives have replaced people who were incapable of making any sort of commitment.

What really causes this demand for speed in concepts is growing up with the commercial offers for greatest-hits records—you know, the all-time favorite hits of Slim Whitman, one of the great superstar singers of all time whom nobody ever heard of; forty hits from Ricky Nelson; or with the excited announcer, as in the Robert Klein parody, saying, "Now, for the first time, all the music ever recorded in the world since Mozart. On one record."

High concept is probably not new in TV, when you come to think of it. Some genius, with the success of Jack Lord's *Hawaii Five-O* in mind, probably approached the big brains at CBS, and said "Tom Selleck. Hawaii. Oahu, not Maui." And the next thing we knew, we got *Magnum, P.I.*

TV as an art form was itself high concept. As Vladimir Zworykin of RCA, the founding father of TV, told General Sarnoff in 1923, "Have I got a medium for you! Like movies, except not so good. Radio—but with pictures."

Said Sarnoff, generalizing: "I got it!"

One year I blamed the terrible decline of television on California weather. Without different seasons, I argued, there can be no creativity.

Strictly speaking, this is not true. As Robin Tyler pointed out at the Radical Humor Conference at NYU (April 1982), they do have seasons out there—the fire season, the earthquake season, the flood season, and the TV season.

After four days in L.A., your brain turns to guacamole.

To be creative you need a city where they shoot you for smiling on the street (e.g., New York). Tension is useful in the creative process.

For the best TV programming you need an exchange of ideas, lots of people you can bounce off, shake hands with, make contact. In a place like L.A. there are no people. At least on the streets. Nobody walks. Groups of people inspire each other. You rub up against people in the streets, in the subways. The cafés have to be crowded. People have to yell at each other, shake hands, touch. It all transmits ideas, as well as germs. Ferment. Excitement.

The only political discussion I ever heard in L.A. was two people arguing about where their state capital is. "North of here, somewhere," one said.

To be creative a place has to have a history. L.A. has no history to speak of. By "history" they mean last week's grosses. And the Nielsen overnights.

People come to L.A. *because* the weather is so nice. That's a mistake. They want the same thing every day. They don't want clouds, or chills, or rain.

"Where else can you wake up," Shimon Wincelberg explained, "go to a friend's estate at Truesdale, play tennis, go for a sauna, swim, dress, and then over to the unemployment line?"

Their notions of creativity are used up in the food. Have you tasted their pizzas? Peanut-butter-on-mayonnaise pizzas . . . one hundred dollars? Bean sprouts? It's like grazing cattle. When you leave New York, somebody once said, take sandwiches.

The good life affects their passions. At Dodger games the fans throw avocado pits and Famous Amos chocolate-chip cookies, rather than beer bottles and cold franks, as New York fans have been known to do. Witness the case of a Mr. Bach, a friend of my pen pal Louisa Tango. He travels in conjunction with his musical career, but has settled mostly in Hollywood. He left New York, Tango told me, "as a sensitive, stimulating, and substantial adult—and now he has gone totally hot tub. Burn-Out City. Herbal Standard Time. Portable vacuum. Every other word out of his mouth is 'fantastic.' He's so laid back he's going in reverse. He's gone beyond superficial—saying that he's all surface would imply that he has at least one dimension—into that zero dimension reserved for gaseous chemicals, hypothetical atomic particles, and Richard Nixon's integrity. As Q (in *Rock Follies*) once said, 'it's all too, too sic transit gloria, darling.' "

Why get upset? There are ideas in the air, ideas to steal.

Steal? Too harsh, you say? TV steals from itself all the time, the true capitalist-cannibalist medium. A fresh idea like *All in the Family* owes much to the British TV show on which it is based, *Till Death Us Do Part*. Even so, *Family* was original theft. Followed then by seven hundred poor copies.

There is a Serendipity Principle, a Theory of Ideas Released as Waves in the Air. Take, for example, one of the exciting ABC smash hits of the 1982–83 season, one that couldn't miss, *Tales of the Gold Monkey*.

In part, it imitated the old Hollywood B − (minus) movies, a TV version of the old-fashioned adventure movies of the 1930's and 1940's, and featured death-defying feats of heroism, including, they said, ripping off *Raiders of the Lost Ark* without being sued by Stephen Spielberg and George Lucas. I have my own theory of origins.

Tales of the Golden Monkey was not Spielberg's *Raiders*, it was more the Oakland Raiders. It was not clear sometimes what Don Bellisario, the producer, was doing, but he was doing it furiously, throwing in everything that he ever saw in the old adventure flicks.

The time is 1939. The islands. The tropics. The bar run by the Frenchman, with slowly turning ceiling fan. It has intrigue, romance, secret agents, Nazis and Japanese, Eurasian beauties and white goddesses. And two-fisted men. Danger. Ferocious beasts. It's a jungle out there. Also, in the bar.

Tales of the Golden Monkey was original in that it doesn't have a lost ark everybody is looking for. They were looking for a gold monkey. A long, long time ago, the legend said, a monkey led a boatload of monks to safety in a storm. For seven days and nights he stood on the bow of the boat pointing the way. And he was miraculously turned into a gold statue one hundred feet high . . .

But why go on? Anyway, it wasn't gold but a heat-resistant alloy, and the Nazis want it. Corporal Schicklgruber—they use period language in the script—himself has dispatched the finest minds in the Third Reich to beat the bushes in the South Seas. He wants the monkey back in Berchtesgarden becuse he is Aryan. I must be making that up.

Stephen Collins is Harrison Ford . . . Jake Cutter, I mean, the handsome, cigar-smoking, two-fisted adventurer pilot who flies a Grumman Goose seaplane. His best friend is a one-eyed dog named Jack, who has the best dialogue in the show. *Tales* also stars monkeys, a special breed of man-sized ferocious Doberman monkeys who guard the old idol, reminiscent of Roddy McDowall in *The Planet of the Apes*, or the young M.B.A. types who guarded Grant Tinker at NBC. I gave the show three bananas.

One noticed a similarity between *Tales of the Golden Monkey* and *Bring 'Em Back Alive*, which opened the same week on CBS. It's amazing how these coincidences happen in TV. Both shows had handsome, two-fisted central characters, who could knock the socks off your grandmother. Bruce Boxleitner played Frank Buck, which should give those who remember the real Frank Buck quite a laugh. Both take place in the same locale and time. Both had the Nazis and Japanese who are chasing our hero. Both had the same kind of bars with the overhead fans. Both were filled with shifty characters who were pale washes of Sydney Greenstreet and Peter Lorre.

And, of course, both were rip-offs of the old TV idea, the Gardner McKay show *Adventures in Paradise*, which in 1959–62 was forgettable. Who knew?

How is it possible that two competing networks in a free-enterprise system without a cultural commissar to tell them what to do, could have independently arrived at two such similar shows with so many similar ingredients?

There is a theory that when you have an idea, it is immediately liberated into the air. You can be sitting at your typewriter, at your desk, and think of a bright idea, like how about having a series based on the adventure movies of the 1940's? A fellow passing by on the street outside your window is suddenly hit by an idea. "Good grief, I've got it," he says, clapping his hand to his head, and rushes to a pay-phone at the corner.

"Hello, Shifty," he says to his agent, "now here's the concept," dictating your idea word for word.

Over the years, I've tried to warn the other critics that L.A. is not the Garden of Eden. And I'm the only one who stays home.

In the meanwhile, send my regards to Hollywood & Vine, and tell all the boys at Century Plaza I won't be there.

Naturally, I was afraid that I would never come back to New Jersey; I was worried that I might finally cave in. "You win," I might say. "I'll stay."

A word about my return, unchanged. Just because I came back on the Red Eye (the all-night flight from L.A., which gets into Kennedy just in time for you to work a full day at Black Rock or 30 Rock without sleep), wearing a four-hundred-dollar set of prewashed, prefaded, preworn, pretorn jeans, and blue-and-white sneakers without socks, a hundred-dollar shirt open three buttons down, bathed in Chaps, deodorized by Halston, and on my arm Shelly Hack—a *wonderful* actress and a *wonderful* friend—don't think that I've gone Hollywood.

I'm just back from the Coast.

Q & A ON T & A,
OR WHY JIGGLY GOT A BAD NAME

We have given violence, money, and Los Angeles sufficient time and space. Let us return for one final analysis of sex, television's greatest contribution to the motion picture, or, at any rate, to the mouth in motion.

I am, let it be said, fond of jiggly.

Naturally, I'd prefer watching great drama like *Mourning Becomes Electra*, especially starring Jaclyn Smith. But what's really wrong with jiggly, anyway? I've seen more jiggly in the shopping malls, and on the jogging tracks, than on television. There is better jiggly on some radio shows than on TV.

And for those who think it's sexist, I'm not against male jiggly. So give Jim Palmer his own show. Let him walk around in his Jockey shorts discussing the meaning of Plato's *Republic* or Pestalozzi's theories of education, or baseball as metaphor. I don't care. Turnabout is fair play: TV should be an equal-opportunity medium.

Still, jiggly got a bad press the last few years. I couldn't even use the familiar acronym in my family newspaper a few years back. *T & A*, I explained (quoting a TV executive), meant "talent and ambition." The paper didn't believe me! (Funny. I believed him.) *T & A* was *verboten*. I suggested using the phrase *dash & dash*, but that probably sounded too erotic. *Jiggling* itself was out. Why not print it J------G, I suggested, even if some will think it stands for jogging? The heck with it, I stormed, change the name. Call it wiggly, higgly, piggly, call it what you will, but will it to continue.

Somebody has got to say this, and I don't care if Pat Robertson calls me a heathen. A lot of people *like* jiggly on TV.

Am I the only one who misses it today? Am I an Immoral Minority of one?

I have a hunch there are others like me. Why do you think so many people are walking around depressed by TV the last few seasons? It's not just a recession, either.

Do the people of America want everybody on TV dressed up like June Allyson? Is boring wholesomeness enough? In short, let's have a plebiscite, another of the famous "Kitman Polls" on major issues of our time. We've got to let the networks know we want it, them, back.*

You could also write a letter to your favorite network. Be sure to include a few misspellings. You don't want to seem educated, but a real person.

I'm always surprised that the Miss Universe beauty contest doesn't have more contestants from Uranus. Or Mars, Pluto, Neptune. Or at least Venus. Every time I tune in to the two-hour annual special, the girls always seem to be from places like Wyoming, as in other beauty contests. The selection procedures used by the Miss Universe Pageant seem to support the contention that there is no form of life in other galaxies.

But in L.A. itself there are many people from other worlds who welcome the chance to appear on a TV show. In the Big Orange, they have seen little green persons from other worlds, talked to them, befriended them, made three-picture deals with them. What an opportunity the Miss Universe Pageant would have if they decided to judge the most beautiful UFO.

Bob Barker could ask (Bob Barker could talk to them. He, too, is from another planet.), "What are your hobbies?"

"Splicing genes," they could say.

As it is, beauty queens speak a common language, I have noticed, listening to Barker "interviewing" semifinalists from such moons as Germany, Finland, Uruguay, Guam, Canada, and Italy. It is composed of beatitudes called platitudes.

Nothing linguistic flaps Bob Barker, though. There are no cultural barriers he cannot leap with a single bounce.

He asked Miss Germany, for example, if she would be seeing the Los Angeles Dodgers when she went to L.A. She smiled. "Does she know who the Dodgers are?" he asked Miss Germany through an interpreter. One could hear *"Was ist?"* and *"Dummkopf."* Finally she said, "No."

---

* Famous Kitman Poll on Jiggly
☐Pro-jiggly
☐Anti-jiggly
1. Check One.
2. Clip and Mail to Jiggly Poll, % Random House, 201 E. 50 St., NY, NY 10022

Why should Miss Uruguay have done so poorly in the interview competition? She was bright, witty, intelligent, bilingual. She spoke little to Bob Barker, and answered his most banal questions in Spanish, talking to the audience and never once mentioning *el stupido*.

The thirty-first annual *Miss Universe Pageant*, live from Lima, Peru, in 1982, turned out to be not as much fun as the Ice Capades, but better looking. At least we learned that Miss Finland was interested in . . . either (a) astrology, or (s) sex. My Finnish isn't that good.

Why can't Bob Barker dance or do something besides ask the same inane questions every year?

Anyhow, 36-24-35 was the winner. It was a travesty of justice. How could the judges *not* have given the prize to 38-25-34? Did you see the evening dress she wore? The stitching on the bias alone should have taken the cake.

I was surprised the audience took the results so calmly. In soccer games in the rest of the universe, they can kill referees for a yellow card. In Peru, you never saw such calmness and tranquillity over the most blatant insult to national pride.

My theory is that the audience in Lima didn't have the slightest idea how the vote—or anything else—was going. Certainly the contestants couldn't have known. We saw the computer numbers about how they were doing superimposed on their navels. Yet they kept smiling all the time! Not a tear or disappointed look. This is the greatest composure in the face of violence to navels since the first stapled binding in *Playboy*.

The results of the competitions were announced to the audience at home by Joan Van Ark, quietly, sort of whispered into the mike. Van Ark, usually one of my favorite actresses, was an extremely low-key reporter. She was so nonplussed she was minus.

The philosophical question, of course, is whether competition is better than cooperation.

I knew, for example, in April 1979, that I should have been watching *The Second Annual National Collegiate Cheerleading Championship* on CBS for the wholesomeness of it all. Cheerleading is good for young people, say high-school gym teachers. It helps build strong bodies twelve ways. It encourages the growth of coordination. It allows young people to express themselves through dance and music. It is a good, constructive way to express school spirit and vent youthful passions. And it's a great way to get fresh air, such as it is these days, and a terrific way to dwell on thighs.

The five teams that I watched in the ninety-minute special were the best (USC, Tulsa U., North Carolina U., Mississippi, Michigan State), the cream of the cheerleading crop in the universe. The top 5 were selected from the 178 squads invited to compete. We were in the big leagues of cheering.

I knew I should have been watching the talented Suzanne Somers, co-hostess of the show, whom I have sworn never to criticize again, and I won't. For one thing, fair's fair. For another, she's got leabanzas that don't quit.

Or watching Joe Namath, the co-host. He has been starring on TV for popcorn, hamburger helper, panty hose, and Brut. (Not all at once.)

And then, in between the cheerleading segments, there were such stunning acting talents as Herve Villechaize. (Again, he's the little one usually on *Fantasy Island* reruns.) Unfortunately, Herve didn't do his "Zee plane, Zee plane!" And there were Donny and Marie Osmond, singing and dancing, too. (The show was taped at the new Osmond Entertainment Center in Provo, Utah.) You know—Donny and Marie have crow's-feet. It happens to the best of us, even non-Indians.

I knew I should have been watching the five cheerleading teams for their neatness, the novelty of their presentations, their precision, and how they related to their music. These were the criteria, we were told, by which the judges would be awarding the trophies. What a distinguished panel of judges, I would like to add in passing, led by the eminent Dr. Joyce Brothers. As Suzanne Somers reported, Dr. B. had been a cheer-leader at Cornell. That woman never ceases to amaze me. She can sing and dance, box, analyze, act the fool in sitcoms, and never once turn a hair or a guy on. A regular Renaissance woman.

With all of those attractions to keep my eyes busily occupied for ninety minutes, somehow all I really noticed about this show was the girls jumping up and down.

Decadent, yes. I just loved those Trojan (USC) women in their little white sweaters, eight nubile beauties emblazoned with their golden letters, eight future Suzanne Somerses, all good dancers with full throats and things, chanting their college praise, shaking it for the world, the universe, and old USC. The Trojans, incidentally, finished last.

Shows you how much I know. I still remember the ABC entertainment special *The 36 Most Beautiful Girls in Texas*, in 1978, the first time the Dallas Cowgirls were presented on television—this time uninterrupted by any damfool football game. Kind of the Wide World of Cowgirls—right from the capital of Cowgirlism, Cowboy Stadium in Irvine, Texas. Cowgirlmania. Starring incredible simulations of thirty-six human beings. The Cow Clones.

Up front I want to confess that I'm prejudiced. Anyone who likes

Beverly Sills in her nightie, as I did while seeing *Manon* really *Live from Lincoln Center*, can't possibly like the Dallas Cowgirls, even thirty-six of them.

Why were the Cowgirls having their own special? Well, they had certainly had a lot of TV exposure the previous year. There were times when it seemed as if the games were half-time segments between their routines. TV made them big, if you'll pardon the pun. TV takes care of its own. Therefore, TV must give them a special. It's the kind of circular reasoning, or rectangular reasoning with rounded-off corners, TV is famous for.

And what did the Cowgirls *do* in their first special? They showed their charms. They shook their double entendres. Now the Cowgirls are not good dancers. They can't sing. They don't tell jokes. They have an IQ of 198—that's the sum total for all thirty-six of them—at least given the way they are presented on TV. The worst thing about them, the darkest secret, is that they are not even true cheerleaders.

"As a woman I found their exhibition demeaning," wrote Julia E. Bingham of Bay Shore, New York, after a Super Bowl appearance. "And as a high school Cheerleader Advisor I found the constant references to them by 'broad'casters as 'cheerleaders' insulting. I saw no actions on the part of these so-called cheerleaders that in any way resembled the talent and ability of true cheerleaders. Real cheerleaders not only lead the crowd in supporting their team, but they also perform prepared and athletically demanding routines. They should be called a Chorus Line or Pom Pom Girls. But don't insult hard-working, dedicated college and high school cheerleaders by calling these show girls cheerleaders."

They were not good enough to be called chorus girls, either. For correct nomenclature, I prefer *dummies*, as in tackling, or *womannekins*.

They don't even wave their pompoms with gusto. I don't care what you do. But, if pompom waving is your thing, long may you wave.

That special was nothing like the Dallas Cowgirls movie, titled *The Dallas Cowgirl Cheerleaders*, on ABSleaze's network January 14, 1979, starring thirty-six dazzling Cowgirls, and the undazzling Bucky Dent in his TV movie debut, giving a foretaste of his later commercial work for Emilio Gucci.

No, the earlier cheerleading championships were so wholesome you could eat them. But still I found myself thinking I was watching the National Bouncing Championships. I should have known that eventually it would come to this. First you start out looking at the girls running down the aisles on *Beat the Clock* reruns. Then you watch *Flying High*. And before you know it, you are seeing jiggly where it is not intended.

And where it is. At 8:00 P.M. on a Monday night in April 1978, we had *Sugar Time* on ABC, *Roller Girls* on NBC, and cheerleaders jumping up and down on CBS. The first competition for MTV. The three shows made up the bountiful Bouncing Olympics of the year, the world series of jiggling. I didn't know where to look first.

Phyllis George was especially eloquent. She explained that she had been a cheerleader for "seven" years at Denton (Texas) High School. Must have been a typo on the cue card. Or maybe she's not so good in math. All that jumping up and down, while pirouetting and carrying pompoms (one in each hand) can affect the brain. Phyllis was still a long way from earning a place in the pro-football booth, with Brent Mooseburger.

Perhaps I'm not the only one suffering from such decadence. During the football season, the cameramen are often temped to spend more time on the cheerleaders than on the games. At the stadiums, half the people watch the game, the others watch the cheerleaders. Surely they are all lovers of the dance.

Such displays were foretold by the French author Réné Barjavel in his novel *Ravage*, back in 1943, which some authorities credit as the first scientific study of what his fellow French call *le jiggle*. Barjavel applauded the idea of jiggling for its usefulness in "hastening the ripening of adolescents," and "preserving the lives of octogenarians." The novel, a look at twenty-first-century Paris, includes a TV broadcast consisting of a chorus line of girls dressed in nothing but helmets and sidearms. For the finale, they turn to display their buttocks, painted in tricolor. A patriotic display, and inspiring in a divided world.

NAKED NESS

Would you believe our Elliot Ness in bed, naked from the waist up? It happened on *Hotel* one night in April, 1984. I saw it by accident. The whole hour. I thought it was a news show.

I didn't usually watch *Hotel* on ABC. But there had been an advisory warning from Don Rickles:

"Everybody on *Hotel* is in heat."

You can listen to the networks' ratings; I'll listen to my main man, Rickles.

Can you believe that NBC flashed the "parental guidance" advisory on clips promoting the first network showing of *On Golden Pond*? Were they warning the young or the old away? Or were they trying to arouse prurient interest falsely? That's what I call *immoral*.

But, back to bed. A lot of stars are photographed in bed in *Hotel*. If you lined up all the beds in *Hotel* headboard to headboard, they'd stretch across Forty-second Street.

Aaron Spelling, the producer, must have gotten the idea for this series from the last sleeper train he took to L.A. The plot is basically this— everybody climbs into their berths while the show lurches to the end. Hey, there's a spin-off for Aaron Spelling—*Pullman*, the story of the women and men who sleep their way across the country!

But I digress. I haven't seen anything so sickening as Robert Stack in bed naked since Pernell Roberts was in bed, naked from the waist up, in the first episode of *Hotel*. As if that wasn't bad enough, he was with Ma Partridge, Shirley Jones. They were also in a bathtub scene. One of those hot tubs.

Stack was for the over-forty crowd. But they also had Bing Crosby's daughter, what's-her-face, in bed for the younger folks. She was also naked from the waist up.

The stars are photographed from the rear, of course. This is known as *backal nudity*. TV blithely goes along showing us naked backs as if there were nothing damaging, as in frontal nudity. You see it all the time in the soap commercials. It's good, clean smut. But what about the poor people who are turned on by backs? How do we know that TV isn't creating a whole new perversion, a fetish with backs? People are turned on by strange or familiar parts of the anatomy, you know, like the people who are into toes—yech—or lobes or nostrils. Some people are turned on by the turn of a shapely ankle, thigh, whatnot. We are mutating all the time watching TV, developing new videoerogenous zones. It may be that the mere mention of the word *back* now arouses some unfortunate wretch's prurient interest. We can't turn our backs on this problem.

Quality shows like the miniseries *Celebrity* also had people in bed with sheets up to their waists. And in the daytime soaps hardly an hour goes by without somebody in bed with the sheets. Of course, in the soaps they overdo it, as usual. They jump out of beds with the sheets wrapped around them. Soaps are supposed to be the most realistic form of TV drama. So people all over America are walking around the house wrapped in sheets these days, vacuuming, taking the mail or the mailman in, and so forth. What is this with the sheets, anyway? Sometimes I think the whole thing is a plot by Dan River, Cannon, and Pepperell. Sheets soon will be seen in better lingerie departments.

Now Dyan Cannon in a Cannon, that would make sense to every Tom, Dick, Charley, Harry, Jane, June, and Lisa.

Such small screen scenes remind me that we've come a long way, sister, from the old Hollywood bedrooms, when one of the lovers always had to keep one foot on the floor, leading to especially interesting perversions and the development of rather peculiar musculature. This was in the days when the earth used to move while people were having sex. All because Hollywood was built on San Andreas's (and everybody else's) Fault.

We knew in Bensonhurst, when I was a boy, what happened when the clouds passed over the moon . . . the surf started pounding on the sandy beach . . . the fire crackled feverishly in the hearth . . .

In the opening two hours of *Malibu*, nineteen people were wending their way to bed, slowly. It's not easy to fill a four-hour movie about people having sex when all you can show is a kiss. Then they cut to people running on the beach. Jogging appears to be the new ABC metaphor for sex. Also, tennis. These are the new train-entering-the-tunnel or embers-burning-low-in-the-fireplace.

The wearing of the sheet, I guess, is pretty explicit. The language is also becoming more permissive. I heard the word *hump* on some show the other night. The only *hump* in the old days was on a camel. And that was in the days of cigarette advertising.

I remember TV when they couldn't use the word *damn*. In a miniseries about the life of Commodore Perry, the hero would have to say *"Bleep the torpedos, full speed ahead." Bartlett's*, prepare to revise!

We can't hide under the sheets to avoid the trend. Call it the new licentiousness.

Is the total moral climate changing in ways that account for the new reckless abandon? I find that hard to believe. People aren't any more immoral today than yesterday. The interest in sex and nudity dates back to 1943, at least.

It is TV that is changing. TV, you see, had been behind the times, and the *National Enquirer*. Wrong to start with not treating sex maturely, as a part of life, they are frantically trying to catch up.

I still think the British have the best techniques. The BBC did sex scenes for a play based on the short story *The Watercress Girl* in the dark. It was wholly erotic just listening to the sounds and dialogue. Of course, I realize what you have then is black-screen radio or radio.

What continues is a weird, schizophrenic, surreal TV attitude toward sex. If you don't see it, it's not there. The ostrich must have descended from the same gene pool as TV executives. The ultimate sex act may be putting your head in the sand.

While TV is showing backs, TV *talks* about sex in endless ways. For example, one had to admire Billie Jean King's courage, the way she dealt with her private problems on May 7, 1981, confessing her lesbian affair to Barbara Walters and the rest of us on *20/20*. And then there was her husband admitting that he had driven her into another's arms.

I hadn't had a TV talk experience like that since the Jenrettes, Rita and John, discussed their marital affairs on *Donahue*, the morning of February 26, 1981. There I was, ironing my shirts and dusting, listening to Rita, the hottest TV superstar of the last fifteen minutes at the time. She was demonstrating how your husband, the congressman, can be a person of poor moral fiber, and you can pose naked for *Playboy*, and your opinions can still be highly desirable on TV talk shows. What a great country we live in! Hooray for the First Amendment.

And then who should call in but the ex-congressman himself, the dishonorable gentleman from South Carolina, disputing various statements his lovely wife had just made. Shocking. Everybody was standing around on the set, including Donahue himself, as the couple traded charges about who cleaned out the joint bank accounts, who took the silverware and furniture. Talk about your audience-involvement programs. It began to sound like a new show, *Ask Rita Jenrette*. Old Philo didn't help at all by asking the caller if he was "still on the booze."

Now in the South, where Rita and John come from, this is called "tacky." It's just not nice to fight about finances and discuss your love life on the *Donahue* show. But on television, it is the right stuff.

By the time Rita got to *20/20* a week or so later, the second major milestone in the saga of this great American schoolteacher-aspiring country-and-western-singer-nude-poseur-congressman's wife, I was really getting sick and tired of her. It made you wish that Margaret Trudeau were back. Rita J. bared her breast, so to speak, for Tom Jarrell, the ABC News correspondent, about how *Playboy* had tricked her into it. She hadn't planned to take off an earring when she went to the nice photographer's studio. And before she knew it, she was naked. Poor thing, the duplicitous photographer had somehow talked her into it. "Isn't it warm in here," he must have said.

Such a discussion hardly matched the candor of John himself, confessing on network news shows what it had been like making love on the steps of the Capitol. Politics makes strange bedfellows? Heck, sex makes strange bedfellows.

Am I the only one who is embarrassed by the new frankness on TV, the new free speech?

There is nothing personally offensive to me about lesbianism, if it's a private life-style. The Statue of Liberty could be sapphic for all I care. I don't mind getting under the sheets with the six wives of Henry VIII on *Masterpiece Theatre*. That's history. In the old days, royalty was always a suitable source for scandal, almost the only one. It was a major function of the crown, creating speculations for the masses below. But Billie Jean isn't royalty, except as a tennis queen. Am I going to have to watch everybody's sex life now, just because they are in the news, or in the sack, briefly?

Not only is all of this confession embarrassing, it's boring.

Barbara Walters was very pained, asking the big question of Billie Jean. She had on her Pained Expression. It hurt her to ask, she told Billie Jean. Not nearly as much as it hurt Mr. or Mrs. King, I have a hunch. And what kept running through my mind during the painful moment was: Why?

Is this what they mean by the public's right to know? Are people nosier today than the old days? Are they hornier? Do they welcome invasions of privacy more than Grenada? The business was a private matter among Billie Jean, her husband, her ex-lover, and maybe the courts. It became a so-called public issue because a lawyer went to the newspapers on his way to the courts. What did this stuff about Billie Jean and her sex life have to do with me? Why was I being invited to become part of the affair, a TV voyeur? So what if Buddy Hackett eats ice pops in bed or Gregory Peck sleeps with a Snoopy doll?

Isn't there a right *not* to know about certain things? People used to want to protect their privacy. Today, it appears, practically nobody wants to keep their secrets secret. Confession is the national sport. There are celebrities who invent vices just to be able to confess. The worst of sins is being ignored by the media.

Perhaps the new phase started with the writer Merle ("Only You, Dick Daring") Miller confessing in *The New York Times Magazine*—on a Sunday morning, yet—that he was a homosexual. And then one day I was shocked to read *New York Times* writer Enid Nemy confessing that she had fat thighs.

But it's not enough to confess in print, which has a long history. Now you have to do it on TV, which has none. This could be a new psychological *mishegoss*, the prurient need to tell anchorpeople or "hosts" under the hot lights about your darkest side. Who knows, this could be the new turn-on, an electronic-age fetish Krafft-Ebing never dreamed of. Confession in print is still somehow a private experience, one-on-one. Doing it in public, in full view of millions, is really getting it on.

Exhibitionism itself has changed because of television. Once it was enough for a guy to flash on the subway, when one or two people could see him. Now he has to do it at the stadium, where fifty thousand can see him plus the millions at home who watch the game. I knew somebody who exposed himself on radio. But, psychiatrists tell me, it's not the same thing.

Confessing to a crime, for instance, can be a gimmick in today's media world. You can confess to anything in the papers or on TV and stay out of jail. The president takes "full responsibility." The public carefully reads and watches all confessions, sifts all dirt, and we find everybody not guilty or who cares? As long as you don't deny it, you can get away with it. The mistake President Nixon made was trying to cover it up at Watergate. Had he said, "I'm a crook," he would still be president today. "Truth," as Dr. Donald Kaplan has observed, "is the last refuge of scoundrels."

Billie Jean began by denying, at first, the lesbian allegation. Some smart media-minded adviser must have told her to get with the new morality. Go to Sister Barbara and confess, cleanse the soul, and wash your dirty linen in the new miracle Dreck. Barbara's confessional box of the air provides instant absolution of sins.

One of the arguments advanced against allowing TV into the courtroom is that it's just a first step, a guise to get the cameras into the judicial process. After the courtrooms, we'll be televising public executions. Cameras will go right into the cell for the last supper, follow the death march, and pick up the benediction by Pat Robertson as they strap the man into the chair: A few brief remarks about how crime doesn't pay since the change in the tax code.

I'm clearly a reactionary about the right to privacy. It's almost a privilege to be invaded today.

ABC announces plans for a made-for-TV movie about the career of Walter Lippman. In his prime time as a columnist for the *New York Herald-Tribune*, Lippman was one of the three most boring writers in America, right up there with his contemporaries Arthur Krock and Arthur Daley of *The New York Times*, all Pulitzer Prize winners. And what aspect of Lippman's rich, full intellectual life would the movie focus on? His affair with a colleague's wife.

We had already seen what they did to *Eleanor and Franklin*. To millions, FDR's contribution to history was his *I Love Lucy* [Mercer] affair.

Everybody has some skeleton in the closet. Now the absence of a skull on the shelf is a scandal in itself.

This is the Barbara Howar school of political science. It concentrates on the private bad, rather than the public good. Public-affairs TV is suddenly, ironically, well named.

ANTI—, OR AUNTIE SEX
(CARSON AND BIRTH CONTROL)

Not all of television leads to the sex act and its consequences. Quite the reverse. Johnny Carson on the *Tonight* show has been one of the most important birth-control devices since the invention of the headache (in 1536, by Anne Boleyn).

Here is his method:

TV viewers watch Carson on the *Tonight* show until it is too late. "Are you crazy?" one of the parties says when the show is over. "I have to go to work in the morning." Instead, Carson's sexual innuendoes become a stand-in (or lie-down) for a sex life, just as fast foods became a surrogate for dining.

When Carson leaves the show in 2021, we must brace ourselves for a population explosion. As with what happened nine months after the last New York blackout. Conception will replace illegal immigration as a control problem. Even those of us in the press, which covers his threat-to-quit story (every two or three years at contract-renewal time during his quarter-century on the air) as if it were news, do not quite grasp the fact that the Carson-NBC controversies are more profound than dollars. Planned Parenthood and Zero Population Growth ought to be working with the network to solve the forseeable problem.

Carson has enlarged one population, however, in that he is responsible for saving many tourists' lives by warning them about the dangers of being mugged in New York. He moved to California.

Carson, too, has done more for vacations than any man. He is often off six days out of five. This results from something in his contract that allows him to take three days off back to back with three days off in between. I have never understood how this worked, really. The fun thing of the Carson show for me has become tuning in just to see if he is there, like playing the lottery.

Carson also has done much for good posture. How does he manage to stand so straight? I found myself wondering during a long stint (three days, or so it seemed) as host of the Academy Awards. "He has his brace on," my friend Max Friedman, a publicist for Bristol-Myers, explained. "Or else he lived in *my* mother's house." Or maybe his suits are made of polyester chain mail. Carson, for all his double and single entendres, is still a mother's dream, the only one who stands up the way not even she could, carrying all that laundry and, sometimes, Dad.

Yes, stand-up Johnny Carson kept more people up at night than Mexican food. He is king. I tell you, the man—both the monument and the myth—is going to be missed, should he ever lie down like a board and retire.

Everybody has their favorite moments from the Carson shows of the past twenty-five years. One of mine involved an accident that befell the great American actress Ann-Margret. She was on her way to a Hollywood party in a beautiful red dress that some fancy couture house had ripped off from the old-fashioned men's undershirt. As an accessory, she wore a shawl. The cameras covered her entrance and strut across the stage to give Johnny the standard hello kiss, when the accident happened. The shawl fell from her shoulders (or was it pushed?). The front of the dress was held up by two pieces of cotton thread. Carson, who reportedly has seen everything, rubbed his eyes with the heel of his right hand and carried on as if nothing unusual had happened. His take was a joy to see, as always. He is the master of understatement and overstatement, brilliant at both double and single entendre in foreign languages (in addition to being a snappy dresser).

Although I've never missed the chance to poke a little fun at him, I secretly liked the man on TV. He is, as Harlan Ellison once observed, the world's oldest Huckleberry Finn.

I met him in the early 1970's, when I was a guest on the *Tonight* show, pushing a book that I had co-written, *George Washington's Expense Account*. To this day, I believe the bright young woman who was talent coordinator on the *Tonight* show in charge of the pre-interview was disappointed that the publisher sent me instead of my co-author, General Washington. During the breaks for commercials, I was stunned to discover that not only had Carson read the book, but he argued with me about historical details. I wanted to stand up and shout, "America, this man is a phony! He can read. Don't be conned by his blatant anti-intellectualism. He plays the fool. But he is a lot smarter than he lets on, deep down." I've kept it all to myself, until now. Charges like these could ruin a man's career.

I did notice that when I tried to exchange a few pleasantries after the show, he had vanished, as if somebody had pushed a button and the trapdoor dropped him into a limousine, which then rushed him off to seclusion.

The heavy schedule of nonappearances by Carson is one of the major reasons offered by NBC as the cause of gradual ratings decline for the *Tonight* show. I don't buy that. There are other considerations. First, a lot of people really don't like Johnny Carson because the best thing he does these days is go on vacation. Second, a lot of people don't really listen to the show anymore. They use it as background music—to sleep by or talk by. It's a habit now, ingrained, like overeating. Third, Johnny is getting tired. He can hardly open his paycheck.

There is a self-satisfied air about our John lately. He seems satisfied to make $2 billion a month and still get sixteen vacations. It's amazing how little in life some settle for.

Trying to beat Carson, of course, has been the stupid pet trick of the year in the TV industry for the last twenty-five years. The field is littered with the bodies of those who have tried.

But another reason for the sometime decline in ratings is economic. Reuven Frank, former head of NBC News, once told me (in the 1970's), "*Tonight* has nine commercial positions of two minutes each, six for network commercials and three for the stations; plus two 'station breaks' of more than a minute and a half each, which are mostly local commercials, for a total of more than twenty minutes out of eighty-eight, not counting titles credits, and other hoo-ha. This means that someone watching *Tonight* spends about a quarter of his time watching something else.* What he wanted to watch, right or wrong, is cut up into slices and slivers so that jokes have to be one-liners and larger, sententious statements of the sort people who visit that program like to make are reduced to slogans. Which may be why fewer people are watching."

I personally never watched the Carson show night after night—even in its prime. My sex life was too healthy for that. Still, my heart goes out to the millions who did.

CORN PORN (CHANNEL J DEPRIVATION)

But without Carson, what's a body to do at night? Recently a colleague of mine, who had moved from the suburbs of Long Island to Manhattan,

---

* And this was before the deregulation orgy of the Reagan years.

"got cable." As part of the package of basic services, he explained on the telephone, along with all the little stations, like CBS, etc., he discovered they had one "porno station," as he called it. This was the infamous Channel J on Manhattan Cable, the most incredible TV channel in the history of TV, it has been said.

My colleague had the same sense of excitement and urgency in his voice that Don Ameche must have had when he invented the telephone. What did I as a critic think of Channel J? he asked, without waiting for an answer. "The stuff they have is unbelievable!" he burbled on ecstatically. "There was one program the other night where a guy was interviewing a call girl. She was in the nude. And he was in the nude."

"That's investigative reporting," I explained. "Real undercover stuff."

"And then the reporter puts his hand on her knee as he is questioning her."

"Just like real reporters," I said.

"And then the commercials," he went on at a fever pitch. "They're worse than the program. They have commercials for an escort service on the air that sounds just like the Mayflower Madam story. . . . Did you know all about this?"

Of course I did, I assured him. "It's sickening. Feh. Yecch. The people who put that kind of programming on the air should be put in prison and throw away the key. Disgusting. I watch it all the time, whenever I go into Manhattan."

I was lying through my teeth, of course. To be sure, I had reported on the Channel J story from time to time. I wrote serious, searching essays about the phenomenon known as *The Ugly George Show*, a program with a cause (the cause being this fellow's determination to get women with large bosoms to take their blouses off in front of his porta-video-pack equipment). Or *Midnight Interludes* (the talk show my friend had in mind), which featured a host who looked like a rabbinical student, interviewing such legendary figures as Angel Cash, who looked like a *Penthouse* dream, 100 percent silicon, bleached white hair, breathlessly saying such things as "I just love to have men squeeze my nipples, if you know what I mean." Or *The Robin Byrd Show*, hosted by what could be the most incredible sex object in Western civilization, if she had never opened her mouth and started to talk, producing the most complete turn-off since saltpeter. Once a year she appears nude. "Never on the right day," one of my sources said, "never when I was watching."

I wrote about all of these things on Channel J from time to time. But people out there in the 'burbs, like my colleague, thought, Oh, there goes Marvin again, being satirical. I was just reporting the truth. They thought I was making it all up.

Of course, I had heard of Channel J, as legendary in the cable world as the pillars of salt in Sodom and Gomorrah. It was one of the reasons I unconsciously rushed to subscribe to cable when it came into our town. Little did I know that where I lived they would have thirty-six channels of CBN, or its equivalent. That's what the people want in my town in New Jersey, apparently not like Manhattan.

There is nothing on my own cable systems comparable to Channel J. Oh, on HBO you might see the topless version of *Swan Lake*, or a nude magic show. And of course you can buy the Playboy Channel or Motel-arama, playing those obscure movies like *Meanwhile Back at the Raunch*.

But Channel J is free access. It's serendipity, the strange world of surprise TV, stumbling on something that you've never seen before. That's what TV was supposed to be about, opening the door to new visual and educational experiences and enlightenment.

This colleague of mine made me feel deprived. As a critic, I'm supposed to know everything. But I can't keep up with all the arts, certainly not from my town in northern New Jersey.

It's a clear case of geographical discrimination. Why should the cable people of Manhattan be subjected to this kind of rubbish and not us in the suburbs, where we really need it?

MARVIN NUDE: MARVELOUS
MARVIN CONFESSES ALL

But enough about them. A question I'm often asked is: "Where do I get the Eighth Avenue A-train?" The question I'm asked less often is: "What made you give up your former life as a famous author to become a TV critic?" Mostly I am asked this by my wife.

"Money," I explain to others. "Believe me, I wouldn't watch TV unless I got paid. I may be crazy, but I'm not stupid."

True, I had been living an exciting life as a free-lance writer. I was doing all kinds of important things, like trying to make a fortune on Wall Street by cornering the market in Chinese railway bonds* (of extinct railroads), and silly things like running for president in the Republican primaries of 1964. I lost. But so did Dick Nixon, Nelson Rockefeller, and Harold Stassen. Barry Goldwater got the nomination that year, despite my campaign slogan that "I'd rather be president than write." The slogan was true enough. At the time I had the biggest writer's block on my block in New Jersey. That election ruined a promising career—I had been undefeated in politics until then, never having run for anything. Overnight I had risen from a political unknown to a political nonentity.

With the publication in 1970 of *George Washington's Expense Account*, I also became a serious historian.

I had written five other books, including one I'd like to list in my curriculum vitae (*The Coward's Almanac*), except that I'm afraid. I was a man-about-Elaine's, also a man-about-remainder-stores, where my books could most often be found. And I suddenly disappeared one day

---

* The Imperial Chinese Government 5 percent Hukuang Railways Sinking Fund Gold Loan of 1911.

in 1969 to turn to TV criticism. At Elaine's, to this day, they think I have died.

It reminded me of an earlier career decision. In 1968, I went to work for a Madison Avenue agency, researching a project for *Monocle Magazine* on why famous people in the literary, artistic, political, and other establishments had sold out. I had never sold out before. In order to acquire the background, I took a job at Carl Ally, Inc., as a senior writer on the Hertz account. I had never written an ad or rented a car. That's the kind of guy Carl Ally was.

Somebody spoke to me at a party a few weeks later: "You hear about Kitman? He sold out."

"I am Kitman," I explained.

This time it was different. I was to disappear, go underground in mass culture for nineteen years, become one of the MIA of the electronic era. And did. For nineteen years I just stayed at home watching TV. I had gone to the land of the living dead, and I was a pod.

Where else had I gone? One of the better-kept secrets (except in this book) is that I live in New Jersey. I don't know why it has to be a secret. Probably they think you can't take anybody seriously who lives in New Jersey. Everybody laughs when you say "New Jersey." People from nowhere, U.S.A., like South Dakota or Nebraska and Idaho, laugh. What do they have to laugh about? Even people from Jersey laugh at themselves.

Billy Crystal was doing his opening monologue on his HBO special, *Billy Crystal*, and he said, "I'm from New Jersey. Where? Exit Fifteen." (A cheap gag: Actually, he's from Long Island.)

I can't even mention the name of the town I live in anymore. For security reasons. This is some commentary on life. All the celebrities who live in Jersey don't want their towns mentioned. The fans would harass all three of us. But I digress.

Here was a major literary figure who used to go to the Century Club (when I could find a member to take me), not only Elaine's. And for the next nineteen years I was suddenly sitting at home watching TV in New Jersey. My house became a kind of electronic bunker, filled with equipment, multi-TV sets in all sizes, VCR players, and hundreds of the latest tapes and cassettes, which nobody else had seen or, in some cases, would want to.

And so I sit in my bunker in northern New Jersey like J. D. Salinger in New Hampshire, free from the pressures of a normal newspaper man.

When *Newsday* asked me to take the job as their TV critic in 1969, I offered to move to Long Island. I even had an average, typical Long Island town picked out—East Hampton. As I explained, there was a nice cottage they could buy for me at a bargain $395,000 (1969 prices). And a private school for the kids. The public schools in the East End of Long Island were even more threatening than New Jersey's.

Newsday said it wouldn't be necessary to relocate, after all. People had the same programs in New Jersey as on Long Island, right? Except in New Jersey, they played *The Untouchables* all the time, didn't they?

So here is the news: My readers in Long Island all these years have assumed that I also live in their Nassau or Suffolk Counties. For nineteen years now they have been looking for me in the shopping malls and on the highways, wanting to let me know what *they* think about TV in person. More than the threat of nuclear annihilation, famine in India, inflation, or crabgrass, they feel very strongly about TV in Long Island. They'd like to let me know what they think—with their hands. Around the neck. But they never see me in Long Island. Because I'm not there.

My neighbors in New Jersey, on the other hand, think I am a Mafioso. I never seemed to go to work. I just sit around in my bathrobe all day watching TV. For nineteen years? Hey, come on now. There is something fishy. And he doesn't even drive a big black car.

This is not necessarily a detriment in New Jersey, being thought of as Mafia, I should point out.

It had all begun in 1967 at the *New Leader*, a small "Trotskyite publication," as its detractors called it; "a leading intellectual journal," as it called itself. I myself never read anything in it but the television page. I had met the editor, Mike Kolatch, in the army at Fort Dix, where I had gone to fight Communism in 1953. Dwight Eisenhower had just been elected president, promising, "I will go to Korea." I remember telling my draft board at the time, "I will go to Korea with Ike—provided I can come back with him."

My job in the U.S. Army, where in only two years I rose to the rank of Pfc, was as a sportswriter. I covered basketball for the *Fort Dix Post*, the camp newspaper. My major contribution to the war effort, though, was baseball statistics. I was the one who introduced the Top Ten Hitters. Nobody had ever done that before in Fort Dix journalism. It gave an extra edge of competitiveness to the rival regimental teams. It was an idea I got while learning to yell "Kill! Kill!" on the bayonet course.

After infantry basic at Fort Dix, I had been assigned to the Ninth Division Truck Driver Training School. I flunked out the first day. They didn't have hydramatic. My eyes were also weak, which I told them all about at the draft board and at 39 Whitehall Street, but they didn't listen.

My mother was very upset at my failure in truck-driver school. She had always wanted me to learn a trade. Kolatch, then the editor of the *Fort Dix Post*, was being discharged that week at Fort Dix—he was one of the little corporals who ran the army—and he arranged for my reassignment to the newspaper.

Fourteen years later I resumed my friendship with Corporal Kolatch. It was at lunch at Farm Foods Restaurant, a vegetarian *boîte* in Manhattan, that he first asked me to become the *New Leader* TV critic and thus reshape the history of TV criticism.

Today, men would kill to get the job. At the time, however, the *New Leader* was having trouble getting a critic. The other one had died. Nobody wanted the job. What could one say about TV in 1967? It had all been said: The programs were bad in 1967. You couldn't even be satirical about TV. You couldn't parody what already was a parody of itself.

Also, there was another problem. I had never watched TV. This was not, in 1967, intellectual snobbery. It's just that I was afraid of losing my mind. We grew up at a time, remember, when there were all these reports that TV damaged the brain. Educators and social scientists were saying that TV was very dangerous (this was before *they* started watching). As a free-lance writer, I was afraid of becoming addicted to TV. The motto on my family crest was "publish—and perish." I was doing badly enough at writing without having to tear myself away from the TV set every day. The only thing that kept the family from starving to death was my not watching TV.

Yet I was culturally disadvantaged, as they call it now. "Really dumb," as they called it then. Whole areas of my mind, where knowledge of TV programs are stored, were totally blank. I was a vast wasteland. For example, my *My Little Margie* studies were nonexistent. I knew absolutely nothing about the development of TV's first speed freak. I was totally unfamiliar with the classics, like *Dobie Gillis*.

I knew nothing about TV, I explained to the editor of the *New Leader*, in declining the honor.

The depth of my qualifications made him double the proposed honorarium. "We want someone who doesn't know anything," the editor said. "It gives you an open mind." That was flattering. It was the first suggestion I had a mind.

"I don't even have a color TV set," I argued.

"Where did you get the notion that because you're becoming a TV critic," said Kolatch, "you need a color TV set? That's for the square writers. And I certainly wouldn't subject a friend to Walter Cronkite reporting the Vietnam War with a turquoise face, red eyes, and violet hair against a yellow background." I think he just was afraid the bill I would submit to the *New Leader* for a professional TV set would make *him* turn green.

"I lack commitment," I went on, listing my shortcomings. "I don't hate the networks with a passion. I'm not even sure TV is bad. My kids never complain about it."

"Watch one program," he said, "and call me back."

I asked my eight-year-old daughter which shoot-'em-up cowboy or private-eye thriller I should watch. "All the kids are watching *Bravo Picasso* on NBC tonight," Suzy recommended. "Would you like to see it on my set?"

The paintings, drawings, ceramics, and sculptures in the Picasso exhibits in Paris and the Dallas/Fort Worth museums came across beautifully on the trans-Atlantic TV special that spring Sunday night in 1967. "Bravos" and a few "olés!" filled the room time after time. But my daughter was puzzled by Yves Montand's narration. Why did NBC hire an actor who couldn't speak English to introduce the work of a great artist to an English-speaking audience? During the first commercial break I dug out a book review from a 1950 *Paris Herald-Tribune* that explained why Frenchmen like M. Montand speak that way.

Georges Guilaine, in *La Langue Anglaise en 30 Leçons,* published at about the time Montand was learning English to make his debut in Hollywood, tells his students "How is your mother?" is pronounced "Haouz iz yor mozeur?"

"But ziz iz a minor ponte," I told my daughter. "Lizzaine tou ouot ze man sezz, not tou haou e zez eet." I soon realized my mistake as Montand went further, into a technical analysis of Picasso's art.

"What is a mistress?" asked my daughter.

"It's like a fiancée," I explained, "except unofficial. Like almost engaged." A picture of a naked mistress suddenly flashed on the screen. I turned away and made a cutting motion with a finger across the throat, which my wife was supposed to interpret as "Get this poor defenseless child out of here." But Carol missed her cue.

"Does a model have to be engaged to an artist before she takes her clothes off?" said Suzy.

I looked at my watch. Only 6:50 P.M. Millions of American children were still awake and at their TV sets. "How could he have two children with somebody he isn't even married to?" my daughter asked.

My God, why aren't they hitting the *bleep* button at 30 Rockefeller Plaza? "What does he mean, 'shared his life now with Françoise?' "

How long had this kind of raw *cinéma vérité* been going on? I asked myself, this *cinéma nudité?* The listing for *Bravo, Picasso* in *TV Guide* hadn't said FOR ADULTS ONLY. I remember what had happened to the moral fiber in my town in New Jersey after Jackie Mason made an adult gesture on *The Ed Sullivan Show.* That finger alone eventually caused 1968 and ended the Vietnam War.

"Go to bed," I said firmly. "You've seen one Picasso, you've seen them all."

"But there's going to be an art auction afterward," she said. A new moral breakdown was starting with this smut, with kids not listening to zere fathers. As a compromise, I turned the sound down, as she said, "What's a whore of Montmartre?"

While I was trying to explain the arrondissement system of Paris, Montand blithely admitted that Picasso was a Communist. My daughter asked, "A Communist?"

"It's a terrible economic system, especially for artists and little girls your age. Communists don't have freedom of expression under communism."

"Neither do I. What's a Communist?"

The picture on our screen dissolved to a painting of a woman with two noses and three eyes. Thank God, things were getting artistic again. "In order to be a great artist, like Picasso," asked my daughter, "do you have to be a mistress *and* a Communist?" In thirty-seven minutes, *Bravo, Picasso* had done more for the cause of communism and free love than all the years of water fluoridation.

Bidding me good night, eventually, now that I was fifteen years older, Suzy said, "Zomday when ai grow up, ai want tou bey a grit artiste laike Pablo Picasso." I smiled. "Or," she said, "a grait mizztress."

I called up the editor and accepted the job as TV critic. If my daughter ever joined the New Left or lived loosely, I would sue NBC. Meanwhile, I planned, on behalf of all the nation's children, to be entirely objective and to destroy the network.

Also, the honorarium was in the high two figures, an offer I couldn't refuse. I guess I was also curious about TV.

As a TV critic that first year or two, I would sit in front of the set watching a minor show like *He and She*, a sitcom (1967–70) about a cartoonist, starring Richard Benjamin and Paula Prentiss, taking notes. If the kids talked or balked, I would say, "Shussh. Can't you see I'm working?"

They laughed at me.

True, I was backward, in media terms, in pop culture. I felt inadequate.

To make up for such disadvantages, I threw myself into TV viewing. My children saw me watching *The Donna Reed Show* with a clipboard, jotting down dialogue. I was bewildered by the plots, trying to figure out, for example, what happened to the other husband in *Bewitched*.

Aspects of this peculiar behavior puzzled my kids. I had been the usual parent, saying, "Don't watch this, don't watch that. It's too violent." My son, Jamie, reminded me I had even banned *The Man From U.N.C.L.E.* because of the violence. And now I, ogre number one, was sitting around watching anything, as long as it moved, spoke, shot, hit, or grinned. My kids used to invite their friends in to look at me doing my work. They even charged a few pennies, I later learned.

My son used to greet me, on my return from a long day in the literary marketplace before I became a TV critic, with "Pop, they're giving away a Triumph Spitfire on *Let's Make a Deal*. Let's go down and get on line." And I would lecture him. Had he been sitting around wasting his youth watching TV?

Now I was sitting at home watching TV all day long. Life's little ironies. Go know!

It was bizarre in a way, managing to grow up without TV. I mean it's one thing if you were a Japanese soldier hiding out in a cave in Saipan after VJ-Day, waiting for the next Pearl Harbor. But my case was one of those aberrations in intellectual history. How had I managed to escape?

(1) Our family didn't own a TV set when I was growing up. We were so poor or out of it. Uncle Miltie was a horse to me, when TV started in the 1940's. Then (2) when I went off to CCNY in 1947, watching TV was outré. Or at least "out." Not to watch TV was a political statement. Rebellious radical youth held their noses about TV. I was an egghead of the worst kind: a nouveau who couldn't breathe.

Of course, (3) I would go to rich girls' houses who had TV sets. But (4) I would neck when we were supposed to be watching TV. I didn't even see Sid Caesar. *Your Show of Shows* wasn't mine, even though it was on every Saturday night all the time.

Then (5) I got married (during the 1951–52 season). Our apartment in Hell's Kitchen, before it was fashionable, was hell on the West Side of Manhattan, too small for a TV, with no room for a telephone. Our first phone was in a drugstore at the corner. And again (6) it was very on-the-cutting-edge to sneer at TV during the Eisenhower years. Not owning a set was again a heavy political protest against . . . I forget what.

In 1957, I bought my first TV set. But that was for my wife to watch while she was nursing our first baby, Jamie Lincoln. Still, I couldn't watch. Oh, I used to watch a little baseball, whenever the Pittsburgh Pirates were playing the Mets on Channel 9. But baseball is not TV. It's baseball.

All this not watching left me deprived, or weird. I suffered a kind of cultural autism. To this day, there are gaps. *F-Troop, Lucy, Gilligan's Island, Gunsmoke, Maverick, The Fugitive, The Twilight Zone*—shows that every sensitive, aware, hip, self-confident intellectual has seen ninety-three times. It's virtually impossible to recoup lost time.

And now I was working like a (*Leave It to*) Beaver to rid myself of electronic illiteracy.

The *New Leader* had few readers compared to *People* or the *National Enquirer* today, but all twenty thousand were opinion leaders. One of them was Bill Moyers, then publisher of *Newsday* and former press secretary to Lyndon Johnson. I later found out it was Bill who had suggested hiring me in 1969, something he never lets me forget. "*Ahh* hired you," he is always saying at crowded public-television cocktail parties. "It was the only mistake *ah* made as a publisher."

Two *Newsday* editors, Dave Laventhol and Lou Schwartz, took me to lunch at Charley O's one week in the fall of 1969. "How would you like to write a column for us on TV?" they asked. I needed time to think about it, I explained. And a minute later, accepted.

It was a chance to finally get paid real money to sit around and watch TV twenty-four hours a day. Forget the eventual MacArthur Foundation grants for geniuses: This was the educational stipend of the century. The Times-Mirror Company, which owns *Newsday*, had become a true patron of the arts.

I had been curious about TV, writing one essay a month. Now that *Newsday* offered me a chance to actually do it full time, I was really pleased. I couldn't believe my good fortune. I finally had a Medici, as I liked to think of the Times-Mirror Company president, Otis Chandler de' Medici. I even wrote to him when he bought *Newsday*, offering to put the shot with him if he ever came to New Jersey, where we do a lot of shooting.

It was on December 7, 1969, that this remarkable experiment began; a day of infamy, of course, as the networks think of it.

The Education of Henry Adams? This was the education of Marvin Kitman.

In Adams's day, the well-educated person didn't have to be concerned about such significant issues as who shot J.R. or can Vanna White spell. I'd like to see old Henry making something out of *The Battle of the Network Stars Challenge*, finding, say, the dynamo of meaning in Valerie Bertinelli and Adrienne Barbeau jumping up and down on the track without bras in their wet T-shirts. Or wondering if Dolly Parton is anorectic on her variety show. Or contrasting Susan Lucci's acting in *Invitation to Hell?* (a TV movie of 1984) with her performance in *Mafia Princess* (1986). As much as we admire the well-rounded man of the nineteenth century, it is tougher being cultured today. TV viewers are inundated by information and entertainment. Never in the history of mankind has there been such an unending assault on the mind. There is such a bombardment of images, issues to decide, facts to decide. In docudramas, who is to know what is fact, what fiction? In TV news shows, we don't know what is news or features. We don't know what's right or wrong on anything.

All you had to do in the old days was read a couple of hundred great books and understand them. Today, one must have *Scruples*, belong to a *Dynasty*, spin in the *Wheel of Fortune*. Becoming *au courant* with the arts today is an incredible achievement.

I am living testimony to this, a perfect example of how it is possible to make one's self over in only nineteen years. Now, I really am concerned about Alexis and Krystle *and* Blake, about Gary Ewing and Abby, will Dolly's variety show work, how they got rid of Uncle Walter, and whether Tom Brokaw is a mechanical doll. Was David (Duh) Hartman as dumb as they say? Is *Dallas* done? Does *Falcon Crest* make an amusing wine? I care, you see, about these matters that have preoccupied Americans for two decades.

You think I'm kidding about how hard it is? Okay. Flash quiz time. Ancient American History I. Here is your chance to prove what an ignoramus you are.

THE GREAT *SATURDAY NIGHT LIVE* BLUEBOOK IQ TEST

1. Francisco Franco is what?
2. Which drugs does Steve Martin endorse?
3. The following things have what in common: (a) Puerto Rican steak (b) Russian jewelry (c) endangered feces (d) Mississippi liver boats (e) presidential erections
4. A White House surgical team had to remove what from the mouth of President Ford?
5. Students at Cornell Medical School were taught what instead of basic cardiovascular surgery?
6. Why didn't the Coneheads' planet send a spaceship to rescue them?
7. Jane is a what?
8. Cite the watchwords of the eighties.
9. How long were the Coneheads supposed to stay on Earth?
10. What has baseball been to Chico Escuela?
11. Complete this line and tell who said it: "It just goes to show you . . ."
12. What do you get with the Rovco All-Flammable Christmas trees?
13. Reincarnation is what?
14. Who always writes the letters to Roseanne Roseannadanna?
15. Where did the Coneheads' ship land?
16. What was the Coneheads' mission on Earth?
17. Why is it worth it to join a health club?
18. Princess Lee had what on her shoes?
19. What do the Coneheads eat with eggs?
20. Mr. Conehead works as a: (a) high school principal (b) Mr. Macho model (c) driving teacher (d) Freddie Silverman lookalike
21. Define Y.E.A.
22. Where were the Blues Brothers from?
23. What does Dan "eat, drink, and snort?"
24. Give the name of the company that makes the Meat Wagon Action Speed Set?
25. What colors do the Rovco All-Flammable Christmas Tree come in?
26. In *The Gift of the Magi*, what did the wife sell?
27. Who is Leonard Pinth-Garnell?
28. Who said, *Our flop story tonight*?
29. How did the Coneheads get back to their home planet?
30. Name the Coneheads.
31. What did President Carter call Secretary of State Vance?
32. Where do the Coneheads tell people they are from?
33. Have you ever had a toenail you couldn't throw away because it was shaped like a boomerang and kept coming back?
34. What won't Steve Martin smoke at dusk, and why?
35. What game do the Coneheads play?
36. New Shimmer is a what?

37. What did Cleveland do when it defaulted?
38. What does Emily Litella call Dan?
39. How much does a slop jockey charge to jump in your cesspool?
40. Where does Brother Elwood keep his harmonica?
41. (a) If you ordered a hamburger at the Olympia Café what would you get?
    (b) Do they have fries?
    (c) Coke?
42. What planet are the Coneheads from?
43. Who had a sweat ball on the tip of her nose?
44. What was the humorous part to the tragic story of Bubbles the Hippo?
45. A January issue of *Ms.* magazine showed President Carter pregnant. What did he have to say about it?
46. What was Mr. Loopner's problem?
47. Who is a putz?
48. If you could say "Hawwy Weasoner cowwectwy," you would be who?
49. Who said, "A corpse is a corpse of horse of horse"?
50. Chico Escuela is: (a) one of four comedy brothers (b) a South American soccer star (c) a dictator of South American country (d) a baseball player (e) all of the above (f) still dead.

Easy Bonus Question

51. Why does Saturn have a ring around it?

Scoring This Test:
Give two points for each correct answer.

What the Test Scores Mean:
   100–90   You are a very well-educated person.
    89–75   You are wasting too much time reading books.
    74–65   You are a borderline case.
    64–0   You were out of the country in the 1970's.

ANSWERS:

1. still dead
2. placebos
3. Never mind!
4. a snowball
5. air-conditioning repair
6. They cut back on their space program.
7. ignorant slut or bitch

8. Let's party.
9. seven centuries
10. "berry berry good"
11. ". . . It's always something." Roseanne Roseannadanna
12. an all-flammable hanging wreath
13. milk taken from dead cows
14. Richard Feder of Fort Lee, New Jersey
15. Lake Michigan
16. to be the timekeepers
17. because you get to see a lot of people that you don't know—naked
18. a little "tinny" piece of toilet paper
19. Fiberglass
20. (c) a driving teacher
21. Yuletide Energy Alert
22. Illinois
23. news
24. Mainway
25. pink, electric blue, and pine
26. her hairbrush
27. host of *Master Joke Theatre*, *Bad Play House*, *Bad Cinema*, etc.
28. Emily Litella
29. They took off on the Chrysler Building.
30. Beldar, Prymat, and Connie
31. a little dink
32. France
33. yes
34. Marijuana, " 'Cause that's when the little fat men will come."
35. ring toss
36. dessert topping and floor wax
37. changed its name and moved to Arizona to get a fresh start
38. Mr. Adenoid
39. eighty-five cents
40. in a locked case, handcuffed to his wrist
41. (a) cheese-burr-gah! (b) no fries, chips (c) no Coke, Pepsi
42. Remulak
43. Dr. Joyce Brothers
44. She rolled over a troop of Brownies and crushed them all to death.
45. "It is obviously a hoax and I haven't been pregnant since I had Amy ten years ago."
46. He was born without a spine.
47. Billy Carter
48. Baba Wawwa
49. Mr. Ed's Widow
50. (d) a baseball player
51. God was playing with a basketball and it got stuck in the hoop.

(FAST FORWARD) (PLAY)

In England, people who went to Oxford, Cambridge, and before that Eton or Harrow all speak the same language. This automatically leaves a few out, i.e., those who didn't go to the same schools. But that's okay. They wouldn't want to talk to anybody who didn't go to the right schools, anyway. They're just not worth talking to. Otherwise they would have gone to your school.

The right people all are equipped to talk about Cicero's account of the Punic Wars, the battle with Hannibal, what Pericles did in 90 A.D., and so forth. That is what they taught at their schools. They all know about it, since they went to the same school. And it all works out very well. It's mutually exclusive. Now there is a phrase I never did quite get the hang of (they didn't teach it at my school). But I think what it means is it excludes those who didn't go to your school and wouldn't be worth talking to, anyway.

Anyway, in this country during the mid-1970's, we, too, had a special language, background, and breeding. It was called *Saturday Night Live*. SNL was the *lingua franca* of the "in"-persons, the native language, the mother tongue that established a bond, a chord that is as strong as the old English school tie, knotted too tightly. They all knew what one Conehead said to the other Conehead in those unforgettable skits. References, jokes, literary allusions, samurai this or that, guest hosts, conceits, metaphors. Every educated person knew that the Father of the Year was Father Guido Sarducci.

The *SNL* thing could really leave a person out of it in conversations, much as the conversations on a weekend with Robert Oppenheimer and the Manhattan Project gang had done in the 1940's.

TV replaced Yiddish as the language of intellectuals. They used to say at Harvard that one knew just enough Yiddish to get across the Yard. The truly educated person today knows some TV. It doesn't matter what his S.A.T. scores are. The common bond that united Arthur Schlesinger, Jr., Nat Hentoff, Sr., Norman Podhoretz II, Michael Harrington the Good, Victory Navasky the Bad, Norman Mailer & Company, and Susan Sontag Herself was the ability to talk TV.

Lately I'm researching a major study of soap operas. I've been into this problem for three years, and have seen one or two plots resolved. Soap time passes so slowly. The people deciphering the Dead Sea Scrolls probably had the same feeling of progress. When I started as a TV critic, people were ashamed of being caught. It was something dirty, a vice you kept in the closet, with the dust mop and . . . well, the soaps. If somebody called on the phone in the afternoon, you ran to turn the sound off. Or when they asked what you were watching, you said "Oh, *Washington Week in Review* and *Playing Shakespeare.*" Now, people talk about their favorites openly.

Everybody has come out of the closets about soaps. Robert MacNeil/ Lehrer (as I think of him) of the NewsHour told me he watches the soaps— but only to catch the news bulletins at the bottom of the screen. Mean Joe Green of the Pittsburgh Steelers, my idol, watches soaps. (Which one? Any one he wants.) I would not be surprised to hear that John Kenneth Gailbraith takes them in at Harvard. I. F. Stone is a *Days of Our Lives* freak. Secretary of State Shultz watches *Guiding Light* at Foggy Bottom. Fans? Thomas Hoving, Martin Borman, Mario Cuomo, Associate Justice Sandra Day O'Connor. Nothing would surprise me.

Brain surgeons' wives, librarians, teachers, women with Ph.D.'s, all the smart women who would be running countries instead of homes, watch soaps without shame—today.

College students—the nation's future leaders—are watching them. Even at City College. Some colleges stopped scheduling classes opposite *General Hospital* at its peak: 1981–83, because the competition was too stiff. If the Russians attacked the United States between 3:00 and 4:00 P.M. on a weekday, nobody would notice.

What's to be ashamed of? What is a soap, anyway, but the study of human behavior. You spend a comparable number of hours in a classroom talking about the same problems they do on the soaps, they give you a degree and call you a social worker. I am a social watcher. I'm not saying the soaps are superb lessons for living. They do teach you things, like sooner or later the blonde always gets it in the end. A brick falls on her head. Dr. Dichter, the psychologist, who is a soap-opera fan himself, once told me, "The blonde is out cold, dead. It ends happily for a while. A lot of people are looking for easy answers to life's problems, which they get on soaps." Slowly.

That's okay. I'm a slow learner.

We had all come a long way—from initial curiosity and attraction, to repulsion and fashionable sneering, to selective, discriminating TV-speak. And I was part of, indeed, soon an arbiter of, this vast ferment.

(STOP) (PAUSE)

(PLAY)

By this time, as you have detected, I think I have the most wonderful job in the world. Can you imagine getting *paid* to watch television? Why, I know several people who would do it for nothing.

One of the most important parts of the job is going out with the stars, like Donna Mills, Cybill Shepherd, and Deidre Hall. Eileen Davidson of *The Young and the Restless* always wanted to sit down and discuss her acting aspirations: Should she appear next in *Uncle Vanya, Moon for the Mis-begotten*, or *Knots Landing*? Lynda Carter, that Wonder Woman, was thinking of converting to Judaism and asked me to be her spiritual adviser. Lindsay Wagner always called to go jogging with me. At night, after Channel 13 had signed off with the Bella Abzug fight song, I'd be off to the glittering parties thrown by producers for me, waving starlets and money. I was always star-studded, with Mary Hart of *ET* or Linda Ellerbee clinging to my arm and hanging on my every word.

I don't actually do any of these things. But as a well-established TV critic for a major newspaper and syndicate, I could. My wife doesn't think it's necessary.

I have to watch football twelve hours a week. At least that's what I told my wife. You never know when a column will come out of it.

It's my work, my children are trained to tell anybody, including my wife. Sometimes she forgets that a TV critic has to watch TV.

Look, I don't want to give the impression this business is as dull as astrophysics. I could have starlets delivered to my house Federal Express, if I was that kind of disgusting person, and if my wife would go shopping, for a month. There are networks that produce shows in New York only so certain executives will be able to fly in from the Coast on a Thursday night to see their bimbos. There are network executives who have put associate producers on the payroll because of their tight purple toreador pants. Everything is handed to me on a silver platter. I can get anything I want from TV.

I can talk medicine with Dr. Westphall of *St. Elsewhere*, discuss the Miranda rights questions with Cagney, Lacey, Kojak, or Bruce Willis, explore the meaning of Martin Buber's books with Vanna White. I could talk to the man who wrote the Peter Principle about Victoria Principal. I could talk ballet with Baryshnikov, or profound with Maynard G. Krebs (Bob Denver), and one day I'll ask Bryant Gumbel what he really thinks of Jane Pauley. I plan to discuss the rumor he is a secret Reagan supporter with Sam Donaldson. All of this is mine because I am a charming, wonderful, witty fellow. But also a bit because of my position.

Is there any wonder that I sometimes think I've been on vacation for the last nineteen years? Mentally, at least. I get paid to do what people do for free, for fun, for disintegration. If I were another kind of critic, I could eat pizza and all the junk food I wanted and nobody could say, Stop eating that poison.

Being a TV critic was once described as a form of punishment. Sisyphus had to push a rock up a hill and down; a TV critic has to watch the new shows endlessly. But being able to (a) stay up late and (b) watch TV, and (c) nobody, including yourself, says you've got to go to work tomorrow, is as good a definition as any of paradise in the 1980's. I've been living in the Garden of Eden. And the only persons who have it better are the TV executives. They actually get paid fortunes to make the junk I have to watch.

(STOP) (REWIND)

(PLAY)

A question I'm often asked is: How much TV does a TV critic actually have to watch?

A. Less time than the average viewer.

The average TV viewer, according to a year-end report by Nielsen Media Research, watched seven hours, seven minutes each day in the 1986–87 season, or forty-nine hours and forty-nine minutes per week per household. Wow! Can you imagine how much they'd watch if there was anything on?

Seven hours a day? I'm not that good. Besides, I'm too busy writing about TV to actually watch much.

Still, I watch a lot more now than before I became a critic, as I've explained. My viewing is way up, percentage-wise, from when I didn't watch TV at all.

In defense, even in my darkest, most ignorant period, before getting paid to watch, I was never against TV for other people. It was simply as a matter of conscience that I chose to be backward. I was never, for example, against it for kids, even my own. Sure, I grumbled about how it would ruin their minds, their manners, their morals, but just so long as they had their health. I never forbade the watching of TV, a form of electronic censorship that works about as effectively as did banning dirty books in Boston. Instead, I encouraged my kids to watch TV, in my way. The first year I became a TV critic I forced them to watch TV. They were given TV as a chore. I had three kids, one for each network. One was responsible for everything on CBS, one for NBC, one for ABC. Thank God for birth control. Nobody wanted to watch PBS. Hey, I'm a father. Who would be so cruel as to force his children to watch public television? This isn't Dickens's day. I'm no monster. Making them watch what was good for them would have been a form of infanticide. But they had to watch what was bad for them.

Whenever I had a question about, say, *Camp Runamuck* on NBC or *The Flying Nun* on ABC or *Joe & Son* on CBS—the appropriate child would be summoned. If he hadn't done his chores, he or she would be assigned extra TV to watch, usually the network evening news, which they hated intensely. No excuses were accepted.

An odd but interesting and unexpected by-product of this is that they all grew up hating TV. It was homework. They looked forward to when prime time was over, and they could read a book. They were even doing it under the covers, when I assumed they were upstairs snug in their beds watching Merv Griffin for me.

It helped me evolve the theory: Schools should require the viewing of commercial-TV programs as assignments. Forget the occasional Shakespeare plays and *Lincoln Center Lives* they like to assign. Give them *The Young and the Restless, Let's Make a Deal*, and *The Newlywed Game every day*. Write an essay on the socio-politico-economic implications of *The Price Is Right*. How is it possible biologically that Lisa Hartman died as C. J. Dunne in *Knots Landing* in the cliff-hanger of 1983 and comes back the next season (1984) disguised as Cathy Geary? At what speed do we move in *As the World Turns*? In two years, nobody will watch TV except teachers and critics. If they assigned car stripping in schools or doing graffiti in the gym, daily, and gave grades, they'd hate it.

My daughter Andrea, the youngest, my 1964 model kid, was particularly discerning. She was my scout, my eyes and ears, and she was too willing to help out in the beginning. She was the one who told me that Fonzie would make it after seeing the first episode of *Happy Days*. Freddie Silverman had the same idea. I just wrote down what Andrea said about the shows, and was acclaimed. But I digress.

Officially, I "watch" no TV. Not when you're watching. Oh, maybe I may watch an hour a week, in a good week. But you have to realize I'm also watching all the time when you're not, and I'm working.

One of the great things about the job is that I get to see the shows in advance—even the Oscars and the Super Bowl. Didn't you know they are taped in a studio? I joke. But other tapes and cassettes from New York and Hollywood arrive at my house in New Jersey by train, boat, and bicycle every morning. They start arriving before 8:00 A.M., usually with the damned Federal Express gal, who's always racing with Emery, Purolator, DHL, and Econo Courier to get to my door, to see who can wake me up first thing with cassettes of the new *My Two Dads* or *Growing Pains*. You know their commercials?

First, they should say, they'll make sure you're sleeping. If you're awake, they'll come back later in the day.

Some days I may watch eleven or twelve hours of cassettes. It depends on how many goodies there are on the schedule. During the "sweeps" periods, it gets intense. The cassettes of the multihour-blockbuster series pile up on the floor in my office. It looks like Crazy Eddie's stockroom.

Which brings me to another standard question: Do I watch all the episodes? "You couldn't watch them all," one of my worried readers (J. L. Liberman) wrote. "You wouldn't watch them all! You shouldn't watch them all. It's bad for the medulla oblongata. Attacks it directly." Indeed, some critics do watch all the hours of a miniseries like Sidney Sheldon's *Master of the Game* or *Windmills of the Gods*. They are muttons for punishment. Deep-dyed masochists. This isn't necessary. You can tell in one cassette (in one hour): Casting, production values, the way they tell a story, whether there is a story, whether they give details of character, development, or whether they just go from violence to violence, with occasional kissing, the hallmarks of shallow television. You can usually tell by the name of the producer. David Gerber tells one kind of story. No matter how many foreign countries he goes to on location, how many stars from British theater he dragoons, a Gerber miniseries—i.e., *The Last Days of Pompeii* or *George Washington*—comes out the same, and never as a wonderful John Hawkesworth (*Upstairs, Downstairs*) or a Kenith Trodd (*Singing Detective*). Sometimes I skip to the last cassette. You wouldn't want to miss the last day of *The Last Days of Pompeii*. It should have started with the volcano.

The great thing about being a critic is you have the freedom to watch as much as you want, when you want them, in any order. My big secret: The desire to see more of something. When I wanted to see more of *Winds of War*, despite Ali MacGraw, who looked as if she studied acting under Lurch in *The Addams Family*, and Robert Mitchum, who seemed to be on Valium, that told me it was going to be a hit. If you come back for eighteen hours, it's usually a sign they've got something, I always say. What a joy to sit at one's desk transfixed by a great series like *Brideshead* or Roy Marsden as Adam Dalgleish in any P. D. James on *Mystery!* and feed the cassettes into your machine as kids put quarters into a video game.

On the other hand, I once went eight days with no TV. On days off, I find that staring at the wall is more fascinating. It allows the imagination to waken, to run rampant. There is more going on on many walls than TV sets: patterns, or cracks or the unevenness with which paint dries over the years. Sometimes you get a little dark speck crawling on the wall, or, where I live, mosquitoes. (They have insignia on their wings. But this is New Jersey, where mosquitoes are the state bird.)

The biggest problem I have is watching TV late at night. Forget the late-night news at eleven. Forget Carson and David Letterman. I'm talking about 10:00 P.M..

Anything after ten, you see, and my wife thinks the romance has gone out of our life. No TV.

We have had long talks about this, unfortunately not during the commercials. This creates a lot of problems for me, as a critic and as a regular person.

Ten o'clock is when most normal people watch TV. Most people watch to get away from the cares of the day. They escape, relax from work. For me, it is my work. I'm always getting enraged about something or other and rushing off to my typewriter, even if I don't actually get there. So my wife has a point. But her embargo on TV after ten carries it to excess.

It's not that she is a Talmudic scholar or a snob. Carol reads her horoscope in the *Daily News* every morning, religiously. It always says: "Stay away from TV after ten."

"It's my job," I explain one night. "I have to watch."

"But I don't," she said.

The problem became especially critical during the period when *Police Woman*, starring Angie Dickinson, was on at 10:00 P.M. on NBC. As a major in TV police science, I had to watch Angie Dickinson walk down those stairs every Wednesday night. And the way she ran after the bad guys in high heels! Every time she pointed that gun, I wanted to hide behind the couch. She was wicked.

"What was that?" my wife would say, seeing the whirling lights from the corner of the set. She didn't even look at the screen.

"It's *Crime and Punishment* . . . on public TV," I lied, mumbling "Fyodor Dostoyevsky."

And then the dumb bongos on the sound track started. "Forget it," she would say. "No police shows after ten." Sometimes I think I am married to Mother Teresa.

I've had this recurring fantasy of someday sneaking out to a motel at night. And I'd be the only one there really watching clean TV.

At that, I work long hours. There is always some emergency that needs my attention, a reader who wants me to look at something scandalous. "*Hawaii Five-O* reruns were switched back to 11:30 P.M. though listed as 12:00 P.M.," a card from reader Simon Nathan of South Orange, New Jersey, explained. "Consequently, I missed the first half of a very important case. What the H- is going on over there at Channel 9?"

It's a job very much like the volunteer ambulance corps or fire dept. You're always on duty.

Q. Okay, already, how much do you really watch?

A. Eighteen hours a day. That's what I tell the editors. A cheap plea for sympathy. Look, I can't watch everything. Basically, I try to keep on the level of your average TV executive, who watches less TV than anyone you know. You'd be appalled at how they spend private time. (Sneak-reading books, one of them.) The only way to change children's TV would be to chain TV executives to their desks at the office on a Saturday morning and make them watch the Saturday-morning ghetto in action.

There is a law here somewhere; the closer you get to the center, in their case to the decision-making process, the less TV you watch. The further away you get, the more you watch. Here is a chart that describes this relationship:

Profession	Average Hours of Watching/Day
TV network vice-president	0. 7
TV critic	0. 8
TV repairman	2. 9
Nonviewers, intellectual	6. 9 (0. 3 hours openly, 6. 6 in closet)
Average viewer	7. 07

If I seem a little hesitant, unwilling, less than candid, you can understand why. The amount of viewing time each critic spends at his job is a trade secret. It's like the amount of thyme or salt a cook puts in. One man's pinch is another man's ¼ tsp. The touch of saffron, though, makes a difference. The amount of time cooking is, however, relevant. If you watch too much TV, you can spoil the broth. Or spoil what is mostly spoiled.

But there is a complex formula that answers the question specifically:

T (The amount of time watching) ÷ (divided by) A (Attention) + S (the square root of a network executive's brain) = Q (Quality) or P (Pulitzer Prize).

If anything, most people who write about TV watch far too much of it. The field doesn't warrant it. Confuses them, having facts.

It's not how long, but the way you look at TV that is significant. Straight on is the worst. The brilliance of the picture can hurt the cornea of the eye. You have to look at TV from the corner of the eye. Peripheral vision! Otherwise you can go crazy, or be an average TV viewer. You can't watch 7.7 hours a day and have anything to say about TV.

You have to look at it obliquely. Preferably with one eye at most. Give it a glancing blow, so to speak. Does TV look better with one eye than two?

The regulars scan, the electronic equivalent of skimming a book. They monitor shows.

Watching TV is an experience like looking at an eclipse. You don't see anything. But you wind up blind.

(STOP) (REWIND)

(PLAY)

The last thing about watching TV professionally I save for the last, it is so terrible. That is the dreaded Critic's Block, the disease of not being able to watch at all, even when there is nothing on that requires attention, which is almost always. You can be watching from 0.7 to 7.0 hours a day, and then suddenly—you can't look one more minute, or you'll scream. Yes, you've got the Block. Not only can't you watch anymore, you can't even be in the same room with a TV set on. It's all in the head, of course. It often strikes when you least expect it, during the start of a new season, when there are nineteen new shows and all you want to do is look at the sky. Or you find yourself picking up a book suddenly, something like *Russia and the West Under Lenin and Stalin* by George Kennan. There are genuine dangers.

Another question I'm often asked is whether I own a TV set, and what kind do professionals use? The answers are yes, yes, no, and not necessarily. Some of my best work has been done without seeing the programs. The medium is the message, McLuhan said. Personally, I always thought the commercials were the messages.

How and where you watch TV is as important as the programs. If a TV program is in a theater, then you call it a movie. If you show it in a museum, it's art. You could run *MacGyver* or *Who's the Boss?* at the Museum of Modern Art, or the Getty, and they'd be lined up around the block. And if you ran them dubbed in French, then they'd be classics, as with Jerry Lewis. Shown on the small screen at home, they are small change.

There has been a radical change in my method. When I started in 1969, I went to private screenings at the networks' luxurious screening rooms. At the CBS headquarters—the marvelous Eero Saarinen piece of art, called Black Rock—a critic sat in a well-padded leather chair near the marble coffee table up front, or reclined on a divan to the rear. P.R. men stood at attention to sharpen your pencil or peel you a grape. At NBC in the RCA Building, "30 Rock," the fourteen modern swivel chairs had their own dials at the armrest for controlling the room's lights and sound, and two telephones. When bored, I used to dial a number at random, say, "You're fired," and hang up. It gave the P.R. people something to think about, in case they weren't sufficiently paranoid.

"The main cause for disappointment in, and for, criticism of television," Marshall McLuhan explains in *The Medium Is the Message*, "is the failure on the part of its critics to view it as a totally new technology which demands different sensory responses." I discovered that critics saw shows on a big movie-type screen. It was very interesting, to see the new programs this way, but it bore little relevance to what my readers would be seeing at home. I was audibly disappointed.

"Is anything wrong?" asked the NBC public-relations man.

"Yes," I explained. "The picture is in focus. And I don't see ghosts on your screen."

There were even greater reasons to be disappointed. During the first pause for a brief message from our sponsors, INSERT COMMERCIAL HERE flashed on the big screen. I started to walk out of the room to get a bite to eat. The show, however, went back on immediately. In four days of screening I didn't get one pretzel, much less a salami-and-egg sandwich.

"Most often the seconds—the commercials—reflect a truer understanding of the medium," McLuhan wrote. My old professor at City College Irving Rosenthal said it even better earlier, in 1951: "I don't mind the commercials. It's the stuff in between that bothers me." How then was it possible for a critic to judge the overall impact of a program without seeing the most creative aspects of the medium?

These misleading practices continue. The usual two-hour made-for-TV movie runs, in the version we see, about ninety minutes. It moves right along. They don't even bother telling us that we'll be right back after these messages. Also, most of my time at the networks was spent in isolation, an unnatural way to watch television shows. I couldn't stand the privacy. The networks in effect are forcing a critic to give his total attention to the programs. His undivided attention. But TV requires divided attention. What makes the medium work for many millions is selective inattention.

Which brings us to the question of how I survive under these hardship conditions; why I am not one of the homeless, given what goes on in my home; why my mind has not turned to mush, to match the medium; or why the medium is so medium at best, except for the good parts; and how I have come to be able to see, or at least sense, the good parts.

It is not just the secret I revealed at the outset, that I have become a VCR. That my mind works on Play, Rewind, Fast Forward, Pause (or

Freeze), and, mainly, in Slo Mo. It is not just that this book has been a series of playbacks, a total recall of what I never intended to remember in the first place. No, it is that I have had some work done. It is time to confess.

(STOP) (REWIND)

(PLAY)

The operation was a success.

The transplant worked.

The new bionic brain is functioning perfectly, thank God.

Not shown is my bionic stomach, which many TV viewers have, anyway.

In the late 1970's, bionic transplants were the biggest thing since bio-feedback. Everybody was trying them. They were part of the self-improvement craze of that era.

We were living then, of course, in the age of bionic broadcasting. We had shows starring the bionic man, the bionic woman, the bionic boy. Still to come were the bionic horse, and the bionic chicken. Bionics were an accident not of genetics or electronics but of geography.

Steve Austin, the original *Six Million Dollar Man* and Jaime Sommers, the six-million-dollar woman (a.k.a. "Bionic Woman"), and all bionic people on television originally came from Bionia, which is just below Carbondale, Illinois. They played a critical role in the development of modern television. *The Six Million Dollar Man* was the forerunner of *That's Incredible*. It catered to our interest in *Real People* (a show title of the era), and their achievements. Bionics seemed the wave of the future, something for a shrewd critic to get into, as plastics was for Dustin Hoffman in *The Graduate*, which led him to become chairman of Monsanto and to restage *Death of a Salesman* as a sitcom.

I had taken some time off from the paper in 1976 to work with the baseball player Jim Bouton on the TV series *Ball Four*, which CBS turned into Strike Three. Before coming back from this busman's holiday, I decided to have the operation.

I used to make fun of Steve Austin and Jaime Sommers in the old days, before the transplant. Now I am their intellectual equal.

Surgically, early bionic transplants were difficult procedures. They were done at home. With a chain saw. Now they have these new solid-state bionic brains. Like quasars, or adding a memory board to a computer. You just take out the old one, when it goes, and slip in the new one. You don't even have to go to the shop.

Mine came to me in the mail. "Use as directed," the directions said.

BEFORE

AFTER

This phrase is the most widely used language in broadcasting, and I'm still not sure what "Use as directed" means. Most of us don't even have a director.

To order the brain kit, you simply write to: Bionic Brain Bank % Grand Central Station, N.Y. Or if you live in South Jersey, Erie Lackawanna Station. They'll send a selection of sixty golden oldies, plus postage and handling. Batteries extra.

Many network executives are satisfied users.

At first I had thought of just changing my name. Kitman is only a nom de plume anyway. My real name is Salinger, J. D. Or of altering my fingerprints. But transplants seemed a more effective way to get a wholly new outlook on things, a different head, to become more with it.

The old brain kept missing the subtleties of TV. It had me saying negative things like "You can put all the good things on TV in a telephone booth, and still have room for Totie Fields." Every day it caused me to complain about the mindlessness of the programming: "Too many cop shows . . ." "Spin-offs lack imagination . . ." "Public-TV pledge weeks are no fun . . ." and that the commercials on commercial-free television were a plague. My comments about the mass medium were boring even myself.

I traded it all in for a brain that will look at TV like a regular person, the average bionic TV viewer's (7.7 hours a day).

After the operation in 1977, my five favorite shows were:

1. *Charlie's Angels*
2. *Laverne & Shirley*
3. *Starsky & Hutch*
4. Any ABC crummy movie-of-the-week (especially about young prostitutes from Minnesota, crazed psycho-killers, girls in jail, teenage witches, and creeps)
5. Channel 13 begathons

With my old brain, I had a photographic memory, total recoil, as I already said Oscar Levant called it, though it could have been Carl Jung. I would wake up in the night sweating, remembering dialogue from *Barnaby Jones*.

With my new brain, I had instant forgetfulness.

Rebraining has made it possible for me to relax, to really get into the new decadence. These are the final days of Western civilization. Why fight it?

Now, I never tire of seeing the same old thing done the same old way.

It is the old-wine-in-new-bottles theory of programming, which I now praise.

Dealing with the brain bank (member, FDIC), I don't mind telling you, had me worried. I could have gotten John O'Connor's brain (the critic of *The New York Times*), which would make me review only Channel 13 programs. Or Kay Gardella's brain (the *New York Daily News* writer), which makes you take TV seriously, as if it were the world. Or Tom Shales's brain (a *Washington Post* TV analyst), which keeps writing that Lorne Michaels of *Saturday Night Live* is beautiful.
(STOP) (PAUSE)

After I wrote about coming out of the closet, vis-à-vis my operation, others also came forward. Wayne Robbins, the music critic at *Newsday*, confessed that he, too, had undergone the procedure. "How do you think I handle Aerosmith, Frankie Valle, the Ramones, and the Bay City Rollers, anyway? Since the operation, I just let the fingers pop."

My old way of watching TV was in an undershirt, with a beer, sitting on the couch. I used to evaluate shows by beer-can ratings (one to six). The better the show, the fewer cans it got. The dreaded Kitman Six-pack was the worst. One show was so bad, I awarded it the Anheuser-Busch Brewery in Newark.

But after the operation I was born again.

I didn't watch any more TV than before. But the new bionic brain helped me watch it faster. I was watching at 60 mph. Standing up. With one eye.

Once, watching TV—a whole night of prime time, for example—tended to make me apathetic. Whatever it was I had in mind when I turned on the set—researching some column idea, looking for evidence—I would forget after fifteen minutes or so. And wind up slack-jawed.

All of that was a thing of the past with my new bionic brain. Because a TV critic is never supposed to sleep, the bionic transplant was not just a luxury, an indulgence, like a face-lift, or silicone injections. It was necessary.

I was never so happy. You could hear the click of my mind as I babbled new nonsense. I no longer had to take the Dramamine pills to deal with *The Love Boat*. *Fantasy Island* was high on my vacation list. Forget little Dix and Caneel, Maui and Cozumel.

The thing about these bionic brains, though, is they sometimes go haywire.

They said it was supposed to help me do the normal things as a TV columnist, like currying favor with the networks and the TV establishment

(Does anybody have a good recipe for curried favor they can share?) The idea was that I would start lunching with Vanna White to discuss her views on the Middle East (Ohio, West Virginia, and western Pennsylvania). I hoped to be able to faint in awe every time the Bell Telephone Hour or Hallmark Hall of Fame got Richard Chamberlain to star in Shakespeare's *Troilanus* or Clavell's *Shogun*. Before my new brain, I could never figure out how this minimally talented fellow got all the top-heavy dramatic roles on TV, which would normally have gone to Sir Lawrence Olivier, who, four illnesses and all, can act.

But I have been having these strange moments.

Lately I can't believe what I see there, on that curious little screen, that strange mirror of life as we never knew it. Whatever happened to Vertical Hold? Can it be that the price ain't right? That the left also has its price? Why did Kojak become a bad guy and start doing commercials for the casinos?

But all will soon be peace. I have just located the button marked OFF.

(OFF)

MEA APOLOGIA

I realize how disappointed you must be, Roone, that there isn't anything about you. But we ran out of tape. Two more words, and my editor says they'd have to charge $42.95. Mea sorrya, Roone. Next time, I do a whole book about you.

THE CRAWL: CLOSING CREDITS

This book was shot on a Royal standard (manual) office typewriter, with a 3.5 aperture. The manuscript was then corrected in pen and Magic Marker. It looked like it was knitted, a piece of tapestry, as my editor said, by which I assumed he meant it was a work of art.

My associate producer, Victoria Johnson, then made the manuscript legible. I would like to thank the wonderful, incredible Vicky for her hard work, patience, vigilance, virtues, and retyping the manuscript so often she can now whistle it in the shower.

The manuscript was then delivered from New Jersey to Random House in New York, a fifteen-minute ride away, by Federal Express, via Memphis.

The manuscript weighed thirty-four pounds, and was sent to a fat farm where my editor, the astounding Sam Vaughan, put it on a diet. It lost eighteen pounds.

I apologize to all those who got left on the cutting-room floor. It was Sam's fault. A consoling word about the errors of omission: Usually, my friends in the TV business say, the best thing I can do for them is not mention them.

The errors of commission are my own.

No columnist is better than his sources. Mine can be divided into two groups: the reliably uninformed sources and the unreliably informed sources. I would like to thank both for having taught me everything I know about TV.

An unsung hero, as one reliably informed TV source, Ed Newman, once explained, is a Chinese sandwich. Among the many unsung heroes in these pages whom I want to take this opportunity to thank or make a hero sandwich, whichever they'd prefer:

Jeff Erdel, Lewis Chesler, Stuart Sucherman, Mark Schubin, Reuven Frank, Roger Ailes, Martin Solow, Tony Gentile, Dick Ebersol, Frank Swertlow, Gene Walsh, Jim Bouton, Glenn Collins, Mike Winship, Brandon Stoddard, Howard Schuman, Glenn Rabney, Howard Stringer, Bob Martin, Ben Halpern, Jerry Agel, Richard Lingeman, Lawrence Grossman, Victor Navasky, Brandon Tartikoff, Janis Hirsch, Esther Shapiro, Alan Levine, Herb Schmertz, Sanford Socolow.

Helen Ricco, Harriet Lesser, Cheryl L. Blum, Rita Solow, Barry Kogan, Dr. Herb Meyers, Allison Wolcoff, Susanna Orling, Mike Kuhns, Dr. Michael Perloff, Julian Downward.

Maria Milito, Don McKinney, Myra Appleton, Tony Insolia, Pearl Perloff, Caroline Miller, Donald Blank.

And Dr. Erika Freeman.

By inference, anything not credited to a source here is original thinking by the author.

I also want to thank the quiz masters. Some people know all the answers; I know all the questions or where to get them. I want to thank Ken Sperling (for the *Saturday Night Live* quiz), John Benevento (*Monty Python*), Glenn Schmid (*Star Trek*), Michael Huppert (sp?) (*M*A*S*H*). I especially want to thank them for the answers to the tests. Without all their years spent in front of TV, I would have flunked.

I want to thank Vladimir Zworkin for inventing TV and Benjamin Franklin for inventing electricity. And my English teacher at Brooklyn Tech, who gave me a C−, eat your heart out, Bubbles Moscowitz, but who was correct.

I also want to thank, in the words of Michael Jackson at the Grammys and the People's Choice Awards, "God." And then I want to thank the People's Choice Awards and the Grammys . . . I'd better stop before this starts sounding like an awards show. Or is it too late?

ABOUT THE AUTHOR

MARVIN is a member of the Brooklyn Tech Alumni Association, the James Beard Foundation, and writes about television for *Newsday*, *New York Newsday*, and the Los Angeles Times Syndicate. He has been on TV himself, having appeared on the *Tonight* show, *Tomorrow*, *Today*, *Merv Griffin*, *Barbara Walters*, *MacNeil/Lehrer*, and *Entertainment Tonight*, among other programs, though not all of these shows have invited him back. Marvin has won the Folio Award and the Playboy Prize for Humor.

LIBRARY
ST. LOUIS COMMUNITY COLLEGE
AT FLORISSANT VALLEY